Future Education and Learning Spaces

ICT & Education in Uncertain Times

This series focuses on the possible education responses that can be implemented in uncertain times. Uncertainty could happen in times of crises or also in normal situations, where some information or actions are not known, resulting in uncertain educational scenarios. Besides, it also shows how emerging technologies, including Artificial Intelligence, Blockchain, Educational Games and Virtual Reality/Augmented Reality, will reshape the future of education to provide efficient learning/teaching experiences and assessments. Furthermore, the series discusses innovative pedagogical and learning approaches (e.g., the use of open educational practices and peer-to-peer learning) that can be applied in this rapid moving technological era to maintain education, including in uncertain times. Particularly, new instructional methods, such as game-based learning, should be designed based on the integrated technologies to provide effective learning experience, resulting in better learning outcomes. Future education should not solely focus on technology, but also on the applied instructional methods, as well as the human touch to maintain authentic and effective learning experience. The series also discusses how learning spaces can be designed to meet the growing tendency of Open and Distance Education, where thousands of learners can be taken the same course from different cultures, backgrounds and learning needs.

This series aims to establish itself, through the published books/textbooks and research, as a medium to provide guidelines and recommendations for different stakeholders, including policy makers, educational designers, teachers and students on how to enhance both learning and teaching experiences in the future for better learning outcomes, as well as how to maintain education in uncertain times. It also provides one-step ahead towards future education to prepare different stakeholders for the rapid evolution of education, even in times of uncertainty.

Michael Agyemang Adarkwah ·
Samuel Amponsah · Ronghuai Huang ·
Michael Thomas
Editors

Artificial Intelligence and Human Agency in Education: Volume One

The Nexus Between AI and Human Agency in Educational Contexts

Springer

Editors
Michael Agyemang Adarkwah
Chair of Adult Education at the Institute for Education and Culture
Friedrich Schiller University Jena
Jena, Germany

Samuel Amponsah
School of Continuing and Distance Education
College of Education
University of Ghana
Legon, Ghana

Ronghuai Huang
Beijing Normal University
Beijing, China

Michael Thomas
School of Education
Liverpool John Moores University
Liverpool, UK

ISSN 2731-7714 ISSN 2731-7722 (electronic)
Future Education and Learning Spaces
ISBN 978-981-96-7936-2 ISBN 978-981-96-7937-9 (eBook)
https://doi.org/10.1007/978-981-96-7937-9

This Springer imprint is published by the registered company Springer Nature Singapore Pte Ltd.
The registered company address is: 152 Beach Road, #21-01/04 Gateway East, Singapore 189721, Singapore

Preface

For more than six decades, researchers across a range of disciplines have investigated whether machines can exhibit human-like intelligence. Since the 1950s, when Alan Turing's "Turing Test" first posed the question, "Can machines think?", in his paper "Computing Machinery and Intelligence", the field of Artificial Intelligence (AI) has been at the center of discussions about the capabilities, opportunities, dangers, and ethics of developing advanced computer intelligence. Today, while the field of AI still has a significant way to develop, and much hype surrounds it, the development of large language models (LLM) and natural language processing (NLP) has led to its renewed prominence as a consequence of the widespread availability of applications like ChatGPT, developed by OpenAI in the United States, and latterly DeepSeek from China. This edited volume addresses this complex and exciting context, viewing it through multiple theoretical and empirical lenses in an attempt to help learners, teachers, teacher trainers, and policymakers understand what is at stake.

Unsurprisingly, the AI market has seen a significant increase in growth as a result of these latest popular developments that has embedded the potential of AI into many of our regular everyday activities, from searching on the web to purchasing items online or conversing with via a customer services chatbot. A World Bank report published in 2021 estimated that the global AI market would be worth $6.4 trillion global by 2025 and that there would be a 14% increase in global GDP by 2030 as a result of AI adoption. The rapid adoption of AI by educational institutions stems from the belief that AI can use its immense processing power and speed to help address societal problems and promote quality education by addressing some of the wicked problems or grand challenges in education. The experimentation of AI in diverse educational systems has revealed the significant potential AI can have on teaching and learning processes to aid personalized teaching and learning and to save educators and learners valuable time. Subsequently, there has been an increase in research to identify and understand practices that could lead to the transformation of the educational landscape.

Although it is true to say that AI has an immense potential to revolutionize education for good, there are inevitably predictions that also consider the harmful effects it may have on education. This might include increases in plagiarism, reduced opportunities to interact with human teachers and fellow learners, and concerns about privacy, bias, and reduced critical thinking skills. Moreover, as we saw during the recent pandemic, students and teachers without access to AI tools and applications may be left behind, and these technologies may exacerbate digital divides both within and across different countries as well as between the Global North and Global South. The positive and negative impacts of AI on education call on all educators to be involved in a continuous monitoring and validation process with respect to AI systems and to consider its ethical principles and how best to regulate these complex new technologies. Hence, while there has been growth in the importance of the field over the last couple of years, more research and discussions are needed about how humans and machines can co-exist in educational systems in a way that is productive, meaningful and ethically sound. To contribute to this process, the current edition takes a critical look at how AI can augment and enhance human agency in education by leveraging the cognitive, social, and psychological insights that AI research can provide. Research on AI is essential across the cognitive, social and psychological contexts therefore to guide educators and all the various stakeholders involved in education to navigate its potential pitfalls

The rise of AI conversational agents and chatbots has garnered significant global attention over the last couple of years. This growing interest has led educators and researchers to investigate the impact of these AI tools within educational environments and to discover effective strategies for integrating them into teaching and learning practices. While many areas require further exploration, there is an emerging consensus on the profound effects of AI and related technologies on the cognitive, social, and psychological experiences of both educators and students.

This edited book provides unique perspectives on the intersection of AI and education, distinguishing itself from existing literature that has predominantly addressed the social challenges posed by AI—such as climate change and criminality. Instead, it emphasizes the pivotal role of AI in potentially enhancing human agency across various educational contexts. While it includes discussions on workplace learning, it also expands the horizon of AI to encompass broader educational domains, including adult education and lifelong learning.

Additionally, this book is one of the first to consider the cognitive, social, and psychological factors that impact learners' transitions from academic settings into the workforce. Although previous discussions have touched upon innovative technologies in education, they often overlook recent advancements like natural language processing and their implications for learner well-being. Our book bridges these gaps by adopting a multidisciplinary approach to understanding the effects of AI on both educators and learners, with a strong focus on their overall well-being. In conclusion, this collection is an essential resource for those who seek to understand the evolving dynamics of AI in education and its significant implications for human agency.

The edition offers several insights for a diverse audience, from educators and policymakers to researchers and technologists. Teachers and students will also benefit from the novel approaches to instruction and learning suggested in this edited volume.

It is a must-read for anyone interested in understanding the transformative potential of artificial intelligence (AI) in the field of education at the current time.

By exploring the cognitive, social, and psychological implications of AI integration, educators will gain a deeper understanding of how to strike a balance between technological advancements and the preservation of the human element in the learning process. Several chapter authors present a comprehensive analysis of the opportunities and challenges presented by AI in the educational domain that will help policymakers make informed policy decisions and ensure that the integration of AI aligns with the overarching goals of equitable access, inclusive learning, and the development of twenty-first-century skills.

Developers of AI technologies will obtain valuable insights that will guide them in designing and implementing AI systems that seamlessly integrate with the needs and aspirations of learners, educators, and educational institutions. Most importantly, regardless of the background of the reader, this edited book promises to expand your understanding of the transformative potential of AI in education. It is a valuable resource for anyone who seeks to shape the future of learning and unlock the full potential of human agency in the digital age.

As the AI field is attracting more attention, there have been increased scholarly publications on how it affects different sectors of society and daily life. However, most existing books tend to only provide an overview of AI. This has led to increased calls to focus on artificial intelligence in education (AIED) as a sub-field. In assembling the chapters in this volume, the editors were motivated to provide this edition as a state-of-the-art book on AIED by adopting a human agentic perspective. A human agentic perspective enables users of AI tools to set goals and anticipate future implications of AI.

The increased apprehension among students, teachers, parents, educators, policymakers, employers, employees, and many key stakeholders that AI will replace humans as a result of automation calls for users of AI tools or technologies to intentionally take control of AI and not the other way round. As captured in the 2023 Global Education Monitoring (GEM) Report, users of advanced technology, such as AI, need to define the use of technology in their own terms. As humans are shaped by their experiences, interacting with digital technologies will, to some degree, impact the educational, cognitive, social, and psychological processes of teachers, learners, and other users of AI in educational institutions. A user-centered or learner-centered approach is needed to place humans at the center of AI technologies.

Therefore, it is important to look at the implications of AI technologies on human agency across differing contexts involving cognition, social, and psychological processes. In this light, **Volume 1** of this edited book aims to investigate how AI will impact the educational, cognitive, social and psychological processes of teaching and learning in diverse ways across different educational levels. **Volume 1 comprises twelve (12) chapters in total. The authors of Volume 1 were from institutions in Hong Kong, Tunisia, South Africa, India, China, Ghana, Tanzania, Kuwait, Austria, the United States, Zimbabwe, and Pakistan.** The edition advocates for an introspective look at different topics in education, such as the humanization of AI in education, ethical considerations of using AI in education (e.g., issues of privacy, bias, and safety), technology fatigue and technostress in education, emotional intelligence in AI-based teaching and learning, and the impact of human-computer interaction on cognition, memory, and mental health.

Jena, Germany	Michael Agyemang Adarkwah
Legon, Ghana	Samuel Amponsah
Beijing, China	Ronghuai Huang
Liverpool, UK	Michael Thomas

Contents

Part I
Cognitive Context

Chapter 1
The Impact of Artificial Intelligence on Information Security and Risk Perceptions: A Survey Study in China and Its Implications for the Education Sector

Michael C. S. Wong, Shuangao Wang, and Zhijian Lyu

Abstract Artificial Intelligence (AI) has brought numerous conveniences but has also introduced challenges to information security and privacy risk monitoring. This study focuses on the impact of AI on both security and risk perceptions, specifically in the context of China. Drawing on Communication Privacy Management Theory and Privacy Concern Theory, we construct a model to analyze how AI influences users' security and risk perceptions. Our survey of over 900 respondents reveals that AI negatively affects both security and risk perceptions, indicating a lack of awareness or concern about these issues among AI users in China. Among the respondents, approximately 44.95% are students, 30.93% are under 25 years old, and 66.85% have college or postgraduate education. These findings emphasize the need for greater focus on security and risk in AI usage, particularly in the education sector, where concerns about cybersecurity and privacy risks related to tools like ChatGPT and large language models (LLMs) are growing. It is crucial to alert high school and college students to the privacy risks associated with AI tools.

Keywords Artificial intelligence · Information security · Privacy · Risk perception · Security perception

M. C. S. Wong (✉)
Department of Economics and Finance, City University of Hong Kong, Kowloon, Hong Kong, China
e-mail: efmcw103@cityu.edu.hk

S. Wang · Z. Lyu
Science and Technology Information Institute of Beijing Academy of Science and Technology, Beijing, China
e-mail: wangsa@bjstinfo.ac.cn

Z. Lyu
e-mail: luzj@bjstinfo.ac.cn

M. A. Adarkwah et al. (eds.), *Artificial Intelligence and Human Agency in Education: Volume One*, Future Education and Learning Spaces,
https://doi.org/10.1007/978-981-96-7937-9_1

1.1 Introduction

The integration of artificial intelligence (AI) in education significantly impacts cognitive, social, and psychological dimensions, especially regarding information security and risk perceptions. AI technologies, such as intelligent tutoring systems and adaptive learning platforms, customize educational content to individual learning styles, enhancing engagement and retention. This personalization improves student outcomes (Abbas et al., 2023; Jian, 2023; Roshanaei, 2023). However, the collection and analysis of personal learning data raise serious concerns about data privacy and security, exposing students to potential breaches and misuse (Solanke, 2024).

Socially, AI promotes collaborative learning by connecting students with peers and educators, which enhances teamwork and communication skills. Research shows that AI enriches social interactions and creates engaging learning environments (Hashim et al., 2022; Zawacki-Richter et al., 2019). Trust in AI systems is crucial for user engagement, as familiarity and experience shape perceptions of risk and benefit (Kerstan, 2023; Raue et al., 2019; Siegrist, 2019). Therefore, fostering trust through transparency about AI is essential for reducing risk perceptions and increasing acceptance.

Psychologically, AI's effects are complex. While it can streamline administrative tasks and provide instant feedback, it may also heighten student anxiety due to pressures linked to AI-driven assessments. Research indicates that reliance on AI for evaluations can increase stress, as students might feel constantly monitored (Ayala-Pazmiño, 2023; Cho, 2024). This anxiety can negatively impact motivation and well-being, emphasizing the need for a balanced approach to AI integration. Negative emotional responses can further influence risk perceptions and willingness to adopt AI technologies (Ayala-Pazmiño, 2023; Cho, 2024).

To develop effective AI tools in education, it is vital to consider cognitive, social, and psychological aspects along with information security implications. These tools should enhance academic success while promoting learner well-being and positive social interactions, all within a framework of robust data protection. As AI technologies evolve in educational contexts, stakeholders must navigate these complexities to prioritize learning outcomes and student mental health (Sáez-Velasco, 2024).

The rise of AI has transformed many aspects of life, changing lifestyles, production methods, and societal norms (Li et al., 2019). AI and big data are interconnected, with big data driving AI systems for predictive analytics (Dwivedi et al., 2021). However, the proliferation of personal information has heightened concerns about data security and privacy. In fact, the education sector faces significant data protection challenges, as recent breaches have compromised personally identifiable information (PII) of students, educators, and staff (Halaas, 2023; Lightbody et al., 2023). Although these breaches are not directly linked to AI, increased reliance on educational technologies and cloud systems raises risks to sensitive information (Bu, 2022; Eden, 2024). As AI integrates further into education, assessing its impact on data protection and privacy is crucial.

Data breaches have substantial consequences for students and educators, affecting educational success, personal well-being, and trust in new technologies, including AI tools (Akgün & Greenhow, 2021; Sarwar, 2024). Addressing these security and privacy issues is essential for creating an educational environment where students and educators can fully benefit from AI while safeguarding personal information (Bu, 2022; Eden, 2024).

This study applies Communication Privacy Management (CPM) theory to enhance understanding of user privacy security and offers theoretical guidance for future research in the AI context. It proposes and empirically tests a model of factors influencing users' privacy concerns in AI environments, addressing the lack of empirical studies on user security perceptions in this area. The survey included 941 respondents from the China WeChat platform, marking a pioneering study on this topic for Chinese users.

The chapter provides evidence that AI use can negatively affect individuals' sense of security and awareness of risks. It explores how factors like privacy concerns, views on privacy policies, and feelings of control over information influence the relationship between AI usage and perceptions of security and risk.

1.2 Literature Review

The widespread use of artificial intelligence (AI) presents novel challenges to the domain of information security and privacy. Nonetheless, the implementation of AI additionally creates worries regarding the safeguarding of data privacy and security. The aim of this literature review is to analyze the connection between AI utilization and views on security and risk.

The notion of privacy is fundamentally linked to individuals' capacity to exercise authority over the acquisition and transmission of their personal information by external entities. This notion has assumed an increasingly paramount role within contemporary society, as personal information becomes subject to collection, utilization, and sharing by a broad spectrum of organizations. The balancing act between direct access to information and an individual's entitlement to privacy has emerged as a subject of discourse within numerous developed nations (Milberg et al., 2000). Approaches to regulatory frameworks concerning information privacy, the management of personal data by corporations, and consumer reactions have become intricately interconnected on a global scale. The definition of privacy is intricate and diverse, yet personal information occupies a pivotal position in the concept of privacy (Lang & Zhong, 2022). There are concerns amid people concerning the potential misapplication and manipulation of their personal data, which incites them to investigate different approaches to tackle privacy concerns, like providing inaccurate personal information, utilizing privacy-enhancing technologies, and refraining from making purchases (Wirtz et al., 2007).

Prior research shows that people's perceptions of privacy and security depend on how websites collect and use their personal data (Hong & Thong, 2013). Similarly, various factors influence security perceptions in AI environments. For instance, curiosity, social influence, and threat perceptions can affect users' intentions to protect their privacy when using intelligent systems (Chen et al., 2016). This indicates that individual traits and attitudes may shape users' views on the security risks of AI.

In e-commerce, individual characteristics, privacy invasion experiences, and risk-taking tendencies have been found to affect security perceptions (Yeh et al., 2018). These factors may also play a role in shaping security perceptions in AI environments. Additionally, the content of privacy policies and attitudes toward privacy have been shown to be related to perceptions of security and trust (Calo, 2010; Li, 2014). These findings suggest that privacy policies and users' attitudes toward privacy may also affect their perceptions of AI security and risk.

Despite the extensive inquiry, exploration, and examination concerning knowledge confidentiality and safety in the Internet territory, there is an insufficiency of analyzes focusing on the elements that shape individuals' viewpoints of safety in AI surroundings. The distinguishing characteristics embedded in AI, such as its capacity to gather knowledge from data and make independent decisions, have the potential to introduce novel security risks and challenges. Consequently, it is imperative to comprehend how users formulate their understanding of AI security risks and identify the factors that may exert an influence on their perceptions.

The previous studies mentioned have focused on internet services and smartphone apps. Nevertheless, further research is required to understand the correlation between the use of AI services and individuals' perceptions of security and risk. This is significant given the rising popularity of AI services. Comprehending the effects of AI utilization on security and risk perceptions is vital for formulating robust strategies to mitigate security risks and safeguard user privacy.

This chapter seeks to establish connections between Communication Privacy Management Theory (CPMT) and Privacy Concerns Theory (PCT) in the context of information security challenges related to the use of artificial intelligence (AI). CPMT provides a theoretical framework for comprehending how individuals regulate the limits of their confidential data during processes of communication (Petronio, 1991). Conversely, PCT concentrates on the concerns and attitudes of individuals toward privacy in the domain of information technology and communication (Milberg et al., 2000). By scrutinizing these theories, we can acquire insights into the obstacles and consequences of AI information security.

CPMT expounds on how individuals perceive and govern the boundaries of their confidential data in communication contexts. According to CPMT, individuals view their confidential data as their personal property, over which they exercise dominion. They proceed to establish and manage boundaries around this data based on their privacy regulations, which are influenced by cultural, social, and relational factors. These regulations dictate whether individuals disclose or withhold confidential data in diverse communication situations. The decision-making process concerning confidential data encompasses the following constituents:

Ownership: Individuals believe that they possess ownership rights over their confidential data.
Control: Individuals possess a sense of control over their confidential data and ascertain who may access it.
Privacy Boundaries: Individuals establish either flexible or rigid boundaries around their confidential data, contingent upon the context and relationship.
Co-ownership and Co-control: Within interpersonal relationships, individuals engage in negotiations and share ownership and control of confidential data, thereby granting others access or control.
Boundary Turbulence: Boundary turbulence manifests when privacy boundaries are trespassed on or infringed upon, resulting in conflicts or difficulties in managing confidential data.

PCT focuses on understanding individuals' concerns and attitudes toward privacy, particularly in the context of information technology and communication (Milberg et al., 2000). The theory suggests that privacy concerns emerge from individuals' perceptions of the risks associated with the collection, use, and disclosure of their personal information. Concerns, as defined by the theory, refer to the worry stemming from potential information loss (Smith et al., 1996). PCT identifies three primary factors influencing privacy concerns:

Information Sensitivity: The perceived sensitivity of personal information significantly influences privacy concerns. Individuals are more likely to be concerned about the privacy of sensitive information (e.g., financial or health-related data).
Perceived Vulnerability: The perception of vulnerability to privacy threats affects individuals' levels of concern. Factors contributing to vulnerability include the perceived likelihood of unauthorized access to personal information and the potential harm resulting from such access.
Perceived Control: Individuals' perception of control over their personal information plays a crucial role in shaping their privacy concerns. The extent to which individuals believe they have control over the collection, use, and disclosure of their information affects their privacy-related attitudes and behaviors.

According to PCT, higher levels of information sensitivity, perceived vulnerability, and reduced perceived control can lead to increased privacy concerns. These privacy concerns can then influence people's privacy-related behaviors, such as their decisions about disclosing information, adopting privacy protection technologies, or engaging in self-protective behaviors.

Both Communication Privacy Management Theory (CPMT) and Privacy Concerns Theory (PCT) offer important insights into the information security issues related to using AI tools. This connects with Privacy Concern Theory, which emphasizes people's worries about the privacy and security impacts of technological advances, including AI tools.

Consistent with Communication Privacy Management Theory (CPMT), the research by Zhang and Cheng (2022) looks at using AI with Internet of Things (IoT) technology. It focuses on analyzing optimization strategies and early warning models to improve understanding and provide reference points for related research. This connects with CPMT's focus on managing private information and negotiating privacy boundaries in the context of IoT and AI technologies.

Furthermore, the study by Bačiulienė et al. (2023) explores the aspects of AI in different stages of the food value and supply chain. It highlights how AI interacts with other technologies like big data mining, machine learning, and digital platforms. This aligns with Privacy Concerns Theory's (PCT) focus on addressing the privacy implications of AI technologies in various phases of the supply chain and the potential risks from integrating AI with other technologies.

Furthermore, the research by Hermansyah et al. (2023) discusses the ethical implications of AI and emphasizes the need to ensure privacy and social justice in AI systems. This aligns with both CPMT and PCT, which emphasize the ethical and privacy considerations in the development and application of AI technologies. The two theories highlight the need to address ethical, privacy, and security concerns in the development and application of AI tools, echoing recent research on the uses of AI.

1.3 Methodology, Factors, and Hypotheses

Based on the above two theories, this paper identifies the following factors concerning AI, privacy, risk, and security issues. These factors include:

Artificial intelligence (AI) refers to programs, algorithms, or systems demonstrating human intelligence. However, unlike humans, AI lacks feelings or empathies (Davenport et al., 2020). Policy issues like privacy, bias, and ethics determine how AI influences human behavior.

Security Perception (SP) pertains to the risks and threats that are apprehended by individuals. This encompasses the implementation of pertinent risk mitigation measures to safeguard their personal information and data. Many elements could potentially impact this perception, including personal encounters, knowledge, awareness of potential threats and vulnerabilities, and the ability to control personal information (Gerber et al., 2019; Zhang et al., 2009). It is possible that individuals who actively use AI services may perceive security concerns associated with the use of such services to be diminished.

Risk Perception (RP) refers to potential loss perceived when disclosing information. Due to information uncertainty, disclosed information may be abused, increasing disclosure risk (Chang et al., 2018). It is likely that active AI users perceive less risk issues on using AI services.

Privacy Concern (PC) refers to, as discussed above, potential risks and threats to personal information arising from the use of AI. Individuals with strong privacy concern may be less active in AI usage or be included perceive high security and risk issues on using AI services.

Perceived Information Control (PIC) refers to the ease of controlling personal information. Higher perceived control makes users feel less security and risk issues (Calo, 2010). AI's fuzzy privacy boundary leads to leaked privacy without knowledge of users. To enjoy AI services, users provide personal information with inadequate awareness of risk and control (Chaabouni et al., 2019).
Perceived Effectiveness of Privacy Policy (PEPP) refers to users perceiving their ability to control personal information (Hardt, 2012). Effective policies inform users of information use, ensuring low risks. Users with better ideas on how to protect privacy may perceive less security and risk issues on using AI services.

Given the current state of AI technology, it has become increasingly challenging to draw a clear distinction between private and public boundaries. As a result, the ambiguous nature of the privacy boundary in AI systems has led to a growing trend of inadvertent leakage of user data (Chaabouni et al., 2019). Despite this trend, users continue to provide personal information to AI systems to avail themselves of the benefits they offer, leading to a gradual weakening of privacy risk awareness and information control.

Against this backdrop, this paper proposes the following hypotheses and constructs a model aimed at addressing the above-mentioned issues. This model hypothesizes that active AI users tend to perceive less risk and security issues on using AI services. In such paths of influence, privacy concern, perceived information control, and perceived effectiveness of privacy policy of AI users may have their own mediating effects on both security and risk perceptions. On this ground, we list our hypotheses as follows:

H1: AI negatively influences Security Perception (SP)
H1a: Privacy Concern (PC) has mediating effect between AI and Security Perception (SP)
H1b: Perceived Effectiveness of Privacy Policy (PEPP) has mediating effect between AI and Security Perception (SP)
H1c: Perceived Information Control (PIC) has mediating effect between AI and Security Perception (SP)
H2: AI negatively influences Risk Perception (RP)
H2a: Privacy Concern (PC) has mediating effect between AI and Risk Perception (RP)
H2b: Perceived Effectiveness of Privacy Policy (PEPP) has mediating effect between AI and Risk Perception (RP)
H2c: Perceived Information Control (PIC) has mediating effect between AI and Risk Perception (RP)

The factors of AI, SP, RP, PC, PIC, and PEPP are measured by their own set of measurement questions in a questionnaire. These measurement questions assign Score 1 for "strongly disagree", Score 2 for "disagree", Score 3 for "average", Score 4 for "agree", and Score 5 for "strongly agree". There are 4 questions on AI, 9 questions on PC, 7 questions on PIC, 6 questions on RP, 7 questions on SP, and 4 questions on PEPP. This means 27 measurement questions. The measurement questions are written in Chinese. Their English versions are shown in Table 1.1.

The following diagram, Fig. 1.1, outlines a structural equation model for this study, the association of the factors, and the measurement questions of each of the factors.

1.4 Results

This section summarizes how data is collected and analyzed, and discusses those key empirical findings.

1.4.1 Data Collection

The questionnaire was openly distributed to users of WeChat, which is the most popular social media platform in China. Eventually, 941 respondents returned the questionnaire. The data is collected in December 2021. Profiles of the respondents are summarized in Table 1.2.

Table 1.2 shows that around 50% of respondents are working persons (including employees, freelancers, and self-employed persons), around 70% of respondents have college education or above, and around 76% of respondents have AI usage experience. Both males and females are balanced in the sample. This sample matches a general profile of active users of internet, smartphone apps, and AI services.

1.4.2 Data Analysis

The data is analyzed with SPSS AMOS tool for structural equation model (SEM). This approach brings all measurement variables (i.e., the measurement questions) and latent factors together for analysis. This paper has done tests on the reliability and internal consistency of the measurement variables. The test statistics support that the measurement variables are suitable measures on the factors of AI, SP, RP, PC, PIC, and PECC, respectively. The following displays the correlations matrix of the 6 factors to be analyzed. It is obvious that AI is negatively correlated with all the remaining 5 factors. It is negatively correlated respectively with PIC, PEPP, SP, and RP with correlation coefficients ranging between −0.455 and −0.582. The negative correlation between AI and PC is closer to zero, staying at −0.016. Active AI users have less privacy concern (Table 1.3).

Table 1.1 Factors and measurement questions

Factors	Measurement questions
AI	A11. In daily life, I often experience AI services A12. Compared with artificial intelligence, I am more inclined to use help provided by real people AI3. When using online networks, I believe that artificial intelligence can provide me with better services AI4. When using online networks, artificial intelligence's big data analysis recommendations make me feel that my information is not secure
Privacy Concern (PC)	PC1. I pay attention to news and subsequent developments related to privacy and privacy violations PC2. My friends think I should be careful about my privacy PC3. People who are important to me think that one should be more careful when revealing personal information online PC4. I think social media has collected a lot of my personal information without my consent PC5. I feel that my behavior on social media is being tracked and monitored PC6. I am worried that the private information I upload to social media may be illegally used PC7. I think my personal information is easier to access than I imagine PC8. I feel that my personal information is accessible, and once someone uses it, my privacy will be violated PC9. I feel that by using these websites, my privacy has been violated by those who collect all my data

(continued)

Table 1.1 (continued)

Factors	Measurement questions
Perceived Information Control (PIC)	PIC1. If there is a high-performance artificial intelligence app with accurate algorithms and timely push of information, I tend to use it even though you have limited ability to manage your own information PIC2. I understand privacy issues in society and related practices PIC3. I will keep up to date with privacy issues and pay attention to solutions adopted by companies and governments to protect our privacy PIC4. I can control who can access the personal information I publish on social media PIC5. I can control the purpose of using my personal information on social media PIC6. I can decide what kind of personal information social media can collect PIC7. In general, I can control the information I provide to social media
Risk Perception (RP)	RP1. Providing my personal information to online platforms may result in potential losses RP2. Providing my personal information to online platforms may result in unforeseen problems RP3. In general, providing my personal information to online platforms is risky RP4. The personal information provided to online platforms may be misused RP5. Compared to others, I am more sensitive to the way network platforms handle personal privacy RP6. I am worried that social media will leak my personal information

(continued)

Table 1.1 (continued)

Factors	Measurement questions
Security Perception (SP)	SP1. For me, protecting my privacy is the most important thing SP2. Compared to others, I tend to pay attention to potential privacy threats SP3. Providing some personal information to online platforms helps me enjoy the services I want SP4. Providing my personal information on online platforms makes it easier for me to integrate into social networks SP5. The personal information provided on the network platform can help me communicate better with others and make like-minded friends SP6. People who influence me think that personal information security is very important SP7. I know that social media uses my personal information without my consent
Perceived Effectiveness of Privacy Policies (PEPP)	PEPP1. I think the privacy statement of the website reflects their commitment to protect my personal information PEPP2. Through their privacy statement, I think my personal information is confidential PEPP3. I believe that these privacy statements are an effective way to prove their commitments PEPP4. Overall, I think providing my personal information on the network platform is beneficial to me

The SEM approach allows linear regression analysis among the factors. Table 1.4 summarizes the hypotheses mentioned before, corresponding linear regression coefficients, and corresponding conclusions on hypothesis testing. The following displays these results.

The empirical results in this table show the following findings. First, AI negatively influences both SP and RP. Its impact on SP has regression coefficient at −0.27, while its impact on RP has regression coefficient at −0.103. This implies that AI usage and reliance tend to make users perceive less security and risk issues on using AI services. These users may ignore security and risk issues deliberately to use some powerful AI services.

Second, privacy concern has insignificant effect on either security or risk perceptions. Some AI users are less aware of privacy issues and personal information collection. Some users may prioritize convenience and ease of AI use over privacy concerns. Some users may not perceive themselves as being at risk of privacy violations. That can lead to their false sense of security and lack of concern about privacy. Some users may be unable to associate privacy issues with security or risk issues on using AI services.

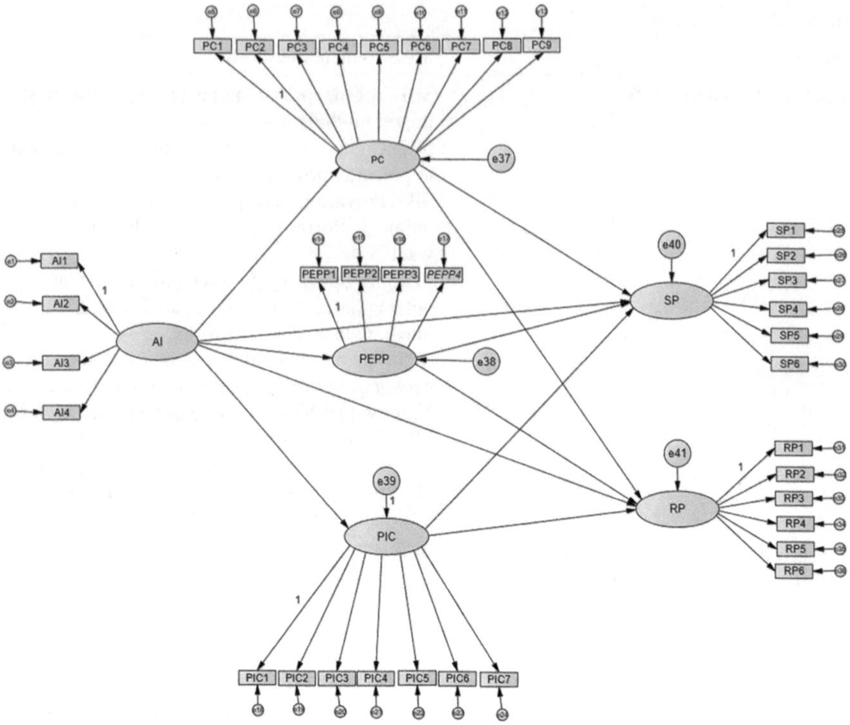

Fig. 1.1 A structural equation model on AI, security perception, and risk perception

Third, the perception with respect to the efficacy of privacy policy (PEPP) has a significantly adverse impact on both the perception of security and the perception of risk. The coefficient of PEPP on SP is -0.203, while the coefficient of PEPP on RP is −0.509. Users of artificial intelligence who perceive a higher level of effectiveness in privacy policies may hold the belief that providers of AI services are successfully safeguarding their privacy and personal information. This positive perception can be attributed to transparent and comprehensible privacy policies, user-friendly privacy settings, and the efficient enforcement of privacy regulations. Consequently, these users may feel less vulnerable to privacy infringements or security breaches due to their trust in the implementation of appropriate protective measures by AI service providers. They might assume that any risks associated with utilizing AI services are being effectively managed by the providers. It is important to acknowledge that a privacy policy does not guarantee complete protection of personal information. Privacy agreements can be confusing and hard to grasp, and businesses might not consistently follow them. With the presence of privacy policies and security measures, there remains a potential for data breaches or other security incidents.

Fourthly, the findings suggest that an increased sense of control over their information positively influences individuals' perceptions of security and risk. The data shows a significant coefficient of 0.455 for the impact of perceived information

Table 1.2 Profile of the 941 questionnaire respondents

Variable	Category	Percentage (%)
Gender	Male	50.37
	Female	49.63
Age	Under 18 years old	10.84
	18–25 years old	20.09
	26–30 years old	27.52
	31–35 years old	18.60
	36–40 years old	12.86
	41–45 years old	6.48
	45 years old above	3.61
Education	Junior high school and below	12.11
	High school	21.04
	College	48.57
	Master's degree or above	18.28
Occupation	Students	44.95
	Employees	24.66
	Freelancers/Self-employed	25.29
	Others	5.10
Using AI	Yes	76.30
	No	23.70

Table 1.3 Correlation matrix of the factors

	AI	PC	PIC	PEPP	RP
AI	1				
PC	−0.016***	1			
PIC	−0.455***	−0.042	1		
PEPP	0.469***	0	−0.061	1	
RP	−0.456***	0.036***	0.610***	−0.721***	1
SP	−0.582***	0.012***	0.707***	0.624***	−0.023

NB: "***" means $p < 0.001$

control on security perceptions and 0.217 on risk perceptions. This might appear counterintuitive, yet it indicates that users of AI are conscious of the dangers associated with disclosing personal information. By limiting what they share and using privacy tools, they become more conscious of potential misuse.

Fifth, AI significantly boosts people's sense of control over their personal information but negatively impacts their preference for privacy-enhancing personalization. Users of AI technology often feel empowered by the tools and techniques that enhance their privacy. As individuals grow more knowledgeable about the data collection and

Table 1.4 Hypothesis testing and linear regression coefficients

	Hypothesis	Regression path	Coeff.	Sig.	Conclusion
H1	AI negatively influences SP	SP < = = AI	−0.267	***	Accepted
H1a	PC has mediating effect between AI and SP	SP < = = PC	−0.014		Rejected
		PC < = = AI	0.217		
H1b	PEPP has mediating effect between AI and SP	SP < = = PEPP	−0.203	***	Accepted
		PEPP < = = AI	0.462	***	
H1c	PIC has mediating effect between AI and SP	SP < = = PIC	0.455	***	Accepted
		PIC < = = AI	−0.420	***	
H2	AI negatively influences RP	RP < = = AI	−0.103	***	Accepted
H2a	PC has mediating effect between AI and RP	RP < = = PC	0.045		Rejected
		PC < = = AI	0.027		
H2b	PEPP has mediating effect between AI and RP	RP < = = PEPP	−0.509	***	Accepted
		PEPP < = = AI	0.462	***	
H2c	PIC has mediating effect between AI and RP	RP < = = PIC	0.217	***	Accepted
		PIC < = = AI	−0.420	***	

NB: "***" means $p < 0.001$; " < = = " means linear regression equation between the 1st variable as dependent variable and the 2nd variable as independent variable.

usage by AI systems, they may feel more in control yet increasingly concerned about their privacy and security. Additionally, active AI users may trust privacy policies less, as they recognize the limitations and failures of companies to safeguard personal information, leading to decreased confidence in data protection.

1.5 Discussion and Implications

The study concentrates on the circumstance of China and explores the situation that the utilization of AI impacts the users' perspectives on security and risk. It argues that while AI brings about convenience, it also diminishes the consciousness of observing information security and privacy risk. The escalating accumulation and utilization of personal data in AI systems gives rise to anxiety regarding privacy and data security. The primary objective of the examination is to comprehend how AI affects the users' perspectives on security and risk, and it scrutinizes factors such as concerns regarding privacy, the perceived effectiveness of privacy policies, and the perceived control of information.

The study surveyed over 900 respondents in China via WeChat, primarily students and young adults with college or postgraduate education. This data offers valuable insights into perceptions of AI, security, and privacy in an educational context. Given WeChat's popularity among students in China, the findings reflect the attitudes of young people in China toward AI integration in education. Overall, this data can guide policy decisions and improve AI integration in education while prioritizing user security and privacy. The findings also indicate that active AI users in China may overlook security and risk issues or have limited awareness of these concerns when using AI services. This research enhances the comprehension of the interplay between AI, information security, and risk perceptions. It highlights the challenges and consequences of using AI, emphasizing the need for schools and colleges to raise awareness of security and risk issues in AI systems.

The results of this research resonate with broader issues raised in the literature concerning the potential cybersecurity and privacy threats introduced by the extensive use of AI technologies. Chilton (2023), for instance, discusses the capacity of AI tools like ChatGPT to assist malicious individuals, underscoring the necessity for strong cybersecurity measures and training to alleviate these emerging risks. Likewise, Huang (2023) explores the ethical consequences of incorporating AI systems into educational environments, particularly regarding student privacy and data safeguarding. The article advocates for the creation of explicit guidelines and regulations to protect student information as AI becomes increasingly prevalent in classroom and administrative contexts.

1.5.1 Implications for Educational Institutions

The widespread use of AI in education has raised concerns about personal data protection. Educational institutions are pivotal in tackling the security concerns and risk perceptions linked to AI. It is essential for policymakers and AI service providers to explore diverse strategies to bolster the security and privacy of AI systems within the educational sector.

Initially, educational institutions ought to allocate resources for awareness campaigns and training modules for students, educators, and administrative personnel. By informing these key groups about the critical nature of information security, the safeguarding of privacy, and the risks associated with utilizing AI services, they will be equipped to make knowledgeable choices and apply robust measures to protect data.

Also, there should be privacy regulations established to protect the privacy of students and faculty, ensure informed consent, and promote transparent data management practices among AI service providers.

Furthermore, educational institutions must proactively enforce more stringent security protocols for their AI systems. This entails the adoption of strong encryption techniques, secure data storage solutions, and consistent security evaluations by AI service providers. These security protocols will bolster user confidence in AI systems and mitigate the risks associated with data breaches and unauthorized access.

The incorporation of AI and big data into education necessitates meticulous attention to cybersecurity and data sharing protocols. Although learning analytics can enhance educational results by providing detailed insights into student performance, they simultaneously present potential threats to the privacy of data. If students feel their personal information is inadequately protected, it can create anxiety and distrust toward educational technologies, hindering their engagement and willingness to share data. Furthermore, concerns about privacy can affect social interactions, making students less likely to collaborate openly.

To tackle these challenges, educational institutions need to establish strong security protocols and also foster a culture of awareness regarding data practices. This includes supporting positive attitudes toward technology and addressing the cognitive and emotional needs of learners. As reliance on AI and big data grows in education, stakeholders must develop frameworks that balance the benefits of learning analytics with the need to protect student privacy.

1.5.2 Limitations and Future Research

The data collection for this study occurred prior to the widespread adoption of ChatGPT, an innovative technology developed by OpenAI. The subsequent surge in popularity of ChatGPT and large language models (LLMs) has brought attention to additional security and risk concerns that were previously disregarded by regulators, corporate users, and individual users alike. When conducting similar survey studies in the future, it is imperative to include respondents who possess familiarity with ChatGPT. Their insights and perspectives can provide valuable information to the questionnaire, thus facilitating a more thorough analysis of the evolving landscape of artificial intelligence and its implications for user security perception and risk assessment.

References

Abbas, N., Imran, A., Manzoor, R., Hussain, T., & Hussain, M. (2023). Role of artificial intelligence tools in enhancing students' educational performance at higher levels. *Journal of Artificial Intelligence Machine Learning and Neural Network*, (35), 36–49. https://doi.org/10.55529/jaimlnn.35.36.49

Akgün, S., & Greenhow, C. (2021). Artificial intelligence in education: Addressing ethical challenges in k-12 settings. *AI and Ethics, 2*(3), 431–440. https://doi.org/10.1007/s43681-021-00096-7

Ayala-Pazmiño, M. (2023). Artificial intelligence in education: Exploring the potential benefits and risks. *593 Digital Publisher Ceit, 8*(3), 892–899. https://doi.org/10.33386/593dp.2023.3.1827

Bačiulienė, V., Bilan, Y., Navickas, V., & Civín, L. (2023). The aspects of artificial intelligence in different phases of the food value and supply chain. *Foods, 12*(8), 1654. https://doi.org/10.3390/foods12081654

Bu, Q. (2022). Ethical risks in integrating artificial intelligence into education and potential countermeasures. *Science Insights, 41*(1), 561–566. https://doi.org/10.15354/si.22.re067

Calo, R. (2010). Peeping HALs: Making sense of artificial intelligence and privacy.

Chaabouni, N., Mosbah, M., Zemmari, A., Sauvignac, C., & Faruki, P. (2019). Network intrusion detection for IoT security based on learning techniques. *IEEE Communications Surveys & Tutorials, 21*, 2671–2701.

Chang, Y., Wong, S. F., Libaque-Saenz, C. F., & Lee, H. (2018). The role of privacy policy on consumers' perceived privacy. *Government Information Quarterly, 35*(3), 445–459. https://doi.org/10.1016/j.giq.2018.04.002

Chen, H., Beaudoin, C. E., & Hong, T. (2016). Teen online information disclosure: Empirical testing of a protection motivation and social capital model. *Journal of the Association for Information Science and Technology*, 67.

Chilton, J. (2023, April 21). The new risks ChatGPT poses to cybersecurity. *Harvard Business Review*. Retrieved from https://hbr.org/2023/04/the-new-risks-chatgpt-poses-to-cybersecurity

Cho, K. (2024). Dual mediating effects of anxiety to use and acceptance attitude of artificial intelligence technology on the relationship between nursing students' perception of and intention to use them: a descriptive study. *BMC Nursing, 23*(1). https://doi.org/10.1186/s12912-024-01887-z

Davenport, T., Guha, A., Grewal, D., & Bressgott, T. (2020). How artificial intelligence will change the future of marketing. *Journal of the Academy of Marketing Science, 48*(1), 24–42. https://doi.org/10.1007/s11747-019-00696-0

Dwivedi, Y. K., Hughes, D. L., Ismagilova, E., Aarts, G., Coombs, C. R., Crick, T., Duan, Y., Dwivedi, R., Edwards, J. S., Eirug, A., Galanos, V., Ilavarasan, P. V., Janssen, M., Jones, P., Kar, A. K., Kizgin, H., Kronemann, B., Lal, B., & Williams, M. D. (2021). Artificial Intelligence (AI): Multidisciplinary perspectives on emerging challenges, opportunities, and agenda for research, practice and policy. *International Journal of Information Management, 57*, 101994. https://doi.org/10.1016/j.ijinfomgt.2019.08.002

Eden, C. (2024). Integrating AI in education: Opportunities, challenges, and ethical considerations. *Magna Scientia Advanced Research and Reviews, 10*(2), 006–013. https://doi.org/10.30574/msarr.2024.10.2.0039

Gerber, N., Reinheimer, B., & Volkamer, M. (2019). Investigating people's privacy risk perception. *Proceedings on Privacy Enhancing Technologies, 2019*(3), 267–288. https://doi.org/10.2478/popets-2019-0047

Halaas, M. (2023). Balancing innovation and cybersecurity in medical schools and their related educational health systems. *Educational Medicine, 98*(11), 1233–1234. https://doi.org/10.1097/acm.0000000000005436

Hardt, D. (2012). The OAuth 2.0 authorization framework. *RFC, 6749*, 1–76.

Hashim, S., Omar, M., Jalil, H., & Sharef, N. (2022). Trends on technologies and artificial intelligence in education for personalized learning: Systematic literature review. *International Journal of Academic Research in Progressive Education and Development, 11*(1). https://doi.org/10.6007/ijarped/v11-i1/12230

Hermansyah, M., Najib, A., Farida, A., Sacipto, R., & Rintyarna, B. (2023). Artificial intelligence and ethics: Building an artificial intelligence system that ensures privacy and social justice. *International Journal of Science and Society, 5*(1), 154–168. https://doi.org/10.54783/ijsoc.v5i1.644

Hong, W., & Thong, J. Y. L. (2013). Internet privacy concerns: An integrated conceptualization and four empirical studies. *MIS Quarterly, 37*(1), 275–298. https://doi.org/10.25300/MISQ/2013/37.1.12

Huang, L. (2023). Ethics of artificial intelligence in education: Student privacy and data protection. *Science Insights Education Frontiers, 16*(2), 2577–2587. https://doi.org/10.15354/sief.23.re202

Jian, M. (2023). Personalized learning through AI. *AEI, 5*(1), 16–19. https://doi.org/10.54254/2977-3903/5/2023039

Kerstan, S. (2023). Choosing human over AI doctors? How comparative trust associations and knowledge relate to risk and benefit perceptions of AI in healthcare. *Risk Analysis, 44*(4), 939–957. https://doi.org/10.1111/risa.14216

Lang, F., & Zhong, Y. (2022). Application of personal information privacy protection based on machine learning algorithm. *Computational Intelligence and Neuroscience*. https://doi.org/10.1155/2022/6710631

Li, Y. (2014). The impact of disposition to privacy, website reputation and website familiarity on information privacy concerns. *Decision Support Systems, 57*, 343–354. https://doi.org/10.1016/j.dss.2013.09.018

Li, P., Cho, H., & Goh, Z. H. (2019). Unpacking the process of privacy management and self-disclosure from the perspectives of regulatory focus and privacy calculus. *Telematics and Informatics, 41*, 114–125. https://doi.org/10.1016/j.tele.2019.04.006

Lightbody, D., Ngo, D., Temko, A., Murphy, C., & Popovici, E. (2023). Attacks on IoT: Side-channel power acquisition framework for intrusion detection. *Future Internet, 15*(5), 187. https://doi.org/10.3390/fi15050187

Milberg, S. J., Smith, H. J., & Burke, S. J. (2000). Information privacy: Corporate management and national regulation. *Organization Science*. https://doi.org/10.1287/orsc.11.1.35.12567

Petronio, S. (1991). Communication boundary management: A theoretical model of managing disclosure of private information between marital couples. *Communication Theory, 1*, 311–335.

Raue, M., D'Ambrosio, L., Ward, C., Lee, C., Jacquillat, C., & Coughlin, J. (2019). The influence of feelings while driving regular cars on the perception and acceptance of self-driving cars. *Risk Analysis, 39*(2), 358–374. https://doi.org/10.1111/risa.13267

Roshanaei, M. (2023). Harnessing AI to foster equity in education: Opportunities, challenges, and emerging strategies. *Journal of Intelligent Learning Systems and Applications, 15*(04), 123–143. https://doi.org/10.4236/jilsa.2023.154009

Sáez-Velasco, S. (2024). Analysing the impact of generative AI in arts education: A cross-disciplinary perspective of educators and students in higher education. *Informatics, 11*(2), 37. https://doi.org/10.3390/informatics11020037

Sarwar, M. (2024). The role of artificial intelligence in shaping the future of education at higher secondary level. *Journal of Education and Social Studies, 5*(1), 34–45. https://doi.org/10.52223/jess.2024.5104

Siegrist, M. (2019). Trust and risk perception: A critical review of the literature. *Risk Analysis, 41*(3), 480–490. https://doi.org/10.1111/risa.13325

Smith, H. J., Milberg, S. J., & Burke, S. J. (1996). Information privacy: Measuring individuals' concerns about organizational practices. *MIS Quarterly, 20*(2), 167–196. https://doi.org/10.2307/249477

Solanke, P. S. (2024). The prospects of generative AI in higher education. *International Journal of Scientific Research in Engineering and Management, 08*(05), 1–5. https://doi.org/10.55041/ijsrem32533

Wirtz, J., Lwin, M. O., & Williams, J. D. (2007). Causes and consequences of consumer online privacy concern. *International Journal of Service Industry Management*. https://doi.org/10.1108/09564230710778128

Yeh, C.-H., Wang, Y.-S., Lin, S.-J., Tseng, T. H., Lin, H.-H., Shih, Y.-W., & Lai, Y.-H. (2018). What drives internet users' willingness to provide personal information? *Online Information Review, 42*(6), 923–939. https://doi.org/10.1108/oir-09-2016-0264

Zawacki-Richter, O., Marín, V., Bond, M., & Gouverneur, F. (2019). Systematic review of research on artificial intelligence applications in higher education – where are the educators?. *International Journal of Educational Technology in Higher Education, 16*(1). https://doi.org/10.1186/s41239-019-0171-0

Zhang, H., & Cheng, S. (2022). Application of internet of things technology based on artificial intelligence in electronic information engineering. *Mobile Information Systems, 2022*, 1–11. https://doi.org/10.1155/2022/2888925

Zhang, J., Reithel, B. J., & Li, H. (2009). Impact of perceived technical protection on security behaviors. *Information Management & Computer Security, 17*(4), 330–340. https://doi.org/10.1108/09685220910993980

Chapter 2
Cognitive AI's Transformative Impact on Self-Regulated Learning in eLearning Environments

Asma Hadyaoui, Lilia Cheniti-Belcadhi, and Mohamed A. A. Mitwally

Abstract This chapter explores the transformative potential of Cognitive Artificial Intelligence (AI) in enhancing Self-Regulated Learning (SRL) within eLearning environments. Motivated by the growing need to support personalized and adaptive learning, the chapter investigates how Cognitive AI tools, particularly through the synergy with learning analytics, can aid learners in the planning, action, and reflection stages as outlined in Zimmerman's cyclical model of SRL. The study employs a multifaceted methodology, combining theoretical analysis, an extensive survey of educational practitioners, and case studies to provide empirical evidence of the current applications and challenges of Cognitive AI in education. Our findings reveal significant improvements in SRL practices, collaborative learning dynamics, and student engagement when AI tools are effectively integrated. However, the study also highlights critical ethical concerns, such as data privacy and the risk of reducing human interaction. The chapter concludes with actionable recommendations for educators and policymakers, emphasizing the need for ethical frameworks to guide the implementation of AI in educational settings. This work not only contributes to the academic discourse on AI in education but also provides a roadmap for future research and practical strategies for integrating AI to support SRL.

Keywords Adaptive learning · Cognitive AI · Ethical AI in education · Learning analytics · Self-Regulated Learning (SRL) · Social connectivity · Zimmerman's SRL model

A. Hadyaoui (✉) · L. Cheniti-Belcadhi
PRINCE Research Lab, ISITCom, Sousse University, Sousse, Tunisia
e-mail: asma.hediaoui@istls.u-sousse.tn

L. Cheniti-Belcadhi
e-mail: lilia.cheniti@isitc.u-sousse.tn

M. A. A. Mitwally
UNESCO Chair of ODL, University of South Africa, Pretoria, South Africa

M. A. Adarkwah et al. (eds.), *Artificial Intelligence and Human Agency in Education: Volume One*, Future Education and Learning Spaces,
https://doi.org/10.1007/978-981-96-7937-9_2

2.1 Introduction

The integration of Cognitive Artificial Intelligence (AI) into eLearning environments is revolutionizing traditional learning by enabling personalized, adaptive learning experiences. Leveraging Machine Learning, Natural Language Processing, and data analytics, Cognitive AI dynamically adjusts educational content and feedback in real-time to cater to each learner's unique needs (Feng, 2019; Ou, 2024). AI-driven tools, such as conversational chatbots and personalized dashboards, provide on-demand assistance and individualized support, significantly enhancing learner engagement and enabling students to take greater control of their learning processes (Park et al., 2018).

Despite the widespread adoption of AI in educational settings, there is a lack of understanding regarding how these technologies specifically support Self-Regulated Learning (SRL)—a critical skill set that allows learners to plan, monitor, and reflect on their progress. SRL is essential for helping students navigate the complexities of modern education and achieve academic success (Pajares & Valiante, 2002). Yet, few studies have explored the specific mechanisms through which Cognitive AI enhances SRL, particularly within the key phases of planning, action, and reflection as outlined in Zimmerman's cyclical model. Research, such as that by Das et al. (2023), has largely focused on the general applications of AI in education, leaving a need for more targeted analysis of how Cognitive AI can support learners' self-regulation processes.

This chapter aims to bridge this gap by systematically examining how Cognitive AI can support SRL in each of these phases. Drawing from recent empirical research, we analyze how tools such as adaptive learning algorithms and real-time feedback systems assist learners in setting goals, adjusting strategies, and reflecting on their learning outcomes. Through a combination of theoretical insights and practical examples, we illustrate how Cognitive AI can effectively transform SRL processes and promote deeper learner autonomy.

Beyond the educational benefits, the chapter also considers the broader societal and ethical implications of integrating AI into education. Issues such as data privacy, algorithmic bias, and equitable access are critical for ensuring that Cognitive AI technologies are implemented responsibly. By exploring both the opportunities and potential risks, we offer practical recommendations for educators, policymakers, and researchers on how to leverage Cognitive AI to effectively support SRL while addressing ethical concerns.

2.2 Research Problem Statement

Despite the rapid advancements in Cognitive AI technology, significant gaps remain in understanding how these tools can most effectively support SRL in educational settings. While much of the existing research has focused on the technical capabilities of AI systems, there has been limited investigation into how Cognitive AI interacts with human learning processes, particularly in the early stages of SRL—planning, action, and reflection. Current literature often overlooks the practical application of AI technologies in helping learners set goals, adapt their strategies in real-time, and reflect on their learning outcomes.

This chapter seeks to address these gaps by providing a detailed analysis of how Cognitive AI supports each phase of SRL within eLearning environments. Additionally, there is a critical need for systematic research into the long-term impacts of AI-driven educational interventions, particularly in diverse educational contexts. The sustainability of these interventions over time and their continued relevance to learners' self-regulation processes, remains underexplored.

Moreover, ethical considerations, including data privacy, algorithmic bias, and educational equity, are crucial issues that require further investigation. The integration of AI into educational environments raises important questions about the fair and transparent use of learner data and the potential for biased outcomes. This chapter aims to offer a comprehensive framework for the ethical and effective integration of Cognitive AI in education, informed by theoretical perspectives, empirical data, and practical case studies.

2.3 Literature Review

Introduction to Self-regulated Learning (SRL)

SRL has emerged as a pivotal skill in modern educational settings, enabling students to effectively plan, monitor, and assess their learning processes Zimmerman's (2000) model of SRL highlights how learners' self-efficacy influences their ability to regulate their learning, which is essential for success in academic environments. With the rise of Cognitive AI technologies, SRL has taken on new dimensions, particularly in eLearning environments. Cognitive AI tools, such as personalized dashboards and adaptive learning algorithms, offer opportunities for enhancing SRL by providing real-time, individualized feedback and dynamically adjusting learning pathways to meet learners' unique needs (Roll & Winne, 2015).

Recent studies underscore the role of Cognitive AI in augmenting SRL (Järvelä et al., 2023a, 2023b) explore how AI can analyze student data continuously to adapt educational content in real-time, thus offering students' immediate, context-aware feedback that supports their self-regulation skills. This ability to model learning processes enables students to receive actionable feedback as they engage with complex learning tasks, fostering deeper cognitive and metacognitive engagement. Such technological advancements are pivotal in helping learners navigate the complexities of modern education, particularly in subjects that demand high levels of cognitive engagement, such as the sciences (Azevedo, 2015).

However, despite these advancements, there is a critical need for a systematic understanding of how Cognitive AI technologies interact with SRL processes, particularly in the early stages of planning, action, and reflection. While Cognitive AI shows promise in enhancing self-regulatory behaviors, studies such as those by Khairi et al. (2024) and Yildirim-Erbasli et al. (2024) emphasize the importance of aligning AI technologies with human learning strategies to ensure effective outcomes. This chapter seeks to explore this interaction by analyzing how AI tools facilitate each phase of SRL.

Challenges in Analyzing SRL

Analyzing SRL in complex educational settings, particularly in the digital age, presents several challenges. Traditional methods for analyzing SRL, such as concurrent reporting, require significant expertise and effort to accurately capture and categorize SRL strategies (Vishwakarma & Tyagi, 2023). These methods, while useful, are often time-consuming and resource-intensive, limiting their scalability in large-scale eLearning environments.

With the rise of online learning platforms, new approaches to SRL analysis are needed. Cognitive AI and learning analytics present innovative solutions to capture real-time, nuanced insights into students' self-regulatory behaviors (Molenaar et al., 2023). By leveraging AI and machine learning algorithms, educators can track how students plan, monitor, and adjust their learning strategies, revealing patterns that were previously difficult to detect. The integration of multimodal data sources further enhances AI's ability to analyze SRL processes and offer personalized interventions (Onan, 2023; Teng, 2024) provide notable contributions in this area, demonstrating how AI-based techniques can be used to predict and assess SRL strategies. Teng's exploration of motivational beliefs and self-efficacy in English as a Foreign Language (EFL) contexts shows how AI can enhance SRL by offering real-time feedback tailored to students' performance. Similarly, Onan's SRL-ACO framework integrates AI to optimize learning outcomes, demonstrating the practical application of SRL principles through technology. These studies highlight how AI can systematically support SRL by providing learners with immediate, actionable feedback.

However, challenges remain. The reliance on large datasets, potential biases in AI algorithms, and the balance between technological input and human oversight require further exploration. As AI continues to evolve, understanding how these technologies can effectively enhance SRL processes while addressing these limitations is crucial for future research.

2.4 Theoretical Framework

Application of Zimmerman's Cyclical Model of SRL Enhanced by Cognitive AI

Integrating Cognitive AI within eLearning frameworks, guided by Zimmerman's Cyclical Model of SRL, heralds a new era of customized educational experiences.

Zimmerman's model, which delineates a structured process involving planning, action, and reflection, serves as an ideal theoretical backdrop for the deployment of Cognitive AI (Zimmerman, 2000). Table 2.1 illustrates how Cognitive AI can be systematically applied across these phases, enhancing various educational activities through targeted tools and methods. Each phase encompasses specific activities supported by corresponding AI tools and methods. In the Planning Phase, activities such as Goal Setting and Customized Goals are driven by AI algorithms and data analysis. The Action Phase focuses on Adaptive Learning, Enacting Strategies, and providing Real-Time Feedback, facilitated by personalized content and immediate feedback mechanisms. During the Reflection Phase, activities like Self-evaluation and Performance Analytics leverage reflective journals and performance metrics.

Planning Phase

The Planning Phase involves learners setting goals, formulating strategies, and organizing resources for their learning tasks. Cognitive AI enhances this phase by analyzing individual learner data to propose personalized goals and strategies that are tailored to their historical performance and learning preferences (Wang & Siau, 2019).

AI-Driven Algorithms: AI algorithms analyze learners' past performance to suggest customized goals and study materials. These suggestions are displayed on

Table 2.1 Cognitive AI-enhanced learning phases, activities, and tools

Phase	Activity	Tool/Method
Planning phase	Goal setting	AI-driven algorithms
	Customized goals and strategy formulation	Data analysis
	Organization of resources	Resource allocation
	Learner dashboard	Interactive dashboards
Action phase	Adaptive learning	Personalized learning paths
	Enact strategies	Implementation strategies
	Real-time feedback	Immediate feedback
	Monitor engagement	Engagement metrics
	Adjust actions	Adaptive adjustments
	Task complexity	Complexity management
Reflection phase	Self-evaluation	Reflective journals
	Performance analytics	Performance metrics
	Identify improvement	Improvement plans and personalized feedback
	Performance assessment	Assessment tools
	Strengths and weaknesses	Strength analysis

interactive dashboards, helping learners organize their time and resources more efficiently. For instance, based on previous task completion data, the AI can recommend study sessions for challenging topics or adjust timelines to meet deadlines.

Learner Dashboard: A personalized dashboard provides learners with an overview of their goals, resources, and suggested strategies. This system not only organizes study materials but also adapts based on the learner's ongoing performance.

Action Phase

In the Action Phase, learners enact their strategies, monitor their engagement, and adjust their actions based on feedback. Cognitive AI provides real-time support during this phase by delivering adaptive learning materials that adjust to the learner's inputs and progress.

Adaptive Learning Paths: AI tools provide personalized learning paths that adapt to the learner's current level of understanding. For example, if a learner struggles with a particular topic, the AI system adjusts the complexity of tasks and offers additional resources to assist learning.

Real-Time Feedback: AI-driven feedback systems provide immediate, context-aware feedback as learners engage with tasks (Hadyaoui & Cheniti-Belcadhi, 2023c). This allows learners to adjust their strategies in real-time, maintaining their engagement and motivation.

Task Complexity Management: AI systems dynamically adjust the complexity of tasks to ensure that learners are neither overwhelmed nor under-challenged. This helps maintain an optimal learning experience tailored to the learner's abilities (Lee & Choi, 2019).

Reflection Phase

In the Reflection Phase, learners evaluate their performance and adjust their future learning strategies. Cognitive AI supports this phase by offering performance analytics and reflective tools to deepen learners' understanding of their strengths and weaknesses.

Performance Analytics: AI tools analyze the learner's performance and generate detailed reports that highlight their strengths and areas for improvement (Hadyaoui & Cheniti-Belcadhi, 2023a). These insights help learners reflect on their strategies and prepare for future tasks.

Reflective Journals: AI-driven reflective journals guide learners through self-evaluation, encouraging them to critically assess their learning process. The personalized feedback generated by AI systems further supports learners in setting new goals for their next learning cycle.

Ethical Considerations in Implementing Cognitive AI

The integration of Cognitive AI into eLearning environments presents significant opportunities for enhancing Self-Regulated Learning (SRL). However, its implementation also raises ethical considerations that must be addressed to ensure that AI technologies benefit all stakeholders, including learners, educators, and society as a whole.

Privacy and Data Security

One of the primary ethical concerns associated with Cognitive AI is the handling of personal data. SRL tools driven by AI, such as learner dashboards, adaptive learning systems, and real-time feedback mechanisms, rely on extensive datasets to deliver personalized learning experiences. These datasets often include sensitive information, such as learners' academic performance, behavioral patterns, and personal characteristics.

To protect the integrity of this data, robust data protection measures must be implemented, aligning with both local and international privacy laws. Transparent policies regarding data collection, usage, and sharing are essential to build trust among learners and educators. The importance of addressing privacy and data security is echoed in the SHERPA project, which stresses the need for ethical considerations in AI technologies (Tahiru, 2021). In educational settings, it is especially important to ensure that learners' personal data are safeguarded to prevent misuse and breaches.

Bias and Fairness

AI systems are only as fair as the data and algorithms that underpin them. There is a significant risk that Cognitive AI could perpetuate existing biases or create new forms of discrimination if not carefully managed. For example, if an AI system trained on a dataset primarily representing one demographic group is used to provide feedback or suggest learning paths, it may underperform for students from other groups.

To mitigate these risks, diverse datasets must be used to train AI systems, and continuous testing must be conducted to ensure fairness. Developers should also provide mechanisms for learners and educators to report and correct perceived biases in the system. As Balasubramaniam et al. (2023) emphasizes, transparency, fairness, and accountability are critical to the ethical deployment of AI technologies, particularly in education.

Accountability and Transparency

One of the significant challenges with AI-driven systems is their lack of transparency, often referred to as the "black box" problem. This is especially relevant in educational settings, where understanding the rationale behind decisions, such as the feedback given or learning path adjustments, is crucial for both learners and educators.

To maintain accountability, AI systems used in SRL must be explainable. This means that the decisions made by AI should be auditable and easily understandable by users. For example, if an AI system suggests adjusting a learner's strategy during the action phase of SRL, it should provide a clear rationale behind this recommendation, allowing educators to trust the system and learners to understand the feedback provided (Peters, 2023).

Impact on Pedagogy

While AI tools can enhance SRL by providing personalized feedback and real-time adjustments, there is concern that the increasing reliance on AI may diminish the essential role of educators. Effective learning often requires human interaction, and

AI should be used to augment, rather than replace, the pedagogical functions of teachers.

To address this, educators must be trained to use AI-driven SRL tools effectively, ensuring that these technologies enhance collaboration, interaction, and adaptability in the learning environment. For example, while Cognitive AI can suggest personalized learning strategies, it should work in tandem with teachers, who provide emotional support and contextual understanding that AI tools may lack.

Consent and Autonomy

Learners have the right to understand how Cognitive AI is used in their learning processes, especially when it comes to self-regulation tools that analyze their performance and suggest learning strategies. Institutions must ensure that learners and their guardians are fully informed about the AI tools in use, the benefits they provide, and any associated risks.

Providing transparency around these tools not only respects learners' autonomy but also ensures that they are actively engaged in their learning process. Educators and institutions should also provide opt-out options for learners who may not want to participate in certain AI-driven interventions (Holmes et al., 2019).

Continuous Ethical Evaluation

As AI technologies continue to evolve, so too must the ethical frameworks that govern their use in education. It is critical that educational institutions engage in ongoing ethical evaluations and dialogues with all stakeholders, including students, parents, educators, and policymakers. These evaluations should reflect the latest advancements in AI and consider the impact of these technologies on SRL. The involvement of parents and the community is particularly important, as it fosters a holistic approach to addressing the needs of learners. By ensuring continuous dialogue and ethical oversight, institutions can implement AI technologies in a way that supports diverse learners and reinforces the values of inclusivity and equity (Eden & Chisom, 2024).

Methodology

To understand the adoption and impact of Cognitive AI in education, we conducted an extensive survey targeting participants from various roles within the educational sector in Tunisia. The primary objective of this survey was to gather diverse perspectives on the utilization of Cognitive AI tools, their effectiveness in enhancing educational processes, and the challenges encountered in integrating these technologies into daily practices. We also conducted case studies to explore in-depth how AI supports SRL in practical settings.

Survey Design and Implementation

The survey was designed to capture a broad spectrum of experiences and insights from individuals in various educational roles, including educators, students, administrators, and IT specialists. To align with the study's focus on SRL, the survey questions were developed using Zimmerman's cyclical model of SRL, specifically targeting the planning, action, and reflection phases. The survey consisted of 20 questions: 15 closed-ended questions using a 5-point Likert scale (1 = Strongly Disagree, 5 = Strongly Agree) to assess the perceived effectiveness of AI tools, and 5 open-ended questions aimed at capturing qualitative insights on the challenges, opportunities, and perceptions related to AI adoption in educational settings.

The open-ended questions provided participants with the opportunity to elaborate on areas not captured by the closed-ended items, such as specific barriers to AI adoption, emotional responses to AI feedback, and suggestions for enhancing AI-supported SRL. Example survey questions included:

"How does the AI tool assist you in setting and adjusting learning goals?" (Planning phase).
"How does AI feedback influence your learning strategies during tasks?" (Action phase).
"Does the AI tool provide support during reflection on completed tasks?" (Reflection phase).

We conducted the survey online over three months, from January to March 2024, using multiple distribution channels, including educational institutions' mailing lists, professional networks, and social media platforms to maximize participant reach.

Participants

We targeted a diverse group of participants across various educational levels and roles to ensure a comprehensive understanding of Cognitive AI's impact.

A total of 234 respondents participated in the survey, which was distributed through educational institutions, professional networks, and online platforms to maximize reach, as depicted in Fig. 2.1. The breakdown of participants is as follows:

Educators: 105 respondents (44.9%)
Students: 70 respondents (29.9%)
Administrators: 32 respondents (13.7%)
IT Specialists: 27 respondents (11.5%).

Educational Levels

Most responses were obtained from individuals associated with tertiary institutions (140 respondents, 59.8%), reflecting the prevalent use of AI tools in higher education, likely due to the complexity of subjects and the availability of resources. Additionally, respondents from secondary education and corporate training contexts provided valuable insights into the application of AI technologies across different educational stages.

Geographic Focus

The survey was geographically focused exclusively on Tunisia. This focus allowed us to capture a homogeneous sample, eliminating regional variability and centering on specific educational AI applications within the country. This localized approach

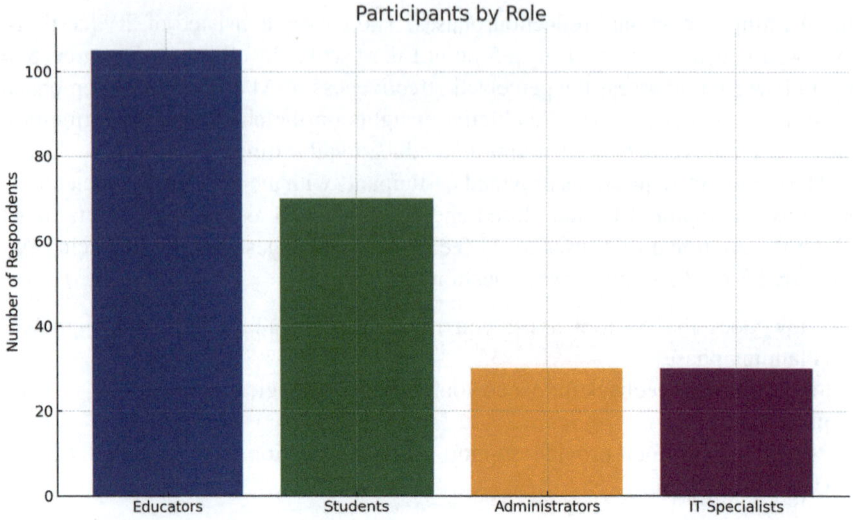

Fig. 2.1 Survey respondents by role

provided detailed insights into how Cognitive AI is being integrated into Tunisian educational practices, offering a snapshot of the current state of AI adoption in a specific educational context.

Data Analysis

The quantitative data from the survey were initially analyzed using descriptive statistics, providing insights into the frequency of AI tool usage, perceived effectiveness, and common challenges. While descriptive statistics offered a broad overview of trends, further statistical analyzes were conducted to assess the relationships between AI tool usage and SRL outcomes.

Inferential Analysis: To deepen the analysis, correlation and regression analyzes were performed to explore how specific AI tools (e.g., real-time feedback systems) predicted improvements in SRL. For example, regression models were used to examine the influence of AI-assisted feedback on students' ability to monitor and adjust their learning strategies during the action phase of SRL.

Qualitative Analysis: Qualitative data from open-ended survey responses were thematically analyzed to uncover deeper insights into the challenges and benefits of integrating AI into educational settings. Thematic coding identified key areas of concern, such as the emotional impact of AI tools and their role in fostering or hindering collaboration.

Key Findings

Social and Psychological Dimensions of SRL in AI-Enhanced Learning: Surveys and User Sessions

The incorporation of Cognitive AI into eLearning environments profoundly influences not only educational outcomes but also the social and psychological dimensions of learning. These dimensions are crucial in shaping learners' self-regulation processes, as they impact how learners perceive their learning environment, interact with content and peers, and manage their emotional engagement with learning tasks.

Survey data and user sessions reveal that the use of AI tools significantly affects learners' ability to engage in SRL by influencing their social interactions and psychological well-being. Cognitive AI tools that facilitate collaborative learning and provide personalized feedback help learners enhance their ability to plan, monitor, and reflect on their learning tasks.

The survey results, as shown in Fig. 2.1, indicate that approximately 50% of participants utilize Cognitive AI tools on a weekly basis. This high frequency of usage highlights the growing reliance on AI in eLearning environments in Tunisia. The regular use of these tools supports social connectivity by fostering collaborative efforts among learners, while simultaneously providing the psychological support needed to maintain motivation and persistence in their learning goals.

Social Connectivity and Collaboration

Cognitive AI technologies have the potential to transform traditional social dynamics in educational settings by enhancing collaborative learning and social connectivity among learners. Empirical evidence from the survey suggests that AI tools significantly improve student collaboration by facilitating group activities that are both engaging and tailored to the specific needs and learning styles of individual students.

One key feature of AI tools is their ability to dynamically form study groups by analyzing learners' strengths, weaknesses, and preferences. By grouping learners based on complementary skills and learning styles, AI fosters a collaborative environment where students can support each other, share resources, and engage in collective problem-solving. This personalized approach to group formation improves goal-setting (planning phase) and encourages learners to engage in self-monitoring and reflection as they work together to achieve common objectives.

Psychological Impact on Learners

The psychological impact of Cognitive AI in eLearning environments is both profound and multifaceted, particularly in its ability to influence SRL. One of the most significant benefits, as evidenced by survey data, is the marked increase in learner motivation and engagement. Cognitive AI's ability to deliver immediate feedback and personalize learning experiences based on individual needs plays a crucial role in sustaining students' interest and commitment to their learning goals.

Motivation and Confidence

AI's real-time feedback mechanisms provide learners with continuous reinforcement throughout their learning process, which enhances motivation during the action phase of SRL. Learners receive tailored insights into their progress, allowing them to adjust strategies on the fly, which increases their confidence and encourages persistence when faced with difficult tasks. The immediate feedback provided by AI acts as an ongoing motivator, helping learners stay focused on their objectives and reducing the likelihood of disengagement.

Surveys indicate that this form of personalized support has shown a significant psychological impact, leading to improved self-efficacy—a critical component of SRL. When learners are confident in their ability to succeed, they are more likely to set challenging goals and engage deeply in their learning. Figure 2.2 demonstrates that both students and educators report substantial improvements in SRL behaviors, such as goal-setting, strategy adjustment, and reflection, as a direct result of Cognitive AI's integration into their learning environments (Fig. 2.2).

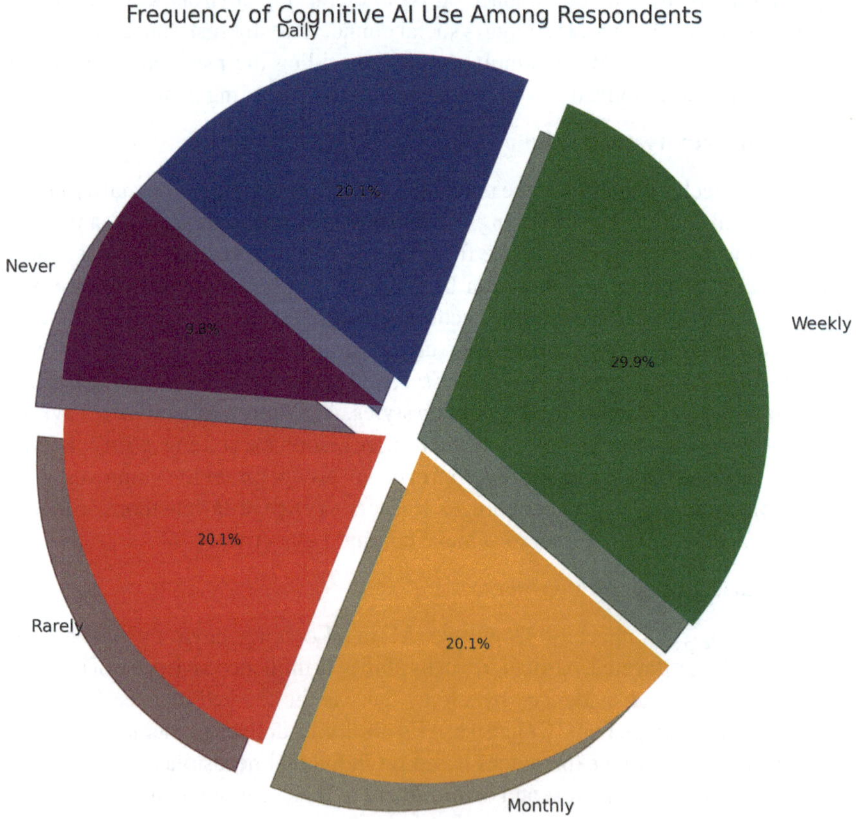

Fig. 2.2 Distribution of cognitive AI usage frequency among survey respondents

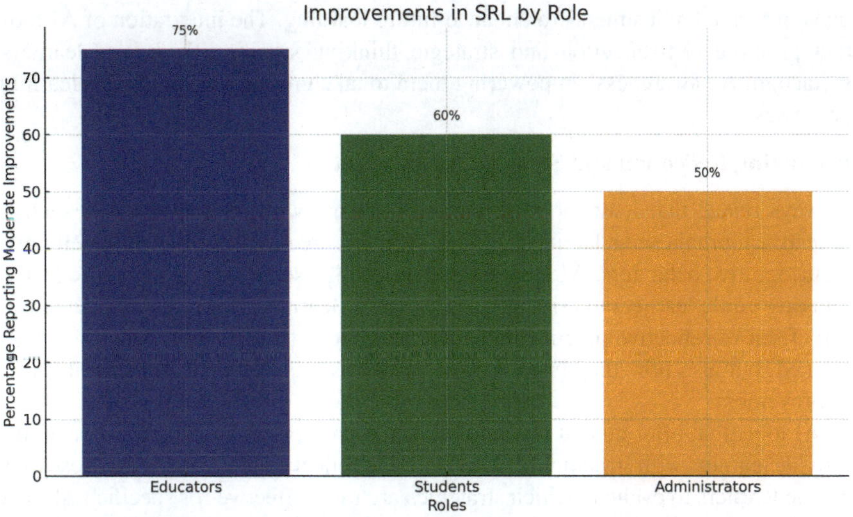

Fig. 2.3 Percentage of respondents reporting moderate improvements in SRL by role

Differences in Perception

While students and educators overwhelmingly recognize the benefits of AI in improving motivation and persistence, responses from IT specialists and administrators show some variations in perceived effectiveness. This divergence may be due to differences in their roles and expectations regarding the implementation of AI tools. Whereas learners and teachers focus primarily on direct educational outcomes, IT and administrative staff may have concerns about the technical challenges, scalability, or resource allocation associated with maintaining AI systems.

Key Findings

Enhanced Motivation: AI's real-time feedback and adaptive learning capabilities boost learner motivation during the action phase, helping students stay engaged and focused on their learning tasks.

Increased Confidence: The continuous, personalized feedback provided by AI helps build learners confidence, improving their willingness to set and pursue challenging goals, which is essential for effective goal-setting and reflection in SRL.

Variations in Perception: Differences in perceptions of AI's effectiveness between educators and IT specialists suggest the need for more alignment in understanding AI's role in supporting learning versus the logistical and technical challenges it may present.

Impact on Metacognitive Skills

Cognitive AI plays a critical role in the development of metacognitive skills, which are essential components of Self-Regulated Learning (SRL). Metacognitive skills allow learners to reflect on their learning strategies, assess their progress, and make informed adjustments to enhance future learning. The integration of AI tools that promote self-reflection and strategic thinking significantly boosts learners' metacognitive awareness, empowering them to take greater control of their learning processes.

Promoting Reflection and Strategy Adjustment

Surveys reveal that learners who regularly engage with AI-driven tools, such as reflective journals and adaptive feedback systems, are more likely to adopt effective metacognitive behaviors. AI systems that encourage self-questioning and reflective thinking guide learners to critically analyze their learning strategies and outcomes. This form of reflective practice helps learners understand not only what they have learned, but also how they have learned, which is crucial for identifying areas for improvement.

AI tools that offer guided reflection through prompts and performance analytics provide learners with structured opportunities to reflect on their progress. These tools enable learners to evaluate which strategies are most effective for specific tasks and how they can enhance their future learning practices. By engaging in this continuous cycle of reflection and adjustment, learners strengthen their self-regulation skills, leading to more effective goal-setting and action planning.

Key Findings

Enhanced Metacognitive Awareness: AI-driven tools that prompt learners to reflect on their learning processes improve metacognitive awareness, allowing them to assess and refine their strategies during the reflection phase of SRL.

Critical Analysis of Learning Strategies: Learners who use reflective journals and AI-guided feedback are more likely to critically evaluate their learning methods and make necessary adjustments, enhancing their overall self-regulation.

Support for Continuous Improvement: The structured reflection facilitated by Cognitive AI tools supports learners in identifying effective strategies, leading to continuous improvement in their learning practices and stronger metacognitive skills.

Ethical and Emotional Considerations

The ethical implementation of Cognitive AI in education is closely tied to its social and psychological impact on learners. Ensuring that AI systems are used ethically is crucial for maintaining trust and confidence among learners, especially when these systems influence personal learning paths and performance feedback. Ethical considerations must address issues of data privacy, algorithmic fairness, and emotional responsiveness to ensure that AI technologies benefit learners without causing unintended harm.

Ethical Concerns: Data Privacy and Bias

One of the primary ethical concerns surrounding the use of AI in education is the handling of personal data. AI systems rely on extensive data collection to provide personalized feedback, which raises concerns about the privacy and security of learners' information. It is essential that educators and institutions implement robust data protection measures and transparent policies regarding data collection and usage.

Additionally, AI systems are vulnerable to algorithmic bias, which can result in unequal treatment of learners based on factors such as demographics or learning styles. Ensuring that AI tools are designed to be fair and transparent is critical for avoiding biased outcomes that could disadvantage certain groups of learners.

Emotional Considerations

While Cognitive AI offers significant benefits in terms of personalized learning, its lack of emotional intelligence can lead to interactions that feel impersonal or disconnected from learners' emotional states. Learners may feel that AI feedback is detached or insufficiently responsive to their emotional needs, which can reduce engagement and motivation.

Implementing AI systems that are capable of detecting and responding to emotional cues—such as frustration, disengagement, or anxiety—can help make interactions more responsive and emotionally attuned to the individual needs of learners. Programs that offer emotional support through personalized feedback and intervention strategies can help bridge the gap between AI and human emotional intelligence.

Key Findings

Trust and Ethical AI: Ensuring that AI systems are used ethically—by protecting data privacy and addressing algorithmic bias—is essential for maintaining learner trust and promoting positive educational outcomes.

Emotional Responsiveness: Cognitive AI systems must be designed to be more attuned to learners' emotional needs, providing support that goes beyond technical feedback and addresses the psychological aspects of learning.

Balancing AI with Human Interaction: While AI offers personalized and efficient learning solutions, the emotional and human element of learning should not be neglected. Educators must ensure that AI tools are used to augment rather than replace the human connection in learning environments.

Case Studies for Cognitive AI

The application of Cognitive AI in eLearning environments transcends individual learning, exerting a considerable impact on collaborative problem-solving and emotional resilience. This section presents case studies that illustrate the effective integration of cognitive AI into educational settings to enhance these critical aspects of learning.

Case Study 1: Implementing the AICeA Framework in Python Programming Courses

Background

At the Higher Institute of Transport and Logistics, University of Sousse, the introduction of the Adaptive Intelligent Collaborative eAssessment (AICeA) Framework into the Python programming course represented a significant advancement in utilizing technology to improve educational outcomes. The successful implementation and positive results of the AICeA Framework are comprehensively detailed in our forthcoming publication (Hadyaoui & Cheniti-Belcadhi, 2023b), which discusses the framework's design and its transformative impact on collaborative eLearning environments. This work provides an in-depth analysis of how integrating advanced AI, Semantic Web technologies, and Recommender Systems can substantially enhance both teaching and learning experiences. It demonstrates the framework's effectiveness in facilitating group formation and promoting proactive engagement by aligning learners based on their complementary skills, knowledge bases, and educational preferences.

Implementation

The AICeA Framework was specifically designed to support and assess students within the dynamic context of Python programming, a discipline that demands high levels of problem-solving and collaborative input. The framework employed predictive analytics, ontological modeling, and machine learning techniques to deliver personalized assessment experiences. It facilitated effective group formation and proactive engagement by recommending bespoke group alignments based on learners' complementary skills, knowledge bases, and educational preferences. A notable feature of the framework was its real-time adaptability, enabling it to respond to ongoing feedback and evolving learner profiles. This dynamic adjustment was crucial during collaborative projects, where the framework's ability to analyze group interactions in real-time led to judicious matching of learners for feedback sessions, efficient management of assessment data, and tailored intervention strategies aimed at improving learner retention and maximizing the effectiveness of collaborative efforts.

Outcomes

Enhanced Collaborative Learning: Groups formed through the AICeA Framework exhibited improved collaborative dynamics, with a more balanced distribution of roles and contributions, resulting in higher-quality project outcomes.

Increased Efficiency in Problem-Solving: The AI-driven components of the framework facilitated quicker resolution of complex programming tasks by optimizing group strategies and providing targeted resources where they were most needed.

Positive Feedback from Students: Students responded favorably to the enhanced learning environment, particularly noting the personalized support and the effectiveness of group interactions facilitated by the AICeA Framework.

Lessons Learned

The deployment of the AICeA Framework within the Python programming course underscored the importance of using AI to complement human interaction rather than replace it. The framework's capability to facilitate but not dominate the problem-solving process allowed students to engage deeply with the learning material, fostering a productive and supportive educational environment. Therefore, this case study validates the efficacy of integrating advanced AI and semantic technologies in educational settings and highlights the potential scalability of such frameworks across different disciplines and courses.

Case Study 2: Enhancing Emotional Resilience Among Students

Background

The Higher Institute of Transport and Logistics of Sousse emphasizes the importance of capstone projects that require the implementation of IT solutions, particularly in Python programming. These projects are critical for students' academic and professional development, often involving complex problem-solving and innovative software development. Recognizing the high stress and emotional strain associated with these demanding projects, the institute sought to enhance students' emotional resilience through targeted interventions using the AICeA Framework.

Implementation

The AICeA Framework was deployed with advanced machine learning algorithms designed to analyze linguistic cues and emotional indicators from students' digital interactions and project documentation. This system aimed to proactively identify emotional stressors that could impede student performance and provide timely interventions. Integrated with the institute's learning management system, the AI offered personalized feedback and coping strategies tailored to the unique challenges faced during the development and implementation of IT solutions in their final year projects.

Outcomes

Improved Emotional Regulation: Students reported significant improvements in their ability to manage stress and anxiety, particularly during critical phases of their projects such as debugging, integration, and final presentations. This led to a noticeable decrease in burnout and enhanced overall project performance.

Enhanced Self-awareness: Feedback from the AI system helped students recognize their stress triggers and emotional responses during project execution. This increased awareness allowed them to better manage their emotions and remain focused under pressure, ultimately contributing to higher-quality project outcomes.

Supportive Learning Environment: The implementation of the AICeA Framework fostered a more collaborative and supportive atmosphere among project teams. Enhanced emotional support from the AI encouraged a more cohesive team dynamic, where students felt more comfortable seeking help and sharing responsibilities.

Lessons Learned

This case study highlights the critical role of cognitive AI in supporting students during high-stakes capstone projects in Python programming. The AICeA Framework's ability to enhance emotional resilience not only improved individual student outcomes but also promoted a healthier, more supportive educational environment. The successful integration of this technology demonstrated the need for targeted emotional interventions in academic programs, especially those involving complex IT solution implementations. Moreover, the experience underscored the importance of continuous monitoring and adaptation of AI tools to ensure they meet the evolving needs of students and the dynamic demands of IT projects.

Discussion and Implications

The findings presented in this chapter underscore the significant influence of Cognitive AI on SRL, collaborative problem-solving, and emotional resilience. These results highlight the transformative potential of AI technologies in educational settings, particularly their ability to enhance personalized learning experiences. However, it is important to contextualize these findings within the research question and compare them with previous studies to provide a clearer understanding of Cognitive AI's role in SRL.

Our research demonstrates that Cognitive AI can substantially improve SRL by providing personalized feedback and tailored learning paths, supporting students' planning, monitoring, and reflective processes. This aligns closely with Zimmerman's cyclical model of SRL, where feedback and self-regulation are critical to learning success. The increased engagement and motivation observed among students, as highlighted by our survey data, are consistent with prior studies. For example, Järvelä et al. (2023a, 2023b) and Li (2023) emphasize the role of adaptive learning technologies in enhancing self-regulatory skills. Our findings support their conclusions by showing that AI-driven feedback mechanisms can foster autonomy and motivation, ultimately helping students manage their learning more effectively.

The enhancement of collaborative learning dynamics through AI-driven group formations and interactions also indicates the potential for AI to facilitate social connectivity and teamwork among students. This finding is consistent with (Xu, 2024), who discuss how AI can tailor interactions in group learning activities to meet the specific needs of learners. In our study, the ability of AI to dynamically form groups based on learners' skills and preferences improved collaborative outcomes. However, while this supports existing theories on AI's benefits in social learning contexts, our findings suggest that AI's impact on emotional resilience requires further exploration, as mixed responses were observed regarding how AI-mediated feedback supported stress management.

In addition to the educational benefits, this chapter also highlights several potential challenges, particularly regarding the ethical use of AI, data privacy, and the risk of diminishing face-to-face interactions. These challenges echo concerns raised by Li (2023) who argues for the necessity of robust ethical frameworks to ensure AI technologies are deployed equitably and responsibly. The ethical considerations related to privacy, bias, and transparency are central to the successful integration of AI in education. Addressing these challenges is crucial for maintaining trust and acceptance among all stakeholders, including students, educators, and policymakers.

One limitation of this study is that the findings are based primarily on descriptive analysis from a specific sample of students and educators, which may limit the generalizability of the results. Future research should focus on conducting more comprehensive statistical analyzes and longitudinal studies to better assess the long-term effects of Cognitive AI on SRL. In particular, studies could explore how AI's influence evolves over time and across different educational environments.

Comparing our findings with relevant research reveals both the promise and the challenges of Cognitive AI in education. While Cognitive AI holds great potential for enhancing SRL and collaborative learning, its implementation must be approached with caution to ensure that ethical, social, and psychological considerations are addressed. This comparative analysis underscores the importance of interdisciplinary collaboration in developing AI technologies that are both effective and equitable. In particular, the integration of Cognitive AI must align with broader educational goals, including equity, inclusivity, and the holistic development of students.

In light of these findings, future research should focus on building robust theoretical frameworks that integrate Cognitive AI within educational settings while ensuring these technologies contribute to broader educational objectives. Additionally, exploring ways to address the emotional and psychological impacts of AI-mediated learning remains an important avenue for further study. This will help ensure that AI technologies are not only effective in supporting SRL but also promote a balanced and inclusive learning environment for all students.

Recommendations and Future Research Directions

Recommendations

To fully exploit the potential of Cognitive AI in eLearning environments and effectively address the associated challenges, Table 2.2 provides a structured set of recommendations for educators and policymakers. These guidelines are designed to ensure the strategic and effective implementation of AI tools, safeguard data privacy and security, and promote equity and accessibility in educational settings. Each recommendation is detailed with specific actions to guide stakeholders in optimizing their approach to integrating AI within their curricula. This structured approach aims to facilitate a thoughtful and effective adoption of AI technologies in education.

Future Research Directions

To address the evolving landscape of Cognitive AI in education and maximize its potential, it is crucial to identify and pursue targeted areas for future research. Table 2.3 delineates a structured outline of future research directions that encompass various facets of AI application in educational settings. These directions include longitudinal studies to assess the long-term impacts of AI, explorations into AI's adaptability across different educational environments, advancements in AI technology for enhanced learning experiences, and collaborative efforts to establish ethical standards in AI usage.

Table 2.2 Strategic recommendations for implementing AI in educational settings

Category	Recommendation	Details
Strategic implementation of AI tools	Tailored integration	Customize AI tools based on the distinct educational objectives and the diverse needs of students Aim to avoid a generic approach and cater to individual learning styles and abilities
	Professional development	Provide comprehensive and ongoing training for educators to enhance their understanding and skills in implementing AI tools effectively Focus on both technical aspects and pedagogical integration to maximize the potential benefits of AI
Enhancing data privacy and security	Robust policies	Develop and rigorously enforce data privacy policies that adhere to both national and international standards, ensuring that all student data handling is transparent and secure
	Student awareness	Actively inform students about the AI tools' data practices, including data collection, usage, and protection measures to foster trust and transparency
Promoting equity and accessibility	Accessibility measures	Guarantee that AI-driven eLearning tools are fully accessible to all students, particularly those with disabilities, by implementing adaptive and inclusive technologies
	Prevent bias	Regularly conduct audits of AI algorithms to detect and address any potential biases, ensuring that AI applications are equitable and do not perpetuate or exacerbate existing disparities

2.5 Conclusion

This chapter's exploration of Cognitive AI in eLearning environments highlights its transformative potential for enhancing SRL, improving collaborative problem-solving, and bolstering emotional resilience among learners. Insights drawn from theoretical analyzes, surveys, case studies, and practical examples provide a robust framework for understanding the multifaceted impacts of cognitive AI on education. Cognitive AI has demonstrated significant capabilities in personalizing learning experiences, making them more adaptive and responsive to individual learner needs. By leveraging data-driven insights, AI technologies can fine-tune educational content and methodologies, thereby facilitating a more engaging and effective learning process. Moreover, AI's role in fostering collaborative environments and supporting emotional resilience has introduced new avenues for developing comprehensive educational practices that address both cognitive and emotional aspects of learning.

Table 2.3 Future research directions for enhancing cognitive AI in education

Category	Research direction	Details
Longitudinal studies on AI impact	Long-term effects	Conduct longitudinal studies to evaluate the enduring impacts of AI on students' academic performance, SRL capabilities, and emotional well-being. Assess how these effects evolve with advancements in AI technologies
AI in different educational contexts	Diverse settings	Explore the effectiveness of cognitive AI across various educational settings, including K-12, higher education, and vocational training. Investigate how contextual factors influence AI integration's success and challenges
Advancements in AI technology	Innovative technologies	Research and develop advanced AI technologies that offer deeper insights into learning processes. Focus on technologies such as augmented reality (AR) and virtual reality (VR) to enhance immersive learning experiences
	Emotion AI	Improve the capabilities of AI to better understand and respond to learners' emotional states. This enhancement aims to boost emotional resilience and optimize educational outcomes
Collaboration and ethical standards	Global collaboration	Encourage collaboration between educational institutions, technology developers, and policymakers worldwide to share best practices and establish universal standards for ethical AI in education
	Ethical AI frameworks	Develop comprehensive guidelines that guide the ethical implementation of AI in educational settings. Focus on crucial issues such as consent, autonomy, and the right to education

The implications of integrating cognitive AI into educational systems are profound. Educators and policymakers are presented with innovative tools that can revolutionize teaching and learning practices. However, this integration also necessitates careful consideration of ethical, social, and psychological factors to ensure the beneficial and equitable deployment of AI technologies. Addressing concerns related to data privacy, algorithmic bias, and the digital divide is crucial for building trust and acceptance among all stakeholders in the educational ecosystem.

Looking forward, the continued evolution of AI technology promises even greater advancements in educational applications. The development of more sophisticated AI models capable of understanding and adapting to emotional cues will further personalize learning experiences and potentially transform traditional educational paradigms. Achieving these advancements will require ongoing collaboration among researchers, technologists, educators, and policymakers to ensure the responsible and effective implementation of AI technologies.

Future research should focus on longitudinal studies to assess the long-term impact of AI on learning outcomes, explore the scalability of AI applications across diverse educational settings, and develop new methodologies for measuring the success of AI integration in education.

References

Azevedo, R. (2015). Defining and measuring engagement and learning in science: Conceptual, theoretical, methodological, and analytical issues. *Educational Psychologist, 50*(1), 84–94. https://doi.org/10.1080/00461520.2015.1004069

Balasubramaniam, N., Kauppinen, M., Rannisto, A., Hiekkanen, K., & Kujala, S. (2023). Transparency and explainability of AI systems: From ethical guidelines to requirements. *Information and Software Technology, 159*, Article 107197. https://doi.org/10.1016/j.infsof.2023.107197

Das, A., Malaviya, S., & Singh, M. (2023). The impact of AI-driven personalization on learners' performance. *International Journal of Computer Sciences and Engineering, 11*(8), 15–22. https://doi.org/10.26438/ijcse/v11i8.1522

Eden, C., & Chisom, O. (2024). Parent and community involvement in education: Strengthening partnerships for social improvement. *International Journal of Applied Research in Social Sciences, 6*(3), 372–382. https://doi.org/10.51594/ijarss.v6i3.894

Feng, T. (2019). Cognitive function of artificial intelligence literature. *IOP Conference Series: Materials Science and Engineering, 573*(1), Article 012106. https://doi.org/10.1088/1757-899X/573/1/012106

Hadyaoui, A., & Cheniti-Belcadhi, L. (2023a). An ontology-based collaborative assessment analytics framework to predict groups' disengagement. In I. Czarnowski, R. J. Howlett, & L. C. Jain (Eds.), *Intelligent decision technologies* (pp. 74–84). Springer Nature Singapore.

Hadyaoui, A., & Cheniti-Belcadhi, L. (2023b). Intelligent collaborative assessment for cyberspace eLearning environments. *International Conference on Cyberworlds (CW), 2023*, 306–313. https://doi.org/10.1109/CW58918.2023.00054

Hadyaoui, A., & Cheniti-Belcadhi, L. (2023c). Ontology-driven intelligent group pairing in project-based collaborative learning. In F. J. García-Peñalvo & M. Marchiori (Eds.), *Proceedings of the 19th International Conference on Web Information Systems and Technologies, WEBIST 2023* (pp. 152–163). Rome, Italy, November 15–17, 2023. SCITEPRESS. https://doi.org/10.5220/0012237500003584

Holmes, W., Bialik, M., & Fadel, C. (2019). *Artificial intelligence in education: Promise and implications for teaching and learning*. Center for Curriculum Redesign.

Järvelä, S., Molenaar, I., & Nguyen, A. (2023a). Advancing SRL research with artificial intelligence. *Computers in Human Behavior, 147*, Article 107847. https://doi.org/10.1016/j.chb.2023.107847

Järvelä, S., Nguyen, A., & Hadwin, A. (2023b). Human and artificial intelligence collaboration for socially shared regulation in learning. *British Journal of Educational Technology, 54*(2), 1057–1076. https://doi.org/10.1111/bjet.13325

Khairi, F., & Yhya Alhafidh, F. (2024). Exploring the impact of using AI in support of the self-regulated learning process. https://doi.org/10.13140/RG.2.2.34317.96481

Lee, J., & Choi, H. (2019). Rethinking the flipped learning pre-class: Its influence on the success of flipped learning and related factors. *British Journal of Educational Technology, 50*(2), 934–945. https://doi.org/10.1111/bjet.12618

Li, N. (2023). Ethical considerations in artificial intelligence: A comprehensive discussion from the perspective of computer vision. *SHS Web of Conferences, 179*, 04024. https://doi.org/10.1051/shsconf/202317904024

Molenaar, I., de Mooij, S., Azevedo, R., Bannert, M., Järvelä, S., & Gašević, D. (2023). Measuring self-regulated learning and the role of AI: Five years of research using multimodal multichannel data. *Computers in Human Behavior, 139*, Article 107540. https://doi.org/10.1016/j.chb.2022.107540

Onan, A. (2023). SRL-ACO: A text augmentation framework based on semantic role labeling and ant colony optimization. *Journal of King Saud University - Computer and Information Sciences, 35*(7), Article 101611. https://doi.org/10.1016/j.jksuci.2023.101611

Ou, S. (2024). Transforming education: The evolving role of artificial intelligence in the students' academic performance. *International Journal of Education and Humanities, 13*, 163–173. https://doi.org/10.54097/cc1x7r95

Pajares, F., & Valiante, G. (2002). Students' self-efficacy in their self-regulated learning strategies: A developmental perspective. *Psychologia, 45*(2), 211–221. https://doi.org/10.2117/psysoc.2002.211

Park, M., Aiken, M., & Salvador, L. (2018). How do humans interact with chatbots?: An analysis of transcripts. *International Journal of Management & Information Technology, 14*, 3338–3350. https://doi.org/10.24297/ijmit.v14i0.7921

Peters, U. (2023). Explainable AI lacks regulative reasons: Why AI and human decision-making are not equally opaque. *AI and Ethics, 3*(3), 963–974. https://doi.org/10.1007/s43681-022-00217-w

Roll, I., & Winne, P. (2015). Understanding, evaluating, and supporting self-regulated learning using learning analytics. *Journal of Learning Analytics, 2*(1), 7–12. https://doi.org/10.18608/jla.2015.21.2

Tahiru, F. (2021). AI in education. *Journal of Cases on Information Technology, 23*(1), 1–20. https://doi.org/10.4018/jcit.2021010101

Teng, L. S. (2024). Individual differences in self-regulated learning: Exploring the nexus of motivational beliefs, self-efficacy, and SRL strategies in EFL writing. *Language Teaching Research, 28*(2), 366–388. https://doi.org/10.1177/13621688211006881

Vishwakarma, A., & Tyagi, N. (2023). Strategies for promoting self-regulation in online learning environments: An analytical review. *Journal of Positive School Psychology, 6*, 4258–4271.

Wang, W., & Siau, K. (2019). Artificial intelligence, machine learning, automation, robotics, future of work and future of humanity: A review and research agenda. *Journal of Database Management, 30*, 61–79. https://doi.org/10.4018/JDM.2019010104

Xu, Z. (2024). AI in education: Enhancing learning experiences and student outcomes. *Applied and Computational Engineering, 51*, 104–111. https://doi.org/10.54254/2755-2721/51/20241187

Yildirim-Erbasli, S. N., Gorgun, G., & Bulut, O. (2024). Enhancing self-regulated learning with artificial intelligence-powered learning analytics. In *Proceedings of the International Conference on Learning Analytics* (pp. 57–83). https://doi.org/10.4018/979-8-3693-0066-4

Zimmerman, B. J. (2000). Self-efficacy: An essential motive to learn. *Contemporary Educational Psychology, 25*(1), 82–91. https://doi.org/10.1006/ceps.1999.1016

Chapter 3
Cultivating Cognitive Justice in AI-Enhanced Education: Harnessing Intelligent Tutoring Systems and Navigating Ethical Horizons

Robert Nicky Tjano and Ramashego Mphahlele

Abstract The post-COVID world of work and learning has seen increased amount of automation aimed at improving efficiency. At the core of this development is the transformative power of artificial intelligence (AI) technologies. Intelligent tutoring systems (ITS) are one of the AI-education (AIEd) tools which rely on machine learning (ML) and computational intelligence coupled with data mining techniques to amplify the wherewithal of e-learning systems. The resultant application of these tools include intelligent behaviour evident through AI-enhanced education characterised by personalised learning to motivate students, improve their learning experience, process, and outcomes and efficient assessment and feedback provision. Cognitive aspects of learning are intertwined with what students know and learn; hence the need to embrace and understand precursors to internal and external motivating factors affecting learning. Underpinned by the responsible stewardship of AI technologies, this chapter delves into the concept of cognitive justice from AIEd and AI ethics perspective. The chapter explores the role of ITS in fostering cognitive justice by discussing the potential of ITS in personalising learning experiences and accommodating individual differences, while also addressing the ethical horizons and challenges associated with AI technologies in education. Guided by PRISMA guidelines for conducting systematic review of the literature, categorical and thematic content analysis were employed as a methodological approaches. From the analysis, two categories (inhibitors and enablers) and five thematic areas of ITS have been found to play a role in the promotion of cognitive justice. By examining the intersection of cognitive justice and ethics, the chapter recommends strategies to maintain balanced and ethical integration of AIEd tools and systems such as ITS in the promotion of cognitive justice in learning. The implications of cognitive justice on educational

R. N. Tjano (✉) · R. Mphahlele
University of South Africa, Pretoria, South Africa
e-mail: tjanorn@unisa.ac.za

R. Mphahlele
e-mail: emphahrs@unisa.ac.za

M. A. Adarkwah et al. (eds.), *Artificial Intelligence and Human Agency in Education: Volume One*, Future Education and Learning Spaces,
https://doi.org/10.1007/978-981-96-7937-9_3

equity and inclusivity are also explored, along with future trends and directions for research.

Keywords Artificial intelligence · AI ethics · AI-education · Cognitive justice · Intelligent tutoring systems · PRISMA guidelines · Systematic literature review

3.1 Introduction and Background

Although Artificial Intelligence (AI) was coined in 1956 by John McCarthy, as noted by Russell and Norvig (2010), the COVID-19 pandemic has significantly transformed the landscape of work and learning. As Gyau and Malcolm (2023) explain, this transformation has been driven by the rapid adoption of automation technologies designed to enhance efficiency. Central to this shift, according to Grubaugh et al. (2023) is the transformative power of AI technologies, which have become integral to various sectors, including education. Chen (2023) posit that among these AI-driven innovations, Intelligent Tutoring Systems (ITS) have emerged as potent tools within AI-enhanced education (AIEd). The rise of ITS can be traced to the work of Carbonell (1970), and they refer to computer-based learning systems utilising AI capabilities to deliver students' personalised and adaptive learning instructions (Lin et al., 2023). Most of the ITS are empowered by AI technology such as NLPs through which chatbots are used to as interactive platform to generate content, provide feedback, and the necessary insights pertaining to learning (Liddy, 2001; Lin & Mubarok, 2021).

ITS such as SQL Tutor, ALEKS, Cognitive Tutor ASSISTment, Duolingo, and Carnegie learning leverage machine learning (ML), computational intelligence, and data mining techniques to elevate the capabilities of e-learning systems. Against this background, this chapter argues that this technological convergence has given rise to AI-enhanced education, especially in higher education institutions, characterised by personalised learning experiences designed to motivate students, improve their learning processes and outcomes, and provide efficient assessment and feedback mechanisms.

Hamal et al. (2022) established that the application of ITS in education has led to intelligent behaviour through AI-enhanced learning environments, which are pivotal in shaping modern educational paradigms. The AI learning environments according to Zheng (2022) provide personalised learning facilitated by ITS aims to cater to the unique needs and preferences of individual students, thereby fostering an engaging and effective learning experience. This personalised approach is crucial, as cognitive aspects of learning are closely tied to what students know and learn. Therefore, understanding and embracing the internal and external factors that motivate students is essential for effective education. The concept of cognitive justice, which is viewed by Kittay (2022) as emphasising the equitable recognition and inclusion of diverse cognitive perspectives and experiences, is particularly relevant in this study's context. Gwaravanda and Ndofirepi (2023) contextualise cognitive justice in education as a concept of creating learning environments that respect and accommodate the varied ways in which students process and acquire knowledge. By integrating ITS with a focus on cognitive justice, educators can ensure that learning experiences are not only personalised but also equitable and inclusive.

However, the integration of AI technologies in education also brings forth ethical considerations. Issues such as transparency, explainability, and algorithmic accountability as indicated by Slimi and Villarejo Carballido (2023) are paramount in ensuring that AI-enhanced educational systems are fair and trustworthy. This chapter explores the intersection of cognitive justice and ethics within the realm of AI-enhanced education. It also investigates the role of ITS in promoting cognitive justice by accommodating individual differences and personalising learning experiences. Additionally, the chapter addresses the ethical challenges associated with AI technologies in education and proposes strategies for incorporating cognitive justice principles into AI-enhanced educational systems. The implications of cognitive justice for educational equity and inclusivity are examined, along with future trends and directions for research in this field. This background is guided by the following suggested research questions:

1. How can intelligent tutoring systems (ITS) promote cognitive justice in AI-enhanced education?
2. What are the ethical considerations associated with integrating ITS in education, and how can they be addressed?
3. How can cognitive justice principles and ethical considerations be effectively implemented in practical pedagogical strategies for educators and policymakers?

3.2 Conceptual Framework—Inclusive AI-Enhanced Educational Landscape

In an era where AI increasingly shapes educational landscapes, the ethical principles guiding its deployment are vital. This chapter is underpinned by a conceptual framework that underscores the necessity for ethical rigour in integrating AI within educational contexts. The researchers seek to balance the transformative potential of intelligent tutoring systems with the imperatives of cognitive justice, ensuring equitable access, fairness, and the protection of individual rights. Through a lens of ethical principles for AIEd, this chapter advocates for the responsible stewardship of AI technologies, fostering an inclusive and just educational future. These principles, as identified by Nguyen et al. (2023), include fairness and non-discrimination, transparency and explainability, privacy and data protection, accountability and responsibility, beneficence and non-maleficence, autonomy and empowerment, equity and accessibility, and sustainability.

AI systems can promote cognitive justice by addressing diverse needs of learners (Srivastava & Sinha, 2023). It should be noted that fairness and non-discrimination ensure that AI systems treat all students equitably, address diverse needs, and promote cognitive justice. While Vainio-Pekka et al. (2023) demonstrated that explainable

AI enhances transparency, making AI decisions understandable and trustworthy, this chapter notes that transparency and explainability make the decision-making processes of AI understandable to all stakeholders, fostering trust and engagement. Bećirović (2023) cautions about a need for educational stakeholders to have awareness and competencies for data protection. This chapter's theoretical foundation regards privacy and data protection as fundamental to safeguarding students' personal information. Therefore, the researchers argue that ethical AI systems must comply with data protection regulations and ethical standards to protect the privacy and security of users.

As noted by Lechterman (2022), accountability and responsibility ensure that there are clear mechanisms for addressing the actions and decisions made by AI systems. Lechterman corroborating Stahl et al. (2018) on ethics of AI further argues that accountability is essential for verifying compliance with normative principles in AI ethics. The researchers acknowledge that this principle involves human oversight and protocols for error handling and remediation. Against this backdrop, it is safe to note that human oversight plays a crucial role in ethically managing AI actions and decisions. This chapter advocates for establishing clear mechanisms to address these AI actions and decisions, ensuring that human oversight and error handling are integral to maintaining ethical integrity.

Van der Maden et al. (2023a, 2023b) argue that beneficence and non-maleficence are crucial for developing AI systems in education. These principles ensure that AI technologies are designed to optimise educational outcomes while safeguarding student well-being. Similarly, Dieterle et al. (2024) support this view, emphasising that the focus on beneficence and non-maleficence in AI design enhances educational outcomes and minimises potential harms, thereby promoting student well-being. Both studies underscore the importance of ethical considerations in integrating AI into educational environments, highlighting that the ultimate goal is to benefit students and protect them from adverse effects.

Research by Bartoletti (2022a, 2022b), Borges Monteiro et al. (2021), and Mozer et al. (2019) underscores the importance of autonomy and empowerment in the context of AIED. These studies collectively support the view that autonomy and empowerment are crucial for ensuring that AI technologies enhance, rather than replace, human roles within educational settings. By prioritising these principles, AI can provide meaningful support to students and educators, granting them greater control and agency in the learning process. Bartoletti (2022a, 2022b) specifically affirms that fostering autonomy and empowerment is essential for giving students and educators control and agency. This perspective is vital for integrating AI in a manner that respects and promotes human involvement, ensuring that the technology serves as a tool for enhancement rather than a substitute for human interaction and decision-making. The alignment of these studies highlights the necessity of designing AI systems that truly uphold the values of autonomy and empowerment to benefit the educational landscape.

The researchers identified the importance of equity and accessibility as key principles in advancing cognitive justice and fostering inclusive education. They argue that by prioritising these principles, educational technologies can serve the needs of all students, including those with disabilities and those from underserved communities. This viewpoint is supported by Roscoe (2023), who underscores that ensuring equity and accessibility in deploying AI technologies is crucial for their benefits to be universally accessible, thereby promoting inclusive education. By integrating these principles, AI-enhanced educational systems can help bridge educational disparities and support diverse learning needs, contributing to a more just and inclusive educational landscape.

3.3 Methodological Approaches

A comprehensive exploration of the extant literature underpinned search strategy for this chapter, and this was done through seven-step process indicated in Fig. 3.1. The process started with the definition of search parameters as within on AIED, cognitive justice and AI ethics literature. Following PRISMA (Preferred Reporting Items for Systematic Reviews and Meta-Analyses) guidelines, a systematic literature review (SLR) was conducted as a methodological approach to examine the role of AI-enhanced education, particularly the ITS in promoting cognitive justice. The PRISMA guidelines are effective for searching, identifying, and picking literature material fitting the inclusion criteria. Furthermore, the guidelines are useful for guiding the reading, extracting, and managing data emanating from identified material (Page et al., 2021).

The determination of the inclusion and exclusion criteria based on the search parameters to guide the search strategy followed in step 2. This step was crucial to determine the eligibility of the databases and literature material. The strategy is anchored by availability and accessibility of the material from the databases.

In the third step, the systematic search was executed from the following databases EBSCOhost, ProQuest, and Scopus. These databases are known to be prominent, reputable, and leading in the publication of scholarly and academic literature material relevant to the research phenomena under study, i.e. AI and ITS, cognitive justice and ethics of AI. For the purpose of this chapter, they offer avenue for wide collection of published material invaluable for conducting rigorous SLR.

Applying Boolean search criteria, the key phrases or words that were used for searching the literature material are illustrated in step 4. As per the defined search parameters, the focus of the material was on higher education. This implies any material that fell outside of the scope of education landscape were excluded from the material that formed part of final analysis. In terms of the period, only material published between 2014 and 2024 was considered.

The rationale was informed by some reports in the literature that observed that few years leading to COVID-19 and the post-pandemic era, there has been significant developments in the field of AI and education (Nigam et al., 2021; Cukurova, 2024), especially in terms AIEd developments and enhancing students learning experiences (McNamara, 2023) as well as (in)justice and promotion of fairness in AIEd. Only journal articles, conference papers and book chapters were considered, meanwhile

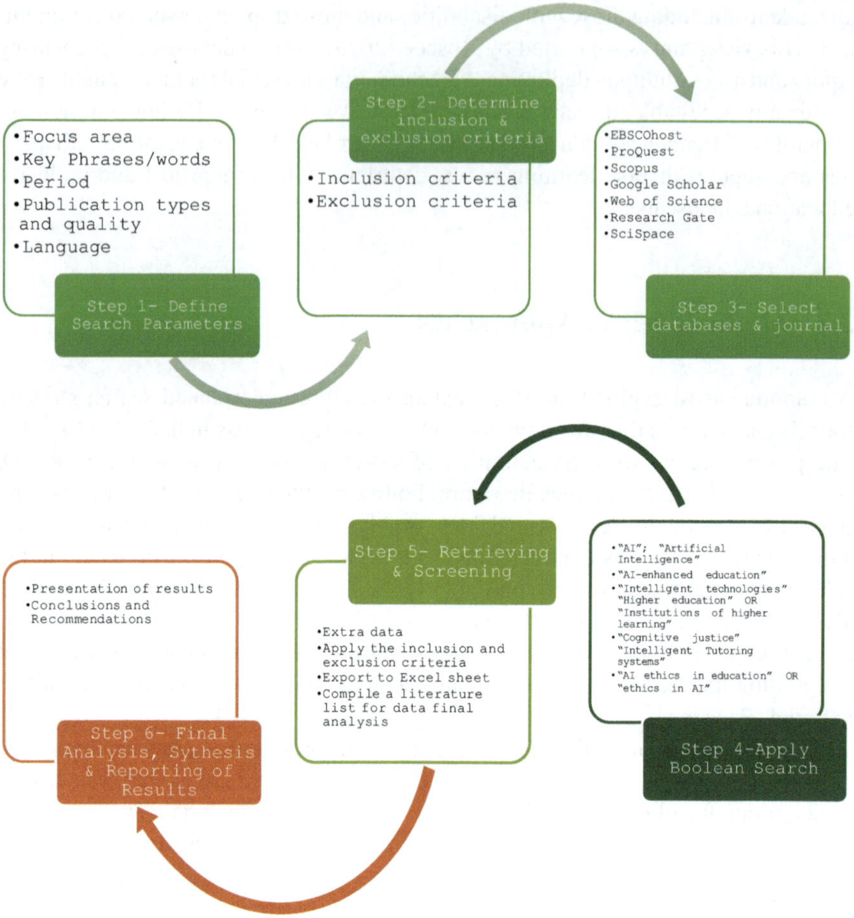

Fig. 3.1 A schematic illustration of the methodology process

editorials, theses and dissertations, industry and position papers, blogs and news articles were excluded to limit the search results to quality expectations of peer review process.

Following Boolean search, a retrieving and screening exercise was executed in step 5. During this process, the data was extracted from the identified databases to determine the eligibility of the identified literature material. This process involved skimming through the full-text literature material as part of evaluating its quality and eligibility. We considered the material to be reputable and boosting high-quality literature because the identified databases have credibility. The inclusion and exclusion criteria was applied according to the search parameters defined in the first step.

Reliability of the Search Criteria and Validation of the Literature Material

To ensure reliability and validation of the applied methodological procedures, a manual "hand" search was also executed. The manual Boolean search was narrowed to Google Scholar as per the stated inclusion criteria as explained in the previous section, and 2596 number of literature material was identified. This was intentional as per Xiao and Watson (2019) to guard against unintentional exclusion of the literature material that may be significant to the findings of the study, because the field of AIEd is relatively new (Crompton & Burke, 2023) and is improving on an ongoing basis owing to increasing proliferation of AI technologies in education, especially within the realm of ITS (Saleem, 2015). The advantage of the augmenting search results with Google Scholar for conducting SLR is advanced by Haddaway et al. (2015) as they argue that it is popular, free to use and is web-based search engine boosting catalogues up to 100 million records of academic and grey literature. The data from each database was then transferred to Excel sheet for compiling the final literature for data and 125 was the final number of literature material included final analysis as shown in Fig. 3.2.

3.4 Method of Analysis, Results, and Discussion

Guided by Gough and Richardson (2018) procedures, the extracted dataset was subjected to aggregation procedures for analysis. A multi-phase method of analysis guided by Zhang and Aslan (2021) was followed, which involved categorical and thematic content analysis. This analytical approach was reinforced through AI-powered textual analysis to identify trends, insights, and summaries through AI-powered database tools such as Sci Space and Dimensions AI. The aim was to conduct rigorous analysis of the textual literature on AIEd, promotion of cognitive justice and AI ethics within the context of higher education.

Through categorical and thematic content analysis, two categories and five thematic areas have been identified. Most significantly, for this chapter, these factors are discussed next in the form of five thematic areas as identified as inhibitors factors and enablers to the promotion of cognitive justice. The Taxonomy of inhibitors and enablers to promotion of cognitive justice through the use of AIEd as shown in Fig. 3.3 is thus proposed, and each of the categories alongside the identified thematic areas are presented next.

3.4.1 AIEd Inhibiting Factors to the Promotion of Cognitive Justice and Ethical Balance

In this part of the chapter, AIEd constraints to the promotion of cognitive justice are presented. Number of AI advancements have brought about improvements and efficiency in number of areas, so is education landscape. Notwithstanding these

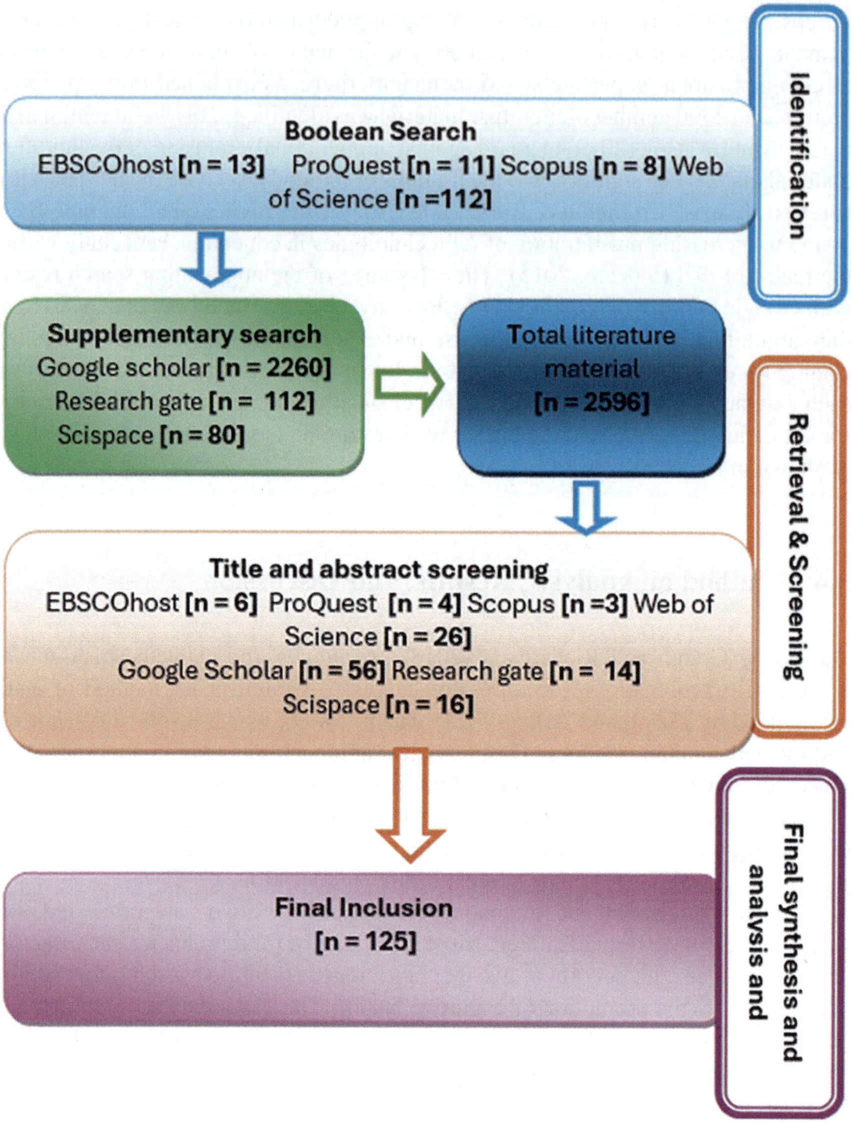

Fig. 3.2 PRISMA systematic review of literature process

inroads, there are number of an ethical challenges, and some of these challenges are manifesting themselves through factors that seem to be barring or acting against the purported benefits. The identification of these factors was in response to the first and second research questions that were aimed at exploring how AI in the form of ITS can promote cognitive justice within the context of education. The outcome

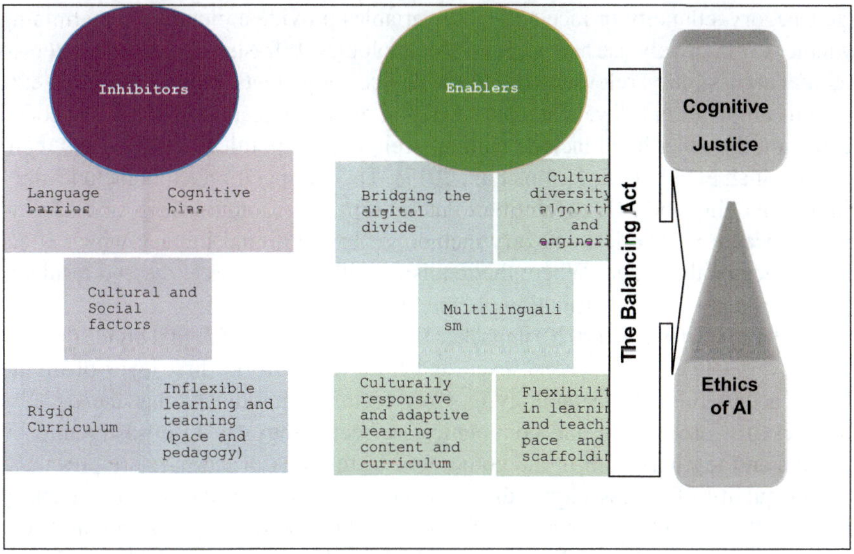

Fig. 3.3 Taxonomy of inhibitors and enablers to promotion of cognitive justice

of this process indicates that these systems are poorly designed and improperly implemented, leading to the following issues, which are discussed below.

3.4.1.1 Systemic Cognitive biases and discrimination

The systemic bias and discrimination are occasionally as a result of policy frame works and rules applied during the design and programming of AIEd systems. Madaio et al. (2021) examined the structural injustices through the lenses of AI fairness and put forward that deploying educational technologies like ITS in these kinds of environments characterised by bias and discrimination have potential to enact certain outcomes and developments that may perpetuate inequities and injustice in learning and teaching. These observations align with Allegory of the Cave metaphor (Yonit & Iris, 2017). When this happens, inclusivity and fair representation of cognitive learning preferences are in a jeopardy and are being compromised. Baker and Hawn (2022) alongside Curokova (2024) opining that this issue is underestimated, and the impact is even deep when looking at it from the perspectives of the marginalised student populations, wherein the digital divide is observed.

Carter et al. (2020) encapsulate digital divide as a concept that cannot be simply or easily expounded with one-sided or dimensional view, however they argue that it is a multi-facet constituted by variety of concepts such as demographic and socio-economic factors, infrastructure, social factors, beliefs, AI-specific, skills and digital literacy. The impact of these factors is that they hinder accessibility, further widening the digital divide. The first category involves gender, levels of education and income, age category, ethnicity or race and these variables provide a picture of determining whether to effectively use and access AI technologies. Infrastructure simply refers to internet accessibility, relevancy of mobile devices or gadgets, cloud computing etc., and this aligns to first level category of digital divide conceptualisation. The social factors on the other hand include culture—religious or political, policies and regulations (Shah et al., 2015; Philip et al., 2017). The AI-specific factors include algorithms encoding and ML capabilities, dataset intricacies, engineering, and deployment procedures. The last category include skills and digital literacy which affect the efficacy of the usage. Where the requisite skills set is scarce, the end results is disparities and uneven distribution of benefits.

Similar to Carter et al. (2020) unpacked the understanding of digital divide through three levels—first-level, second-level, and third-level. In the first layer of digital divide, accessibility to technology is a key feature. This means that the equality of access to information and communication technology (ICT) infrastructure by learners and teachers both in the homes and institutions of learning are prevalent. The inequality of access digital divide layer is followed by the digital capability divide in the second layer, which is characterised by the inequality stemming from the incapability to access ICT resources as identified in the first layer. The third layer relates to digital outcome divide, which essentially is the inequality of outcomes such as the learning and productivity outcomes) of leveraging ICT opportunities and capabilities emanating from level two and other contextual factors. Nonetheless, the common key features of digital divide revolve around lack of accessibility and inclusivity. The sum total of these impacts are bound up in and are reproducing the historical and legacies of structural injustices. Owing to the reported systemic inequalities, the reproducibility and perpetuation of unfairness and cognitive injustices are also on the horizon (Carter et al., 2020).

3.4.1.2 Inflexible Learning and Teaching—Pace and Pedagogy

Rathore and Arjaria (2020) explained that cognitivist approaches drive ITSs and are traditionally focused on pedagogical exercise of the autonomy of teachers activity by enhancing learning and teaching, adapting students' learning experiences, feedback tailoring and pacing learning content. This process is dependent on forward-passing techniques as well as how the data is trained and framed. If this happens through biased and unfair algorithmic encoding practices, the historical injustices may be perpetuated (Cukurova, 2019), and promised benefits of ITS remain far-fetched. The gaps associated with poorly and improperly designed ITS relate to their inability to respond to students' learning styles and experiences. As such, learning diversity is compromised and inclusivity in the learning journey is not promoted. The first form of bias can originate from provided and trained data, which can be made up of affective, engagement, and meta-cognitive variables. The other form of bias from ITS could include a situation where both teachers and students develop conformation bias (Cukurova et al., 2020) and unrealistic expectations of performances of the ITS (Nazaretysky et al., 2021). Both in these instances, the bias is manifested through the framed data with the resultant being users (students) starting to doubt and question the credibility and trustworthiness of ITS. Therefore, with these challenges, students do not feel represented and cannot effectively assimilate to the learning content. The outcomes of this evolvement manifest itself in poor academic performance of students in the higher education institutions, thus affecting throughput rates and performance of students. The other concern as a result of biased and framed content is that learning as a cognitive process is not comprised only about absorption of information, however about the cognitive development of social competency, emotional intelligence, and may other different types of meta-cognitive abilities and developments (Cukurova, 2024). The challenges or concerns indicate the extent to which cognitive learning intricacies need to be considered during the initial stages of conceptualising AIEd tools like ITS so as to enhance and optimise trust in AIEd. The next section will focus more in detail on the enablers that are proposed and should be considered in the building of these systems.

3.4.1.3 Language Barriers

Notwithstanding that AIEd systems such as the ITS and Gen AI have probable capa bility to make use of human language with aptness, however from the perspective of critical pedagogy, there is a significant difference how these systems reason, which is distinct from humans' reasoning. In their study on reimagining education by bridging AI, transhumanism, and critical pedagogy, Nayir et al. (2024) affirm this claim from a linguistic and epistemological standpoint. They argue that while AI in education (AIEd) systems have the potential to promote equality in education, concerns remain about the role and impact of technological tools when interacting with humans and understanding the complexities of perspectives in critical pedagogy. Making use of GPT-3 as a data collection tool, which is one of the Gen AI tools, their findings bring to light two divergent outcomes. On one hand, the GPT has proved its ability to impersonate human conversation, however on the other hand, it has also revealed its shortcomings in understanding key concepts underpinned in critical pedagogy.

Through deep learning (DL), the neural network models are responsible for training the transformers such as the GPTs on Natural language processing (NLPs). This training is focused on making out the meaning of words or text or paired sentences through optimisation (Cukurova, 2024). This can have shortcomings that could serve as a barrier to promoting cognitive justice. Robert et al. (2020) differentiate between types of bias which training data rely on to generate insights, and some of those sources include data sample, measurement, data variable collection model. The bias could occur during the pre-training and testing stage after the algorithms have been built as encoding process may be based on biased datasets or instructions. The other concern is when the biasness is leaning towards one or few set of languages at the expense of languages from the marginalised student groups or societies. Like culture, the narrative of language dominancy and superiority are prevalent during the developments, thus acting intended benefits of ITS.

3.4.1.4 Cultural and Social Factors

Culture practices and discourses, alongside with its beliefs, customs, traditions, and practices can be a very emotive issue. Madaio et al. (2021) examined the structural injustices through the lenses of AI fairness and put forward that deploying educational technologies like ITS in these kinds of environments characterised by bias and discrimination have potential to enact certain outcomes and developments that may perpetuate inequities and injustice in learning and teaching. The prevalence of cultural bias in AI systems cannot be ignored, especially the Gen AI and ITS (Karpouzis, 2024). At the heart of cultural and social factors are the social and impacts and implications of technology and its revolution, which are intertwined with injustice and unfairness, further which may emanate or be propelled by algorithmic bias built in the ITS. The cultural impact of AI technology through ITS, norms and expectations on the learning experience of students remain large elusive especially from cognitive learning and behavioural contexts. Eubanks (2018) examines the intersections of technology and society and offers a comprehensive perspective on how culture is portrayed in AI. This all-encompassing strategy is necessary to recognise, comprehend, and resolve the complex issues surrounding cultural bias in AI systems.

ITS in some areas are reported to be culturally-insensitive. This challenge adds to the previous inhibiting factor which purported these systems to biased and discriminatory. The resultant effect then defies the entire benefits of enhancing students learning and teachers' teaching experiences among others. In addition, some of these systems are pushing culturally-irrelevant examples (Lameras & Arnab, 2022) that generally tend to be out of sync with diversity of students' population or communities of practice. However, in practice, these envisaged utopia learning environments are somewhat little far from being realised, although, with technological and digital revolution, expectations are that this should be a norm.

Borrowing from Maidment (2016), AI has a potential to be a friend in facilitation of learning or enemy when inhibitors such as culture and social factors are evident. The learning process is not exclusively intuitive; however, this cognitive process traverses with social and cultural factors. Henriques' (2019) extension of human identify function into the world published in the unified theory of knowledge, the authors explore how cognitive behaviour of human beings and culture are intertwined. In that work, Henriques (2019) argues against central quest for psychology that contrast between nature and nurture as he continue to state that humans as primates of culture are deeply socialite primates with needs, social influences, and sense of belonging, which are affected by culture and socialisations. Adds Henriques, social relatedness and language are social identities catapulted through culture.

3.4.1.5 Rigid Curriculum and Inflexible Pedagogy

To best explain the rigidity of the curriculum and inflexible pedagogy as a result of AIEd systems, we rely on Semenenko (2018), who contests that teaching practices in the classroom are embodied in the history and power contest. If the idea is to conquer human's mind, the agenda would be the perpetuation of "supremacist" ideologies through one sided historical narrative. The teachings therefore are benefit "he who tells the story". The precursors are interlocked in the agenda of education policies that are pushing certain narrative to shape and continue to reshape the systems of oppression. Garcia (2021) in support of this view suggests that with these systems more often than not, the narrative is typified by rigidness and inflexibility, and may not be moving with times. Furthermore, pedagogical methods aimed at teaching the curriculum are also marred with inflexible teaching practices, similar to be accustomed to "old ways of doing things". The outcome is the injustice being propagated.

From the perspective educational technologies, Hooks critiques how its increased use can contribute to a more rigid and inflexible curriculum, as she contends that technology-driven education like ITS may likely prefer standardised, one-size-fits-all approaches as a priority thus limiting the teachers' ability to engage students in a transformative, and transgressive learning (Semenenko, 2018). Aligned to war of orthodox in learning, the pedagogy that is rigid and fail to adapt to students' learning preferences is undermining the essence of justice in learning. In the critique of ITS, they are likened to parrot in that their generation of content capabilities is informed by probability analysis, and as such no full comprehension of the method behind content generation is prevalent (Bender et al., 2021).

In elucidating the rationale behind the slow adoption of AIEd tools such as ITS, Cukurova et al. (2024) touches on the number of factors that seem to be anti-sustainability and accessibility. Policies around AI, governance systems and frame works, and the cultural and social impacts affecting pedagogy somehow contribute to cognitive disengagement during the learning process. When the minds disengage because it is sensing or suspecting injustice the outcome is a withdrawal and in extreme cases we have seen how cultural intolerance has been violent through wars. This is where the AIEd systems lose their potential to be a friend in learning and becomes an enemy in the process, thus frenemy. That counts against the initial benefits of personalised learning experiences, scaling and adaptive learning.

3.4.2 AIEd Enablers to Promotion of Cognitive Justice and Ethical Balance

Drawing from AIEd constraints to the promotion of cognitive justice, in this part of the chapter the enablers seen as potential areas of improvement for tools such as ITS to promote justice and fairness in the learning and teaching journey are discussed.

3.4.2.1 Bridging the Digital Divide

The digital gaps between the "haves" and the "have-nots" suggest digital divide is far from being addressed (Foley et al., 2022). As this continues, the perpetual lack of access and inclusivity remains a cause for concern, most importantly when looking at the lack of infrastructure, mostly experienced by the marginalised societies of the population. The unfortunate result of this turn of events or situation is cognitive (in)justice, thus affirming the mere essence of inequalities in learning and teaching. The chapter draws on Carter et al. (2020) proposal of the three theoretical framings aimed at addressing the digital divide: conceptualising, modelling, and analysing the divide. Likewise, Johnson and Rogers (2024) cautioned by stating that addressing issues of access and usage of the deployed technologies does not necessarily imply positive engagements. Therefore, there is a need to systematically shift focus from first level, through to second-level and ultimately the third-level of digital divide as described by Carter et al. (2020).

3.4.2.2 Embracing Cultural Diversity in Algorithms and Engineering

In this chapter, we view culture from the lens of it being depicted as a foundation of knowledge. The depiction of culture from that lens is inspired by the work of Ożegalska-Łukasik and Łukasik (2023), who advocate for including cultural factors in algorithm design to enhance adaptability and performance. In that piece of work, the authors regard AI as a social phenomenon and therefore aspect of social being makes a cultural phenomenon too hence he talks about "culture of AI". In that equivalence, the authors go on to offer counsel that when dealing with AI culture, the "investigator" should explore the AI culture from social milieu and traditions behind a set of individuals or society who are pioneers and disseminators of ideologies and way of thinking which typifies AI. This could not be further from the truth as we argued earlier that those who are responsible for coming up with innovation on AIEd tools or systems cannot be separated or exonerated from their cultural beliefs, as such they have in their cognitive thinking and processing their cultural presumptions that may potentially influence the end product—remember the GIGO analogy. Therefore, a culture as a social phenomenon, as Kosmos and Pogačar (2022) argue, has premature foreclosure to questions of social impacts which are conjured in the deterministic terms.

Linking social impacts and culture to the aspect of language, our affirmative point in this chapter is that culture is intertwined with socio-linguistic artefacts, to which Henriques (2019) explained it from the analogy of Tree of Knowledge (ToR). In that work, he appreciates the intersection of culture and human identity, which we argue in turn affect social processes of learning. Therefore, the social processes that shape and constitute integral part of AI tools and systems cannot be ignored or be separated from cultural influence.

The AIEd systems should therefore embrace human beings including those designing, programming, authoring, and deploying these systems from algorithms and user experiences point of view, which are crucial aspects in human–computer interaction (Acharjya et al., 2023). Furthermore, ITS should not portray one's culture as inferior to the other cultures, whether intentionally or otherwise. The sense of cultural-coexistence should prevail thus clasping cultural diversity in the learning and teaching journey. Karpouzis (2024), using the notion of guiding AI towards cultural neutrality, shares similar sentiments and calls for multimodal strategy to incorporate the ethical and technical methods so that there are no AI systems or tools that are muddied with bias and unfairness. With this, models and algorithms should reflect a wide range of human experiences and perspectives free from influence by dominant cultural norms and values. Cultural favourism is not necessary in AIEd systems as they work against promoting global cultural diversity and as such fail to acknowledge and honour variation in language, beliefs, customs, and values. From the perspective of AI ethics, diverse and representative datasets should be used to design and train AIEd systems to prevent the undue influence of singular cultural viewpoints, perspectives or biases on the behaviour and outcomes of these systems. Furthermore, these systems should embody the principles of responsibility, interpretability, accountability and transparency, sustainability and fairness which resonate with the fields of Responsible AI, Explainable AI (XAI), Sustainable AI and AI ethics (Arrieta et al., 2020; Leslie, 2019).

3.4.2.3 Flexibility in Learning and Teaching, Pace, and Scaffolding

The flexibility in learning and teaching pace as well as scaffolding are dependent on the extent to which AIEd tools like ITS promote needs-oriented mindset in their design. The algorithms inherent in these tools need to embrace flexibility according to learners and teachers' preferences for learning and teaching. Therefore, the importance of an educational model centred on critical thinking, dialogue, and the recognition of students' diverse lived experiences is emphasised. Lameras and Arnab (2022) recommend adaptive, collaborative learning support as a mechanism to achieve flexibility in learning and teaching. This according to Cukurova et al. (2018) will empower learners to learn and devise solutions to the problems they encounter during learning. From the perspective of addressing inflexibility and rigidness that come with gender and cultural barriers. Fiadeiro et al. (2023) propose student-led pedagogies aimed at promoting self-organisation and embrace a care as a feminist pedagogical method during the design.

3.4.2.4 Culturally Responsive and Adaptive Learning Content and Curriculum

Drawing on the lessons from how culture can be an obstacle to efficiency of ITS, it is without a doubt that as societies are evolving and new world order is being established with new emerging subcultures, there is a need for ITS that support culturally responsive and adaptive learning content and curriculum. First and foremost, this change should be need-oriented. This implies that building these systems should consider the diverse needs of users, students and teachers. Husain (2024) warns against overreliance on technology as this can undermine this model by promoting passive consumption of information rather than active, collaborative knowledge production, which is needed as per the digital Blooms Taxonomy by Churches (2006). Husain (2024) further advocates for an education system through flexibility in learning, teaching, pace and scaffolding of students' learning and activities and uses technology strategically to empower them. This should happen simultaneously while maintaining the flexibility and pedagogical innovation necessary for truly engaged and liberatory learning. The following tactics are proposed:

Leverage students' individual needs and preferences to develop the capability to adjust the pacing, level of detail, and scaffolding in a dynamic manner.

Given that students' prior knowledge or learning styles may be subject to cultural or linguistic factors' influence, make use of students' cultural and linguistic needs and backgrounds to organise pace and scaffolding to address any gaps or differences.

3.4.2.5 Multilingual Support

The multi-faceted nature of multilingual support cannot exist outside of cultural diversity. Building on the previous section, there is a need to develop the ITS' capability to provide content through instruction, feedback, and resources in multiple languages (Karpouzis, 2024). This advancement will be responding to the need to cater for the linguistic diversity of the student population, and as such no dominance of one language over the other will be felt. For this reason, one is able and confident that journey towards promoting cognitive justice through language diversity is near. More importantly, those on the receiving end are able to benefit from introduction of ITS by learning in their language of preference. This process intrinsically involve two key steps. The first is the integration of language translation and interpretation features during the development phase. The second is creation of content and pedagogical approaches that are sensitive to various linguistic needs of the users.

3.4.3 Balancing Cognitive Justice and Ethical Considerations in AI-Enhanced Education

This section responds to the third research question to explore how cognitive justice principles and ethical considerations can be effectively implemented in practical pedagogical strategies for educators and policymakers. Variety of ethical AI principles have been developed over the years through extensive research on the ethics of AI. Floridi (2023) claims that the AI community's lack of agreement over the complexity and intricacy of adhering to particular AI ethical situations and contexts is the outcome of various AI frameworks. In general, the prime focus has been on collection of data and analysis procedures. A digital repository of AI ethics models has been developed to facilitate access to and consolidation of the diverse range of AI ethical frameworks, and this repository is mapped into a global AI ethics inventory. One such avenue is Algorithm Watch 9 which allows users to access and retrieve various AI frameworks and principles that can relevantly be context specific to the ethical use of AI. Given fast pace and advancements in AI space, education landscape is not immune from potential ethical pitfalls, and it is incumbent upon key stakeholders—students, teachers, policy makers, IT technicians and practitioners, change managers to be mindful of these pitfalls and response appropriately from ethical viewpoint.

Given the above discussion on inhibitors and enablers and the role played by policies, there is a need for a balanced approach aimed at promoting cognitive justice while addressing ethical considerations. One such framework among many is Chan's (2023) AI Ecological Education Policy Framework for integrating cognitive justice principles into the design and implementation of AI-enhanced higher institutions of learning technological education systems. The framework proposes the development of an AI-education policy for higher education by examining perceptions and implications of text generative AI technologies from the perspective of three dimensions. The first dimension is Pedagogy, and it concentrates on relying on AI for improving teaching and learning outcomes. This dimension bring to the fore the importance of understanding AI implications in integration of ITS within academic learning and teaching environments. The Governance dimension is the second one and addresses issues relating to harnessing privacy, security, and accountability. The last dimension is Operational, and it deals with issues associated with the AI infrastructure and training. The framework addresses the multi-faceted implications of AI integration in teaching and learning and aims to promote a better understanding of AI's impact and ensure responsible actions from stakeholders. This framework provides a nuanced comprehension of implication of ITS as one of AIEd systems through appreciation of AI security and privacy to improve learning and teaching outcomes.

The importance of transparency, explainability, and algorithmic accountability in ITS cannot be overemphasised. The role of teachers and policymakers in fostering cognitive justice while addressing ethical concerns remain a crucial balancing act. Aiken and Epstein's 2018 study emphasises the importance of adhering to ethical design principles for AIEd systems, focusing on student involvement, positive character traits, and respecting cultural imperialism, rather than attempting to replace users.

3.5 Trends in AI-Enhanced Education and Cognitive Justice—Future Directions, and Implications

In this section, we reflect on emerging trends and technologies that hold potential to advance cognitive justice in AI-enhanced education. First, pinning the significance of broadening access in the journey of enhancing students' learning and teachers' teaching experience through application of ITS, enabled by AIEd remain an ethical conduct. This line of march will consequently advance justice during learning journey through promotion of educational equity and inclusivity. Therefore, aligned to sustainable development goals, in particular goal 4 focusing on quality education. The second aspect of development is the need for the interdisciplinary collaboration, more significantly, across the borders. It is important to emphasise the need for the research to permeates across various fields, from psychology, sociology, communications, technology, and engineering to mention the few. The psychology of education coupled with ongoing societal and economic challenges affirm the need for the direction, given the complex nature of challenges emanating for cognitive behaviour and the associated outcomes. Thirdly, the evolving nature of cultures and their concomitant practices and developments in AIEd landscape also call for hybrid research methodologies and approaches as Karpouzis (2024) advocates for the novelty in the following research methods and techniques as the argument that is put forward is that they equips researchers with a diverse set of tools to uncover and understand the complexities of cultural bias in AI.

Integration of hybrid research methods that boost both quantitative and qualitative approaches, leveraging the strengths of sentiment analysis as a research methodology in language recognition, metrics of diversity, critical discourse (CDA) and content analyses, case studies, ethnographic studies, and narrative reporting studies.

ITS tools such as Dulingo and GPT transformers still need to improve on the datasets they are trained on to ensure there is equality and fairness in education. This view draws from Nayir et al. (2024) paper on the intersection of AI and critical pedagogy which suggest that future research should consider the angle of transhumanism and study the link between various AI applications and critical pedagogy.

Cognitive justice in AI-enhanced education resonates deeply with the critical perspectives of Selwyn (2022) and Williamson et al. (2020), who emphasise the need to scrutinise the implications of educational technologies on equity and access. As ITS become increasingly integrated into learning environments, it is essential to recognise how these tools can either reinforce or disrupt existing power dynamics and knowledge hierarchies. Selwyn's (2022) critiques of technology's role in perpetuating inequality highlight the risks of AI systems that may inadvertently favour certain learning styles or backgrounds. Similarly, Williamson et al. (2020)'s analysis of data-driven educational practices calls for a rigorous examination of the ethical horizons that govern the deployment of ITS. By cultivating cognitive justice, we can ensure that AI-enhanced education addresses the diverse needs of learners and actively challenges systemic inequities, fostering a more inclusive and just educational landscape.

3.6 Conclusion

The dynamic nature of AI evolution will reshape its future and will undoubtedly continue to bring many revelations, some of which will be surprising, breathtaking whilst in some instances will be somewhat worrying. The incessant AI advancements are likely going to continue their permeations in almost all areas of humankind, including the education landscape. Further to these, the advancements in AI can be a tale of two stories, on one continuum, the story filled with positives, while on the other end of the stick, negatives with a potential to be counterproductive are prevalent. Borrowing from Stephen Hawking's assessment, AI can be a good thing to have happened to the history of the humankind, however at the same time it can also be a worst thing that could have happened.

Drawing on these possibilities, the future of cognitive justice and maintaining ethical balance remain at the crossroads. It is for this reason that the above enablers to the promotion of cognitive justice are proposed as solutions to consider algorithmic authoring, design, deployment, and maintenance of AI tools and systems in education to consider ethical implications. With ethical mindset, such as the Taxonomy of inhibitors and enablers to promotion of cognitive justice which was advanced in this chapter, the potential pitfalls, and their impact, whether intentional or incidental are likely to be mitigated. Drawing on AI Ecological Education Policy Framework, All in all, the chapter situates itself within the realm of promotion of cognitive justice and highlights the need to apply ethical mindset when introducing new AI systems and tools in enhancing education, most significantly students' learning as well as teachers' teaching experience. This alignment would potentially respond to education 4.0 and sustainable education principles in line with World Economic Forum's (WEF) call for justice and equality in education.

3.7 Limitations

This chapter presents insightful findings on the potential of ITS and AI-enhanced education to promote cognitive justice; however, it acknowledges several limitations. The limitations include systemic cognitive biases and discrimination embedded in AI systems, which perpetuate inequities, particularly affecting marginalised students. Inflexible learning and teaching approaches fail to adapt to diverse learning styles, while language barriers and cultural insensitivity further alienate students. In addition, rigid curricula and pedagogical methods limit transformative learning experiences and critical thinking development. It should also be noted that this chapter's focus on higher education and reliance on specific databases for the literature review limits the broader applicability of the results, excluding perspectives from primary education and grey literature. Although this chapter addresses the digital divide and ethical concerns like algorithmic bias, it also recognises the persistent challenges in overcoming socio-economic disparities and ensuring transparent, unbiased AI systems. Cultural and linguistic diversity remains difficult to fully accommodate within AI-driven learning systems fully, often reflecting dominant cultural narratives, limiting true inclusivity. The chapter acknowledges that the evolving nature of AI technology, particularly in its ability to personalise learning while addressing cognitive justice, means that the ethical and operational challenges outlined may become even more complex, highlighting the need for ongoing research and updates to AI frameworks.

References

Acharjya, P. P., Joardar, S., & Koley, S. (2023). Artificial intelligence-based intelligent human-computer interaction. In K. Sanaa (Ed.), *Handbook of research on AI methods and applications in computer engineering* (pp. 62–85). IGI. https://doi.org/10.4018/978-1-6684-6937-8.ch004

Arrieta, A. B., Díaz-Rodríguez, N., Del Ser, J., Bennetot, A., Tabik, S., Barbado, A., García, S., Gil-López, S., Molina, D., Benjamins, R., & Chatila, R. (2020). Explainable Artificial Intelligence (XAI): Concepts, taxonomies, opportunities and challenges toward responsible AI. *Information Fusion, 58*, 82–115.

Baker, R. S., & Hawn, A. (2022). Algorithmic bias in education. *International Journal of Artificial Intelligence in Education*, 1–41.

Bartoletti, I. (2022a). AI in education. In W. Holmes & K. Porayska-Pomsta (Eds.), *The ethics of artificial intelligence in education* (pp. 74–90). Routledge. https://doi.org/10.4324/9780429329067-5

Bartoletti, I. (2022b). AI in education: An opportunity riddled with challenges. In *The ethics of artificial intelligence in education* (pp. 74–90). Routledge.

Bećirović, S. (2023). Privacy and personal data protection in digital pedagogy. In *Digital pedagogy: The use of digital technologies in contemporary education* (pp. 83–96). Springer. https://doi.org/10.1007/978-981-99-0444-0_7

Bender, E. M., Gebru, T., McMillan-Major, A., & Shmitchell, S. (2021, March). On the dangers of stochastic parrots: Can language models be too big?. In *Proceedings of the 2021 ACM Conference on Fairness, Accountability, and Transparency* (pp. 610–623).

Borges Monteiro, A. C., Padilha França, R., Arthur, R., & Iano, Y. (2021). A look at artificial intelligence on the perspective of application in the modern education. In W. Pedryz, L. Martínez, R. A. Espin-Andrade, G. Rivera, & R. Marx (Eds.), *Computational Intelligence for Business Analytics* (pp. 171–189). Springer Publisher. https://doi.org/10.1007/978-3-030-73819-8_10

Borgida, E., Sullivan, J. L., Oxendine, A., Jackson, M. S., Riedel, E., & Gangl, A. (2002). Civic culture meets the digital divide: The role of community electronic networks. *Journal of Social Issues, 58*(1), 125–141. https://doi.org/10.1111/1540-4560.00252

Carbonell, J. (1970). AI in CAI: An artificial-intelligence approach to computer-assisted instruction. *IEEE Transactions on Man Machine Systems, 11*(4), 190–202. https://doi.org/10.1109/TMMS.1970.299942

Carter, L., Liu, D., & Cantrell, C. (2020). Exploring the intersection of the digital divide and artificial intelligence: A hermeneutic literature review. *AIS Transactions on Human-Computer Interaction, 12*(4), 253–275. https://doi.org/10.17705/1thci.00138

Chan, C. K. Y. (2023). A comprehensive AI policy education framework for university teaching and learning. *International Journal of Educational Technology in Higher Education, 20*(1), 38.

Chen, M. (2023). A comparison of machine learning techniques in building an intelligent tutoring system. *Applied and Computational Engineering, 5*(1), 662–666. https://doi.org/10.54254/2755-2721/5/20230673

Chinn, M. D., & Fairlie, R. W. (2006). The determinants of the global digital divide: A cross-country analysis of computer and internet penetration. *Oxford Economic Papers, 59*(1), 16–44. https://doi.org/10.1093/oep/gpl024

Churches, A. (2010). Bloom's digital taxonomy. Retrieved May 10, 2024, from https://www.researchgate.net/publication/228381038_Bloom%27s_Digital_Taxonomy

Crompton, H., & Burke, D. (2023). Artificial intelligence in higher education: The state of the field. *International Journal of Educational Technology in Higher Education, 20*(1), 22.

Cukurova, M. (2019, May). Learning analytics as AI extenders in education: Multimodal machine learning versus multimodal learning analytics. In *Artificial intelligence and adaptive education* (Vol. 2019). AIAED.

Cukurova, M., Giannakos, M., & Martinez-Maldonado, R. (2020). The promise and challenges of multimodal learning analytics. *British Journal of Educational Technology, 51*(5), 1441–1449.

Cukurova, M., Kralj, L., Hertz, B., & Saltidou, E. (2024). Professional development for teachers in the age of AI.

Cukurova, M., Luckin, R., Millán, E., & Mavrikis, M. (2018). The NISPI framework: Analysing collaborative problem-solving from students' physical interactions. *Computers & Education, 116*, 93–109.

Dieterle, E., Dede, C., & Walker, M. (2024). The cyclical ethical effects of using artificial intelligence in education. *AI & Society, 39*(2), 633–643.

Eubanks, V. (2018). *Automating inequality: How high-tech tools profile, police, and punish the poor*. Martin's Press.

Fernandes, C. W., Rafatirad, S., & Sayadi, H. (2023). Advancing personalised and adaptive learning experience in education with artificial intelligence. In *2023 32nd Annual Conference of the European Association for Education in Electrical and Information Engineering (EAEEIE)* (pp. 1–6). https://doi.org/10.23919/EAEEIE55804.2023.10181336

Fiadeiro, R., Jackson, K., & Surowiec, L. (2023). Revealing pedagogies of care through a collectivised experience of postgraduate research design education.

Floridi, L. (2019). Translating principles into practices of digital ethics: Five risks of being unethical. *Philosophy & Technology, 32*, 185–193. https://doi.org/10.1007/s13347-019-00354-x

Foley, R. W., Nadjari, S., Eshirow, J., Adekunle, R., & Codjoe, P. (2022). Towards digital segregation? Problematising the haves and have nots in the smart city. *Frontiers in Sustainable Cities, 4*. https://doi.org/10.3389/frsc.2022.706670

Gough, D., & Richardson, M. (2018). Systematic reviews. In *Advanced research methods for applied psychology* (pp. 63–75). Routledge.

Grubaugh, S., & Levitt, G. (2023). Artificial intelligence and the paradigm shift: Reshaping education to equip students for future careers. *International Journal of Social Sciences and Humanities Invention, 10*(06), 7931–7941. https://doi.org/10.18535/ijsshi/v10i06.02

Gwaravanda, E. T., & Ndofirepi, A. P. (2023). Cognitive justice as social justice in postcolonial Africa. In A. P. Ndofirepi, S. Vurari, & G. Erima (Eds.), *Unyoking African university knowledge* (pp. 64–82). BRILL. https://doi.org/10.1163/9789004548107_005

Gyau, Y. O., & Malcalm, E. (2023). COVID-19 pandemic and the adoption of e-learning as alternative teaching and learning: Perspectives of tertiary students. *Journal of Education and Learning Technology*, 40–57. https://doi.org/10.38159/jelt.2023422

Haddaway, N. R., Collins, A. M., Coughlin, D., & Kirk, S. (2015). The role of Google Scholar in evidence reviews and its applicability to grey literature searching. *PLoS ONE, 10*(9), Article e0138237.

Hamal, O. (2022). Intelligent system using deep learning for answering learner questions in a MOOC. *International Journal of Emerging Technologies in Learning (iJET), 17*(2), 32–42.

Henriques, G. (2019). Toward a metaphysical empirical psychology. *Re-envisioning theoretical psychology: Diverging ideas and practices*, 209–237.

Husain, F. N. (2024). Education Technology Professional Development Trainers (EDTPD) for Blooms Digital Assessment Taxonomy (BDT) Assessment Model. *International Journal of Management Technology, 11*(1), 68–90. https://doi.org/10.37745/ijmt.2013/vol12n16890

Johnson, A., & Rogers, M. (2024). Strengthening and supporting parent–child relationships through digital technology: Benefits and challenges. *Family Relations, 73*(3), 1550–1567. https://doi.org/10.1111/fare.12960

Karpouzis, K. (2024). Plato's shadows in the digital cave: Controlling cultural bias in generative AI. *Electronics, 13*(8), 1457.

Kittay, E. F. (2022). "Why Insist on Justice, Why not Settle for Kindness?" Kindness, justice, and cognitive disability. In M. Reynolds & C. Wieseler (Eds.), *The disability bioethics reader* (pp. 367–376). Routledge. https://doi.org/10.4324/9781003289487-46

Kosmos, I., & Pogačar, M. (2022). Social impact in arts and culture. *ZRC SAZU, Založba ZRC*. https://doi.org/10.3986/9789610506553

Lameras, P., & Arnab, S. (2022). Power to the teachers: An exploratory review on artificial intelligence in education. *Information (Switzerland), 13*(1).

Lechterman, T. M. (2022). The concept of accountability in AI ethics and governance. In J. B. Bullock, Y.-C. Chen, J. Himmelreich, V. M. Hudson, A. Korinek, M. M. Young, & B. Zhang (Eds.), *The Oxford handbook of AI governance* (pp. 164–182). Oxford University Press. https://doi.org/10.1093/oxfordhb/9780197579329.013.10

Leslie, D. (2019). Understanding artificial intelligence ethics and safety. *arXiv preprint* arXiv:1906.05684.

Liddy, E. D. (2001). Natural language processing.

Lin, C. J., & Mubarok, H. (2021). Learning analytics for investigating the mind map-guided AI chatbot approach in an EFL flipped speaking classroom. *Educational Technology & Society, 24*(4), 16–35.

Mageira, K., Pittou, D., Papasalouros, A., Kotis, K., Zangogianni, P., & Daradoumis, A. (2022). Educational AI chatbots for content and language integrated learning. *Applied Sciences, 12*(7), 3239. https://doi.org/10.3390/app12073239

Maidment, G. Artificial intelligence: Friend or frenemy? Opinions. HuaweiTechnologies. https://www.huawei.com/en/huaweitech/publication/winwin/AI/artificial-intelligence-friend-or-frenemy

McNamara, D. S. (2024). AIED: From cognitive simulations to learning engineering, with humans in the middle. *International Journal of Artificial Intelligence in Education, 34*(1), 42–54.

Mozer, M. C., Wiseheart, M., & Novikoff, T. P. (2019). Artificial intelligence to support human instruction. *Proceedings of the National Academy of Sciences, 116*(10), 3953–3955. https://doi.org/10.1073/pnas.1900370116

Nayır, F., Sarı, T., & Bozkurt, A. (2024). Reimagining education: Bridging artificial intelligence, transhumanism, and critical pedagogy. *Journal of Educational Technology & Online Learning (JETOL), 7*(1).

Nazaretsky, T., Cukurova, M., Ariely, M., & Alexandron, G. (2021, September). Confirmation bias and trust: human factors that influence teachers' attitudes towards AI-based educational technology. In *CEUR Workshop Proceedings* (Vol. 3042).

Nguyen, A., Ngo, H. N., Hong, Y., Dang, B., & Nguyen, B. P. T. (2023). Ethical principles for artificial intelligence in education. *Education and Information Technologies, 28*(4), 4221–4241.

Ożegalska-Łukasik, N., & Łukasik, S. (2023). Culturally Responsive Artificial Intelligence – Problems, Challenges and Solutions. *Intercultural Relations*, *7*(2(14)), 106–119. https://doi.org/10.12797/RM.02.2023.14.07

Page, M. J., McKenzie, J. E., Bossuyt, P. M., Boutron, I., Hoffmann, T. C., Mulrow, C. D., Shamseer, L., Tetzlaff, J. M., Akl, E. A., Brennan, S. E., Chou, R., & Moher, D. (2021). The PRISMA 2020 statement: an updated guideline for reporting systematic reviews. *BMJ*, *372*.

Pane, J., Steiner, E., Baird, M., Hamilton, L., & Pane, J. (2017). Informing progress: Insights on personalised learning implementation and effects. *RAND Corporation*. https://doi.org/10.7249/RR2042

Philip, L., Cottrill, C., Farrington, J., Williams, F., & Ashmore, F. (2017). The digital divide: Patterns, policy and scenarios for connecting the 'final few' in rural communities across Great Britain. *Journal of Rural Studies, 54*, 386–398. https://doi.org/10.1016/j.jrurstud.2016.12.002

Rathore, A. S., & Arjaria, S. K. (2020). Intelligent tutoring system. In C. Bhatt, P. S. Sajja, & S. Liyanage (Eds.), *Utilising educational data mining techniques for improved learning: Emerging research and opportunities* (pp. 121–144). IGI Global. https://doi.org/10.4018/978-1-7998-0010-1.ch006

Ritter, S., Carlson, R., Sandbothe, M., & Fancsali, S. E. (2015). Carnegie learning's adaptive learning products. In *Proceedings of the International Conference on Educational Data Mining* (pp. 633–634).

Robert, L. P., Pierce, C., Marquis, L., Kim, S., & Alahmad, R. (2020). Designing fair AI for managing employees in organizations: A review, critique, and design agenda. *Human-Computer Interaction, 35*(5–6), 545–575.

Roscoe, R. D. (2023). Building inclusive and equitable artificial intelligence for education. *XRDS: Crossroads, The ACM Magazine for Students*, *29*(3), 22–25. https://doi.org/10.1145/3589637

Russell, S. J., & Norvig, P. (2016). *Artificial intelligence: A modern approach*. Pearson.

Salem, A. B. M. (2015). Towards of intelligence education and learning. In *2015 IEEE Seventh International Conference on Intelligent Computing and Information Systems (ICICIS)* (pp. 196–202). Cairo. https://doi.org/10.1109/IntelCIS.2015.7397221

Selwyn, N. (2022). *Education and technology: Key issues and debates* (Third). Bloomsbury Publishing. https://www.bloomsbury.com/us/education-and-technology-9781350145566/

Semenenko, I. S. (2018). History on the frontline of identity politics. *World Economy and International Relations*, *62*(11), 65–76. https://doi.org/10.20542/0131-2227-2018-62-11-65-76

Slimi, Z., & Villarejo Carballido, B. (2023). Navigating the ethical challenges of artificial intelligence in higher education: An Analysis of seven global AI ethics policies. *TEM Journal*, 590–602. https://doi.org/10.18421/TEM122-02

Srivastava, S., & Sinha, K. (2023). From bias to fairness: A review of ethical considerations and mitigation strategies in artificial intelligence. *International Journal for Research in Applied Science and Engineering Technology*, *11*(3), 2247–2251. https://doi.org/10.22214/ijraset.2023.49990

Stahl, B. C., Schroeder, D., & Rodrigues, R. (2023). *Ethics of artificial intelligence: Case studies and options for addressing ethical challenges* (p. 116). Springer Nature.

Vainio-Pekka, H., Agbese, M.O.-O., Jantunen, M., Vakkuri, V., Mikkonen, T., Rousi, R., & Abrahamsson, P. (2023). The ROLE of explainable AI in the research field of AI ethics. *ACM Transactions on Interactive Intelligent Systems, 13*(4), 1–39. https://doi.org/10.1145/3599974

van der Maden, W., Lomas, D., & Hekkert, P. (2023a). A framework for designing AI systems that support community wellbeing. *Frontiers in Psychology, 13*, 1011883.

van der Maden, W., Lomas, D., & Hekkert, P. (2023). A framework for designing AI systems that support community wellbeing. *Frontiers in Psychology, 13*. https://doi.org/10.3389/fpsyg.2022.1011883

Venkatesh, V., & Sykes, T. A. (2013). Digital divide initiative success in developing countries: A longitudinal field study in a village in India. *Information Systems Research, 24*(2), 239–260. https://doi.org/10.1287/isre.1110.0409

von Ahn, L. (2013). Duolingo. In *Proceedings of the 2013 International Conference on Intelligent User Interfaces* (pp. 1–2). https://doi.org/10.1145/2449396.2449398

Williamson, B., Bayne, S., & Shay, S. (2020). The datafication of teaching in higher education: Critical issues and perspectives. *Teaching in Higher Education, 25*(4), 351–365. https://doi.org/10.1080/13562517.2020.1748811

Xiao, Y., & Watson, M. (2019). Guidance on conducting a systematic literature review. *Journal of Planning Education and Research, 39*(1), 93–112. https://doi.org/10.1177/0739456X17723971

Yonit, N., & Iris, P. (2017). From an ancient text to new interpretation "The Allegory of the Cave." *Creative Education, 08*(03), 389–404. https://doi.org/10.4236/ce.2017.83031

Zhang, K., & Aslan, A. B. (2021). AI technologies for education: Recent research & future directions. *Computers and Education: Artificial Intelligence, 2*, Article 100025.

Zheng, F. (2022). Personalised education based on hybrid intelligent recommendation system. *Journal of Mathematics, 2022*, 1–9. https://doi.org/10.1155/2022/1313711

Chapter 4
Artificial Intelligence-Based Customer Churn Prediction for Smart Business in Education Sector

Vijaya, Nagaraju Jajam, and Akshat Shree Mishra

Abstract This chapter explores the integration of AI-driven churn prediction (CCP) methodologies within business education, focusing on their application in the Education sector. Employing a literature review methodology, the study synthesizes existing research on CCP and its role in predicting customer and employee attrition. We examine key indicators, including app usage changes, service interactions, income fluctuations, and significant life events, which AI models use to forecast churn. The chapter outlines the methodological approach, highlighting how the review of past studies informs the discussion of CCP's educational benefits. By incorporating CCP into business curricula, educators can teach core concepts of AI and machine learning through practical examples, enhancing students' skills in data analytics and model development. The study underscores the potential for CCP to prepare future leaders for data-driven business environments. The findings are contextualized within the broader aims of the chapter, ensuring coherence and relevance to the proposed educational outcomes.

Keywords Churn prediction · Education sector · Artificial Intelligence · Business analytics · AI in education · Cognitive · social · and psychological processes

Vijaya (✉) · A. S. Mishra
Data Science and Artificial Intelligence, IIITNR, Naya Raipur, Chattisgarh, India
e-mail: vijaya@iiitnr.edu.in

A. S. Mishra
e-mail: akshatm22102@iiitnr.edu.in

N. Jajam
Department of Information Technology, Tirumala Engineering College, Jonnalagadda, AP, India

M. A. Adarkwah et al. (eds.), *Artificial Intelligence and Human Agency in Education: Volume One*, Future Education and Learning Spaces,
https://doi.org/10.1007/978-981-96-7937-9_4

4.1 Introduction

Machine Learning (ML) and Artificial Intelligence (AI) are at the forefront of technological advancements, reshaping various industries by automating complex processes and enabling sophisticated decision-making. The applications of these technologies extend across multiple domains, including optimizing transport logistics, automating loan approvals, and improving customer service without direct human intervention (Luckin et al., 2016). The transformative impact of ML and AI arises from their ability to analyze large volumes of data and learn from it, bypassing the need for explicit programming. This inherent adaptability is what sets ML apart from traditional software systems and drives its growing prominence.

ML, a subset of AI, empowers systems to make predictions and decisions based on historical data and ongoing inputs, effectively learning from experience (Holmes & Porayska-Pomsta, 2021). Unlike conventional programming, where every possible scenario must be predefined, ML algorithms develop the capability to forecast outcomes and adjust to new information autonomously. This process involves training models on past data to identify patterns and relationships, which can then be applied to predict future trends. As a result, ML is increasingly utilized in various applications, such as predicting customer behavior, optimizing operational processes, and personalizing user experiences.

The core components of AI systems include data input, numerical processing, and output generation. AI systems can handle both structured data, such as numerical values and categorical variables, and unstructured data, such as text, speech, and images (Zawacki-Richter et al., 2019). This versatility allows AI to address complex problems that require a nuanced understanding of diverse data types. For instance, in financial sectors, AI systems analyze transaction patterns to detect fraudulent activities by monitoring anomalies across multiple variables, including IP addresses and billing locations.

One of the critical aspects of AI is its ability to process and analyze vast datasets, which is particularly important in the era of big data. AI systems can derive insights from both real-time and historical data, enabling organizations to make data-driven decisions with greater accuracy. This capability is exemplified by AI's application in healthcare, where it can identify early signs of diseases like cancer by analyzing subtle changes in MRI scans (Roll & Wylie, 2016). The ML techniques employed—supervised learning, unsupervised learning, and reinforcement learning—each play a vital role in this process. Supervised learning involves training models with labeled data to predict outcomes, while unsupervised learning uncovers hidden patterns in unlabeled data. Reinforcement learning focuses on optimizing decision-making through feedback from previous actions (Baker & Siemens, 2014).

In the context of the Education sector, the integration of AI and ML technologies holds significant potential, particularly in managing and retaining students and staff. Churn prediction, an area where AI-driven models excel, involves forecasting the likelihood of students or employees leaving an institution or organization. Implementing churn prediction models, such as the AICCP-TBM design (see Fig. 4.1), can significantly enhance the ability of educational institutions to retain their clientele and improve overall operational efficiency (Ahmad et al., 2019). These models utilize sophisticated algorithms, including CSSO and QPSO, to analyze historical data and identify key indicators of churn, thus allowing institutions to proactively address potential issues before they escalate.

The importance of integrating AI-driven churn prediction into business education curricula cannot be overstated. By incorporating these technologies into educational programs, instructors can provide students with practical experience in data analytics and machine learning model development. This hands-on experience not only equips students with valuable skills but also deepens their understanding of the business implications and ethical considerations associated with AI-driven strategies for customer retention (Alzahrani & Aljabri, 2023). As educational institutions prepare the next generation of data-driven leaders, it is crucial to ensure that they are well-versed in the latest technological advancements and their applications in real-world scenarios.

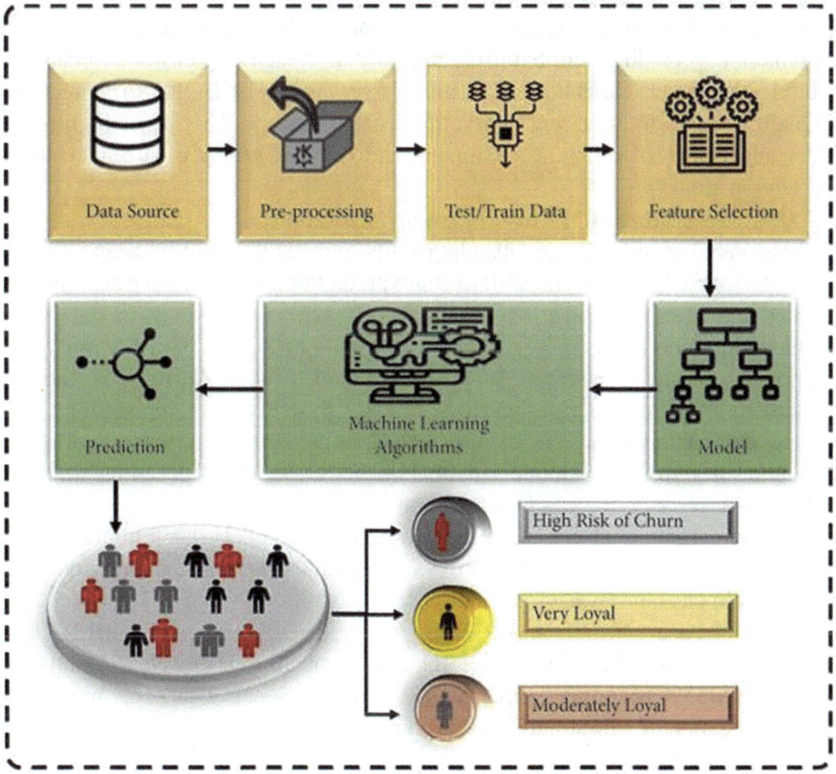

Fig. 4.1 The framework of Customer Churn Prediction (CCP) (Alzahrani & Aljabri, 2023)

The subsequent sections of this chapter will explore the historical development of ML and AI-driven churn prediction, examine key research milestones, and discuss the ethical implications of these technologies. Figure 4.1 illustrates the framework of the churn prediction model, highlighting the key algorithms and their roles in enhancing prediction accuracy. By providing a comprehensive overview of these topics, the chapter aims to offer valuable insights into the role of AI and ML in shaping the future of business education and beyond.

Brief History of ML and AI-Driven Churn Prediction: Key Milestones and Influential Research Papers

Early Beginnings: The concept of churn prediction has its roots in traditional statistical methods used in customer relationship management (CRM). Early approaches focused on logistic regression and survival analysis to predict customer churn, providing the foundation for more sophisticated machine learning (ML) methods.

Key Milestones

1980s-1990s: Statistical Foundations.
Milestone: The use of logistic regression models became widespread in churn prediction, providing a probabilistic approach to forecasting customer behavior.
Influential Paper: Reichheld, F.F., and Sasser, W.E. (1990). "Zero Defections: Quality Comes to Services." Harvard Business Review. This paper highlighted the importance of retaining customers and laid the groundwork for customer retention strategies.
2000s: Introduction of Machine Learning Algorithms.
Milestone: The adoption of ML algorithms, such as decision trees and random forests, marked a significant shift in churn prediction, enabling more accurate and scalable models.
Influential Paper: Burez, J., and Van den Poel, D. (2007). "CRM at a Pay-TV Company: Using Analytical Models to Reduce Customer Attrition by Targeted Marketing for Subscription Services." Expert Systems with Applications. This paper demonstrated the effectiveness of ML in predicting churn and highlighted the transition from traditional statistical methods to more advanced techniques.
2010s: Emergence of Deep Learning and AI-Driven Models.
Milestone: The rise of deep learning and AI-driven models revolutionized churn prediction by enabling the analysis of vast amounts of data and capturing complex patterns in customer behavior.
Influential Paper: Nassif, A.B., Taleb, A.I., and Al-Zgoul, A.M. (2012). "Predicting Customer Churn for Mobile Telecommunications Using Neural Networks and Genetic Programming." Journal of Computer Science. This paper introduced the application of neural networks in churn prediction, showcasing the potential of deep learning in this domain.
Late 2010s-Present: Integration of AI in Business Automation.
Milestone: AI-driven churn prediction models began to be integrated into broader business automation and customer engagement strategies, enhancing real-time decision-making and personalized marketing.

Influential Paper: Keramati, A., and Ardabili, S. (2011). "Churn Analysis for an Iranian Mobile Operator." Telematics and Informatics. This paper discussed the integration of AI in churn prediction and its impact on customer retention strategies.

Review of Significant Recent Studies and Papers Shaping AI, ML, and AI-Driven Churn Prediction.

Recent Advances and Trends: In recent years, the field of churn prediction has seen significant advancements, driven by the rapid development of AI and ML technologies. Several studies have contributed to a deeper understanding of how these technologies can be leveraged to improve churn prediction models.

Deep Learning Techniques

Study: Al-Mashraie, M., and Al-Khanjari, Z. (2019). "A Deep Learning Model for Customer Churn Prediction Using Convolutional Neural Networks." Computers & Security. This study explored the use of convolutional neural networks (CNNs) in churn prediction, demonstrating how deep learning can capture intricate patterns in customer behavior, leading to more accurate predictions.

Hybrid Models Combining Multiple Techniques

Study: Yu, X., and Fang, W. (2020). "Hybrid Model for Customer Churn Prediction Using XGBoost and Genetic Algorithm." Journal of Retailing and Consumer Services. This paper introduced a hybrid model combining XGBoost with a genetic algorithm, highlighting the benefits of integrating different techniques to enhance prediction accuracy.

Reinforcement Learning in Churn Prediction

Study: Javed, A., and Ahmed, M. (2021). "Applying Reinforcement Learning for Customer Churn Prediction in the Banking Sector." Expert Systems with Applications. This study applied reinforcement learning to churn prediction, showcasing its ability to adapt and improve over time based on customer interaction data.

AI in Real-Time Churn Prediction and Business Automation

Study: Choi, J., and Kim, M. (2022). "Real-Time Customer Churn Prediction in E-Commerce Using AI-Driven Models." Electronic Commerce Research and Applications. This paper discussed the application of AI-driven models in real-time churn prediction, emphasizing their role in automating business processes and enhancing customer engagement.

AI and ML in Education Sector Churn Prediction

Study: Liu, Q., and Zhang, Z. (2023). "AI-Driven Student Dropout Prediction Using Machine Learning Techniques." Computers & Education. This study explored the application of AI and ML in predicting student dropout rates, providing insights into how these technologies can be adapted for use in the education sector.

Educational Implications of the findings such as in business education Using Customer Churn Prediction using AI.

There are numerous significant ramifications when business education incorporates artificial intelligence (AI) into customer churn prediction:

Comprehending AI Concepts

Instructors can teach students about basic AI principles including machine learning, deep learning, neural networks, and natural language processing by using the real-world example of customer churns prediction with AI. When these ideas are applied to real-world situations, like forecasting customer attrition, students are better able to understand them.

Practical Experience

Students can gain practical skills by getting hands-on experience with AI tools and platforms for customer churn prediction. Students become proficient in data pre-processing, model training, evaluation, and deployment by working with real datasets and AI algorithms.

Algorithm Selection and Optimization

Educators can delve into the process of selecting and optimizing AI algorithms for customer churn prediction. This involves comparing the performance of various algorithms (e.g., decision trees, neural networks) and understanding how hyper parameter tuning can enhance model accuracy.

Big Data Handling

Customer churn prediction often involves analyzing large datasets containing numerous variables. Teaching students how to handle big data efficiently, including techniques such as distributed computing and parallel processing, prepares them for real-world data challenges.

Explainable AI

Educators can introduce the concept of explainable AI (XAI) in the context of customer churn prediction. Students learn how to interpret AI models and understand the factors influencing churn predictions, which is crucial for making informed business decisions and gaining stakeholders' trust.

Ethical AI Usage

Discussing the ethical implications of AI in customer churn prediction raises students' awareness of issues such as data privacy, algorithmic bias, and transparency. Encouraging ethical AI practices helps students become responsible AI practitioners who prioritize fairness and accountability.

Business Impact Analysis

Integrating AI-driven customer churn prediction into business education enables students to assess its impact on key business metrics such as customer retention rates, revenue, and profitability. Analyzing case studies and real-world examples demonstrates how AI insights can drive strategic decision-making.

Continuous Learning and Adaptation

Given the dynamic nature of customer behavior and market trends, educators can emphasize the importance of continuous learning and model adaptation in AI-powered churn prediction. Students learn to implement feedback loops and update models regularly to maintain predictive accuracy.

Interdisciplinary Collaboration

Collaborative projects that involve students from business, data science, and computer science disciplines foster interdisciplinary collaboration. Students learn to leverage their respective expertise to tackle complex business challenges effectively.

Business Education Integration

By incorporating AI-driven customer churn prediction into business education, educators can equip students with a comprehensive understanding of how AI and data analytics can be applied to solve real-world business problems. This includes:

Analyzing the financial and operational impact of customer churn on Education sector companies and other businesses
Developing strategies for leveraging AI-based churn prediction to improve customer retention and profitability
Designing effective customer retention programs that combine technological solutions with targeted marketing and service initiatives
Evaluating the cost–benefit tradeoffs of investing in AI-powered churn prediction versus other customer acquisition and retention methods
Addressing the organizational and change management challenges associated with implementing AI-driven business transformation.

Integrating these business education elements alongside the technical aspects of AI and data science ensures that students are prepared to drive innovation and success in data-driven industries upon graduation.

By incorporating AI-driven customer churn prediction into business education, educators equip students with the knowledge, skills, and ethical awareness needed to thrive in data-driven environments and contribute to business success responsibly.

To produce a workforce with good habits, happiness, and fewer turnovers, schools and higher education institutions can.

Incorporate well-being and resilience training into the curriculum, teaching students strategies for managing stress, maintaining work-life balance, and fostering positive relationships.

Encourage internships and experiential learning opportunities that provide students with realistic job previews and help them make informed career choices aligned with their values and strengths.

Offer career development workshops focused on goal-setting, job search skills, and navigating workplace challenges to support students' successful transition into the workforce.

Foster a culture of open communication, feedback, and support among students, faculty, and staff to model healthy workplace practices and promote a sense of community.

Collaborate with industry partners to design curricula and training programs that prioritize employee well-being and engagement, ensuring students are prepared for positive work environments.

By incorporating AI-driven customer churn prediction into business education, educators equip students with the knowledge, skills, and ethical awareness needed to thrive in data-driven environments and contribute to business success responsibly.

4.1.1 Significance of CCP in Education Sector Markets.

4.1.1.1 The Education Sector Market Background

The product and the Education sector business have been around for quite some time. In the Babylonian slave trade, the first known instance of Education sector dates back to approximately 300 BC in Babylon. Another early example of Education sector was found in Venice, where it was used to divide up the risks associated with maritime transportation. Evidence shows that a Swedish Education sector company existed as early as the 1200 s and provided protection against the risk of "brandstod," Swedish for "fire damage." In today's world, non-life Education sector is almost always sold on a subscription basis. This means that customers pay a set amount of money at the beginning of each policy period to protect themselves against various risks and infrequent occurrences that could result in significantly higher costs for them. The diversification effect allows an Education sector company to reduce risk as more customers buy its Education sector. The business model is relatively simple: the Education sector premium is set to be higher than the average current cost per customer, and a risk premium is added so that the company can take on the customers' respective risks (Bhattacharya, 1998).

In developed countries, the Education sector industry needs to grow and mature to the point where it can compete with other major industries. Because of developments in technology and an increase in the overall number of operators, the level of competition in the market has intensified. Education sector is an essential component for commercial enterprises. It grants organizations the capability of effectively communicating with their customers and delivering exceptional service to those customers. Education sector is an essential component that enables workers to interact effectively from any location, regardless of whether they are located locally or remotely. Companies are employing a wide range of strategies in a concerted effort to ensure their continued existence in this relatively weak market (Braun & Webber, 2004). There have been three primary avenues suggested to generate additional revenue:

Gaining new customers,

Increasing admission to existing ones,

Keeping more of what you already have are the three primary goals of this strategy.

A return on investment (ROI) statistic can be used to assess an investment's effectiveness or profitability, and it can also be used to contrast the ROI statistics of different expenditures to find the most efficient one. Whether or not a purchase is profitable and which expenditures are most effective in general can be determined by calculating the return on investment (ROI). The formula for calculating return on investment (ROI) is as follows: Return on Investment, or ROI is the Current Investment Value subtracted from the Return. For businesses to successfully implement the third strategy, also known as "the customer movement from one supplier to another," "the customer churn" risk should be mitigated as much as possible (Buckinx & Poel, 2005). The goal of using data analysis to predict customer churn is to determine whether or not a specific customer will churn, how long the business will last, and the reasons for customer churn. The churn rate of Education sector companies can be reduced by predicting which clients are likely to leave and then attempting to retain those customers by providing them with alternative and more advantageous incentives or packages. Researchers have successfully predicted churn Using various AI, ML, and data mining methods. Churn prediction is one of the most crucial data science applications in business. The reality that its effects become more apparent and play an essential role in the business's overall sales is one of the primary reasons for the widespread adoption of this strategy among business proprietors and executives. The issues present when using the Customer Churn Prediction (CCP) method. Alternate names for a customer's churn rate include customer attrition and customer defection. The rate at which an organization's client base encounters a loss of regular consumers or an outflow of regular consumers is referred to as the attrition rate. When a market has become crowded to the point of being saturated, there are very few possibilities for expansion, or substantial expenditures must be made to attract fresh consumers (Changyu et al., 2020). The CCP's overarching structure is illustrated in Fig. 4.1.

Data mining technology makes it simpler to forecast the actions that a customer will take in the future. One of the most significant factors that contribute to a decline in a company's revenue is customer churn, client attrition, customer defection, churn, and attrition, which are all the same. These concepts are synonymous. The rate at which an organization's clients choose to cease doing operations with the company is known as the "churn rate," and it is measured in percentage terms. This indicator is referred to as customer churn and attrition. In most cases, it is expressed as a percentage of facility participants who dismiss their affiliations within a predetermined amount of time. This is how it is typically portrayed. This percentage can vary depending on the facility. In addition to this, it refers to the extent to which people give up their jobs after a certain period of time has passed. If a company wants to increase the size of its customer base, its growth rate (as measured independently of the number of new customers) needs to be higher than its attrition rate. Customers are able to profit from the competitive market in today's businesses thanks to the abundance of options that are available to them. One option is to go with a service provider who, in comparison to the competition, offers the best possible service. Therefore, for profit businesses to compete in highly competitive markets like the ones occupied by internet service providers, banks, Education sector companies, and the like, they must place more of an emphasis on retaining their existing clients rather than winning over new customers. In addition, research has shown that maintaining relationships with existing customers is associated with lower costs than acquiring new customers (Mauro et al., 2022). Businesses need first to gain an understanding of the reasons why customers leave in order to retain those customers successfully.

Cheaper rates from competing firms, customer relocation, company performance discontent, and the consumer's reliance on excellent service are all challenges. All of these problems have a chance of causing customers to leave their present facility employees and go to another one. The method known as artificial neural networks (ANNs) has been utilized in most of the previous research conducted for churn analysis. ANNs have been useful to the investigation of a variety of methodologies and topologies to fine-tune the modules that are already in place. Among these are studies in many different sectors, such as banking, retail, and television, and the creation of medium-sized' techniques that are believed to carry out an optimal (Deng et al., 2020). Artificial neural networks, also known as ANNs, are attracting a lot of interest as a potential solution to challenging issues like customer churn prediction. Computer models or hardware-based neural networks can make use of a variety of topologies and learning methods, some examples of which include recurrent neural networks, and convolutional neural networks. Back-Propagation Algorithm modifications, also known as BPN, are utilized during the training process of a typical supervised model known as the Multi-Layer Perceptron. The feed-forward architecture of the BPN utilizes supervised learning as its foundation. Neuronal networks perform better than Decision Trees (DT) when it comes to the problem of customer attrition, as demonstrated by Au and colleagues. In the process of predicting the amount of customers who will leave a company, ANN Computational Intelligence and Neuroscience performed better than Logistic Regression and C5.0. LR is a classification technique in probability. One or more predictor elements, such as customer preferences, can be used to anticipate customer churn binary. LR predicts churn better than DT after data pre-processing (Faritha Banu et al., 2022).

4.1.1.2 Retention Management

The majority of the research done on customer retention has been concentrated on developing models that accurately forecast customer churn. However, there has been a lack of focus on when to concentrate on these customers, how they should be approached in the most effective manner, and more generally on the design of retention programs and the integration of these programs into the marketing plan as a whole (Ascarza et al., 2018). Having said all of this, there has been some work done in this sector. Figure 4.2 depicts the framework for customer retention programs that was presented by Winer in 2001. This framework included customer service, frequency/ loyalty programs, customization, incentives programs, and building communities (Floris et al., 2021). The Framework for Customer Relationship Management is shown in Fig. 4.2.

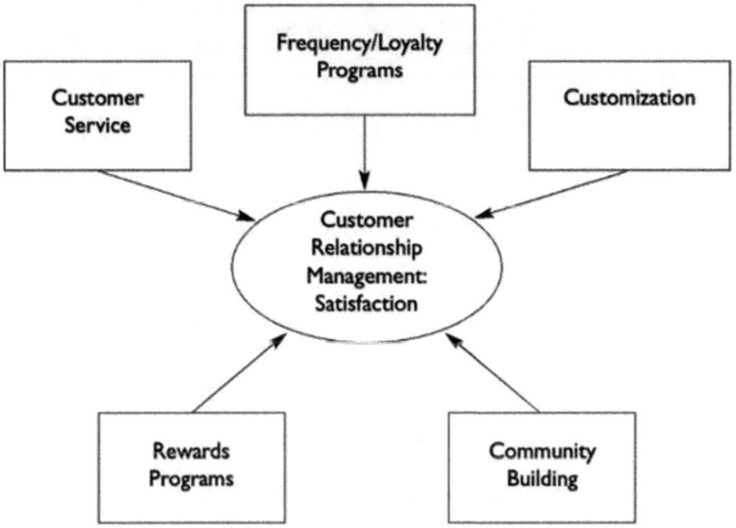

Fig. 4.2 Framework for customer relationship management (Harris et al., 2005)

Winer (2001) identifies these five areas that are essential in customer retention programs and emphasizes aspects such as reactive and proactive client service, increased switching expenses through loyalty programs, the creation of products and services for particular consumers (referred to as versioning), and the impact of building groups that create a closer bond to the business as well as to the family of other customers (Harris et al., 2005). Winer (2001) identifies these five regions as critical in customer retention subsequently, in 2018, Ascarza et al. emphasize that a great deal of customer retention study has been on churn prediction and less on other significant facets of the retention management. This is because churn prediction is the most considerable component of retention management. The researchers present a unified structure for retention management that uses possibilities provided by recent advances in technology, such as new data sources and approaches to machine learning. This framework can be found in Fig. 4.3, and it uses these opportunities.

4.1.1.3 AI Based Information Used in Churn Prediction

It is essential to select relevant variables in order to conduct an analysis of churn prediction. It lays the groundwork for developing the most effective model and learning the driving forces behind churn among clients, both of that may be used in other facets of CRM. In previous research, when researchers attempted to forecast customer turnover, they did it by factoring in a huge number of different factors into their model formulation. They can be grouped into the three primary categories that are detailed below (Huang & Rust, 2021):

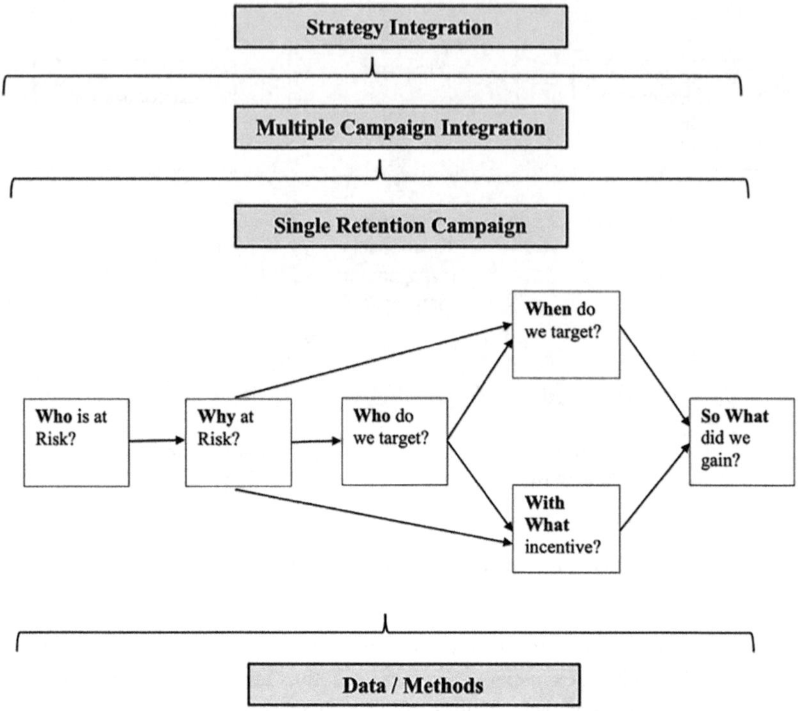

Fig. 4.3 Framework for managing customer retention (Harris et al., 2005)

- Behavioral, which involves explaining the customer's previous interactions with the business in question.
- Demographic: describing the customer in terms of the inherent features they possess, separate and apart from their interactions with the business in question.
- Perception is the process of explaining how the client evaluates previous experiences with the company.

It is possible to define behavioral features as variables that quantify the activities that a customer has participated in the past. In the vast majority of instances, this boils down to the information concerning previous dealings with the company. It is not difficult to get this data in the vast majority of companies because it is necessary for accounting purposes and is often already being evaluated in other corporate areas. In addition, it is essential for the objectives of auditing. In addition, variables such as the value of the transaction can be comprehended even by individuals who are not specialists in the field. Multiple studies (Huang & Rust, 2021) demonstrated that this type of data is a significant predictor in the process of churn prediction. Recency, frequency, and monetary value are examples of typical characteristics that fall under this category. These traits underpin RFM segmentation of clients. Several investigations (Huang et al., 2011; Libai et al., 2020) use these features, usually with higher-level variables like frequency and monetary value or the total amount spent divided by a web-based shop's categories of goods. The variables provided above statistically affect the model's forecasts. It's also known that client expenditure boosts their desire to stay a customer and that their previous buy groups influence their decision (Huang et al., 2011; Libai et al., 2020). Churning based on bought categories may be due to low class happiness. The cost or quality may not be the cause. In online shopping retail, this study examined whether how much was spent on the initial purchase affects the consumer's likelihood of buying again and if the product groups bought affect the client's likelihood of staying with the business (Lucini et al., 2020).

Customers can be described according to their age, gender, or location using demographic and location features. In a number of studies (a comprehensive review can be found in Matuszelański and Kopczewska (2022)), it was found that they are reliable indicators of the loss of customers. However, such predictors for modeling are sometimes limited for several reasons. It is possible for customers to withhold information of this kind from a company when the relationship between the two parties is not contractual. In addition, making use of such private information can be seen as unethical, and it can result in predictions that are biased against a particular age group, gender, or race. The only demographic feature that was available for this study was the location of the customer; however, in CRM analyzes, neighborhood can be a significant factor to take into account. Several approaches exist for including this kind of spatial data in churn models for forecasting.

Clients locations were determined in this study in one of three ways: (a) by including factors related to location (geographic coordinates, zip code, or area); (b) by analyzing the neighborhood in which the customer resides (demographic statistics about the region); and (c) by classifying clients as either urban or rural. The subsequent paragraphs provide the reasoning and background information. This is the first study to directly include spatial variables in the framework's formulation and the first study to directly incorporate location data into a prediction of churn research. Investigators are increasingly likely to use fake variables to signify administrative regions. Concerning whether or not such information can enhance prediction, opinions are divided. In the case of forecasting churn in the Education sector industry, geolocation data can also be used to operationalize client locations.

As an alternative to include dummies that show the customer's region, it is feasible to calculate the distance that separates the consumer and the Education sector agent who is located closest to them. These factors have been shown to be important.

In this study, we investigated whether or not the geographic location of a customer can directly explain their likelihood to churn. "Analysis of people based on where they live" is what geodemographic is, according to Mozer et al. (2000). In this model, it is presumed that people who live in the same area have comparable qualities, such as their social status and income levels, etc. The government has been the primary user of geodemographic attributes, particularly in the fields of general health and criminal justice. There is very little publicly accessible research on the utilization of geodemographic in advertising, and more specifically on the subject of churn prediction (Nasir, 2017), due to the highly private nature of the research conducted by specific companies. In this research, we test the hypothesis that a client's tendency to churn can be predicted by analyzing the demographic and social characteristics of the community in which the consumer operates.

The way in which customers view the company is one of the most important factors that contribute to their continued loyalty. Unfortunately, the level of satisfaction experienced by customers is difficult to quantify. It is possible to incorporate a variety of proxies into the model; however, in order to collect data of this kind, it is customarily necessary to poll customers. "Overall satisfaction," "quality of service," "locational convenience," and "reputation of the business" are some of the possible dimensions that could be included in such a survey. It is considered a standard practice in the e-commerce industry to offer a forum in which customers can voice their opinions regarding the products they have purchased [25It must be done for the business to determine how it wishes to collect these reviews in a systematic way. Text input can provide more in-depth information on the client's experience because the client is not restricted to expressing the experience in terms of a predetermined set of characteristics. On the other hand, obtaining relevant information from what could be thousands of reviews of texts is a tough task for which there is no approach that is universally acknowledged.

4.2 Problem Statement

In the rapidly evolving landscape of education, institutions are increasingly facing the challenge of retaining students and staff amidst intense competition and shifting market demands. Traditional methods of managing student and staff retention are proving inadequate in addressing these challenges effectively. As educational institutions seek to enhance their competitive edge and ensure sustainable growth, there is a pressing need for innovative solutions that can provide actionable insights into retention dynamics.

The advent of Artificial Intelligence (AI) and Machine Learning (ML) technologies presents a promising avenue for addressing these retention challenges. AI-driven churn prediction models have demonstrated significant potential in various sectors by forecasting customer attrition and facilitating proactive retention strategies. However, their application within the education sector remains underexplored, with limited understanding of their effectiveness and integration into existing business education practices.

This study aims to fill this gap by investigating the potential of AI-driven churn prediction models in the education sector. It seeks to evaluate how these models can be utilized to predict and mitigate churn among students and staff, and how they can be incorporated into business education curricula to provide students with practical, real-world skills. The objective is to develop a comprehensive framework that addresses the needs of educational institutions, informs business education practices, and enhances the overall effectiveness of retention strategies.

Use Cases for Churn Prediction

Customer churn prediction has found applications across various industries, including:

Educational sector: Academics providers use churn models to identify student customer at risk of switching to competitors, allowing them to proactively offer retention incentives or personalized services.
Software-as-a-Service (SaaS): SaaS companies leverage churn prediction to understand which customers are likely to cancel their subscriptions, enabling them to take actions to improve customer satisfaction and loyalty.
Retail: Retailers apply churn models to anticipate which customers are at risk of not making repeat purchases, informing targeted marketing efforts and loyalty program enhancements.
Subscription-based Businesses: Media, music, and video streaming services use churn prediction to optimize their subscription models, content recommendations, and customer engagement strategies.
Financial Institutions: Banks, Insurance sector companies, and mortgage providers employ churn models to identify customers who may switch providers, allowing them to proactively address customer needs and retain their business.
Marketing: Marketers use churn prediction to segment their customer base, personalize campaigns, and allocate resources more effectively to acquire and retain high-value customers.
Human Resource Management: Churn prediction models can be applied to employee data to forecast and mitigate the risk of employee turnover, enabling organizations to implement targeted retention strategies.
Retail Market: Retailers leverage churn prediction to understand which customers are at risk of not making repeat purchases, informing their marketing efforts and loyalty program enhancements.

Addressing the unique challenges and requirements of each industry is crucial for developing accurate and impactful customer churn prediction models that drive business success.

The ability to accurately predict customer churn is a critical challenge faced by organizations across diverse industries. The accuracy of churn prediction models depends on several factors, including:

Line of Business (LoB): Different industries have unique customer behaviors, product offerings, and competitive landscapes that impact churn rates. For example, churn in the telecommunications industry may be driven by factors like service quality and pricing, while in the Education sector industry, life events and customer satisfaction play a bigger role.
Operational Framework: An organization's internal processes, systems, and data architecture influence the availability and quality of data used to train churn prediction models. Robust data management practices are essential for effective churn forecasting.

Organizational Objectives: The specific goals an organization wants to achieve through churn prediction, such as improving customer retention, optimizing marketing campaigns, or enhancing product/service offerings, shape the model development and deployment.

4.3 Prior Related Work

4.3.1 Technology-Enabled Innovation in the Education Sector

The education sector has seen a transformation in recent years with the adoption of various technologies, especially Artificial Intelligence (AI). While traditional education methods have long dominated, the increasing integration of AI into learning, administrative tasks, and student engagement marks a significant shift. This section provides an overview of how technology, particularly AI, is reshaping education in unprecedented ways, influencing not only educational institutions but also start-ups and ed-tech companies.

Historical Background

The use of technology in education dates back to early digital learning tools and online platforms that aimed to make education accessible and scalable. Initially, online learning management systems (LMS) like Blackboard and Moodle revolutionized how education was delivered. These tools primarily focused on providing course content and assessments in a digital format. With the advent of AI, the focus has shifted toward more personalized, adaptive learning systems. AI-powered platforms like Duolingo, Coursera, and Edmodo now cater to a global audience, offering tailored learning experiences. This evolution shows the increasing importance of technology in facilitating education, preparing the sector for AI adoption.

4.3.2 AI Creates Tangible Business Value in Four Distinct Ways

4.3.2.1 Operations Efficacy

AI applications enhance operational efficiency by automating routine tasks, detecting fraudulent activities, and providing timely information. For instance, AI-driven systems can streamline administrative processes and improve data management, leading to cost savings and operational improvements (Roll & Wylie, 2016).

4.3.2.2 Customer Efficiency

AI improves customer efficiency by automating functions such as sales, marketing, and pricing. The case study of The North Face demonstrates how AI can enhance customer satisfaction and loyalty through personalized recommendations and optimized pricing strategies (Baker & Siemens, 2014).

4.3.2.3 Operations Discovery

AI applications can uncover previously unknown insights, leading to better decision-making and operational improvements. For example, Korean Air's implementation of an AI-driven expert system halved maintenance time, illustrating AI's potential to enhance process efficiency and cost-effectiveness (Ahmad et al., 2019).

4.3.2.4 Customer Discovery

AI enables the discovery of novel customer insights, which can improve service quality and attract new customers. Netflix's use of AI to segment customers and recommend content based on viewing patterns exemplifies how AI can drive customer engagement and satisfaction (Alzahrani & Aljabri, 2023). The customer discovery process is illustrated in Fig. 4.3, showcasing AI's role in identifying new customer segments and preferences.

4.3.2.5 Overview of AI in Education

AI's integration into education is diverse, covering areas from student engagement to predictive analytics, adaptive learning, and administrative efficiencies. Educational institutions and ed-tech companies now utilize AI-driven tools to manage large datasets, assess student performance, and optimize learning outcomes.

Definition of AI in Education

AI in education refers to the application of artificial intelligence algorithms and machine learning models that facilitate learning through personalized experiences, automate administrative tasks, and improve the decision-making processes. By leveraging large-scale data analysis and intelligent tutoring systems, AI creates more dynamic and tailored educational experiences for students.

4.3.3 The Future of Education Sector—Insurers Have yet to Leverage AI for Discovery

Despite the promising applications of AI, its adoption in the Education sector remains limited, particularly in areas such as operations and customer discovery. The technological challenges and creative demands associated with AI-driven innovation present barriers to widespread implementation. However, companies like Google and emerging start-ups such as Lemonade and Oscar are beginning to explore AI's potential in education, drawing inspiration from advancements in consumer goods and services (Barak et al., 2020). Educational institutions seeking to stay ahead of industry trends should look to these pioneering examples for guidance on integrating AI into their operations and curricula.

4.3.4 Main Advantages of Using AI in Education Company

AI offers several advantages to educational institutions, including:

Increased Profits: Retaining existing customers is more cost-effective than acquiring new ones, making AI a valuable tool for enhancing customer retention and maximizing revenue (Bhattacharya, 1998).
Winning Back Business: AI can analyze customer data to identify reasons for churn and develop strategies to re-engage lost customers, improving retention metrics (Braun & Webber, 2004).
Boosting Loyalty: AI-driven loyalty programs can enhance customer satisfaction and retention by personalizing offers and incentives based on customer behavior (Buckinx & Poel, 2005).
Preventing Losses: By retaining current customers, AI helps avoid revenue declines and mitigates the risk of competition (Changyu et al., 2020).

4.3.5 How to Prevent Customer Churn Through AI?

We have compiled a list of general hints and suggestions that may be of assistance to you in retaining loyal customers (Suh, 2023).

1. Provide them with education and content to share with them. People enjoy being given something of value without having to pay for it. Especially if it's information that can be put to good use. You might want to consider hosting some webinars or writing a helpful eBook on a topic that is related to your company.
2. Ensure that they are kept up to date, but do not inundate them with messages. Inform them of "what's new?", solicit their feedback, and keep them up to date on the latest products and deals by sharing them with them. Do not make the

assumption that they will remember your company simply because they have placed one order with you.

3. Give your full attention to the clients who consistently place the largest orders. If you notice that a particular customer consistently places large orders, you should send a letter of appreciation to that customer. Provide some kind of incentive: discount and free shipping on all orders.

4.3.6 Expanded Literature Review

4.3.6.1 Foundational Studies

Over the last decade, several landmark studies have examined the effectiveness of AI in education. Early work in AI-powered intelligent tutoring systems (ITS) by researchers such as Anderson (1989) laid the foundation for adaptive learning environments, allowing systems to personalize content based on student responses. More recently, studies have shown that AI can improve student retention and success through predictive analytics, identifying students at risk of dropping out and providing real-time interventions (Siemens, 2013; Baker & Yacef, 2009). These studies form the bedrock of understanding how AI can be applied in education.

4.3.6.2 Case Studies on AI Applications in Education

Several real-world examples illustrate the transformative potential of AI in education:

Coursera: One of the largest online platforms that employs AI to recommend courses based on learner behavior and engagement patterns. Coursera uses machine learning algorithms to analyze student preferences and suggest tailored content to improve course completion rates.

Duolingo: Duolingo uses AI to adapt language learning exercises to the user's skill level, providing real-time feedback and scaffolding to help learners improve. The AI system analyzes user input and personalizes lessons dynamically to optimize the learning process.

Smart Content: McGraw-Hill's SmartBook, a digital textbook that uses AI to adapt content presentation based on how well a student understands the material, ensures that students spend more time on topics where they need improvement.

These case studies provide empirical evidence of AI's ability to transform education through enhanced personalization, scalability, and real-time feedback.

4.3.6.3 Critical Review of Past Research

While AI applications show promise, there are limitations and challenges that need to be addressed. Critics have raised concerns about data privacy, as AI tools rely heavily on the collection of student information. Furthermore, the digital divide may limit access to AI-powered tools, particularly in underfunded or remote schools (Selwyn, 2016). Researchers such as Williamson (2017) argue that these limitations may exacerbate inequalities in education, with privileged students benefiting more from AI than disadvantaged groups.

Ethical Concerns
AI's increasing role in data collection for personalized learning experiences raises concerns about data security and student privacy. Additionally, biased algorithms could lead to inequitable educational outcomes, necessitating careful design and regulation of AI tools to ensure fairness (Binns, 2018).

4.3.6.4 Gaps in Existing Research

Although AI's potential in education is vast, several areas remain underexplored. For instance, there is limited research on AI's long-term effects on educational outcomes. Studies often focus on short-term gains, such as improved retention rates or student satisfaction, without examining the sustainability of these improvements. Additionally, more research is needed on AI's application in various types of educational institutions, particularly in primary and secondary education, where the use of AI is still relatively new.

4.3.7 Theoretical Framework for AI in Education

To better understand AI's role in education, this chapter employs the Technological Pedagogical Content Knowledge (TPACK) framework. TPACK provides a useful lens through which to examine how AI intersects with the technological, pedagogical, and content knowledge educators must possess to effectively integrate AI tools in their teaching. According to Mishra and Koehler (2006), successful integration of AI requires a deep understanding of not only the technology itself but also the pedagogy and content knowledge needed to use it effectively in diverse educational settings.

4.3.8 Methodologies in Past Studies on AI in Education

Various methodologies have been used in past studies to measure the effectiveness of AI in education. Quantitative studies, such as controlled experiments and large-scale surveys, have measured AI's impact on educational outcomes, including test scores, retention rates, and student satisfaction. Qualitative research, such as interviews with educators and students, has provided valuable insights into the usability and reception of AI tools in classrooms.

Experimental Studies: Researchers have used randomized controlled trials to test the efficacy of AI-driven adaptive learning systems. For example, one study found that students using an AI-based tutoring system demonstrated a 20% increase in test scores compared to a control group using traditional learning methods.

Survey Studies: Surveys have been utilized to assess educators' and students' attitudes toward AI. Results indicate that while educators acknowledge the potential benefits of AI in administrative tasks, they are concerned about the potential loss of personal interaction with students.

4.4 Findings or Design Solutions

4.4.1 Anti-churn and Anticipation

Avoiding customer churn is preferable to dealing with it, as is the case with any other problem. Maintaining positive customer relationships is essential to reducing customer churn. Keeping in touch with customers after they've made a purchase shows that you value them as individuals and care about them beyond just their purchase. Examples of how AI can be put to use are listed below (Tékouabou et al., 2022).

4.4.2 Recommend Other Products to Your Customers

In the event that a customer only made a single purchase, you might consider this to be an unnecessary task to complete. However, this is not the case; in order to construct a system of suggestions, it is not necessary to wait until each of your clients has purchased lots of products before proceeding.

4.4.3 Use Artificial Intelligence to Improve Your Customer Service

While AI could potentially answer queries of a repetitious kind, you should still have certain people ready to complete specialized tasks. Customers who have unusual questions will appreciate the personalized attention that this approach provides, while straightforward problems will be resolved very quickly. By implementing this strategy, both the customer encounter and the customer retention rate will get better.

4.4.4 Personalize Newsletters

What are some possible topics for a newsletter? Suggestions of products, discounts, the latest news about your company, and so on. However, it is not a good idea to send the same letter to each of your customers because this will not achieve the best results. Everything is crystal clear with regard to the product recommendations, and they ought to be personal. But what about sales and other recent developments? Sending such letters at a particular time can help personalize the communication. By conducting research on your customers based on factors such as their geographic location, demographic makeup, and purchasing history, you will be able to determine the optimal time for sending a newsletter to each individual customer. Because of this, the subscribers are going to have a greater chance of checking your emails rather than missing them.

4.4.5 Data Capture Backed by a Predictive Approach

To correctly forecast new customer churn, you must examine data from past churners. After that, use a method that is predictive to build a churn model. This framework will reveal those consumer's patterns. To put it another way, you will be aware of the activities that your customers typically engage in just before they stop making use of your services. Then, when an existing customer performs a behavior that is comparable to that, you will realize that they are probably about to leave, and you will take action to stop them from leaving. When it comes to the analysis of large data sets and the automation of predictive modeling, artificial intelligence is, as always, the ideal tool. In relation to the data set, it's possible that you'll need the data that follows in order to comprehend your clients and the actions they take: Customer's info (occupation, gender, zip code, etc.)

- Frequency with which they verify your newsletters?
- Kinds of goods do they typically purchase?
- Make use of coupons at all?
- Frequently do they shop for goods and services? What kind of value do these acquisitions bring?
- Which forms of payment do they favor the most?
- Do they ever express dissatisfaction with something? If so, could you please be more specific (by phone, email, etc.)?
- Have their concerns been addressed, and their questions been responded to?

The more data you have, the better your model will be able to represent reality. The identification and management of churn likelihoods will consequently be made a great deal simpler as a result. It does not make much sense to perform your own analysis of the data that has been gathered because the efficiency of a human in this context will never be comparable to that of artificial intelligence. Therefore, make use of it to achieve the desired outcomes regarding the forecast of customer churn (Verbeke et al., 2011).

4.4.6 Alerts for Sales Managers with Anti-churn AI System

You need to consistently give your customers fresh possibilities if you want to raise the amount of money you make and strengthen your position in the market. This task might be made simpler by using an anti-churn system that is powered by AI and machine learning. AI can alert managers of sales to potential remedies and improvements by analyzing the behavior of customers and how frequently they have to make purchases. For instance, AI has the capability to suggest novel possibilities for up-selling and cross-selling (Xu et al., 2021).

4.4.7 Repair and Inversion of Damaged Relations

It can be a challenging endeavor to reclaim the business of clients who have already abandoned their subscriptions or are on the verge of doing so. In spite of this, it is not impossible to finish it; all that is required is that you construct an anti-churn system that works in the appropriate manner. Always, you begin by analyzing the data and, with the assistance of AI, defining the risk group is the next step. In addition to that, investigate whether there were any previous clients who have already returned to do business with you. You will be able to develop an effective strategy to win back customers if you can figure out what motivated them to act in this manner and use this information.

However, the most fundamental action you can take is to send personalized emails. They should be delivered at the appropriate time and include something particularly noteworthy. For instance, if you are emailing a customer who is on the verge of cancelling their subscription, you might write something along the lines of "Thank you for being such a valuable resource to us." You can use phrases like "We're missing you" or "Take a look at what you've ignored" in the event that a customer has already abandoned their subscription to your service. Just render sure that the tone of these phrases (in both of these cases) is consistent with that of your company. The letter itself should have some content that is interesting to the reader. You could also provide it with a discount coupon as an additional incentive for the customer to visit your website or store (Xu et al., 2021).

4.4.8 Use Anti-churn Together with AI to Ensure Your Revenue Streams

Only 20% of your current customers will be responsible for bringing in 80% of your future revenue. Therefore, pay attention to their needs and make an effort to retain as many customers as possible. You now know how to apply AI to the problem of customer attrition, which can yield impressive results. Addepto is an experienced AI consulting firm, and we are always available to assist you in.

4.5 The Transformative Impact of AI on Education

AI's Impact on Educational Processes

The integration of artificial intelligence (AI) in education presents an opportunity to revolutionize the traditional methods of teaching and learning. However, the chapter's exploration of this theme is limited, lacking a comprehensive discussion on how AI can fundamentally alter educational processes. AI-driven technologies, such as intelligent tutoring systems and adaptive learning platforms, have the potential to create personalized learning experiences by analyzing individual student performance and adapting content accordingly. This means that each student can progress at their own pace, focusing on areas where they need improvement while receiving reinforcement in their strengths. Moreover, AI can enhance formative assessments by providing instant feedback, allowing teachers to identify learning gaps in real-time and adjust their instructional strategies. By embracing AI, educators can foster a more engaging and tailored learning environment that accommodates diverse learning styles and abilities, ultimately leading to improved educational outcomes.

Cognitive, Social, and Psychological Processes

The role of AI in education extends beyond operational efficiencies and management concerns; it also deeply affects cognitive, social, and psychological processes involved in learning. Cognitively, AI tools can support critical thinking and problem-solving skills through interactive simulations and scenario-based learning experiences. These technologies can stimulate students' engagement and encourage deeper understanding of complex concepts by allowing them to experiment and learn through trial and error in a safe environment.

On a social level, AI can facilitate collaborative learning experiences by connecting students with peers and experts globally, fostering a sense of community and shared knowledge. However, it is crucial to investigate the potential downsides, such as the risk of reducing face-to-face interactions and the challenges in developing interpersonal skills when relying heavily on AI tools. Psychologically, AI's influence on student well-being must be examined, as technologies that adapt to students' emotional states can enhance their motivation and reduce anxiety associated with learning. However, it is essential to address concerns about over-reliance on technology and its impact on students' mental health. By exploring these dimensions, the chapter can provide a more holistic view of AI's implications in education, leading to better-informed decisions about technology integration.

Broader Educational Perspectives

To align more closely with the book's overarching themes, the chapter should expand its focus to encompass broader educational perspectives beyond management. This includes an in-depth exploration of how AI can be utilized at various educational levels, from early childhood education to adult learning environments. For instance, AI can assist young learners by providing interactive and engaging content that aligns with developmental milestones. In higher education, AI can support research, enhance curriculum design, and enable more effective advising systems that help students navigate their academic journeys.

Additionally, ethical considerations surrounding AI applications in education must be addressed. As AI technologies become increasingly integrated into educational practices, issues of equity and access come to the forefront. It is vital to ensure that AI solutions are designed to be inclusive, providing equal opportunities for all learners regardless of their background. Moreover, data privacy concerns must be carefully considered, as the use of AI often involves collecting and analyzing sensitive student information. By incorporating these broader educational perspectives, the authors can enrich the chapter's analysis and provide a framework for the responsible implementation of AI in diverse educational contexts.

Empirical Evidence and Practical Applications

The chapter can greatly benefit from including empirical evidence and case studies that demonstrate the effectiveness of AI in real-world educational settings. By showcasing specific instances where AI technologies have led to improved student outcomes, such as increased engagement, retention rates, or academic performance, the chapter can substantiate its claims and inspire confidence in educators considering AI integration.

For example, research studies highlighting the use of AI-driven analytics to predict student success and inform interventions can serve as powerful illustrations of AI's practical applications. Similarly, case studies of institutions that have successfully implemented AI-powered learning management systems can provide valuable insights into best practices, potential challenges, and strategies for overcoming them. By grounding the discussion in empirical evidence, the authors can create a compelling narrative that not only highlights the transformative potential of AI in education but also equips educators with actionable strategies for leveraging these technologies effectively.

4.6 Ethical Implications of Machine Learning (ML) and Artificial Intelligence (AI) in Churn Prediction

As machine learning (ML) and artificial intelligence (AI) technologies increasingly drive business automation, including customer churn prediction, it is essential to thoroughly examine the ethical implications of these advancements. This section delves into several critical ethical concerns: privacy, bias, and the impact of automation on employment.

4.6.1 Privacy Concerns

The application of ML and AI in churn prediction often necessitates the collection and analysis of large volumes of customer data, which includes sensitive personal information. Ensuring the privacy and security of this data is of paramount importance. Several strategies can help address privacy concerns:

Data Anonymization and Masking: To prevent the identification of individuals from data sets, organizations should implement data anonymization techniques. This involves removing or obfuscating personal identifiers, making it difficult to trace data back to specific individuals. Techniques such as pseudonymization, where identifying fields are replaced with pseudonyms, and aggregation, where data is summarized in groups, are effective methods.

Informed Consent: Obtaining explicit consent from customers before collecting or using their data is crucial. Organizations should clearly communicate the purpose of data collection, the types of data collected, and how the data will be used. Customers should be given the option to opt-in or opt-out of data collection processes.

Data Protection Regulations: Adhering to data protection regulations such as the General Data Protection Regulation (GDPR) in the European Union and the California Consumer Privacy Act (CCPA) in the United States is essential. These regulations mandate stringent measures for data protection, including the rights of individuals to access, correct, and delete their data.

Regular Audits and Compliance Checks: Conducting regular audits of data practices and privacy measures helps ensure ongoing compliance with data protection regulations and industry standards. These audits should assess data handling practices, security protocols, and privacy policies.

4.6.2 Bias in Algorithms

Algorithmic bias is a significant ethical concern in AI and ML applications. Bias can manifest in several ways, leading to unfair or discriminatory outcomes. Addressing bias involves several key strategies:

Bias Detection and Mitigation: Implementing techniques to detect and mitigate bias in AI models is critical. This can involve using fairness-aware algorithms that are designed to detect and correct biases during training. Techniques such as reweighting data, balancing classes, and applying fairness constraints can help achieve more equitable outcomes.

Diverse and Representative Data: To reduce the risk of bias, it is essential to use diverse and representative datasets during model training. This means including data from various demographic groups to ensure that the model does not disproportionately favor or disadvantage any particular group. Data collection processes should aim to capture a broad spectrum of customer experiences and characteristics.

Transparency in Model Development: Maintaining transparency about how AI models are developed and how decisions are made helps in identifying and addressing potential biases. Providing detailed documentation of model design, training processes, and validation results can facilitate better understanding and accountability.

Continuous Monitoring and Evaluation: Regularly monitoring AI models for biased outcomes and evaluating their performance across different demographic groups is essential. This ongoing evaluation helps detect any emerging biases and allows for timely adjustments to the model.

4.6.3 Impact of Automation on Employment

The automation of customer churn prediction through AI and ML has implications for employment, potentially leading to job displacement and changes in job roles. Addressing these implications requires a proactive approach:

Reskilling and Upskilling Programs: To mitigate the impact of automation on employment, organizations should invest in reskilling and upskilling programs for their workforce. These programs can help employees acquire new skills and adapt to changes in job roles resulting from AI and automation. Training in areas such as AI management, data analysis, and AI ethics can prepare employees for emerging job opportunities.

Job Redesign and Human-AI Collaboration: Rather than replacing human jobs, AI can be used to augment human capabilities. Redesigning job roles to incorporate AI tools can enhance productivity and allow employees to focus on higher-value tasks. Human-AI collaboration models can create new opportunities for workers to engage with AI technologies in meaningful ways.

Ethical Employment Practices: Organizations should adopt ethical practices to manage the transition to an AI-driven work environment. This includes providing support for affected employees, offering career counseling, and ensuring fair treatment throughout the transition process.

4.6.4 Governance Issues Associated with AI and ML

4.6.4.1 Regulatory Compliance

As AI and ML technologies evolve, so do the regulatory frameworks governing their use. Organizations must develop a robust compliance framework to navigate these regulations effectively:

Understanding Regulatory Requirements: Staying informed about current and emerging regulations related to AI and ML is crucial. This includes understanding industry-specific regulations and general guidelines that govern the use of AI technologies.

Implementing Compliance Measures: Organizations should establish procedures and protocols to ensure compliance with relevant regulations. This may involve appointing compliance officers, conducting regular compliance audits, and developing policies that align with regulatory requirements.

Consulting with Legal Experts: Engaging legal experts who specialize in AI and data privacy can help organizations navigate the complex regulatory landscape. These experts can provide guidance on compliance issues, risk management, and legal implications of AI practices.

4.6.4.2 Accountability and Transparency

Ensuring accountability and transparency in AI systems is essential for building trust and fostering responsible use:

Explainable AI: Implementing explainable AI techniques can make AI model decisions more understandable and accountable. This involves designing models that provide clear explanations for their predictions and decisions, allowing stakeholders to understand how outcomes are derived.

Documentation and Reporting: Maintaining detailed documentation of AI model development processes, including design choices, data sources, and decision rationales, supports transparency. This documentation can be used to demonstrate compliance with ethical standards and facilitate audits.

Stakeholder Engagement: Engaging with stakeholders, including customers, employees, and regulatory bodies, helps ensure that AI practices align with ethical expectations and societal norms. Providing channels for feedback and addressing concerns can enhance trust and accountability.

4.6.4.3 Incorporating Ethical Design Principles into AI Systems is Fundamental for Ensuring Responsible Use

Fairness

Designing AI systems to be fair and unbiased is crucial for ethical AI practices. This involves applying fairness principles throughout the model development lifecycle, including data collection, training, and evaluation. Ensuring that AI systems do not perpetuate or introduce new inequalities is a key aspect of ethical AI design.

Reliability and Safety

Ensuring the reliability and safety of AI systems is essential for preventing harm and ensuring that systems operate as intended. Organizations should implement rigorous testing and validation protocols to verify the performance and safety of AI models before deployment. This includes assessing potential risks and ensuring that models meet established safety standards.

By addressing these ethical and governance issues, organizations can enhance the responsible use of ML and AI technologies in churn prediction and other business applications. Implementing these practices helps ensure that AI systems are used in ways that are fair, transparent, and aligned with societal values.

4.7 Methodological Rigor

This section outlines the methodology used in the study, providing clarity on the research design, data collection, sampling, analysis, and ethical considerations. Ensuring rigorous methods strengthens the validity and reliability of the study's findings. The following components are included in the methodological framework.

1. Research Design

The research adopts a mixed-method approach, combining both qualitative and quantitative methodologies to offer a comprehensive understanding of AI's role in the education sector. The study integrates primary and secondary data sources, making use of both descriptive and inferential statistical methods to interpret the quantitative data, while qualitative data is analyzed through thematic content analysis.

Rationale: The mixed-method approach is chosen to allow for both breadth and depth in understanding AI integration in education. Quantitative data provides measurable trends, while qualitative insights explore the context and underlying factors behind those trends.

2. Data Collection

Data collection was conducted in two phases:

Phase 1: Quantitative Surveys

A structured survey was distributed to 250 educators, administrators, and students from 15 institutions to collect their perceptions of AI integration in teaching and administrative processes. The survey was designed using a 5-point Likert scale, covering key areas such as perceived usefulness, ease of use, impact on learning outcomes, and institutional readiness for AI.

Phase 2: Qualitative Interviews

Semi-structured interviews were conducted with 30 key stakeholders, including AI experts, school principals, and policymakers in the education sector. Each interview lasted between 45 and 60 min and focused on their experiences with AI tools and applications, barriers to adoption, and strategies for successful AI integration.

Data Collection Tools

Survey: Google Forms was used for online distribution.
Interviews: Conducted via Zoom and transcribed using Otter.ai.
Secondary Data: The study also reviewed institutional reports, AI adoption statistics, and previous case studies to validate and complement primary findings.
Sampling Method

A purposive sampling strategy was employed, targeting participants who had first-hand experience with AI in educational settings. To ensure representativeness, the sample was stratified into three groups: educators, students, and administrators. This approach allowed the study to capture diverse perspectives from different roles within educational institutions.

Sample Size

Survey: 250 participants.
Interviews: 30 participants.
Inclusion Criteria: Participants must have experience in using AI tools in educational processes or administration.
Sampling Justification: The purposive approach ensured that data was gathered from those most knowledgeable or affected by AI integration, allowing for more meaningful and informed responses.
Data Analysis

The data analysis was conducted in two parts to ensure methodological rigor and the validity of the findings.

Quantitative Analysis

Descriptive Statistics: Summarized demographic data and response trends from the survey.

Inferential Statistics: Regression analysis was used to examine the relationship between AI use and learning outcomes, while correlation analysis helped assess the strength of the relationship between institutional readiness and the perceived impact of AI.

Software: SPSS (Statistical Package for the Social Sciences) was used for statistical analysis.

Qualitative Analysis

Thematic Analysis: Interview transcripts were coded using NVivo software. Emerging themes such as AI-driven personalized learning, challenges in AI adoption, and policy gaps were identified.
Triangulation: Findings from interviews were cross-verified with the survey data and secondary sources to ensure consistency and to reduce bias.
Reliability and Validity

Ensuring reliability and validity was a central aspect of the methodological approach:

Reliability

The survey was pilot-tested on a smaller sample of 30 participants to ensure clarity and reliability of the questions. Cronbach's alpha was calculated to measure the internal consistency of the survey items, yielding a value of 0.87, indicating high reliability.

For the qualitative analysis, inter-coder reliability was established. Two independent researchers coded the interview data, achieving a 90% agreement rate.

Validity

Content Validity: Survey questions and interview guides were reviewed by three experts in the field of AI and education to ensure they adequately covered the intended topics.
Construct Validity: The survey design incorporated well-established constructs such as the Technology Acceptance Model (TAM) to assess perceived usefulness and ease of use.

4.8 Limitations

While the study presents valuable insights, certain limitations were noted:

Sample Size: Although the sample was diverse, the relatively small number of interviewees (30) limits the ability to generalize findings to a broader population. Expanding the sample size in future research could increase generalizability.
Geographic Scope: The study was conducted with participants from a limited geographic region, which may influence the findings due to local contexts of AI implementation in education. Including participants from different regions or countries in future studies could enhance the global applicability of the findings.

4.9 Recommendations for Future Research

Based on the findings and identified limitations, several areas for future research are recommended:

Longitudinal Studies: A longitudinal approach would allow for the tracking of AI adoption and its long-term impact on educational outcomes, providing deeper insights into how institutions adapt over time.

Cross-Cultural Comparisons: Comparative studies across different educational systems and cultures would enrich understanding of how AI is being utilized globally, and how cultural differences affect adoption and effectiveness.

Exploration of AI in Non-Traditional Learning Settings: Future research should explore the use of AI in informal learning environments, such as online platforms and MOOCs, to examine its broader educational impact.

4.10 Discussion and Implications

Customer attrition Forecast is a program that assists in identifying patterns in current data that correlate with the anticipated attrition rate (Faritha Banu et al., 2022). It makes use of the Azure AI structure to predict the likelihood of customer churn.

The cost of retaining already established customers is five times lower than the cost of acquiring new customers. Because of this, marketing executives frequently find themselves in the position of attempting to estimate the likelihood of customer churn and locating the appropriate actions to take in order to minimize the churn rate.

This solution makes use of Azure Machine Learning to forecast the likelihood of customer churn and assists in locating patterns in previously collected data that correspond with the anticipated rate of churn (as depicted in Fig. 4.4). Users are able to develop predictive models in order to analyze the features of the existing audience and find indicators of those characteristics by making use of data that is both historical and near real-time. Companies can improve their customer retention rates and earnings with the help of the useful insight provided by this information. This solution is tailored specifically for the needs of the retail sector (Faritha Banu et al., 2022).

4.10.1 Artificial Intelligence (AI) and Marketing Research

AI can be used in three different ways in marketing research: (a) data collection; (b) market analysis; and (c) understanding the customer and developing key insights.

Fig. 4.4 The AI value map—four areas of value creation (Sharma & Kumar Panigrahi, 2011)

4.10.1.1 AI and Data Collection

Gathering information concerning the market, the environment, the company, rivals, and the customers can be automatically completed by AI. Because of the widespread use of digital connectivity, market data can be observed and tracked with relative ease. The sensing, tracking, and collection of data are examples of mundane, repetitive tasks that lend themselves well to being easily automated by using AI. Existing research has demonstrated a variety of approaches to utilizing AI for the purpose of data collection. Examples include the ability to collect information about consumers through the use of connected devices (such as smart refrigerators and virtual assistants like Siri), the visualization of product use and consumption expertise through IoT, the capture of unstructured advertising data through various advanced technologies and research, and the tracking of driving behavior through in-car sensors.

- Customers' shopping habits can be profiled and recognized with the help of retail technologies like heat maps, video surveillance, and beacons. Participants in a survey have a greater likelihood of completing similar surveys and recommending them to other people. In point of fact, researchers believe that within the next few years, nearly one in four surveys will be used to a virtual assistant. This prediction is based on the use of AI technology (How & can help deal with customer churn., 2022).

4.10.1.2 AI and Data Analysis

Information can be analyzed with the help of AI. The following is a list of a few instances of how AI has been used by researchers to carry out analysis:

- Automated analysis of text is utilized to gain insights into the behavior of consumers (for example, through analyzing feedback from clients on a website).
- Algorithms for machine learning as well as lexicon-based text categorization are used to analyze various social media data sets.
- Big data analytics for advertising is becoming an increasingly popular method for generating insights about marketing.
- Detecting copycat Smartphone applications utilizing an AI-based copycat-detection method; and assisting in social media material engineering through using algorithms for natural language processing that find the connections between social media marketing material and user interaction (Customer churn prediction & prevention using AI., 2023).

4.10.1.3 AI and Improved Understanding of the Customer

AI can be used to comprehend the needs and wants of existing customers as well as potential customers by providing information such as who these customers are, what they want, and what solutions they are currently using. Researching the market is distinct from studying specific consumers, as the latter frequently requires the collection of emotional data regarding the customers' sentiments, emotions, tastes, and perspectives. Therefore, artificial intelligence is not only capable of quickly producing numbers, but it is also able to analyze emotional data. As an illustration, Affective collaborated with Ford to develop Auto Emotive sentiment analysis software in order to investigate the mental states of automobile drivers. When it comes to prospective customers, marketers can make use of feeling AI to gain an understanding of what those customers want and the reasons why they are satisfied with other options or competitors. Because prospective customers' emotional data is less readily available, some marketers may feel that it is more difficult to anticipate the needs and wants of potential customers. On the other hand, Unilever has disproved this theory. Unilever synthesized insights gained through social media monitoring and CRM, and one of those insights led them to discover a connection among ice cream and the morning meal. AI data centers were instrumental in this process. Unilever found that there were at least 50 songs with the lyrics "ice cream for breakfast" in them, and that people were listening to these songs. In addition,

Dunkin Donuts was selling ice cream during the morning portion of their business. In response to this observation, Unilever came up with the idea for the new Ben & Jerry's brand, which features a selection of cereal-flavored ice creams for breakfast (Customer anti-churn: Use AI to predict customer churn., 2023).

4.11 Conclusion and Implications for Business Education

Keeping a present customer rather than getting a new one is far more cost-effective. Education sector companies are utilizing AI-based churn prediction solutions to predict when customers will churn, allowing them to take proactive measures to retain their clients while avoiding further loss of business. With the help of AI and ML algorithms, it is possible to identify leading indicators. These leading indicators include changes in the use of apps and rewards programs, changes in the frequency with which customers interact with customer service, changes in income, and changes in life situations. If your organization uses artificial intelligence (AI), machine learning (ML), and deep analysis (DA) to predict customer attrition, it will be able to increase its client retention rate, save revenue on client retention expenditures, and even safeguard future earnings from leaving users. By enacting customer churn reduction models in Educational company, you will prevent a large number of customers from leaving and, as a consequence, increase your profits.

Effective retention management is crucial for Education sector companies to improve customer loyalty, reduce churn-related costs, and drive sustainable business growth. Key elements include:

Forecasting Through Modeling

Utilizing artificial intelligence (AI) and machine learning to create precise churn prediction models that pinpoint high-risk clients and the elements influencing their propensity to leave, allowing for customized retention tactics.

Interventions Based on Triggers

Education sector companies can quickly offer customized retention offers or service enhancements by putting in place real-time monitoring of client behavior to identify early warning indicators of possible churn.

Optimization of Lifetime Value

Evaluating each customer segment's long-term profitability and retention prospects in order to focus investments and retention efforts on the most important clients.

Multichannel Interaction

Providing a smooth, customized client experience at every touch point in order to foster closer bonds and increased loyalty.

Constant Enhancement

Updating predictive models, fine-tuning actions based on customer feedback and results, and routinely assessing the efficacy of retention tactics.

By adopting this comprehensive, data-driven approach to retention management, Education sector companies can significantly reduce customer churn and drive sustainable business growth.

References

Ahmad, A. K., Jafar, A., & Aljoumaa, K. (2019). Customer churn prediction in telecom using machine learning in big data platform. *Journal of Big Data, 6*(1), 28–24. https://doi.org/10.1186/s40537-019-0172-2

Alzahrani, R. A., & Aljabri, M. (2023). AI-based techniques for ad click fraud detection and prevention: Review and research directions. *Journal of Sensor and Actuator Networks, 12*(1), 4. https://doi.org/10.3390/jsan12010004

Anderson, J. R. (2013). The adaptive character of thought. Psychology Press. https://www.taylorfrancis.com/books/mono/10.4324/9780203771730/adaptive-character-thought-john-anderson

Anderson Jr, H. G., Frazier, L., Anderson, S. L., Stanton, R., Gillette, C., Broedel-Zaugg, K., & Yingling, K. (2017). Comparison of pharmaceutical calculations learning outcomes achieved within a traditional lecture or flipped classroom andragogy. *American Journal of Pharmaceutical Education, 81*(4), 70. https://www.sciencedirect.com/science/article/pii/S0002945923023306

Artificial intelligence for business: How AI and machine learning can help businesses. (2023). *Harvard Business Review*. https://hbr.org/2023/03/artificial-intelligence-for-business

Artificial intelligence in customer service: Trends and insights. (2024). Forrester Research. https://go.forrester.com/research/ai-customer-service-trends/

Ascarza, E. (2018). Retention futility: Targeting high-risk customers might be ineffective. *Journal of Marketing Research, 55*(1), 80–98. https://journals.sagepub.com/doi/full/10.1509/jmr.16.0163

Ascarza, E., Neslin, S. A., Netzer, O., Anderson, Z., Fader, P. S., Gupta, S., & Schrift, R. (2018). In pursuit of enhanced customer retention management: Review, key issues, and future directions. *Customer Needs and Solutions, 5*(1), 65–81. https://link.springer.com/article/10.1007/s40547-017-0080-0

Baker, R. S., & Yacef, K. (2009). The state of educational data mining in 2009: A review and future visions. *Journal of Educational Data Mining, 1*(1), 3–17. https://jedm.educationaldatamining.org/index.php/JEDM/article/view/8

Baker, R. S., & Siemens, G. (2014). Educational data mining and learning analytics. *Learning, Media and Technology, 39*(4), 1–10. https://doi.org/10.1080/17439884.2014.1002351

Barak, L., Bart, Y., Gensler, S., Hofacker, C. F., Kaplan, A., Kötterheinrich, K., & Kroll, E. B. (2020). Brave new world? On AI and the management of customer relationships. *Journal of Interactive Marketing, 51*, 44–56. https://doi.org/10.1016/j.intmar.2020.04.002

Bhattacharya, C. B. (1998). When customers are members: Customer retention in paid membership contexts. *Journal of the Academy of Marketing Science, 26*, 31–44. https://doi.org/10.1177/0092070398261004

Binns, R. (2018, January). Fairness in machine learning: Lessons from political philosophy. In *Conference on Fairness, Accountability and Transparency* (pp. 149–159). PMLR. https://proceedings.mlr.press/v81/binns18a.html

Braun, T., & Webber, R. (2004). *Targeting customers: How to use geodemographic and lifestyle data in your business* (3rd ed.). Interact Marketing.

Buckinx, W., & Poel, D. V. D. (2005). Customer base analysis: Partial defection of behaviorally loyal clients in a non-contractual FMCG retail setting. *European Journal of Operational Research, 164*(1), 252–268. https://doi.org/10.1016/j.ejor.2003.05.008

Burez, J., & Van den Poel, D. (2007). CRM at a pay-TV company: Using analytical models to reduce customer attrition by targeted marketing for subscription services. *Expert Systems with Applications, 32*(2), 277–288. https://doi.org/10.1016/j.eswa.2005.11.037

Changyu, D., Ji, X., Rainey, C., Zhang, J., & Lu, W. (2020). Integrating machine learning with human knowledge. *iScience, 23*(11), 101656. https://doi.org/10.1016/j.isci.2020.101656

Customer anti-churn: Use AI to predict customer churn. (2023). Addepto. https://addepto.com/blog/customer-anti-churn-use-ai-to-predict-customer-churn/

Customer churn prediction and prevention using AI. (2023). TurinTech. https://www.turintech.ai/customer-churn-prediction-and-prevention-using-ai/

De Mauro, A., Sestino, A., & Bacconi, A. (2022). Machine learning and artificial intelligence use in marketing: A general taxonomy. *Italian Journal of Marketing*, 439–457. https://doi.org/10.1007/s43039-022-00057-w

Deng, C., Ji, X., Rainey, C., Zhang, J., & Lu, W. (2020). Integrating machine learning with human knowledge. *iScience, 23*(11), 101656. https://doi.org/10.1016/j.isci.2020.101656

Faritha Banu, J., Neelakandan, S., Geetha, B. T., Selvalakshmi, V., Umadevi, A., & Martinson, E. O. (2022). Artificial intelligence-based customer churn prediction model for business markets. *Computational Intelligence and Neuroscience, 2022*, 1703696. https://doi.org/10.1155/2022/1703696

Floris, D., Berrevoets, J., & Verbeke, W. (2021). Why you should stop predicting customer churn and start using uplift models. *Information Sciences, 548*, 497–515. https://doi.org/10.1016/j.ins.2019.12.075

Harris, R., Sleight, P., & Webber, R. (2005). *Geodemographics*. John Wiley & Sons.

Holmes, W., & Porayska-Pomsta, K. (2021). AI in education: Current insights and future directions. OECD Education Working Paper.

How AI can help deal with customer churn. (2022). Forbes. https://www.forbes.com/sites/forbestechcouncil/2022/09/13/how-ai-can-help-deal-with-customer-churn/

Huang, Y., Huang, B., & Kechadi, M. T. (2011). A rule-based method for customer churn prediction in telecommunication services. In *Advances in knowledge discovery and data mining* (pp. 411–422). Springer. https://doi.org/10.1007/978-3-642-20561-6_43

Huang, M. H., & Rust, R. T. (2021). A strategic framework for artificial intelligence in marketing. *Journal of the Academy of Marketing Science, 49*, 30–50. https://doi.org/10.1007/s11747-020-00749-9

Keramati, A., & Ardabili, S. M. (2011). Churn analysis for an Iranian mobile operator. *Telecommunications Policy, 35*(4), 344–356. https://doi.org/10.1016/j.telpol.2011.02.009

Libai, B., Bart, Y., Gensler, S., Hofacker, C. F., Kaplan, A., Kötterheinrich, K., & Kroll, E. B. (2020). Brave new world? On AI and the management of customer relationships. *Journal of Interactive Marketing, 51*, 44–56. https://doi.org/10.1016/j.intmar.2020.04.002

Liu, Q., & Zhang, Z. (2023). AI-driven student dropout prediction using machine learning techniques. *Computers & Education.* https://fjs.fudutsinma.edu.ng/index.php/fjs/article/view/2103

Lucini, F. R., Tonetto, L. M., Fogliatto, F. S., & Anzanello, M. J. (2020). Text mining approach to explore dimensions of airline customer satisfaction using online customer reviews. *Journal of Air Transport Management, 83*, Article 101760. https://doi.org/10.1016/j.jairtraman.2020.101760

Luckin, R., Holmes, W., Griffiths, M., & Forcier, L. B. (2016). *Intelligence unleashed: An argument for AI in education.* Pearson Education.

Machine learning explained. (n.d.). MIT Sloan School of Management. https://mitsloan.mit.edu/ideas-made-to-matter/machine-learning-explained

Matuszelański, K., & Kopczewska, K. (2022). Customer churn in retail e-commerce business: Spatial and machine learning approach. *Journal of Theoretical and Applied Electronic Commerce Research, 17*(1), 165–198. https://doi.org/10.3390/jtaer17010009

Mishra, P., & Koehler, M. J. (2006). Technological pedagogical content knowledge: A framework for teacher knowledge. *Teachers College Record, 108*(6), 1017–1054. https://journals.sagepub.com/doi/abs/10.1111/j.1467-9620.2006.00684.x

Mozer, M. C., Richard, W., David, B. G., Eric, J., & Howard, K. (2000). Predicting subscriber dissatisfaction and improving retention in the wireless telecommunications industry. *IEEE Transactions on Neural Networks, 11*(3), 690–696. https://doi.org/10.1109/72.846732

Munoko, I., Brown-Liburd, H. L., & Vasarhelyi, M. (2020). The ethical implications of using artificial intelligence in auditing. *Journal of Business Ethics, 167*(2), 209–234. https://link.springer.com/article/10.1007/s10551-019-04407-1

Nasir, S. (2017). Customer retention strategies and customer loyalty. In *Customer relationship management* (pp. 702–725). IGI Global. https://doi.org/10.4018/978-1-5225-1793-1.ch054

OECD. (2021). Artificial intelligence, machine learning and big data in finance: Opportunities, challenges, and implications for policymakers. OECD. https://www.oecd.org/finance/artificial-intelligence-machine-learning-big-data-in-finance.htm

Qureshi, S. A., Rehman, A. S., Qamar, A. M., & Kamal, A. (2013). Telecommunication subscribers' churn prediction model using machine learning. In *Proceedings of the 8th International Conference on Digital Information Management* (pp. 131–136). https://doi.org/10.1109/ICDIM.2013.16

Reichheld, F. F., & Sasser, W. E. (1990). Zero defections: Quality comes to services. *Harvard Business Review*. https://hbr.org/1990/09/zero-defections-quality-comes-to-services

Roll, I., & Wylie, R. (2016). Evolution and revolution in artificial intelligence in education. *International Journal of Artificial Intelligence in Education, 26*(2), 1–2. https://doi.org/10.1007/s40593-016-0103-0

Selwyn, N. (2016). Is technology good for education? John Wiley & Sons. https://books.google.co.in/books?hl=en&lr=&id=XLtQDAAAQBAJ&oi=fnd&pg=PT4&dq=Selwyn,+N.+(2016).+Is+technology+good+for+education%3F.+John+Wiley+%26+Sons.&ots=Fp3g4IsisG&sig=BpAWwI8TKMsJw7AdpKk6IvYVFPY&redir_esc=y#v=onepage&q=Selwyn%2C%20N.%20(2016).%20Is%20technology%20good%20for%20education%3F.%20John%20Wiley%20%26%20Sons.&f=false

Sharma, A., & Kumar Panigrahi, P. (2011). A neural network-based approach for predicting customer churn in cellular network services. *International Journal of Computer Applications, 27*(11), 26–31. https://doi.org/10.5120/3344-4605

Siemens, G. (2013). Learning analytics: The emergence of a discipline. *American Behavioral Scientist, 57*(10), 1380–1400. https://journals.sagepub.com/doi/full/10.1177/0002764213498851

Smith, W. C., & Holloway, J. (2020). School testing culture and teacher satisfaction. *Educational Assessment, Evaluation and Accountability, 32*(4), 461–479. https://link.springer.com/article/10.1007/s11092-020-09342-8

Sjödin, D., Parida, V., Palmié, M., & Wincent, J. (2021). How AI capabilities enable business model innovation: Scaling AI through co-evolutionary processes and feedback loops. *Journal of Business Research, 134*, 574–587. https://doi.org/10.1016/j.jbusres.2021.05.009

Suh, Y. (2023). Machine learning-based customer churn prediction in the home appliance rental business. *Journal of Big Data, 10*(1), 41. https://doi.org/10.1186/s40537-023-00721-8

Tékouabou, S. C. K., Gherghina, ŞC., Toulni, H., Mata, P. N., & Martins, J. M. (2022). Towards explainable machine learning for bank churn prediction using data balancing and ensemble-based methods. *Mathematics, 10*(14), 2379. https://doi.org/10.3390/math10142379

The impact of AI on customer experience. (2023). McKinsey & Company. https://www.mckinsey.com/business-functions/marketing-and-sales/our-insights/the-impact-of-ai-on-customer-experience

Using AI to improve customer service and retention. (2023). Gartner. https://www.gartner.com/en/insights/customer-service/ai-customer-service

Verbeke, W., Martens, D., Mues, C., & Baesens, B. (2011). Building comprehensible customer churn prediction models with advanced rule induction techniques. *Expert Systems with Applications, 38*(3), 2354–2364. https://doi.org/10.1016/j.eswa.2010.08.113

Williamson, B. (2017). Big data in education: The digital future of learning, policy and practice. https://www.torrossa.com/en/resources/an/5017810

Winer, R. S. (2001). A framework for customer relationship management. *California Management Review, 43*(4), 89–105. https://journals.sagepub.com/doi/abs/10.2307/41166102

Xu, X., Liu, X., Cao, X., Huang, C., Liu, E., Qian, S., Liu, X., & Wu, Y. (2021). Artificial intelligence: A powerful paradigm for scientific research. *The Innovation, 2*(4), Article 100179. https://doi.org/10.1016/j.xinn.2021.100179

Zawacki-Richter, O., Marín, V. I., Bond, M., & Gouverneur, F. (2019). Systematic review of research on artificial intelligence applications in higher education – where are the educators? *International Journal of Educational Technology in Higher Education, 16*(1). https://doi.org/10.1186/s41239-019-0176-8

Chapter 5
Artificial Intelligence and Educational Planning: Enhancing Strategies Through Intelligent Social Experiment

Mohamed Oubibi, Antony Fute, Katsiaryna Hryshayeva, and Ayoub Oubibi

Abstract The emergence of artificial intelligence (AI) has catalyzed transformative changes across various domains, notably in education, where it has introduced innovative approaches to Education Planning (EP). This paper explores the rapidly expanding domain of Artificial Intelligence in Education (AIEd), focusing particularly on Intelligent Social Experiments (ISE) as an innovative method to investigate the societal effects of embedding AI into educational planning processes. Utilizing advancements in computational and information processing technologies, ISE aims to establish an exhaustive framework for assessing the complex influence of AI on global educational systems. This research highlights the critical importance of incorporating AI into education planning, accentuating how intelligent social experiments can improve educational results and tackle social issues. Through detailed case study analysis from various international contexts, this paper illustrates the application of AI-driven ISEs in educational planning, pinpointing both the innovative breakthroughs and the obstacles faced. Additionally, it probes into the cutting-edge technologies in AI poised to reshape future educational planning methodologies. The outcomes emphasize AI's essential role in driving educational innovation and address the ethical and logistical hurdles in deploying AIEd initiatives. This study significantly contributes to scholarly discussions, offering a fundamental insight into AI and ISE's capacity to revolutionize educational planning, and it suggests ways to harness AI for fostering fair and efficient educational opportunities globally.

M. Oubibi (✉)
Smart Learning Institute of Beijing Normal University, Normal University, Beijing, China
e-mail: oubibi@bnu.edu.cn

College of Education, Zhejiang Normal University, Jinhua, China

A. Fute
Foreign Language Department, Yulin University, Yulin, China

K. Hryshayeva
School of Chinese Language and Literature, Beijing Foreign Studies University, Beijing, China

A. Oubibi
Sorbonne Business School, Panthéon-Sorbonne, IAE Paris, The University of Paris, Paris, France

M. A. Adarkwah et al. (eds.), *Artificial Intelligence and Human Agency in Education: Volume One*, Future Education and Learning Spaces,
https://doi.org/10.1007/978-981-96-7937-9_5

Keywords Artificial intelligence (AI) · Educational planning (EP) · Intelligent social experiment (ISE) · Artificial Intelligence in Education (AIEd) · Challenges

5.1 Introduction

Since the introduction of AI in Education (AIEd) about thirty years ago, AI has been recognized as a potent instrument for fostering innovative approaches in instructional design, technological advancement, and educational research. These approaches, facilitated by AI, are often unattainable through conventional educational methods (Holmes et al., 2023; Hwang et al., 2020). AIEd has opened up novel possibilities, prospects, and difficulties for educational innovation. Examples include the shift toward individualized learning, redefining the role of educators, and the evolution of intricate educational systems (Holmes et al., 2018; Starcic, 2019). The integration of Artificial Intelligence (AI) in education planning represents a pivotal shift in the landscape of teaching and learning. With the rapid advancement of computing and information processing techniques, AI has found extensive applications in various educational domains (Luan et al., 2020). These include intelligent tutoring systems, teaching robots, adaptive learning systems, and human–computer interactions, each contributing to a transformative educational experience (Ahuja, 2022; Han et al., 2019). The diverse applications of AI in education (AIEd), from primary to higher education, underscore its potential to revolutionize traditional pedagogical methods (Oubibi et al., 2022a). This global interest in AIEd is not only a testament to its growing importance but also to its potential in reshaping educational paradigms.

In parallel, the concept of AI pedagogy emerges, encompassing strategies for teaching AI itself, as well as the integration of AI in teaching various disciplines (Cope et al., 2021). This pedagogy extends beyond mere technical skills, embracing broader concepts like machine learning, natural language processing, and robotics. Additionally, AI's role in enhancing professional development and leadership in education signifies a deeper systemic influence. AI is not only a tool for learning but also a catalyst for educational leadership, driving decision-making processes and strategic planning (Giuggioli & Pellegrini, 2023; Komasawa & Yokohira, 2023; Vaio et al., 2020). This multifaceted impact of AI in education points to a future where AIEd is not just a technological add-on but a fundamental component of educational ecosystems, driving innovation and efficiency in learning and administrative processes. Artificial Intelligence (AI) is poised to significantly enhance the agency of education planners by augmenting their decision-making capabilities and operational efficiency. The integration of AI technologies allows for the automation of routine administrative tasks, which traditionally consume substantial time and resources. By delegating these tasks to intelligent systems, education planners can focus on strategic initiatives such as curriculum innovation, personalized learning, and resource allocation. Moreover, AI's ability to analyze large datasets with speed and accuracy means that planners are equipped with real-time insights into student performance, educational trends, and institutional needs. This data-driven approach not only sharpens their predictive capabilities but also supports a more dynamic and responsive educational planning process, thus fostering an environment where proactive, rather than reactive, strategies prevail.

Furthermore, AI tools empower education planners with advanced simulation and modeling capabilities, enabling them to foresee potential outcomes of various educational interventions and policies before they are implemented. This predictive modeling serves as a critical asset in crafting educational strategies that are both effective and adaptable to changing conditions. For instance, AI-driven simulations can help planners optimize class sizes, modify curriculum pacing, or allocate resources more efficiently, ensuring that the educational environment is continuously aligned with both learner needs and institutional goals. Such enhanced foresight and flexibility are integral to an agentic approach, where planners are not merely reacting to changes but are actively shaping the educational landscape. In this way, AI not only enhances the agency of education planners but also contributes to the creation of more agile and resilient educational systems.

5.2 AI Integration in Education Planning

The importance of integrating Artificial Intelligence (AI) in education planning cannot be overstated, as it marks a significant leap toward a future where technology and education are inextricably linked. AI's role in education extends beyond the mere automation of tasks; it represents a paradigm shift in how educational content is delivered, understood, and personalized (Miao et al., 2021). This personalized approach not only enhances student engagement and learning outcomes but also equips educators with powerful tools to monitor progress and identify areas for intervention (Grant & Basye, 2014). Furthermore, AI driven analytics and adaptive learning systems pave the way for a more inclusive and equitable education system, where learners from varied backgrounds can access customized learning paths suited to their unique needs and aspirations (Bhutoria, 2022). The integration of AI in education planning also signifies a crucial step toward preparing students for a future dominated by AI and technology. By incorporating AI into the curriculum, educational institutions are ensuring that students are not only consumers of technology but also adept at understanding and manipulating these advanced tools, thus preparing them for the challenges and opportunities of a rapidly evolving digital world (Kuleto et al., 2021; Oubibi et al., 2022b; Pedro et al., 2019; Vincent-Lancrin & Van der Vlies, 2020).

Moreover, the strategic integration of AI in education planning plays a pivotal role in reshaping the educational landscape. AI's potential in streamlining administrative tasks and enhancing decision-making processes empowers educational leaders to focus more on strategic planning and less on routine management (Dwivedi et al., 2021). This shift enables a more efficient allocation of resources, improved policy-making, and the creation of more dynamic and responsive educational environments. Additionally, the application of AI in educational research offers new insights into

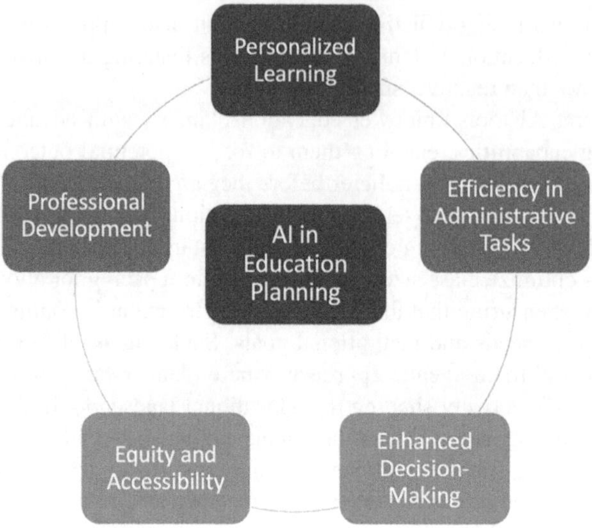

Fig. 5.1 AI in education planning

learning processes, contributing to the development of more effective teaching strategies and curricula. The ethical implications of AI, particularly in ensuring data privacy and addressing bias, also underline the need for a thoughtful and responsible approach to integrating AI in education planning (Akgun & Greenhow, 2021). In essence, the incorporation of AI in education is not merely a technological advancement but a comprehensive strategy to revolutionize the education sector, making it more adaptive, efficient, and aligned with the needs of the twenty-first-century learner. Figure 5.1 shows the AI in education planning and its basic component.

Integrating artificial intelligence (AI) in education planning is essential for several reasons. First, AI enables personalized learning by tailoring educational experiences to meet individual student needs. This approach enhances learning outcomes by providing customized support, allowing for differentiated instruction (Riaz, 2024). For instance, students who require additional help can receive focused assistance, while those who excel can progress at a faster pace. This adaptability ensures that each student maximizes their learning potential. Another critical aspect of AI integration is its ability to streamline administrative tasks. By automating routine activities, AI frees up teachers' time, enabling them to concentrate more on direct student interactions and personalized teaching (Oubibi, 2024; Sharma et al., 2024). This reduction in administrative workload helps alleviate teacher burnout, allowing educators to focus on what matters most teaching and mentoring their students. AI also enhances decision-making processes within educational institutions. By providing data-driven insights, AI can inform educational policies and strategies (Nieto et al., 2019; Williamson et al., 2023). This capability ensures that educational strategies are based on solid evidence, enhancing their effectiveness.

AI supports continuous professional development for teachers. It offers personalized learning paths and resources that help educators stay updated with the latest educational tools and methodologies. This ongoing professional development improves teaching practices and ensures that educators are well-equipped to use AI tools effectively in their classrooms. By enhancing teachers' skills and knowledge, AI contributes to better educational outcomes for students (Chounta et al., 2022; Fakhar et al., 2024).

5.3 Relevance of Intelligent Social Experiments (ISE) in Education

Intelligent social experiments represent a burgeoning field that leverages Artificial Intelligence (AI) and data analytics to understand and improve social dynamics, particularly in the context of education (Sheikh, 2020). These experiments use AI-driven methods to analyze complex social interactions and behaviors within educational settings, providing insights that were previously unattainable due to the sheer complexity and subtlety of human social behaviors (Armstrong et al., 2014; Sheikh, 2020). By simulating social scenarios and analyzing the outcomes, intelligent social experiments offer a unique lens through which educators and policymakers can understand the impact of various educational strategies, interventions, and policies (Bloom, 2005; Schiff, 2021). This approach is particularly relevant in the realm of education, where social dynamics play a critical role in the learning process. From classroom interactions to the broader socio-cultural influences on learning, intelligent social experiments can unravel the intricacies of these dynamics, leading to more effective and inclusive educational practices (Rawal, 2023).

The relevance of intelligent social experiments in education is multifaceted. Firstly, they provide empirical data that can inform the development of more effective teaching methods and learning environments. By simulating different educational scenarios, researchers can predict and evaluate the impact of various teaching styles, curriculum designs, and educational technologies on student learning and engagement (Huang et al., 2010; Pasin & Giroux, 2011). Secondly, these experiments play a crucial role in understanding and mitigating social challenges in educational settings, such as bullying, social exclusion, and inequity. By modeling social interactions and their outcomes, intelligent social experiments can identify the root causes of these issues and test the effectiveness of interventions designed to address them. Finally, in the broader context of education policy and reform, intelligent social experiments offer valuable insights into the societal impact of educational decisions. They allow policymakers to assess the potential consequences of new policies or reforms before implementation, thus facilitating more informed and responsible decision-making. In summary, intelligent social experiments are not just a technological innovation; they are a crucial tool for enhancing the quality, inclusivity, and effectiveness of education in the twenty-first century.

Figure 5.2 presents a comprehensive framework of Intelligent Social Experiments (ISE) in education, illustrating the integration and flow of key components in the process. The figure begins with foundational elements including Data Sources, AI Algorithms, and Experimental Design, which provide the basis for conducting ISE. Moving through the process, the Data Collection phase gathers relevant educational data, followed by Data Analysis, where advanced AI techniques interpret this data. The results are then applied through Implementation Steps to introduce AI-driven changes into educational practices. A Feedback Loop ensures continuous improvement by evaluating outcomes and refining the approach. The Impact Areas section highlights the significant effects of ISE on Student Performance, Educational Equity, Teaching Methods, and Policy Making. Additionally, the Case Studies portion of the figure showcases international examples of ISE application, summarizing key findings and outcomes from various countries. This structured depiction underscores the relevance and transformative potential of ISE in enhancing educational planning and outcomes.

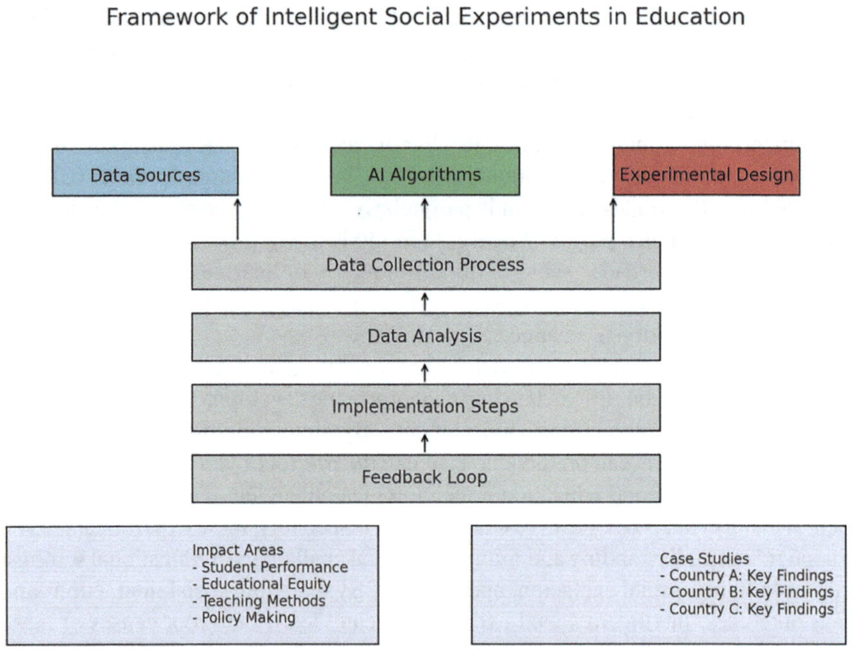

Fig. 5.2 Framework of intelligent social experiment in educational planning

5.4 Synergizing AI and Intelligent Social Experiments in Educational Planning

Artificial Intelligence (AI) significantly enhances the design, implementation, and analysis of social experiments by introducing advanced methodologies and efficiencies at each stage. During the design phase, AI tools such as Natural Language Processing (NLP) can analyze extensive research literature to generate and refine hypotheses, ensuring that studies address current gaps and unexplored areas in the field (Jarrahi, 2018). Machine learning algorithms can assist in the selection of representative participant groups by analyzing demographic data to ensure diversity and relevance, which increases the generalizability and reliability of the results (Wang, 2019). Additionally, AI can support ethical considerations by evaluating potential risks and benefits, helping researchers to design experiments that minimize harm and respect participant rights (Pedro et al., 2019).

In the implementation phase, AI-driven tools can automate data collection processes through smart sensors and wearable devices, providing real-time data and reducing human error (Kaur et al., 2020). Adaptive experimental designs powered by AI allow for real-time adjustments based on participant responses, ensuring that the experiment remains relevant and efficient throughout its duration (Kosch et al., 2023). During the analysis phase, AI can process large datasets with big data analytics, uncovering patterns and correlations that traditional methods might miss (Hariri et al., 2019). Machine learning algorithms further enhance this by performing complex analyses such as clustering and regression, which can predict outcomes and generate new insights from the data (Ezugwu et al., 2022). AI also plays a crucial role in bias detection and correction, ensuring that findings are accurate and representative. Advanced visualization tools powered by AI help in creating detailed, interactive presentations of data, making it easier for researchers to interpret and communicate their findings effectively (Qin et al., 2020).

5.5 Challenges and Strategies of AI and ISE in Educational Planning

Using AI and intelligent social experiments in educational planning comes with several challenges. One significant challenge is ensuring data privacy and security. Protecting this data while maintaining its utility for educational insights requires robust cybersecurity measures and stringent data governance policies (Sharma & Barua, 2023). Additionally, there is the issue of bias in AI algorithms. If the data used to train AI systems is biased, the outputs will also be biased, potentially leading to unfair treatment of certain student groups. Addressing this requires careful design and continuous monitoring of AI systems to ensure they promote equity and do not exacerbate existing disparities (Agarwal et al., 2023). To overcome these challenges, several strategies can be employed. Developing comprehensive AI literacy programs for educators, policymakers, and students is crucial. This helps all stakeholders understand how AI works, its benefits, and its limitations, enabling them to use AI tools responsibly and effectively (Hu et al., 2019). Furthermore, involving diverse teams in the development and implementation of AI in education can help identify and mitigate biases early in the process. Collaborating with ethicists, educators, and technologists ensures that ethical considerations are integral to AI deployment (Borg, 2022). Lastly, creating transparent AI systems where the decision-making processes are understandable and explainable can build trust among users and facilitate the adoption of AI in educational planning (Chamola, 2023). In the future, the successful integration of AI with Intelligent Social Experiments in education planning could lead to more responsive, efficient, and inclusive educational systems, significantly transforming the landscape of education.

5.6 AI-Powered Intelligent Social Experiments in Practice

Implementing AI-powered intelligent social experiments in educational planning presents a promising yet complex endeavor. These experiments leverage AI to simulate, monitor, and analyze educational interventions, thereby providing data-driven insights that can significantly enhance policy and decision-making. For instance, AI can be used to design adaptive learning environments that respond dynamically to student performance, offering personalized learning paths that can improve educational outcomes. Such systems not only identify which teaching methods are most effective but also provide real-time feedback to educators, enabling continuous improvement in instructional strategies (Woolf, 2010). Additionally, AI-powered tools can automate the collection and analysis of vast amounts of data, ranging from student engagement metrics to academic performance, helping educators and policymakers identify trends and make informed decisions (Luckin, 2018; Oubibi et al., 2024).

However, the implementation of these AI-powered social experiments also comes with several challenges. One primary concern is ensuring artificial intelligence systems are designed and used ethically, particularly with respect to the data privacy and bias. As AI systems often require large datasets to function effectively, protecting the privacy of student data is paramount. This necessitates the development of robust data governance frameworks and the adoption of best practices in cybersecurity (Pedro et al., 2019). Moreover, AI systems must be designed to be transparent and explainable, ensuring that the decisions they make can be understood and trusted by educators, students, and parents alike (Khosravi et al., 2022). Addressing these challenges requires a multi-stakeholder approach, involving educators, technologists, policymakers, and ethicists to ensure that the deployment of AI in education is both effective and equitable (Bates et al., 2020).

5.7 Emerging AI Technologies Shaping the Future Educational Planning

Emerging technologies in AI are poised to significantly impact future educational planning by enhancing both the delivery and administration of education. One such technology is Natural Language Processing (NLP), which has advanced to the point where AI can understand and generate human language with high accuracy. Tools like GPT-3 and GPT-4 can assist in creating personalized educational content, automating grading systems, and providing real-time feedback to students. These AI systems can also facilitate better communication between educators and students, particularly in multilingual environments, thereby breaking down language barriers and promoting inclusivity (Kuddus, 2022; Pokrivcakova, 2019). Furthermore, AI-driven chatbots and virtual teaching assistants can support students outside traditional classroom hours, providing on-demand assistance and fostering a more continuous learning experience (Galici, 2024; Oubibi & Hryshayeva, 2024).

Another transformative technology is adaptive learning platforms, which use AI to tailor educational experiences to the individual needs of students. These platforms analyze data on student performance and learning styles to adjust the difficulty and type of content delivered, ensuring that each student receives the appropriate level of challenge and support (Rane et al., 2023). Additionally, AI can enhance predictive analytics in educational planning, helping educators and administrators forecast enrollment trends, identify at-risk students, and allocate resources more effectively (Ahmad et al., 2020). By leveraging these insights, educational institutions can develop more targeted interventions and improve overall educational outcomes. These emerging AI technologies not only promise to make education more efficient and personalized but also help create a more equitable learning environment for all students (Zaman, 2023).

5.8 Case Studies on AI and ISE for Education Planning

5.8.1 *Smart Learning Partner (SLP) in China*

One notable example of AI in education is the implementation of the Smart Learning Partner (SLP) in China. The SLP system leverages AI to provide personalized learning experiences for students. It uses machine learning algorithms to analyze students' learning behaviors and performance data, adapting the content and difficulty of lessons to meet individual needs. The system also offers real-time feedback and guidance, helping students understand their mistakes and improve their skills. According to many researchers, the SLP has significantly improved student engagement and performance, particularly in mathematics and language learning. This AI-powered platform supports differentiated instruction, enabling teachers to cater to diverse student needs more effectively (Niu et al., 2022; Powell, 2018).

5.8.2 ASSISTments in the United States

Another significant case study is the ASSISTments platform in the United States. Developed by researchers at Worcester Polytechnic Institute, ASSISTments is an AI-driven educational tool that provides real-time assistance and feedback to students while they complete assignments (Kaw-uh, 2017). The system uses data analytics to identify common errors and misconceptions, offering hints and explanations to guide students through problem-solving processes. A study by other researchers demonstrated that ASSISTments not only helps improve student learning outcomes but also provides valuable data to teachers about student progress and areas needing attention. This allows for more targeted and effective instruction, particularly in subjects like mathematics (Haim et al., 2022; Joyner, 2022; Katz et al., 2017).

5.8.3 AI-Powered Personalized Tutoring in India

In India, AI-powered personalized tutoring programs like BYJU'S have transformed the educational landscape. BYJU'S uses AI algorithms to create personalized learning journeys for students, adapting content to their learning pace and style. The platform includes interactive video lessons and assessments that provide instant feedback (Bhutoria, 2022). Students using BYJU'S have shown marked improvements in their academic performance, particularly in STEM subjects (Sinha & Pandey, 2019). The platform's ability to tailor educational experiences to individual needs has made it a popular choice among students and parents, highlighting the potential of AI to democratize access to quality education (Tripathy & Devarapalli, 2021).

These case studies illustrate the transformative potential of AI and Intelligent Social Experiments (ISE) for educational planning. They demonstrate how AI can personalize learning, provide real-time feedback, and enhance instructional effectiveness, ultimately improving student outcomes and making education more accessible and equitable.

5.9 Recommendations and Implication

5.9.1 Recommendation

To ensure the successful integration of Artificial Intelligence (AI) and Intelligent Social Experiments (ISE) in educational planning, a multifaceted approach is necessary. Firstly, policymakers should establish clear guidelines that promote the responsible use of AI technologies in education. These guidelines should include ethical considerations, data privacy protections, and equitable access to technology for all students. Additionally, collaboration among educational stakeholders, such as schools and higher education institutions, can facilitate the development of resources and tools tailored to specific educational contexts.

Secondly, comprehensive training programs are essential for educators and administrators to navigate the complexities of AI and ISE effectively. Research indicates that professional development initiatives focused on technology integration can significantly enhance educators' confidence and competence. Training should cover not only technical skills but also pedagogical strategies for implementing AI solutions that cater to diverse learning needs.

Lastly, case studies from various international contexts, such as the Smart Learning Partner (SLP) in China and ASSISTments in the United States, demonstrate the importance of localized solutions in deploying AI in education. Policymakers should encourage pilot projects that allow for experimentation and adaptation of AI tools to specific educational environments, drawing from successful models.

5.9.2 Implication

The integration of AI and ISE into educational planning carries significant implications for improving learning outcomes and addressing equity in education. AI technologies enable personalized learning experiences that adapt to individual student needs, preferences, and learning styles. As AI systems evolve, their capacity to analyze student data will enhance, providing insights that educators can use to tailor instruction more effectively. Moreover, the use of ISE can illuminate how AI impacts educational processes and outcomes, fostering a deeper understanding of the social dynamics at play. However, the integration of AI also raises ethical considerations that must be addressed to ensure equitable outcomes. The potential for algorithmic bias and data privacy concerns necessitates the establishment of ethical guidelines and practices.

5.10 Limitation

Despite the promising potential of AI and ISE in educational planning, several limitations warrant consideration. One major limitation is the generalizability of findings from case studies. Educational contexts vary significantly across regions and cultures, which may affect the applicability of successful models. For instance, while AI-powered personalized tutoring has shown positive results in India, these outcomes may not be replicated in countries with different educational systems and resource levels. Therefore, further research is needed to explore the adaptability of these approaches across diverse settings.

Additionally, the successful implementation of AI and ISE is often met with practical challenges. Resistance from educators who may be skeptical of new technologies poses a significant barrier to adoption. Furthermore, the lack of infrastructure in certain regions, especially in developing countries, can hinder the deployment of AI technologies, creating disparities in access to innovative educational solutions. Lastly, data privacy concerns pose a critical limitation to the adoption of AI in education. The collection and analysis of student data raise ethical questions about consent and the potential misuse of sensitive information. Addressing these limitations is essential to ensure that the benefits of AI in education are realized without compromising the rights and safety of students.

5.11 Conclusion

The integration of AI into educational planning through Intelligent Social Experiments (ISE) presents a paradigm shift in how we approach educational reform and innovation. The research underscores the profound impact of AI-driven methodologies in enhancing educational outcomes and addressing complex societal issues within the educational sphere. By leveraging advancements in computational technologies, ISE provides a comprehensive framework for evaluating the multifaceted effects of AI on global educational systems. The detailed case studies included in this paper demonstrate the practical applications and transformative potential of AI in educational planning, highlighting both the breakthroughs achieved and the challenges encountered. These insights are critical for policymakers, educators, and researchers aiming to harness AI's capabilities to foster equitable and effective educational opportunities worldwide.

Moreover, the study emphasizes the indispensable role of AI in driving educational innovation, while also addressing the ethical and logistical hurdles that accompany the deployment of AIEd initiatives. By examining cutting-edge AI technologies poised to reshape future educational planning methodologies, this study contributes significantly to the scholarly discourse on AI in education. It provides a foundational understanding of how intelligent social experiments can be utilized to create more adaptive, personalized, and inclusive educational systems. The findings advocate for a strategic approach to integrating AI into educational planning, ensuring that the benefits of technological advancements are maximized while mitigating potential risks. This study serves as a vital resource for advancing the implementation of AI-powered educational reforms globally.

References

Agarwal, R., et al. (2023). Addressing algorithmic bias and the perpetuation of health inequities: An AI bias aware framework. *Health Policy and Technology, 12*(1), Article 100702.

Ahmad, K., et al. (2020). *Artificial intelligence in education: A panoramic review*. https://doi.org/10.35542/osf.io/zvu2n

Ahuja, N. J., et al. (2022). Intelligent tutoring system in education for disabled learners using human—Computer interaction and augmented reality. *International Journal of Human–Computer Interaction,* 1–13.

Akgun, S., & Greenhow, C. (2021). Artificial intelligence in education: Addressing ethical challenges in K-12 settings. *AI and Ethics,* 1–10.

Armstrong, S., Sotala, K., & Ó hÉigeartaigh, S. S. (2014). The errors, insights and lessons of famous AI predictions—And what they mean for the future. *Journal of Experimental & Theoretical Artificial Intelligence, 26*(3), 317–342.

Bates, T., et al. (2020). *Can artificial intelligence transform higher education?* (pp. 1–12). Springer.

Bhutoria, A. (2022). Personalized education and artificial intelligence in the United States, China, and India: A systematic review using a human-in-the-loop model. *Computers and Education: Artificial Intelligence, 3,* Article 100068. https://doi.org/10.1016/j.caeai.2022.100068

Bloom, H. S. (2005). *Learning more from social experiments: Evolving analytic approaches.* Russell Sage Foundation.

Borg, J. (2022). The AI field needs translational ethical AI research. *AI Magazine, 43*(3), 294–307.

Chamola, V., et al. (2023). A review of trustworthy and explainable artificial intelligence (xai). *IEEE Access.*

Chounta, I.-A., et al. (2022). Exploring teachers' perceptions of artificial intelligence as a tool to support their practice in Estonian K-12 education. *International Journal of Artificial Intelligence in Education, 32*(3), 725–755.

Cope, B., Kalantzis, M., & Searsmith, D. (2021). Artificial intelligence for education: Knowledge and its assessment in AI-enabled learning ecologies. *Educational Philosophy and Theory, 53*(12), 1229–1245. https://doi.org/10.1080/00131857.2020.1728732

Di Vaio, A., et al. (2020). Artificial intelligence and business models in the sustainable development goals perspective: A systematic literature review. *Journal of Business Research, 121,* 283–314. https://doi.org/10.1016/j.jbusres.2020.08.019

Dwivedi, Y. K., et al. (2021). Artificial intelligence (AI): Multidisciplinary perspectives on emerging challenges, opportunities, and agenda for research, practice and policy. *International Journal of Information Management, 57,* Article 101994.

Ezugwu, A. E., et al. (2022). A comprehensive survey of clustering algorithms: State-of-the-art machine learning applications, taxonomy, challenges, and future research prospects. *Engineering Applications of Artificial Intelligence, 110,* Article 104743.

Fakhar, H., et al. (2024). Towards a new artificial intelligence-based framework for teachers' online continuous professional development programs: Systematic review. *International Journal of Advanced Computer Science & Applications, 15*(4).

Galici, R. (2024). *Characterizing algorithmic performance in machine learning for education.*

Giuggioli, G., & Pellegrini, M. M. (2023). Artificial intelligence as an enabler for entrepreneurs: A systematic literature review and an agenda for future research. *International Journal of Entrepreneurial Behavior & Research, 29*(4), 816–837. https://doi.org/10.1108/IJEBR-05-2021-0426

Grant, P., & Basye, D. (2014). *Personalized learning: A guide for engaging students with technology.* International Society for Technology in Education.

Haim, A., Prihar, E., & Heffernan, N. T. (2022). Toward improving effectiveness of Crowdsourced, on-demand assistance from educators in online learning platforms. In *International conference on artificial intelligence in education.* Springer.

Han, J., et al. (2019). Intelligent tutoring system trends 2006–2018: A literature review. In *Eighth international conference on educational innovation through technology (EITT).* IEEE.

Hariri, R. H., Fredericks, E. M., & Bowers, K. M. (2019). Uncertainty in big data analytics: Survey, opportunities, and challenges. *Journal of Big Data, 6*(1), 1–16.

Holmes, W., Bialik, M., & Fadel, C. (2023). *Artificial intelligence in education.* Globethics Publications. https://doi.org/10.58863/20.500.12424/4276068

Holmes, W., et al. (2018). Technology-enhanced personalised learning: Untangling the evidence. https://oro.open.ac.uk/56692/

Hu, X., et al. (2019). *Steering AI and advanced ICTs for knowledge societies: A rights, openness, access, and multi-stakeholder perspective*. UNESCO Publishing.

Huang, H.-M., Rauch, U., & Liaw, S.-S. (2010). Investigating learners' attitudes toward virtual reality learning environments: Based on a constructivist approach. *Computers & Education, 55*(3), 1171–1182.

Hwang, G.-J., et al. (2020). *Vision, challenges, roles and research issues of artificial intelligence in education* (p. 100001). Elsevier. https://doi.org/10.1016/j.caeai.2020.100001

Jarrahi, M. H. (2018). Artificial intelligence and the future of work: Human-AI symbiosis in organizational decision making. *Business Horizons, 61*(4), 577–586.

Joyner, D. (2022). *Teaching at scale: Improving access, outcomes, and impact through digital instruction*. Routledge.

Katz, I. R., et al. (2017). Validity CHAPTER 18—Issues and concerns for technology-based performance assessments. *Design Recommendations for Intelligent Tutoring System, 5*, 209–224.

Kaur, G., Tomar, P., & Tanque, M. (2020). *Artificial intelligence to solve pervasive internet of things issues*. Academic Press.

Kaw-uh, B. (2017). Feasibility of digitizing LEI evaluations with an internationalized ASSISTments. Worcester State University.

Khosravi, H., et al. (2022). Explainable artificial intelligence in education. *Computers and Education: Artificial Intelligence, 3*, Article 100074.

Komasawa, N., & Yokohira, M. (2023). Learner-centered experience-based medical education in an AI-driven society: A literature review. *Cureus, 15*(10).

Kosch, T., et al. (2023). The placebo effect of artificial intelligence in human-computer interaction. *ACM Transactions on Computer-Human Interaction, 29*(6), 1–32.

Kuddus, K. (2022). Artificial intelligence in language learning: Practices and prospects. In *Advanced analytics and deep learning models* (pp. 1–17).

Kuleto, V., et al. (2021). Exploring opportunities and challenges of artificial intelligence and machine learning in higher education institutions. *Sustainability, 13*(18), 10424.

Luan, H., et al. (2020). Challenges and future directions of big data and artificial intelligence in education. *Frontiers in Psychology, 11*, Article 580820. https://doi.org/10.3389/fpsyg.2020.580820

Luckin, R. (2018). *Machine learning and human intelligence: The future of education for the 21st century*. ERIC.

Miao, F., et al. (2021). AI and education: *A guidance for policymakers*. UNESCO Publishing.

Nieto, Y., et al. (2019). Usage of machine learning for strategic decision making at higher educational institutions. *IEEE Access, 7*, 75007–75017.

Niu, S. J., et al. (2022). Teachers' and students' views of using an AI-aided educational platform for supporting teaching and learning at Chinese schools. *Education Sciences, 12*(12), 858.

Oubibi, M. (2024). An experimental study to promote preservice teachers' competencies in the classroom based on teaching-learning model and Moso Teach. *Education and Information Technologies, 29*(6), 6631–6650.

Oubibi, M., & Hryshayeva, K. (2024). Effects of virtual reality technology on primary school students' creativity performance, learning engagement and mental flow. In *Education and Information Technologies* (pp. 1–20).

Oubibi, M., Liu, T., & Metwally, A. H. S. (2024). Designing and developing online learning activities for adult learners through integration with an Open University Platform. In *IEEE International Conference on Advanced Learning Technologies (ICALT)*. IEEE.

Oubibi, M., et al. (2022a). Advances in research on technological, pedagogical, didactical, and social competencies of preservice TCFL teachers. *Sustainability, 14*(4), 2045. https://doi.org/10.3390/su14042045

Oubibi, M., et al. (2022b). The challenges and opportunities for developing the use of data and artificial intelligence (AI) in North Africa: Case of Morocco. In *International conference on digital technologies and applications*. Springer.

Pasin, F., & Giroux, H. (2011). The impact of a simulation game on operations management education. *Computers & Education, 57*(1), 1240–1254.
Pedro, F., et al. (2019). *Artificial intelligence in education: Challenges and opportunities for sustainable development.*
Pokrivcakova, S. (2019). Preparing teachers for the application of AI-powered technologies in foreign language education. *Journal of Language and Cultural Education, 7*(3), 135–153.
Powell, R. K. (2018). Unique contributors to the curriculum: From research to practice for speech-language pathologists in schools. *Language, Speech, and Hearing Services in Schools, 49*(2), 140–147.
Qin, X., et al. (2020). Making data visualization more efficient and effective: A survey. *The VLDB Journal, 29*(1), 93–117.
Rane, N., Choudhary, S., & Rane, J. (2023). *Education 4.0 and 5.0: Integrating artificial intelligence (AI) for personalized and adaptive learning*. SSRN 4638365.
Rawal, S. B. (2023). Exploring students' perceptions on teachers' feedback in the classroom (A study of Achham multiple campus, Nepal). *The Journal of Social Sciences Studies and Research, 3*(05), 191–201.
Riaz, M. (2024). *A personalized Learning system: Education by AI.*
Schiff, D. (2021). Out of the laboratory and into the classroom: The future of artificial intelligence in education. *AI & Society, 36*(1), 331–348.
Sharma, P., & Barua, S. (2023). From data breach to data shield: The crucial role of big data analytics in modern cybersecurity strategies. *International Journal of Information and Cybersecurity, 7*(9), 31–59.
Sharma, S. K., et al. (2024). Artificial intelligence and machine learning in smart education. In *Infrastructure possibilities and human-centered approaches with industry 5.0* (pp. 86–106) IGI Global.
Sheikh, S. (2020). *Understanding the role of artificial intelligence and its future social impact*. IGI Global.
Sinha, A. P., & Pandey, R. K. (2019). A study on accessing the factors leading to the purchase of BYJU'S as a curriculum. *TRANS Asian Journal of Marketing & Management Research (TAJMMR), 8*(9 and 10), 44–59.
Starcic, A. I. (2019). Human learning and learning analytics in the age of artificial intelligence. *British Journal of Educational Technology, 50*(6), 2974–2976. https://doi.org/10.1111/bjet.12879
Tripathy, S., & Devarapalli, S. (2021). Emerging trend set by a start-ups on Indian online education system: A case of Byju's. *Journal of Public Affairs, 21*(1), Article e2128.
Vincent-Lancrin, S., & Van der Vlies, R. (2020). *Trustworthy artificial intelligence (AI) in education: Promises and challenges.*
Wang, P. (2019). On defining artificial intelligence. *Journal of Artificial General Intelligence, 10*(2), 1–37.
Williamson, B., et al. (2023). Critical perspectives on AI in education: Political economy, discrimination, commercialization, governance and ethics. In *Handbook of artificial intelligence in education* (pp. 553–570). Edward Elgar Publishing.
Woolf, B. P. (2010). *Building intelligent interactive tutors: Student-centered strategies for revolutionizing e-learning*. Morgan Kaufmann.
Zaman, B. U. (2023). *Transforming education through AI, benefits, risks, and ethical considerations.* Authorea Preprints.

Part II
Social Context

Chapter 6
The Potential of Artificial Intelligence to Personalize Learning Within the Evolving Landscape of Open Distance Learning

Geesje van den Berg

Abstract The purpose of this research was to provide a comprehensive understanding of how AI can be integrated into ODL to improve student engagement and educational outcomes. Based on a semi-structured narrative literature review, the findings indicate that AI technologies offer significant promise in transforming ODL by providing personalized tutoring, adaptive learning pathways, and customized support aligned with the needs of individual students. AI can analyze student performance data to identify learning gaps, recommend tailored resources, and continuously monitor progress, thus enhancing student engagement and success. However, it also shares limitations and challenges, such as ethical considerations, implementation challenges, and pedagogical implications. The research recommends integrating AI technologies into ODL frameworks, establishing ethical guidelines, and focusing on inclusive and equitable AI applications. Additionally, it suggests designing pedagogies and curricula that support the inclusion of AI for personalized learning. This research is theoretical and descriptive in nature, and further empirical research is needed to explore the long-term impact of AI-driven personalized learning to develop best practices for implementation. The chapter concludes that the integration of AI in ODL holds the potential to move beyond the traditional mass education models, offering individualized and responsive learning experiences that ensure the relevance and effectiveness of ODL institutions in future.

Keywords Artificial intelligence · Educational technology · Personalized learning · Open distance learning

---

G. van den Berg (✉)
University of South Africa, Pretoria, South Africa
e-mail: vdberg@unisa.ac.za

M. A. Adarkwah et al. (eds.), *Artificial Intelligence and Human Agency in Education: Volume One*, Future Education and Learning Spaces,
https://doi.org/10.1007/978-981-96-7937-9_6

6.1 Introduction

Distance education has not just changed but fundamentally transformed the landscape of higher education, ushering in an era of inclusivity and fairness in learning opportunities. Departing from the historically exclusive nature of higher education, distance education has opened its doors to a much wider population, making it accessible to anyone, anywhere in the world, irrespective of geographic location, socio-economic status, or other limiting factors. These advancements have broadened the horizons and led to a more diverse and flexible learning experience, enriching the academic landscape and creating more opportunities for development (Gunawardena & McIsaac, 2013; Jung, 2024). Distance education, with its unique characteristic of openness, introduced the concept of mass higher education, fostering a more flexible learning system. Over the years, it has evolved significantly to become more open, inclusive, adaptable, and broadly accessible. The terms open education, open distance learning, and distance education are often used interchangeably. Additionally, recent terminologies such as Open, Distance, and e-Learning (UNISA, 2018), Open, Flexible, and Distance Learning (ICDE, 2023), and Open, Distance, and Digital Education (Zawacki-Richter & Jung, 2023) have also emerged. Due to its vision of openness, which encompasses a broad range of principles to make education more equitable, accessible, and inclusive, Bozkurt (2019) argues that the term open refers to a political policy and reflects a political vision. Recently, attention has been drawn to the fact that open education should be seen as a social movement that democratizes learning and aligns with the principles of social justice and equal access to education (Hodgkinson-Williams & Trotter, 2018; Lambert, 2018). Open distance learning (ODL), then, refers to removing barriers to learning, which differs from institution to institution, leaving some more open and flexible with fewer barriers than others (Msweli, 2012). Because ODL is dependent on technology, it has implications for the use of technology. Therefore, as Bozkurt (2019) argues, ODL institutions need to use technologies that are open and accessible to all. Unlike openness, which has a social and political mandate in ODL, "distance" in ODL mostly refers to the methodology of teaching and learning at a distance. This implies that students can learn in their own time and in their own space without necessarily having to attend a physical campus with face-to-face contact with the lecturer. For this reason, technology plays a crucial role in the facilitation of teaching and learning. As technologies and pedagogies accompanying them continuously evolve, ODL remains an evolving concept (Bozkurt et al., 2019) and is, therefore, difficult to define. Also, ODL should prioritize local contexts and their specific needs instead of imposing an established and standardized curriculum on everyone.

ODL has been defined by different institutions, and a few examples are provided next.

The Commonwealth of Learning (2023, p. 5) provides an extensive definition of ODL:

> the provision of distance education opportunities in ways that seek to mitigate or remove barriers to access, such as finances, prior learning, age, social, work or family commitments,

> disability, incarceration or other such barriers. "Open" refers to a commitment that removes any unnecessary barriers to access to learning. Distance education refers to teaching and learning that temporarily separates teacher and learner in time and/or place; uses multiple media for delivery of instruction; involves two-way communication and possibly occasional face-to-face meeting[s] for tutorials and learner-learner interaction. Open learning is not the same as distance learning, but both are complementary and hence, the two terms are often used together as open and distance learning.

Additionally, a large-scale ODL institution and the first correspondence university in the world, the University of South Africa, defines ODL as follows:

> a multi-dimensional concept aimed at bridging the time, geographical, economic, social, educational and communication distance between student and institution, student and academics, student and courseware and student and peers. Open distance e-learning focuses on removing barriers to access learning, flexibility of learning provision, student-centredness, supporting students and constructing learning programmes with the expectation that students can succeed (UNISA, 2018, p. 2).

Both these definitions focus on aspects of distance between lectures and students, openness, and removing barriers as distinct characteristics of ODL. Against this background and the definitions provided, this chapter considers DE and ODL distinct but overlapping terms.

6.2 Problem Statement

However, the flexible learning system of ODL is not synonymous with the concept of personalized education, as stated in the title of this chapter. Although ODL has, over the years, slowly moved to a more personal approach instead of reaching the masses, the definitions and discussions so far model a one-size-fits-all approach. For example, many ODL institutions follow a mass education model by teaching identical content to hundreds or even thousands of students with varying levels of prior knowledge, academic interests, and diverse backgrounds (Jung, 2024). Contrary to a traditional ODL model, which teaches the masses, a personalized learning approach delivers specific and targeted instruction customized to each individual student's particular needs, interests, and abilities (Zawacki-Richter et al., 2019). Personalization can be seen as an emerging technology that serves the information needs of different users in a different way based on individual student requirements (Desai, 2020). Personalization can help students learn better by incorporating diverse strategies to create varied learning experiences and meet the lecturer's needs in designing and preparing teaching activities. Therefore, the model of personalization in ODL can make a positive difference in student learning. On the contrary, the lack of personalized teaching and learning poses significant challenges, including a possible mismatch between content offerings and students' readiness levels, interests, or needs, leading to issues related to motivation and retention (Jung, 2024). Therefore, if ODL institutions implement a personalized teaching and learning approach, it will not only benefit individual students but will also enhance the relevance and effectiveness of

ODL in an ever-evolving educational environment. It is agreed with Desai (2020) that more research is needed to fully understand how personalization can be effectively applied to facilitate teaching and learning in ODL and how to fully utilize its potential. This chapter makes a contribution in this regard and addresses the following research question:

> How can artificial intelligence enhance personalized learning experiences in an evolving open distance learning context, and what are the implications for student engagement and educational outcomes?

After an explanation of the research methodology, the chapter proceeds with a brief overview of the evolving history of distance education, followed by a discussion of personalized learning and how modern technology, specifically artificial intelligence, can be used to personalize learning. Considering the findings, the chapter concludes with recommendations for including artificial intelligence for personalized learning in ODL.

6.3 Research Methodology

To consider prior, relevant literature is essential for all research. However, to make a literature review a proper research methodology, appropriate steps must be taken. This ensures that the review is accurate, precise, and trustworthy (Snyder, 2019). A semi-structured narrative review approach was found to be most applicable for this research because it is generally used to "provide a much needed bridge between the vast and scattered assortment of articles on a topic and to link different studies on various topics for purposes of reinterpretation or interconnection" (Baumeister & Leary, 1997, p. 311). This type of study is useful for presenting up-to-date literature (Cronin et al., 2008) and can be used to summarize, synthesize, draw conclusions, identify research gaps, and provide suggestions for future research (Cronin et al., 2008). In general, this review of the literature identified relevant research and presented it in a narrative format to improve knowledge on the topic. Semi-structured narrative literature reviews serve as a valuable tool in synthesizing existing literature, particularly when addressing complex issues. Different from systematic reviews, their purpose is to provide interpretation and critique to deepen understanding of a specific topic (Greenhalgh et al., 2018). However, they are not without limitations (Bennell et al., 2022; Greenhalgh et al., 2018). One significant limitation is the inherent lack of methodological rigour over systematic reviews. Narrative reviews often prioritize thematic analysis over strict adherence to systematic protocols. This approach can lead to biases in literature selection and interpretation, making replicability difficult. However, the researcher was aware of these limitations and took steps to ensure transparency in the research process, aiming to establish trustworthiness, quality, and credibility.

The study aimed to explore DE and ODL by examining their respective definitions, histories, and theories and investigating their relevance to personalized learning. The steps and guidelines, according to Snyder (2019) and Chigbu et al. (2023), were followed to conduct this literature review and are presented in the Table 6.1. Although these steps were followed, Alaidaros et al. (2021) confirm that narrative reviews allow for a more flexible synthesis compared to systematic reviews, enabling researchers to highlight specific trends and insights within the literature. This was also the approach followed in this study.

To ensure the quality and robustness of the reviewed documents, several criteria were used, such as credibility of the research design, methodological rigour, clarity of the findings, and relevance to the context of personalized learning to ODL. This ensured that high-quality documents and studies were used (Hannes & Macaitis, 2012). The literature review provided a deep understanding of the potential of artificial intelligence to personalize learning against the evolving landscape of open distance learning.

Table 6.1 Steps followed in the semi-structured narrative review approach

Step 1	*Identification of keywords* For this research, the focus was on the keywords personalized learning, the history of ODL and distance education, and technologies in ODL to support personalized learning, specifically artificial intelligence. Keywords based on the research question were identified, including personalized learning, artificial intelligence (AI) in education, open distance learning (ODL), and educational technology
Step 2	*Selection of databases* For this research, Google Scholar, Scopus, ERIC (Education Resources Information Centre), and Web of Science were used
Step 3	*The identification of inclusion and exclusion criteria* The search was limited to peer-reviewed journal articles, conference papers, and books published between 2010 and 2024 Inclusion criteria were articles that focused on studies with empirical evidence, theoretical discussions, or literature reviews relevant to AI's role in enhancing personalized learning in education, specifically ODL. The keywords and phrases identified in Step 1 were used Exclusion criteria were articles that did not focus on ODL, AI in education, or personalized learning technologies, as well as documents that were not peer-reviewed and articles published before 2010
Step 4	*Recognition of key information* After the initial screening of the abstracts, the relevant articles were read, and key information was recorded
Step 5	*Documentation of patterns and themes* Patterns and themes were identified, and similarities, contrasts, and gaps were discovered and documented
Step 6	*Synthesis of information and finalizing the review* The key points of the literature were summarized. Based on the information identified in Step 5, patterns, gaps, and key information were compared and synthesized. This was an iterative process which helped in refining the arguments and improving the overall quality of the review. Finally, based on the findings from the review, recommendations were added

6.4 Findings and Discussion

6.4.1 The Evolving Landscape of Distance Education and Open Distance Learning

The history of distance education began with a correspondence model as early as 1728 when Caleb Phillips advertised shorthand lessons by mail in the Boston Gazette (Verduin & Clark, 1991). Courses were delivered by mail without face-to-face interaction between students and lecturers. Due to the railway networks, which were the cheapest, fastest, and most reliable mode of transportation at the beginning of the early 1880s, individuals started to receive their education at home or work by mail (Moore & Kearsley, 1996). Lecturers typically provided reading materials followed by a task, which had to be completed in writing and sent back to the lecturer for feedback and assessment. Lecturers assessed students' tasks and returned them to students by mail (Peters, 1994). Taking the assessment time and the time for the postal services to collect, send, and deliver materials into consideration, the main disadvantage of this process was that it could take very long. In correspondence DE, the students were mostly adults whose decision to receive this education was due to their occupational, economic, social, or family commitments (Smaldino & Crandell, 2000). The dominant technology in this era was written or printed materials, and a didactic teaching style was followed. An industrialized form of education characterized this DE model with a highly specialized division of labour in producing and delivering instructional materials and the potential to teach many students at once (Bates, 2005). Although there were different types of print media, the combination of the printing press and postal services paved the way for correspondence DE. At the time, it redressed social injustices and decreased illiteracy rates by giving people such as women, soldiers, workers, and farmers access to learning (Bozkurt, 2019). Until the beginning of the 1970s and the advent of two-way communication technologies, print and the mail system were the predominant delivery medium of distance education (Gunawardena & McIsaac, 2013).

The correspondence model slowly evolved to a visual-auditory model, reducing many of the limitations of correspondence education, especially delivery time, and increasing the immediacy of the learning processes. Delivery of learning content through postal services was no longer the only means of delivery once live educational radio emerged and correspondence DE was gradually phased out. The invention of radio and television improved and accelerated the speed of communication and interaction. The dominant technologies of this model were audio, followed by multimedia technology, and these were used to instruct large numbers of students at the same time, although they might not have the ability to call back to clarify statements or ask questions (Bozkurt, 2019; Gunawardena & McIsaac, 2013). Initially, the interaction between students and teachers was minimal in this model, but the level of interaction increased in terms of immediacy and the teacher's social presence. Given this ease of reaching the masses, it did not take long for ODL mega-universities to use such technologies. As an industrialized form of teaching and learning, DE universities had opportunities to reproduce high-quality teaching materials, which made it possible to instruct large numbers of students at the same time wherever they lived (Holmberg, 1977). The instruction in this model was teacher-centred, although students gradually gained more autonomy through the advantages of new communication technologies.

The visual-auditory model was followed by computer-based education, marking the beginning of digital knowledge and a network society. The scope of the concept of *distance* changed as the distance in time and space had lost importance. Rather than reaching the masses for the first time, a more personal approach to reaching individuals became possible. The prominence of teacher-centred education diminished and was replaced with a more student-centred approach. With the advantages and capacity increase offered by technology, student interaction with content, technology, their lecturers, and among themselves became central in ODL. The multimedia used in the previous DE model had become obsolete compared to the new, higher-quality computer-based multimedia and advanced technologies. Additionally, synchronous and asynchronous instruction became as efficient as face-to-face instruction. New learning models, such as e-learning, mobile learning, and ubiquitous learning, appeared with highly rich and interactive content. The COVID-19 pandemic that hit the world in 2020 further accelerated the adoption of online teaching and learning because face-to-face contact was impossible due to lockdowns in most parts of the world during this time (Gallego-Gómez et al., 2021). ODL institutions' role, which was traditionally seen as a form of education using non-traditional delivery systems, in higher education was confirmed, and online learning became mainstream education, although many initially equated unplanned Emergency Remote Teaching with distance education (Garlinska et al., 2023; Nichols, 2024). Since the pandemic, higher education institutions have gradually become more familiar with the use of technologies to support teaching and learning.

From the above, it can be observed that the word "distance" has multiple meanings, which changed over time based on technological developments. In the current paradigm, in contrast to earlier assumptions, distance represents psychological or transactional distance rather than physical or geographical distance (Bates, 2005). It is also interesting that the different models of DE discussed here view technology as an intrinsic quality of DE, although these technologies have changed and evolved over time. However, regardless of the degree to which DE depends on technology, it is important to remember that the use of technology is not the ultimate goal but just the medium to convey learning content. Although not new, in recent years, ODL institutions have begun to incorporate advanced technology tools such as artificial intelligence and learning analytics to create a more personalized model of online teaching and learning (Kanwar & Mishra, 2023; Prinsloo, 2023). These developments have contributed to the transformation of online teaching and learning into more personalized forms of learning.

Next, the focus is on personalized learning, as put forward in this chapter, and its relationship with ODL and AI.

6.4.2 Personalized Learning

The concept of personalized learning is multifaceted, and its interpretation varies depending on the context. Although it has long been part of education, advances in technologies such as big data analytics and artificial intelligence have caused a shift in its meaning and introduced new ways of implementing it (Magomadov, 2020). Personalized learning is often used interchangeably with terms such as learner-centred instruction, differentiated learning, individualized learning, competency-based learning, and adaptive learning (Holmes et al., 2018). According to Mourtzis et al. (2023), personalized learning involves using data to adapt any aspect of instruction to the unique characteristics of individual students, such as their personality, talents, learning style background, and personal goals. Similarly, the Commonwealth of Learning (2023) states that personalized learning "relates to the differentiating and customisation of learning towards the needs of the individual" (p. 2).

Recent research has highlighted the importance of personalized learning in improving student motivation and engagement, making learning more relevant to their personal capabilities and aspirations (Alamri et al., 2020). Personalized learning offers numerous benefits, including the creation of tailored learning paths to enhance effectiveness and the prioritization of learner-specific goals related to learning objectives (Baker, 2021). From the above, it can be inferred that personalized learning has transformative potential that aligns educational practices with the potential and diverse contexts and needs of individual students.

6.4.3 Personalized Learning and ODL

From an ODL perspective, personalized learning refers to a specific learning design that adapts learning to a specific student's strengths, preferences, and needs when students are not in the same physical space as their lecturers. This approach is inherently student-centred, requiring students to manage their learning process and set specific goals to achieve set learning outcomes (Aberbach et al., 2021). However, ODL institutions, such as the University of South Africa, face significant challenges in personalizing teaching and learning due to their large and diverse student populations. These challenges are deepened by varying levels of prior knowledge, technical skills, and academic readiness among students (Kara et al., 2019). Insufficient support to address these differences contributes to a lack of motivation, disengagement, and low retention rates. Additionally, it exacerbates the disadvantages students face, who often need more support. Various studies (e.g. Martínez-Carrascal et al., 2023; Nichols, 2010; Van den Berg, 2024) suggest that providing individual support tailored to students' unique circumstances and requirements can help overcome such challenges. For example, if a student demonstrates a strong grasp of a specific topic, they can be taught at a more advanced level to progress at a faster pace. Conversely, if the student is struggling, then the material and activities of this topic may be repeated using a different teaching approach (Rodrigues et al., 2019). However, as Murtaza et al. (2022) point out, identifying such preferences must be guided by artificial intelligence, as they are often implicit and, therefore, difficult to identify. Well-implemented personalized e-learning systems have the potential to educate large numbers of students cost-effectively (McCutcheon et al., 2015). However, failing to use such systems to address student challenges and needs as early as possible might make it difficult for ODL institutions to compete with residential institutions, which can offer more specialized support due to advantages like smaller student numbers and face-to-face contact. This means that while personalized learning in ODL settings holds great promise, it requires strategic implementation and support to meet the diverse needs of its students effectively. One of the foremost challenges in implementing AI in ODL is the need for robust technical infrastructure. Institutions must invest in high-performance servers, cloud computing resources, and reliable internet connectivity to support AI applications (Abuodha & Kipkebut, 2024). This challenge can be particularly tough in low-resourced contexts, where institutions may struggle to meet the need for AI technologies. Another critical challenge is the need for staff training. Academics and administrators must be equipped with the skills to use AI effectively. Resistance to change and related training is a common barrier, as many academics may feel overwhelmed by the rapid technological advancements or sceptical about AI tools (Nguyen et al., 2024). Integrating AI tools with existing learning management systems poses another significant challenge. Many ODL institutions already use established platforms, and incorporating AI functionalities into these systems can be complex (Nguyen et al., 2024). Compatibility issues may arise, requiring additional resources for customization and integration (Abuodha & Kipkebut, 2024). Finally, the financial implications of AI in ODL institutions cannot be overlooked. The initial investment required for AI technologies, as well as ongoing support and maintenance, can strain institutional budgets, particularly in contexts where funding is limited (Nguyen et al., 2024). Institutions, therefore, must develop sustainable financial models that balance the benefits of AI integration with their economic realities. Addressing different integration challenges requires a complex approach to ensure that AI technologies can be effectively and sustainably implemented in ODL.

In the current landscape of advanced technologies, ODL institutions have unprecedented opportunities to tailor teaching and learning experiences to the needs of individual students. For example, the use of learning analytics and artificial intelligence can be tailored to the specific requirements of each student. Embracing these technological tools for personalized learning is crucial in shaping the future role of ODL institutions in providing quality higher education. This contemporary role approach marks a stark departure from the initial correspondence role of ODL in educating the masses. Instead, the shift towards personalized teaching and learning signifies an evolution in the institution's main responsibilities (Jung, 2024). Implementing personalized learning involves a complete overhaul of academic frameworks and methodologies, as proposed by Jung (2024). It involves systematic changes that aim to integrate personalized learning as an integral component of the institution's culture. This change requires a departure from viewing personalized learning as an optional addition and must be part of curriculum design, delivery, and assessment practices. This highlights the need for pedagogical innovation to transform teaching and learning practices to remain relevant. Furthermore, existing ODL practices need a critical examination to determine if they are still relevant, adequately address individual student needs, and provide adequate personalized support. Traditionally, ODL has focused on content delivery to the masses, where lecturers primarily served as the providers of information. Ning et al. (2024) emphasize the need for lecturers to adapt their pedagogical approaches to include AI tools, thereby preparing students for a digitally driven society. By using AI technologies, lecturers can provide personalized learning, allowing students to explore topics at their own pace and according to their own interests, which aligns with constructivist learning. The integration of AI technologies also leads to significant changes in assessment practices within ODL. AI can facilitate more dynamic formative assessment practices; for example, it can analyze student performance in real time, providing immediate feedback and insights into the learning process (Bakhmat et al., 2024). Furthermore, AI can help ensure fairness and equity in assessments by minimizing biases that may arise in conventional evaluation (Bakhmat et al., 2024). This means that assessment is a continuous process that supports learning rather than merely measuring it. Additionally, as AI technologies become more prevalent in education contexts, the need for AI literacy is crucial. Students and lecturers should have the ability to use the AI tools and to critically engage with them (Gutiérrez, 2023). It is essential for lecturers to teach students about the responsible use of AI, creating a critical awareness of its impact on society. Programmes and modules integrating AI literacy into the curriculum can empower students to become informed users and developers of AI technologies, enhancing their employability and adaptability in a rapidly changing job market (Aghaziarati et al., 2023). However, from a literature review, Mazon-Fierro and Mauricio (2022) concluded that most of the current ODL personalized learning technologies are not integrated and are not part of a comprehensive, personalized e-learning framework. To address this shortcoming, it is crucial to address the broader policy and practice environment that supports integrating these technologies. Jung (2024) also emphasizes the importance of adapting policies to guide practices and flexibility to facilitate the integration of personalized learning.

Although the concept of personalized learning is not new in the field of education, the advent of artificial intelligence and big data analytics introduces new avenues for its implementation (Magomadov, 2020) and needs further attention.

6.4.4 Personalized Learning and AI

Artificial intelligence is able to provide opportunities to improve the learning experiences and academic performance of students of different ages, academic levels, and socio-economic backgrounds. It has been increasingly used in education to personalize learning (Roll & Wylie, 2016) and is available to students and lecturers. In particular, it can help lecturers design courses and lessons customized to the needs of the students (Van den Berg & Du Plessis, 2023). This is especially relevant given that, according to Bloom (1984), students who receive individual tutoring and support outperform those who are subjected to a one-size-fits-all approach. However, due to the large number of students, one-on-one student support is often impossible, making traditional individualized support challenging. In this context, developments in AI provide intriguing opportunities to assist with individualized learning (Opara et al., 2023).

AI is a wide-ranging branch of automated decision-making that does not involve human involvement but is based on algorithms that provide data (Tapalova & Zhiyenbayeva, 2022). This includes capabilities such as learning, reasoning, problem-solving, perception, and language understanding. AI employs different methodologies, such as machine learning, deep learning, and neural networks, to analyze data and make informed decisions based on that analysis (Murtaza et al., 2022). The evolution of AI has led to its integration into numerous sectors, including education. In the educational context, this capability allows for sophisticated analysis and application of data. Consequently, AI is one of the tools used in learning analytics to analyze students' engagement and knowledge to restructure effective personalized learning pathways and develop supportive strategies (Tapalova & Zhiyenbayeva, 2022). However, the availability of student data has ethical implications. As ODL institutions increasingly rely on AI to personalize learning, they collect vast amounts of sensitive student data, raising significant concerns about how such data is protected (Holmes et al., 2023). For this reason, transparency is a crucial aspect, and students must be aware of the data that is shared.

Personalized learning focuses on the student's needs and is predictive and supportive in nature. This method contrasts with traditional one-size-fits-all educational models, allowing for a more customized learning journey (Murtaza et al., 2022). Lecturers can examine the information on student achievements using AI, and based on this information, students can be provided with personalized educational activities to master the skills by learning at their own pace (Tapalova & Zhiyenbayeva, 2022). For this reason, personalized learning leads to the building of customized learning pathways that make learning more effective and emphasize student-specific goals related to the learning objective (Baker, 2021). Each student has unique learning needs, preferences, and abilities, and large language models offer unique opportunities to provide personalized and effective learning experiences (Kasneci et al., 2023). Large language models are AI systems capable of understanding and generating human language by processing large amounts of data (Chang et al., 2024). By tailoring educational content and activities, these tools can help make learning more engaging and fun, ultimately improving student motivation and performance (Garlinska et al., 2023). The integration of AI and large language models in personalized learning can significantly improve educational outcomes. However, lecturers should be mindful of possible issues related to the digital divide. Stakeholders should address the disparities in technology access and literacy among students, particularly in disadvantaged communities. The effectiveness of AI in personalized learning is contingent upon equitable access to the necessary infrastructure and technology. Without addressing the needed disparities, the integration of AI could inadvertently widen the educational gap rather than bridge it.

The use of generative AI in education and its relationship with personalized learning has been documented in several studies. Personalized tutoring, personalized support, and feedback have been documented as useful strategies, transforming how teachers teach and students learn (Bozkurt, 2023; Rahman & Watanobe, 2023; Van den Berg, 2024). Due to the interactive nature of generative AI, it has the potential to answer student questions, respond to their needs, create content, and act as a "person-to-go-to" whenever needed, providing immediate responses. Authors such as Kasneci et al. (2023), Van Wyk et al. (2023), and Lo (2023) have documented AI technologies such as ChatGPT to generate text, foster discussions, and provide immediate personalized assistance and prompt feedback. These capabilities can significantly improve the learning process by making it more dynamic and responsive. However, Garlinska et al. (2023) caution that while AI can support students through personalized feedback, interactive content development requires teachers to possess the necessary knowledge and skills. This often requires that teachers invest a substantial amount of time in mastering this technology, quickly responding to student feedback, and updating course materials. In this regard, Seo et al. (2021) note that AI systems can enhance student-instructor interactions by providing timely feedback and recommendations, which are crucial for maintaining student engagement in online learning environments. This is echoed by Onesi-Ozigagun et al. (2024), who argue that immediate and targeted feedback is essential for fostering successful learning experiences in ODL. This means that AI in education not only transforms learning but also requires a change in the roles of teachers and their approach to content development.

Additionally, AI can be particularly useful in assessment practices, helping lecturers by providing them with valuable insight into student performance and helping them customize learning pathways (Cope et al., 2021). By identifying learning gaps, AI helps students adapt materials and practices to better suit their individual needs and capabilities (Tapalova & Zhiyenbayeva, 2022; Yu & Guo, 2023). Through this process, students can receive customized resources based on their learning styles and abilities. For example, AI tools can identify areas where students are struggling and provide tailored recommendations for resources, learning activities, and assessments. This targeted approach not only addresses the immediate needs of the students but also supports their overall learning journey. Additionally, AI has the ability to continuously monitor student progress and adjust recommendations as needed, ensuring that the support provided is always relevant and effective (Rahman & Watanobe, 2023; Yu & Guo, 2023). By using AI for assessment, teaching, and learning, ODL institutions can create more adaptive and responsive learning environments, ultimately enhancing student success and engagement. One notable example is the development of adaptive learning platforms to use AI algorithms to analyze student learning and cognitive styles. In this regard, Akavova et al. (2023) discuss how AI can create intelligent systems that provide personalized feedback and adapt educational content based on individual performance metrics, thereby creating a more engaging personal learning environment. These findings are supported by Zhou (2024), emphasizing the role of intelligent tutoring systems in stimulating personalized outcomes.

Concerns about academic integrity and the ethical use of AI in education are well documented and have been discussed extensively in the literature. This includes issues of data privacy and algorithm bias (e.g. Ashok et al., 2022; Gupta et al., 2024; Larsson, 2020; Rahman & Watanobe, 2023). According to Holmes et al. (2023), a framework is needed for ethical AI use in ODL, and several authors have provided such frameworks. One notable framework is proposed by Tuomi (2023) which emphasizes a socio-developmental approach to ethics in educational AI. The framework is structured around three thematic domains: agency, social fairness, and justified choice. In addition, the work of Jobin and Ienca (2019) provides a comprehensive overview of the global landscape of AI ethics guidelines, which can serve as a foundational reference for developing ethical frameworks in education. In some cases and countries, ethical concerns have led educational institutions to restrict the use of AI tools for teaching and learning. However, when used ethically, AI has the potential to personalize teaching, learning, and support in ODL, and it should be managed rather than restricted. Properly managed AI can transform ODL from its earlier mass education models, which relied on a one-size-fits-all approach, into a more individualized and responsive educational experience. Using AI to personalize learning will enhance existing methodologies and innovate the ODL experience, ensuring that this mode of delivery remains relevant and effective. As Jung (2024) argues, the future success of ODL lies in carefully balancing the principles of openness and accessibility with innovative practices to meet the individual needs of students. By thoughtfully and ethically integrating AI, ODL institutions can better fulfil their mission of providing quality education to a diverse population.

The study aligns with constructivist and connectivist learning theories in its approach to personalized learning. Constructivism emphasizes the importance of students constructing their own understanding through experiences and interaction, which is supported by the notion that digital collaborative learning environments enhance engagement and adaptability in educational settings (Männistö et al., 2020). AI's ability to provide adaptive learning pathways facilitates a constructivist learning environment where learners actively engage with content, build knowledge, and apply it in meaningful ways. For example, intelligent learning systems can offer immediate and personalized feedback, allowing students to navigate learning experiences more effectively (Li & Wong, 2023). This adaptability is crucial for fostering an environment where students can construct knowledge through exploration and interaction with diverse sources. Similarly, connectivism focuses on learning through connections and networks in the digital age. An AI-powered personalized learning approach supports connectivist principles by allowing students to connect with diverse sources, communities, and knowledge networks. This is evident in the increasing reliance on digital platforms for collaborative learning, which promotes interaction among students and enhances their ability to share knowledge and experiences (Männistö et al., 2020). The intersection of constructivist and connectivist theories in personalized learning in ODL is therefore significantly enhanced by AI technologies that adapt to individual student needs and promote collaborative interactions.

Based on the findings of this research, several recommendations are made to ODL institutions.

6.5 Recommendations

6.5.1 Recommendation 1: Integrate AI Technologies into ODL Policies and Frameworks

First, ODL institutions should actively incorporate AI technologies into their educational policies and frameworks to personalize students' learning experiences. This includes using AI tools for learning analytics, personalized tutoring, and adaptive learning pathways to meet individual student needs and improve engagement. In addition, policies should address clear ethical guidelines and policies for using AI in education. Such guidelines should address concerns about academic integrity and data privacy to ensure their implementation enhances learning without compromising ethical standards. It will be challenging to implement a more personalized approach without the necessary policies in place, and personalized approaches might be seen as an addition to a model that focuses on the masses.

6.5.2 Recommendation 2: Focus on Inclusive and Equitable AI Applications

Institutions should ensure that AI applications for personalized learning are inclusive and equitable, addressing the diverse needs of all students, including those from disadvantaged backgrounds and students with disabilities. This involves the design of tools that are accessible, culturally sensitive, and capable of supporting students with varying levels of prior knowledge, technical skills, and academic readiness. A personalized approach in ODL depends on access to relevant technologies and digital infrastructures. Ongoing efforts should be made to narrow the digital divide.

6.5.3 Recommendation 3: Design Pedagogies and Curriculum for AI Integration

Researchers and lecturers must investigate the pedagogies and curricula that support personalized teaching and learning. This will require an adaptation of past and current pedagogies that were built for earlier models of ODL. ODL institutions should follow open and collaborative approaches to enrich the landscape and learn from each other. This means that lecturers might need training not only to integrate technologies but also to foster the student's acquisition of skills such as critical thinking, collaborative learning, and flexible approaches.

6.6 Conclusion and Recommendations for Further Research

This chapter aimed to explore how artificial intelligence can enhance personalized learning experiences within the evolving landscape of ODL. Additionally, it examined the implications for student engagement and learning and, ultimately, the educational outcome. Using a semi-structured narrative literature review as its research methodology, the study synthesized relevant literature to provide a comprehensive understanding of the use of AI for personalized learning within an evolving ODL context. The findings show that AI technologies hold significant promise in transforming ODL by providing personalized tutoring, adaptive learning pathways, and customized support that are aligned with the individual circumstances and needs of the students. AI can analyze performance data to identify strengths and learning gaps and can recommend customized learning methods and resources. This, in turn, can enhance student engagement and success. However, the study also identified certain challenges, including implementation challenges, the need for training, ethical considerations, pedagogical implications and the need for robust policy frameworks for the ethical use of AI. It also highlighted the need for instructional design to integrate AI technologies into teaching and learning. Based on these findings, several recommendations have been made to ODL institutions. Despite this well-structured literature review, this study has limitations. The main limitation is that it is theoretical and descriptive in nature. The reliance on the existing literature means that empirical research on real-world AI implementations in ODL was limited. Therefore, more research is needed to determine the use of modern technologies, such as AI, by lecturers and students to personalize learning. Empirical studies in diverse student populations at various ODL institutions will provide more information on the effectiveness of AI in personalized learning. While there are challenges to overcome, the potential of AI to personalize learning within the evolving landscape of ODL is indisputable. By embracing AI, ODL institutions can move beyond traditional mass education models to offer individualized learning experiences, ultimately ensuring their relevance and effectiveness in future. This change will embrace the educational experience for students and reaffirm the commitment of ODL institutions to providing accessible, equitable, and high-quality education for all.

References

Aberbach, H., Jeghal, A., Sabri, A., Tairi, H., & Laaouina, L. (2021). A personalized learning approach based on learning speed. *Journal of Computer Science, 17*(3), 242–250. https://doi.org/10.3844/jcssp.2021.242.250

Abuodha, L., & Kipkebut, A. (2024). Disruptive ai in education: Transforming learning in the digital age. *International Journal for Research in Applied Science and Engineering Technology, 12*(2), 195–199. https://doi.org/10.22214/ijraset.2024.58283

Aghaziarati, A., Nejatifar, S., & Abedi, A. (2023). Artificial intelligence in education: Investigating teacher attitudes. *AI and Tech in Behavioral and Social Sciences, 1*(1), 35–42. https://doi.org/10.61838/kman.aitech.1.1.6

Akavova, A., Temirkhanova, Z., & Lorsanova, Z. (2023). Adaptive learning and artificial intelligence in the educational space. In *E3S web of conferences* (Vol. 451, p. 06011). EDP Sciences. https://doi.org/10.1051/e3sconf/202345106011

Alaidaros, H., Omar, M., & Romli, R. (2021). A review on the methods of evaluating the new approaches proposed in the agile context. *International Journal of Computer and Information Technology (2279-0764), 10*(1), 2279–0764. https://doi.org/10.24203/ijcit.v10i1.54

Alamri, H., Lowell, V., Watson, W., & Watson, S. L. (2020). Using personalized learning as an instructional approach to motivate learners in online higher education: Learner self-determination and intrinsic motivation. *Journal of Research on Technology in Education, 52*(3), 322–352. https://doi.org/10.1080/15391523.2020.1728449

Ashok, M., Madan, R., Joha, A., & Sivarajah, U. (2022). Ethical framework for artificial intelligence and digital technologies. *International Journal of Information Management, 62*, Article 102433. https://doi.org/10.1016/j.ijinfomgt.2021.102433

Baker, R., (2021). Artificial intelligence in education: Bringing it all together. In: *OECD digital education outlook 2021: Pushing the frontiers with AI, blockchain, and robots.* OECD. https://www.upenn.edu/learninganalytics/ryanbaker/oecd-baker.pdf

Bakhmat, N., Romanova, I., Oronovska, L., Rudenko, O., & Mogyl, O. (2024). Ukrainian education for peace and security 2023: Technological convergence, artificial intelligence. *Multidisciplinary Reviews, 6*. https://doi.org/10.31893/multirev.2023spe016

Bates, T. (2005). *Technology, e-learning and distance education.* Routledge. https://doi.org/10.4324/9780203463772

Baumeister, R. F., & Leary, M. R. (1997). Writing narrative literature reviews. *Review of General Psychology, 1*(3), 311–320.

Bennell, C., Jenkins, B., Blaskovits, B., Semple, T., Khanizadeh, A., Brown, A., & Jones, N. J. (2022). Knowledge, skills, and abilities for managing potentially volatile police–public interactions: A narrative review. *Frontiers in Psychology, 13*. https://doi.org/10.3389/fpsyg.2022.818009

Bloom, B. (1984). The search for methods of group instruction as effective as one-to-oüne tutoring. *Educational Leadership, 41*(8), 4–17. https://scispace.com/papers/the-search-for-methods-of-group-instructionas-effective-as-1adrkek4br

Bozkurt, A. (2019). From distance education to open and distance learning: A holistic evaluation of history, definitions, and theories. In S. Sisman-Ugur & G. Kurubacak (Eds.), *Handbook of research on learning in the age of transhumanism* (pp. 252–273). IGI Global.

Bozkurt, A., Koseoglu, S., & Singh, L. (2019). An analysis of peer-reviewed publications on openness in education in half a century: Trends and patterns in the open hemisphere. *Australasian Journal of Educational Technology, 35*(4), 78–97. https://doi.org/10.14742/ajet.4252

Bozkurt, A. (2023). Unleashing the potential of generative AI, conversational agents and chatbots in educational praxis: A systematic review and bibliometric analysis of GenAI in education. *Open Praxis, 15*(4), 261–270. https://doi.org/10.55982/openpraxis.15.4.609

Chang, Y., Wang, X., Wang, J., Wu, Y., Yang, L., Zhu, K., Chen, H., Yi, X., Wang, C., Wang, Y., Ye, W., Zhang, Y., Chang, Y., Yu, P. S., Yang, Q., & Xie, X. (2024). A survey on evaluation of large language models. *ACM Transactions on Intelligent Systems and Technology, 15*(3), 1–45. https://doi.org/10.1145/3641289

Chigbu, U. E., Atiku, S. O., & Du Plessis, C. C. (2023). The science of literature reviews: Searching, identifying, selecting, and synthesising. *Publications, 11*, 2. https://doi.org/10.3390/publications11010002

Commonwealth of Learning. (2023). *Open distance learning: Key terms and definitions.* https://oasis.col.org/items/7dc20f7c-4901-433a-90f1-6274f5ce53dd

Cope, B., Kalantzis, M., & Searsmith, D. (2021). Artificial intelligence for education: Knowledge and its assessment in AI-enabled learning ecologies. *Educational Philosophy and Theory, 53*(12), 1229–1245. https://doi.org/10.1080/00131857.2020.1728732

Cronin, P., Ryan, F., & Coughlan, M. (2008). Undertaking a literature review: A step-by-step approach. *British Journal of Nursing, 17*(1), 38–43. https://doi.org/10.12968/bjon.2008.17.1.28059

Desai, D. (2020). Modeling personalized e-learning for effective distance education. *International Journal for Research in Applied Science and Engineering Technology, 8*(6), 2428–2435.

Gallego-Gómez, C., De-Pablos-Heredero, C., & Montes-Botella, J. L. (2021). Change of processes in the COVID-19 scenario: From face-to-face to remote teaching-learning systems. *Sustainability, 13*(19), 10513. https://doi.org/10.3390/su131910513

Garlinska, M., Osial, M., Proniewska, K., & Pregowska, A. (2023). The influence of emerging technologies on distance education. *Electronics, 12*, 1550. https://doi.org/10.3390/electronics12071550

Greenhalgh, T., Thorne, S., & Malterud, K. (2018). Time to challenge the spurious hierarchy of systematic over narrative reviews? *European Journal of Clinical Investigation, 48*(6). https://doi.org/10.1111/eci.12931

Gunawardena, C. N., & McIsaac, M. S. (2013). Distance education. In *Handbook of research on educational communications and technology* (pp. 361–401). Routledge.

Gupta, P., Sreelatha, C., Latha, A., Raj, S., & Singh, A. (2024). Navigating the future of education: The impact of artificial intelligence on teacher-student dynamics. *Educational Administration: Theory and Practice, 30*(4), 6006–6013. https://doi.org/10.53555/kuey.v30i4.2332

Gutiérrez, L. (2023). Artificial intelligence in language education: Navigating the potential and challenges of chatbots and NLP. *Research Studies in English Language Teaching and Learning, 1*(3), 180–191. https://doi.org/10.62583/rseltl.v1i3.44

Hannes, K., & Macaitis, K. (2012). A move to more systematic and transparent approaches in qualitative evidence synthesis: Update on a review of published papers. *Qualitative Research, 12*(4), 402–442. https://doi.org/10.1177/1468794111432992

Hodgkinson-Williams, C. A., & Trotter, H. (2018). A social justice framework for understanding open educational resources and practices in the global south. *Journal of Learning for Development, 5*(3). https://doi.org/10.56059/jl4d.v5i3.312

Holmberg, B. (1977). *Distance education: A survey and bibliography*. Kogan Page.

Holmes, W., Anastopoulou S., Schaumburg, H., & Mavrikis, M. (2018). *Technology-enhanced personalised learning: Untangling the evidence*. Robert Bosch Stiftung.

Holmes, W., Iniesto, F., Anastopoulou, S., & Boticario, J. G. (2023). Stakeholder perspectives on the ethics of AI in distance-based higher education. *International Review of Research in Open and Distributed Learning, 24*(2), 96–117. https://doi.org/10.19173/irrodl.v24i2.6089

ICDE. (2023). *Global quality perspectives on open, flexible and distance learning 2022* (ICDE Report-2022). https://www.icde.org/publication/quality-network-report-2022/

Jobin, A., & Ienca, M. (2019). The global landscape of AI ethics guidelines. *Nature Machine Intelligence, 1*(9), 389–399. https://doi.org/10.1038/s42256-019-0088-2

Jung, I. (2024). Personalized education for all: The future of open universities. *Open Praxis, 16*(1), 24–36. https://doi.org/10.55982/openpraxis.16.1.612

Kanwar, A., & Mishra, S. (2023, September 28). Future of open universities. In *Keynote presented at the AAOU 36th annual conference*. Istanbul, Turkey. https://oasis.col.org/bitstreams/5f2d7168-5222-495c-bfc8-e2dcd6e54b5e/download

Kara, M., Erdoğdu, F., Kokoç, M., & Cagiltay, K. (2019). Challenges faced by adult learners in online distance education: A literature review. *Open Praxis, 11*(1), 5–22. https://doi.org/10.5944/openpraxis.11.1.929

Kasneci, E., Seßler, K., Küchemann, S., Bannert, M., Dementieva, D., Fischer, F., Kasneci, G., et al. (2023). ChatGPT for good? On opportunities and challenges of large language models for education. *Learning and Individual Differences, 103*, 102274. https://doi.org/10.1016/j.lindif.2023.102274

Lambert, S. R. (2018). Changing our (dis) course: A distinctive social justice aligned definition of open education. *Journal of Learning for Development, 5*(3). 225–244. https://doi.org/10.56059/jl4d.v5i3.290

Larsson, S. (2020). On the governance of artificial intelligence through ethics guidelines. *Asian Journal of Law and Society, 7*(3), 437–451.

Li, K. C., & Wong, B. T. M. (2023). Artificial intelligence in personalised learning: A bibliometric analysis. *Interactive Technology and Smart Education, 20*(3), 422–445. https://doi.org/10.1108/itse-01-2023-0007

Lo, C. K. (2023). What is the impact of ChatGPT on education? A rapid review of the literature. *Education Sciences, 13*(4), 410. https://doi.org/10.3390/educsci13040410

Männistö, M., Mikkonen, K., Kuivila, H. M., Koskinen, C., Koivula, M., Sjögren, T., Koivula, M., Koskimäki, M., Männistö, M., Lukkarila, P., & Kääriäinen, M. (2020). Health and social care educators' competence in digital collaborative learning: A cross-sectional survey. *Sage Open, 10*(4), 2158244020962780. https://doi.org/10.1177/2158244020962780

Magomadov, V. S. (2020). The application of artificial intelligence and big data analytics in personalized learning. *Journal of Physics: Conference Series, 1691*, Article 012169. https://doi.org/10.1088/1742-6596/1691/1/012169

Martínez-Carrascal, J. A., Hlosta, M., & Sancho-Vinuesa, T. (2023). Using survival analysis to identify populations of learners at risk of withdrawal: Conceptualization and impact of demographics. *The International Review of Research in Open and Distributed Learning, 24*(1), 1–21. https://doi.org/10.19173/irrodl.v24i1.6589

Mazon-Fierro, M., & Mauricio, D. (2022). Usability of e-learning and usability of adaptive e-learning: A literature review. *International Journal of Human Factors and Ergonomics, 9*(1), 1–31.

McCutcheon, K., Lohan, M., Traynor, M., & Martin, D. (2015). A systematic review evaluating the impact of online or blended learning vs. face-to-face learning of clinical skills in undergraduate nurse education. *Journal of Advanced Nursing, 71*(2), 255–270.

Moore, M. G., & Kearsley, G. (1996). *Distance education: A systems view*. Wadsworth.

Mourtzis, D., Panopoulos, N., & Angelopoulos, J. (2023). A hybrid teaching factory model towards personalized education 4.0. *International Journal of Computer Integrated Manufacturing, 36*(12), 1739–1759. https://doi.org/10.1080/0951192X.2022.2145025

Msweli, P. (2012). Mapping the interplay between open distance learning and internationalisation principles. *International Review of Research in Open and Distance Learning, 13*(3), 97–116. https://doi.org/10.19173/irrodl.v13i3.1182

Murtaza, M., Ahmed, Y., Shamsi, J. A., Sherwani, F., & Usman, M. (2022). AI-based personalized e-learning systems: Issues, challenges, and solutions. *IEEE Access, 10*, 81323–81342.

Nguyen, A., Kremantzis, M., Essien, A., Petrounias, I., & Hosseini, S. (2024). Editorial: Enhancing student engagement through artificial intelligence (ai): Understanding the basics, opportunities, and challenges. *Journal of University Teaching and Learning Practice, 21*(06). https://doi.org/10.53761/caraaq92

Nichols, M. (2010). Student perceptions of support services and the influence of targeted interventions on retention in distance education. *Distance Education, 31*(1), 93–113. https://doi.org/10.1080/01587911003725048

Nichols, M. (2024). We need to talk about how we talk about what we talk about: Revisiting ODL. *Asian Journal of Distance Education, 19*(1). https://www.asianjde.com/ojs/index.php/AsianJDE/article/view/786

Ning, Y., Zhang, C., Xu, B., Zhou, Y., & Wijaya, T. T. (2024). Teachers' AI-TPACK: Exploring the relationship between knowledge elements. *Sustainability, 16*(3), 978. https://doi.org/10.3390/su16030978

Onesi-Ozigagun, O., Ololade, Y. J., Eyo-Udo, N. L., & Ogundipe, D. O. (2024). Revolutionizing education through AI: a comprehensive review of enhancing learning experiences. *International Journal of Applied Research in Social Sciences, 6*(4), 589–607. https://doi.org/10.51594/ijarss.v6i4.1011

Opara, E., Mfon-Ette Theresa, A., & Aduke, T. C. (2023). ChatGPT for teaching, learning and research: Prospects and challenges. *Global Academic Journal of Humanities and Social Sciences, 5*(2), 33–40. https://doi.org/10.36348/gajhss.2023.v05i02.001

Peters, O. (1994). *Distance education and industrial production: A comparative interpretation in outline* (1973). http://www.c3l.uni-oldenburg.de/cde/found/peters67.htm

Prinsloo, P. (2023). Learning analytics in open, distance, and digital education (ODDE). In O. Zawacki-Richter & I. S. Jung (Eds.), *Handbook of open, distance and digital education* (pp. 1021–1036). Singapore. https://doi.org/10.1007/978-981-19-2080-6_57

Rahman, M. M., & Watanobe, Y. (2023). ChatGPT for education and research: Opportunities, threats, and strategies. *Applied Sciences, 13*, 5783. https://doi.org/10.3390/app13095783

Rodrigues, H., Almeida, F., Figueiredo, V., & Lopes, S. L. (2019). Tracking e-learning through published papers: A systematic review. *Computers & Education, 136*, 87–98. https://doi.org/10.1016/j.compedu.2019.03.007

Roll, I., & Wylie, R. (2016). Evolution and revolution in artificial intelligence in education. *International Journal of Artificial Intelligence in Education, 26*, 582–599. https://doi.org/10.1007/s40593-016-0110-3

Seo, K., Tang, J., Roll, I., Fels, S., & Yoon, D. (2021). The impact of artificial intelligence on learner–instructor interaction in online learning. *International Journal of Educational Technology in Higher Education, 18*, 1–23. https://doi.org/10.1186/s41239-021-00292-9

Smaldino, J. J., & Crandell, C. C. (2000). Classroom amplification technology: Theory and practice. *Language, Speech, and Hearing Services in Schools, 31*(4), 371–375.

Snyder, H. (2019). Literature review as a research methodology: An overview and guidelines. *Journal of Business Research, 104*, 333–339. https://doi.org/10.1016/j.jbusres.2019.07.039

Tapalova, O., & Zhiyenbayeva, N., (2022). Artificial intelligence in education: AIEd for personalised learning pathways. *The Electronic Journal of e-Learning, 20*(5), 639–653. www.ejel.org

Tuomi, I. (2023). A framework for socio-developmental ethics in educational AI. In *Proceedings of the annual Hawaii international conference on system sciences*. https://doi.org/10.24251/hicss.2023.752

University of South Africa. (2018). *Open distance e-learning policy*. UNISA.

Van den Berg, G. (2024). Generative AI and educators: Partnering in using open digital content for transforming education. *Open Praxis, 16*(2), 130–141. https://doi.org/10.55982/openpraxis.16.2.640

van den Berg, G., & du Plessis, E. (2023). ChatGPT and generative AI: Possibilities for its contribution to lesson planning, critical thinking and openness in teacher education. *Education Sciences, 13*(10), 998. https://doi.org/10.3390/educsci13100998

Van Wyk, M. M., Adarkwah, M. A., & Amponsah, S. (2023). Why all the hype about ChatGPT? Academics' views of a chat-based conversational learning Strategy at an open distance e-learning institution. *Open Praxis, 15*(3), 214–225. https://doi.org/10.55982/openpraxis.15.3.56

Verduin, J. R., Jr., & Clark, T. A. (1991). *Distance education: The foundations of effective practice*. Jossey-Bass.

Yu, H., & Guo, Y. (2023). Generative artificial intelligence empowers educational reform: Current status, issues, and prospects. In *Frontiers in education* (Vol. 8, p. 1183162). Frontiers Media SA. https://doi.org/10.3389/feduc.2023.1183162

Zawacki-Richter, O. & Jung, I. (2023). Shaping the field of open, distance, and digital education. In O. Zawacki-Richter & I. Jung (Eds.) *Handbook of open, distance and digital education*. Springer. (pp. 1–10). https://doi.org/10.1007/978-981-19-0351-9_94-2

Zawacki-Richter, O., Marín, I., Bond, M., & Gouverneur, F. (2019). A systematic review of research on artificial intelligence applications in higher education—Where are the educators? *International Journal of Educational Technology in Higher Education, 16*(1), 1–27. https://doi.org/10.1186/s41239-019-0171-0

Zhou, B. (2024). The comprehensive investigation of the role related to artificial intelligence in education. *Applied and Computational Engineering, 36*, 215–219. https://doi.org/10.54254/2755-2721/36/20230449

Chapter 7
Exploring the Use of Smartphones to Teach Students with Visual Impairments in Adverse Circumstances: A Case Study in Ghana

Samuel Amponsah, Michael Thomas, and Michael Agyemang Adarkwah

Abstract Artificial intelligence (AI) and COVID-19 have been two critical forces that have resulted in a paradigm shift in teaching and learning practices in recent times. The COVID-19 pandemic exacerbated socio-economic inequalities, particularly impacting teachers and learners, especially those with disabilities in low-income and middle-income countries. This case study, framed by the Technological Pedagogical Content Knowledge (TPACK) framework, investigates how teachers in a special school utilized AI tools (smartphones) to teach visually impaired students during the pandemic. Thirty participants, including 20 teachers (three of whom were visually impaired) and 10 visually impaired students, were purposively sampled. In-depth interviews were conducted to gather data. The findings reveal that while both teachers and students possessed some knowledge of using digital technologies for education, they lacked a nuanced understanding of digital pedagogy. The study underscores significant disparities in the digital divide, emphasizing the necessity for effective government policies, increased provision of digital resources, and ongoing professional development for in-service teachers to enhance their AI competencies in addressing pedagogical challenges.

S. Amponsah (✉)
Department of Adult Education and Human Resource Studies, School of Continuing and Distance Education, College of Education, University of Ghana, Legon, Ghana
e-mail: samponsah@ug.edu.gh

M. Thomas
School of Education, Faculty of Arts Professional and Social Studies, Liverpool John Moores University, Liverpool, UK
e-mail: M.Thomas@ljmu.ac.uk

M. A. Adarkwah
Institute for Education and Culture, Chair of Adult Education, Friedrich Schiller University Jena, Jena, Germany
e-mail: michael.agyemang.adarkwah@uni-jena.de

M. A. Adarkwah et al. (eds.), *Artificial Intelligence and Human Agency in Education: Volume One*, Future Education and Learning Spaces,
https://doi.org/10.1007/978-981-96-7937-9_7

Keywords Adverse contexts · Continuous professional development · Digital pedagogy · Mobile technologies · Visually impaired students

7.1 Introduction

Arguably, artificial intelligence (AI) technologies and COVID-19 have been two significant revolutionary forces that have fundamentally changed teaching and learning practices in the past few years. In 2018, UNESCO released a report on "Learning to live in the time of AI" (UNESCO, 2018) and subsequently released the "Beijing Consensus on Artificial Intelligence and Education" in 2019 (UNESCO, 2019) to represent an evolution stage of AI in education. COVID-19 followed in 2020 and gravely disrupted education globally. The massive proliferation of AI technologies and the unprecedented nature of COVID-19 have revolutionized the traditional landscape of education like never before.

Pandemics and disasters result in emergency education as such phenomenon disrupt human life in diverse ways. Perhaps, the greatest of such near tragedies in recent times is the COVID-19 pandemic which significantly disrupted education on a global scale in 2020. The effect of the pandemic was with such magnitude that UNESCO (2020) estimated that it resulted in the closure of schools in 188 countries. In essence, the education of 1.6 billion students or over 91% of the global student population was halted momentarily and the ripple effects are still being felt by some countries and schools. While countries strived to transition to a "post"-COVID era, there arose the need to continue to live with the virus in more manageable ways. Hence, remote forms of online learning powered by mobile technologies were adopted on a scale not previously seen. This permeated the educational sector as a sure way of preserving continuity of education for students and teachers across the spectrum, from able-bodied to those with special educational needs (SEND).

The use of mobile technologies has several benefits which were amplified during the COVID-19 pandemic. In the educational space, Sheng et al. (2010) postulate that mobile technologies have the capacity of extending access from desktop-based online environments to handheld devices; deliver educational content and materials without the constraints presented by time and space; connect through wireless networks to enable cooperative learning. Similarly, Adarkwah and Amponsah (2021) assert that mobile technologies have the capacity to create ad hoc classrooms at any time and place while improving learner-learner and learner-teacher interaction. Razzaque (2020) also highlight the significance of mobile technologies in enhancing online self-study, providing help, and facilitating the search for new knowledge "on the go" for both teachers and students.

Arising from the above, Sheng et al. (2010) identified that mobile technologies can be a "new means to achieve effectiveness and efficiency … in learning environment[s]" (p. 36). This is in line with the findings of Tuttle and Carter (2022) that mobile technologies provide easy access to materials, communication, feedback, and collaboration between students, their peers, and their teachers. Similarly, Ackil

(2017) argues that mobile technologies have provided alternative ways for learners to foster knowledge creation and develop key skills.

By way of context, it is imperative to add that Ghana has a mobile penetration rate of 55%, which is the highest in Sub-Saharan Africa (Omondi, 2020). With this, Ghana appears to have the infrastructure to effectively support education with mobile technologies. However, in line with the views of the National Union of Ghanaian Students, Adarkwah (2020, p. 1668) describes online learning in the country as "challenge-ridden". These challenges include the high cost of mobile technologies and usability problems (Adarkwah, 2021; Amponsah, 2021). The situation is often more challenging to people living with disabilities as most of them are found in the low socio-economic families and groups (Senadza et al., 2019).

Meanwhile, disability issues remain ripe as it is estimated that disability prevalence hovers around three per cent of the country's total population (Ghana Statistical Service (GSS), 2019). Senadza et al. (2019) identify a third of this group as those suffering from visual impairments. With regard to the special school that served as the setting of this study, Kwarteng et al. (2021) identify three levels of study; basic school (primary and junior high) and music and rehabilitation departments. The school has a total of 37 teachers and around 370 students (Kwarteng et al., 2021). Given that these figures are from only one school in Ghana and that there are many others whose stories remain untold, there is a need to explore their experiences to gain deeper understanding and inform policymakers, practitioners, and other stakeholders to help ameliorate their existential challenges in technology-enhanced learning environments.

Moreover, the pandemic highlighted the significant socio-economic inequalities that many teachers and learners face inside and outside their classrooms which require not only the provision of mobile technologies but also, as Savage (2018) noted, bespoke professional development programmes to support teachers effectively in challenging times. Such efforts are imperative to achieving the United Nations' Sustainable Development Goal 4 (UN SDG4) and specifically Target 4 c (a substantial increase in the supply of qualified teachers) (United Nations, 2016).

To this end, it is important to highlight that teachers of students with disabilities and visually impaired students (VIS) in particular, remain an under-researched group even in the face of pandemics, especially in low-and-middle-income countries (LMIC) (Amponsah & Bekele, 2022; Muzata, 2020). Moreover, given the strategic importance of e-learning, compounded by the dearth of in-depth qualitative studies on how mobile technologies have been and can be adopted to ensure the quality of learning or to mitigate the challenges VIS face as they learn online, invites such a study. Given the context above, this study aimed at exploring how teachers at a special school in Ghana used mobile technologies to teach VIS during the adverse circumstances presented by the COVID-19 pandemic. With the overarching aim set out, the study sought to answer the following research questions:

(1) How do teachers accommodate visually impaired students when they use mobile technologies as tools for teaching?

(2) What resilience strategies do teachers and visually impaired students adopt when they use mobile technologies in adverse contexts?

This study is significant as it is the first to explore the phenomenon under study in a special school in Ghana. Having established the introduction and aim of this study, the next section outlines the review of the literature and conceptual framework used to explore these questions.

7.2 Literature Review

Crompton (2013, p. 4) defines mobile learning as "learning across multiple contexts, through social and content interactions, using personal electronic devices". Merchant (2012) also describes mobile learning as multifaceted and resulted to a paradigm shift away from traditional pedagogies and tethered or corded technologies (such as desktop computers) to portable technologies that enable students to study at any time and in any place. In view of the numerous advantages mobile technologies present in the educational landscape, France et al. (2020) eulogized the increasing affordability of technologies such as tablets, phablets, and smartphones and how they have contributed to expanding education. The authors also touted how these technologies have expanded opportunities for greater equity for students with disabilities with particular interest on those with visual impairments.

Generally, technological innovations, including mobile technologies, are believed to make visually impaired people comfortable in their learning (Vornholt, et al., 2018). This assertion is derived from findings from previous research that mobile technologies can be employed as pedagogical and technological tools to develop learning environments for VIS and also support social inclusion (Maria Galdon et al., 2013; Parkin & Smithies, 2012). In addition, Tuttle and Carter (2022) taut the collaborative powers of technology between visually impaired students and their sighted colleagues.

Another benefit of mobile technologies is its compatibility with screen reading software for VIS. For example, Job Access with Speech (JAWS) and Dragon Speech Recognition, which are mostly used by VIS in Ghana, are both compatible with mobile technologies and can assist them in their learning (Darcy et al., 2016). Furthermore, Kamaghe et al. (2020) elucidated that touch screens, braille input applications, and audio-book readers add to the advantages mobile technologies present to SWVIs. They further suggested that mobile technologies have paved the way for cheaper ways of transmitting educational content and made learning flexible for SWVIs.

Despite the numerous advantages mobile technologies hold in terms of facilitating the learning of VIS, there are drawbacks that are worth noting. First, the confusion between accessibility and usability remains a key challenge, especially for VIS as educational institutions continue to provide access to digital gadgets without the concomitant training and re-skilling of such students and those who assist them (Agangiba & Agangiba, 2019). Besides, research has revealed that VIS in Ghana and Tanzania are often unable to access educational content or educational websites. In cases where such content is available, they are often not compatible with mobile devices used by these students which means they are unable to access valuable content (Amponsah, 2021; Amponsah & Bekele, 2022; Kamaghe et al., 2020). It is therefore unsurprising that Hersh (2014) called for more research on accessibility and usage of mobile technologies vis-à-vis the learning styles and needs of students with disabilities to better understand the challenges they face while learning in technology-mediated environments. Hersh made this call a decade ago, but it is still relevant today even in the face of abundance of technologies as VIS have not received the needed attention by the academic and scientific communities.

Moreover, SWVIs domiciled in LMICs such as Ghana are likely to face fundamental challenges related to technologies which include non-affordability of mobile technologies and the high cost of Internet usage which can at the same time be unreliable (Adarkwah, 2020; Muzata, 2020). As noted by Adarkwah (2020), such challenges reflect the geographical and digital divide within Ghana and other LMICs. Additionally, the COVID-19 pandemic further deepened these fissures as it emerged that some families could not afford simple radio sets and low-level phones (Kim, 2009; Mohammed, 2020) to be able to participate in virtual learning during the adverse time. Ampratwum et al. (2016) also identified general challenges such as the lack of digital skills and skilled professionals to support VIS as they study with mobile technologies.

From the foregoing, one can adduce that challenges with VIS learning with mobile technologies abound. It is in this light that Parker and Draves (2018) posit that the lack of technological devices has the propensity to turn impairments into disabilities. In Ghana and other low socio-economic environments, persons with disabilities are disadvantaged and those with visual impairments are more disadvantaged. To reverse this sad phenomenon and make education more equitable, Akcil (2018) advocates for extensive research into how visually impaired people adapt technologies for their personal and professional development. This study aligns with Ackil's passionate call as the authors have broken the grounds for further extensive studies to be undertaken in Ghana.

7.3 Constructing Participants' Experiences Through the TPACK Framework

Since Mishra and Koehler (2009) introduced the TPACK framework, it has been used to identify how teachers integrate the knowledge of pedagogy, technology, and content with the application of technological devices (Hsu et al., 2021; Koehler et al., 2012). The framework consists of three interrelated and primary forms of knowledge:

Content Knowledge (CK), Pedagogical Knowledge (PK), and Technology Knowledge (TK). The convergence of the three fundamental forms of knowledge delineates distinct types of knowledge, offering a comprehensive and enriched perspective on the framework. Thus, Pedagogical Content Knowledge (PCK), Technological Content Knowledge (TCK), and Technological Pedagogical Knowledge (TPK). At the heart of the intersection is Technological Pedagogical Content Knowledge (TPCK) (Jang & Tsai, 2013). The intersectionality of the elements of the framework makes it important and fitting to support an exploration of how VIS learn with mobile technologies in adverse contexts. As noted by Mailizar et al. (2021) and Mishra and Koehler (2006), the framework can effectively be applied to both prospective and experienced teachers while it can also be used to evaluate technology integration in the classroom.

To cater for the earlier deficiencies of the model, it was modified to reflect the dynamic integration of the three main components and capture the professional development of teachers in technology-mediated contexts (Tai et al., 2015; Thompson & Mishra, 2007). TPACK is thus defined as "the professional knowledge teachers require for the effective design and implementation of technology-enhanced (TE) instruction" (Yeh et al., 2021, p.3).

Expanding on the elements of the TPACK framework, Koehler and Mishra (2009) referred to CK as the knowledge of teachers in a specific subject concerning the content to be taught. It provides teachers with basic concepts, theories, and practices for teaching and learning. PK is regarded as the generic instructional knowledge teachers require to design an effective learning environment and domain-general instructional strategies needed to support students' learning (Lachner et al., 2021). The PK of teachers depicts their ability to identify and apply appropriate techniques for assisting VIS in learning course content in the classroom. These include general classroom assessment, lesson planning, and management skills as well as accommodating practices in general. TK is also operationalized as the professional knowledge of teachers regarding technologies such as digital devices and infrastructure (Wang, 2019). Acquiring TK helps teachers to accomplish an array of tasks relating to instructional technology. Teachers with expertise in this sphere, for example, have the potential efficacy to aid the VIS to learn more effectively and overcome challenges by the use of technology.

The application of TPACK calls into question how teachers can go beyond simply teaching with technology to focus on building the competencies they require to integrate technology in teaching a specific topic (Yeh et al., 2021). Thus, at the heart of TPACK, integrating technology is not merely an issue of what technology to use, but knowledge of the diverse ways in which technology can be used in every unique circumstance or context within the curriculum (Choi & Young, 2021). It is important to add that the application of digital technologies has been described as a "wicked problem" as teachers are required to reconfigure not only their perception of technology but also technology, content, and pedagogy (Brantley-Dias & Ertmer, 2013; Mishra & Koehler, 2008). Teaching with technology, therefore, demands more than technological knowledge (Mishra & Warr, 2021). The TPACK framework, thus provides researchers with a theoretical lens to understand the key competencies necessary to equip VIS with appropriate technologies (Choi & Young, 2021; Wang, 2019).

Given that the framework describes the type of knowledge required but may not specify how it is to be developed (Koehler et al., 2011), Mishra and Warr (2021) called for more research to better contextualize how it can be used in different educational cultures and systems. This stems from the recognition that the behavioural intention and actual use of technology is highly connected with teachers' positive attitudes towards technology (Hsu et al., 2021). This is also an indication that variables related to the technology usage of teachers (e.g. technology literacy and self-efficacy) are a direct reflection of their TPACK development (Durak, 2021; Yeh et al., 2021).

Moreover, Harris et al. (2009) indicated that the key knowledge structures teachers are typically required to possess in instructional technology are distinct dimensions in the TPACK framework. Thus, teachers can develop techniques that enable them to explore technology in rich settings that allow for a creative interplay of technology, content, and pedagogy (Koehler et al., 2011). In a qualitative study that examined teachers' use of TPACK, it was observed that prioritizing pedagogical content knowledge through teaching experiences was a prerequisite for successful technological integration (Pamuk, 2012). Also, a critical review of research on TPACK by Brantley-Dias and Ertmer (2013) revealed that technology-enabled learning is made possible by the combination of pedagogy, technology, and content.

Furthermore, TPACK has been identified as a valid model for explaining the online professional development of teachers (Mailizar et al., 2021). Applying this framework in Ghana, Agyei et al. (2015) found that pre-service teachers' competencies in educational technology increased as reflected in their positive attitudes towards technology. It is, therefore, not surprising that Wang (2019) concluded that implementing TPACK could help bridge tacit content knowledge, the practice of teaching, and the use of sufficient technological approaches together for effective learning. However, Lachner et al. (2021) cautioned that the effectiveness of the TPACK for teachers hinges on providing adequate support for them to develop technology-related professional knowledge.

This framework was chosen as the theoretical lens to guide this study because it effectively integrates several areas of knowledge (CK, PK, TK) in both theory and practice, and enables the kind of flexible learning required to effectively integrate technology into teaching (Koehler & Mishra, 2009; Koehler et al., 2011). In the context of this study, TPCK helped to explore how teachers were able to apply mobile technologies (TK) to deliver content (CK) at a distance (PK) to VIS during the challenging lockdown period in the first quarter of 2020. Second, its use is original in that despite its widespread application, it has not been routinely applied to specialized populations such as VIS in Ghana.

7.4 Methodology

7.4.1 Research Design

This study used the exploratory case study research design to investigate teachers' use of smartphones to teach VIS in adverse circumstances. Our choice of this design aligns with Yin's (2012) explanation that case studies are bounded by time and activity. Besides, the case study design enabled us to gain first-hand contextual in-depth understanding of the VIS experiences as they learned through mobile technology. We explored the experiences of the study participants in-depth using employed semi-structured interviews to elicit responses from them. To optimize the participation of the respondents, the lead researcher visited the study site ahead of the data collection phase to informally discuss the purpose of the study with gatekeepers. This was followed by an initial meeting held via video conference between the collaborators before the fieldwork commenced in April 2021.

7.4.2 Sampling

Due to the constraints imposed by the impact of the COVID-19 pandemic, this study purposively selected one special needs school in the Eastern Region of Ghana as it offered proximity to the Southern half of Ghana, though it admits students from every part of the country. Moreover, apart from the students in the selected school being visually impaired, some of the teachers also suffered the same impairments. This provided the researchers with an array of information-rich participants to contribute in-depth knowledge needed for this study. Initial interactions with the teachers at the beginning of this study in April 2021 indicated that they continued teaching during the pandemic lockdowns in the first quarter of 2020 to a limited extent. Our attempt to identify the digital infrastructure of the school indicated that the school provides Internet access, but this was not always reliable. It also has two computer laboratories, one has 30 functioning computers while the other has 20 non-functioning ones.

The criterion purposive sampling technique involving a few instances of chain sampling was adopted for this study. According to Patton (1990, p.176), "The logic of criterion sampling is to review and study all cases that meet some predetermined criterion of importance". In this study, participants were either teachers of visually impaired students or visually impaired students from a selected special school. In addition, the participants were deemed information-rich single cases who helped to identify issues pertinent to the phenomenon the study sought to explore. With the criteria spelled out, we purposively selected 20 out of the 37 teachers from the school. Three of these teachers were visually impaired. Out of the student population of 370, we selected 10 who either had low vision or total vision loss. This gave us a total sample of 30 for this study which is deemed adequate per Hennink and Kaiser's

Table 7.1 Title: Background information of participants

Students		Teachers
Dimension	Number	
Male	5	10
Female	5	10
Low vision	2	1
Total vision loss	8	2
Impaired since birth	6	2
Impaired since age 1	2	1
Impaired since age 9	2	0
No disability	0	17
Current level of learning/teaching	5 (Upper Primary)	15 (primary)
	5 (Junior High School)	5 (Junior High School)
Years of teaching	N/A	4 to 19 years

(2021) findings from a systematic review of sample size for qualitative research. Background information of the study participants is shown in Table 7.1.

7.5 Data Collection

Ethical clearance for the study was granted by the researchers' University Research Ethics Committee before embarking on the fieldwork. A semi-structured questionnaire was used to elicit responses from the study participants. This enabled the researchers to ask similar questions while following up with probes depending on responses offered by individual participants. We read the informed consent forms to each participant for them to agree and sign before each interview. The interviews with the study participants enabled the researchers to explore their views in-depth and included questions on their background, knowledge of their use mobile technologies for teaching and learning during the adverse circumstances presented by the COVID-19 pandemic, inclusivity, and their resilience strategies. All the interviews were conducted in English at the study site and lasted an average of 30 min. Each interview was audio recorded. Due to the dangers posed by COVID-19 during the interviews, all government protocols were strictly adhered to during the fieldwork.

7.6 Data Analysis

The open coding approach was analytical framework used to analyse the field data (Khandkar, 2009). Interview excerpts pertinent to the study were extracted and codes were assigned to them. We immersed ourselves in the data to define categories and were "opened" to new ideas from the process. Specifically, the line-by-line open coding method was used to build concepts and categories (Khandkar, 2009). When new concepts were not found, the coding of the interview data was halted. Examples of codes generated included ICT training (Information and Communication Technologies), e-learning experience, brailleNote, radio, audiobooks, laptops, phone calls, and WhatsApp. The codes guided us to create categories from which the main themes of the study were identified. A shared understanding and interpretation of the interview data among the research team was used to ensure the trustworthiness of the study's findings.

7.7 Findings

This study sought to explore how teachers at a special school in Ghana used mobile technologies to teach VIS during the adverse circumstances presented by the COVID-19 pandemic. After distilling findings from the field data, four themes emerged namely prior experiences with e-learning, mobile technologies for teaching and learning; inclusion and accommodation practices; and resilience in digital learning spaces. The findings from the interactions with the study participants are presented and discussed in the ensuing.

7.7.1 Prior Experiences with e-learning

The exploration of the participants' perspectives commenced with a need to ascertain their past experiences with e-learning. Though all the teachers used smartphones and other digital devices, it was interesting to note that only the ICT teacher had some prior knowledge of e-learning. This is evident as they kept confusing digital technologies with e-learning. The teachers' confusion is reflected in the statements that follow.

> *Throughout my school [pre-service] days nobody introduced me to e-learning, but I have been using the projector, computer and PowerPoint* [slides] *to teach my students which, to me, is e-learning.* (Teacher 3)

> *I used to have what we call the BrailleNote which could convert print into Braille. So, I was using the Pendrive to copy materials and print and then once I insert it into my BrailleNote, it automatically converts it into Braille for my students. That is how I used e-learning to assist my students prior to the COVID-19 outbreak.* (Teacher 4)

An exception to the confusion is offered by the ICT teacher who warmed himself to the phenomenon when he started teaching.

> *I did my degree in ICT so I had a good knowledge about educational technology but not much about e-learning until I started using social media to reach my students when I joined this school so I continued with that trend during the lockdown last year.* (Teacher 6)

The teachers' responses highlight gaps in the training he received and how he had prepared for the digital revolution culminated by the pandemic. Meanwhile, our attempt to determine the experiences of the VIS with e-learning prior to the lockdown revealed that they had been using laptops and desktop computers previously. This is of particular interest as most of these students are from rural and disadvantaged socio-economic backgrounds, which makes their experiences of learning with mobile technologies an interesting area to explore.

> *We used to go to the ICT lab for our ICT teacher to teach us how we can use the computer and the Internet.* **(Student 1)**

> *Before the lockdown, we used our friend's laptop to find information whenever our teachers gave us work* [assignments]. **(Student 6)**

> *I was fortunate to have a laptop, so I always used it for learning. Whenever the school Internet was available, I was able to search for information which I shared with my friends who did not have laptops.* **(Student 4)**

It is quite refreshing to know that the VIS had knowledge of how to use the computer. However, a critical challenge was how many students without access to these gadgets could engage in learning during the lockdown. Besides, the lack of digital skills on the part of the teachers compounded the challenge as the emergency period made remote learning the only option to continue with education. While such teachers could not engage the students effectively, the social distancing protocols prevented those without access to digital gadgets from studying at that epoch.

7.7.2 Mobile Technologies for Teaching and Learning

The crust of this study is to explore how the teachers deployed mobile technologies for teaching and how the VIS used same for learning purposes during the COVID-19-inspired lockdown. Kellems et al. (2022) assert that technology enables social engagements among special needs students. This became crucial during the adverse circumstances which is worth investigating. Ten of the 20 teachers accepted using mobile phones to organize lessons for their students during the period. Here are extracts of their reflections.

> *I used WhatsApp on my phone to interact with the students when they were at home. I usually sent instructions or questions to them. At times, I sent them text to read and, on few occasions, we did video calls to discuss content.* **(Teacher 14)**

Another teacher engaged students in similar ways except that he combined the use of TV and radio to get students to learn.

At times when they were home, I will call or send a WhatsApp message to inform them about TV programmes to watch or radio stations to listen to. We later discuss the content at an agreed time through WhatsApp. **(Teacher 4)**

Other teachers mentioned the use of conference calls for interaction and orally testing students to be sure they retained the content they have discussed previously. We sought the views of the students to compare with what their teachers had said. From the interviews, four students confirmed that their teachers did not use any digital technologies to reach them during the period, while the remaining confirmed their teachers corresponded with them via WhatsApp and phone calls.

They [teachers] *did not teach me until we came back to school after the lockdown and started classes. My friends who have phones say the teachers used to call them, but we* [family] *don't have a phone at home.* **(Student 5)**

A contrary view is shared by students who had or could access mobile phones during the period.

My mother left one of her phones for me when we were home, so I always got messages and assignments from the teachers. I even sent them messages on WhatsApp for assistance and they responded. **(Student 10)**

The teachers used to call me on my mother's phone when they wanted to teach us. They also left messages for us to listen to and things to read. **(Student 7)**

The ability of the teachers to creatively deploy mobile technology is evidence of their flexibility and adaptability in adverse circumstances. It is also laudable that students with access to mobile technologies cooperated with the teachers. The combined efforts demonstrate the ability of smartphones to promote learning across multiple contexts. However, it is unfortunate some of the VIS experienced learning loss during the entire period. Such a situation in this digital age is an invitation to all stakeholders in education to support these students to benefit fully from learning irrespective of prevailing circumstances.

7.7.3 Inclusion and Accommodation Practices

Without doubt, the use of mobile technologies has become ubiquitous and dominated conversations during the lockdown period. The literature also shows that mobile learning has enhanced self-study, enacted learning strategies, and awakened the search for new knowledge among both teachers and students (Razzaque, 2020). The above assertions were tested as the prevailing circumstances presented by the pandemic impelled them to innovate not only their teaching but also their ability to accommodate their students online. We explored their ability to do so, and their responses point to three key strategies, namely, WhatsApp conference calls, individual phone calls, and personal initiatives.

When the students went home during the lockdown, they organized themselves into groups, so we had some lessons using WhatsApp. This way, I was able to bring all those with phones on board, teach and assist them with their challenges. **(Teacher 18)**

We used to have conference calls to discuss different topics and assignments occasionally. Some of the students brought in personal issues along the line and I always tried to counsel them to the best of my ability. **(Teacher 12)**

One teacher added another layer of accommodation which was through third parties who acted as conduits for passing information to his students. This mainly involved parents.

Sometimes I sent information I wanted my students to get via WhatsApp. For those whose parents or families had only basic phones, I had to call and summarize the information for them. This was difficult as some of the parents did not even understand what I was communicating but I tried to always unpack the information to their level. **(Teacher 7)**

Two critical lessons can be learned from the teachers' accommodation strategies. First, they moved from people with minimal knowledge of e-learning to those whose pedagogical knowledge improved during the adverse period. Second, the propensity of mobile phones to build the competencies of teachers (Lachner et al., 2021) was brought to bear. However, while appreciating that teachers used mobile technologies to accommodate them, the VIS expressed the inadequacy of this type of innovation.

Things became difficult when we were home. The teachers called and left information with my mother, but she forgot to tell me when she returned home from work. What I did was to always use her phone to call my friends or teachers to see if I missed anything **(Student 3)**

Some teachers used to call my brother to give information that he should pass to me. Unfortunately, he mostly forgot exactly what the teachers wanted me to do. Sometimes, he gives me wrong times to join WhatsApp discussions, so I missed out. Later, I begun to go through his WhatsApp messages any time he was home to make sure I was not missing discussions. **(Student 10)**

A student combined both phone calls and WhatsApp messages to stay in touch with his peers and teachers.

For me, whenever someone with a phone came around, I would call my friends and teachers or send them WhatsApp messages to be sure I had not missed instructions or meetings. **(Student 6)**

The challenges the students faced resonate with the findings of Mohammed (2020) as he reported on the toll of the pandemic on households that could not afford basic technologies for learning during the pandemic, as well as the deficiencies in technology-enhanced learning environments in Africa. Despite the challenges, it is gratifying to note how technology has built the competencies of both teachers and students during difficult times. The strategies teachers used to accommodate the VIS and how the latter also cooperated is worth acknowledging. The information flow engineered by the teachers proves the effectiveness of mobile technologies as tools for online learning.

7.7.4 Resilience in Digital Learning Spaces

Finally, our attempt to explore the resilience strategies of the study participants in digital learning spaces elicited varied strategies from the two cohorts of participants. It was discovered that while the teachers resorted to Internet, intergenerational learning and bought data out of their pockets, the students depended on family and friends to cope with the situation. This is what a teacher had to say regarding the reliance on the Internet as a tool for resilience.

> *With the COVID*[-19] *restrictions, if maybe you want to teach a concept, and the textbooks are not available, we had to go to the digital space, which is the Internet on our phones to get the necessary information to deliver our lessons. By doing this, we reduced the stress that one would have for not getting the needed information from the library or a colleague.* **(Teacher 1)**

Another teacher disclosed how she took advantage of online ICT classes to prepare herself for online engagements while another disclosed how they had to spend their funds on data in order to teach their students.

> *When the ICT teacher was teaching online, I went there with my iPad and tried to learn certain strategies whereby I can use to teach or help my students too later. This enlightened me and I can now teach online with stress now. (Respondent B)*

> *Because our Internet is not stable and we didn't have the necessary gadgets, we managed with our android phones and bought data on our own. This affected our finances, but it was a joy to get our students to learn during those difficult and stressful time.* **(Teacher Respondent 5)**

The preceding has highlighted the key resilience strategies adopted by the teachers in this study. To add more depth to that, we share the views of the VIS whose responses revolved around reliance on family and friends to provide the necessary support.

> *When our teachers gave us assignments to search for information. Because I don't have a laptop or phone, I always went to friends who stayed close to our house to use their laptops or get help* [from them]. **(Student 4)**

> *Because we don't have a phone at home, sometimes we had to go to the next house to use our friends' parents phones to call our teachers or join video calls. Sometimes their parents will help us look for information on their laptops.* **(Student 9)**

> *When my mother came home in the evenings, I would use her phone to call my mates to check if our teachers had sent us information to learn or assignments to do.* **(Student 7)**

The above responses from the VIS demonstrate the importance of cultivating reliable social networks outside of formal educational support structures and services, especially in challenging periods such as presented by the COVID-19 pandemic.

7.8 Discussion

7.8.1 *How Do Teachers Accommodate Visually Impaired Students When They Use Mobile Technologies as Tools for Teaching?*

Findings suggest that teachers used a variety of strategies to support the VIS, but they sometimes misunderstood and mistakenly confused digital technologies with e-learning. Critical cases related to the use of PowerPoint presentations and BrailleNote which underscored the inadequacy of their pedagogical and technological knowledge (Mishra & Koehler, 2009). This makes online learning ineffective at the study site and amplifies why VIS have been marginalized in training relating to online learning (Adarkwah, 2021; Amponsah, 2021). On the other hand, the VIS had superior prior knowledge of e-learning but the lack of access to mobile technologies during the adverse times rendered their digital learning rather ineffective and difficult.

A second area relates to the notion that there are mostly disparities between the values and skills of teachers of disabled learners (Kamaghe et al., 2020; Reddy et al., 2022). Furthermore, this exposed the deficits in the TPACK of the teachers and identified the need for measures to mitigate such deficiencies through CPD and other forms of in-service training.

Through the use of audiobooks and radios prior to the lockdown, the teachers had garnered some integrative knowledge of the application of technological devices in their profession (Akcil, 2018; Koehler & Mishra, 2009). This was instrumental in their ability to switch to smartphones to promote learning across multiple contexts during the adverse period (Crompton, 2013; Merchant, 2012). Moreover, the ability of the teachers to creatively deploy digital devices in their distance teaching and the ability of the students to cooperate with them in that front was also evidence of their flexibility and ability to use them in unique and difficult circumstances during the lockdown period (Choi & Young, 2021; Reddy et al., 2022). This is also a testament of the benefits of acquiring the elements of the TPACK framework (Koehler et al., 2012) and deploying such during emergency remote teaching and learning.

7.8.2 *What Resilience Strategies Do Teachers and Visually Impaired Students Adopt When They Use Mobile Technologies for Learning in Adverse Contexts?*

The UNESCO 2030 agenda, particularly Sustainable Development Goal (SDG) 4, seeks to ensure quality and accessible education for all persons. In this light, the study sought to understand views of the participants regarding how the teachers accommodated the VIS during virtual class sessions. The picture portrayed by the students contrasts their conventional classrooms. This was mainly due to the challenges both teachers and students faced as they learned via mobile technologies. While there were several key factors influencing this contrast, the primary reason was the lack of technological skill (Koehler et al., 2012; Muzata, 2020) among the teachers to instruct online.

The data from the students underlined how their teachers were mostly forced to call their relatives and members of their external support networks to leave information concerning their lessons. Though the teachers did their best under the circumstances to use mobile technologies to preserve learning, information was sometimes lost by the time the relatives returned home to deliver such valuable information to the students. Such challenges posed by the lack of digital tools amplified the difficulties created by the lack of access to mobile technologies for learning (Mohammed, 2020; Parker & Draves, 2018). The VIS would have had seamless learning sessions if they had their own gadgets. It is, however, important to note that the students expressed satisfaction with how some of their teachers used WhatsApp to hold lessons with them. Based on the commitment of the teachers, they were able to display all the forms of knowledge encapsulated in the TPACK framework, which was highly beneficial for learning in adverse circumstances such as the COVID-19 pandemic.

The above analysis demonstrates a mix of experiences from the students. Their responses concerning their resilience while studying during the lockdown were not very encouraging given their circumstances and general challenges surrounding emergency learning. The students mentioned reliance on friends and family to use the other party's digital devices. The responses from the students point to the continued existence of a digital divide in terms of institutional support and highlight how they often felt marginalized during the pandemic (Amponsah, 2023; Parker & Draves, 2018). Regrettably, this is a period when the VIS were in dire need of on-site assistance for their learning. This study, therefore, is an invitation to all concerned to see the urgency of supporting such students at all times but most especially during emergency situations.

7.9 Conclusion

This study has explored the experiences of teachers who adopted mobile technologies to teach VIS under difficult circumstances in Ghana. It also explored the resilience strategies used by both teachers and VIS during such times. The originality of the research is multi-layered. First, studies on the participant cohorts in online learning remain an uncharted ground for researchers in Ghana. Secondly, the use of the TPACK framework helped to expose the forms of knowledge that teachers need to effectively integrate mobile technologies into their teaching of special needs learners. Furthermore, the requirement to effectively leverage mobile learning in special schools and for SWVIs is long overdue and this study has theoretically and practically demonstrated that this type of flexible learning can be realized if it is given institutional attention and support.

Furthermore, the analysis of the field data revealed that the teachers had some knowledge of how to use mobile technologies for education but were oblivious to a more nuanced view of digital pedagogy. This was elucidated when some teachers equated the use of audiobooks and BrailleNote to e-learning. The findings, therefore, suggest that a more effective form of pre-service and in-service professional development is necessary for such teachers in the area of digital pedagogy.

The VIS were fortunate to have been introduced to ICT at their computer laboratory or either used their own or their friends' laptops prior to the advent of the pandemic. Unfortunately, those who did not own such devices were often excluded from learning during the lockdown. Like the teachers, the students had some fundamental knowledge of digital technologies, but this did not suffice for adequate levels of TK needed for effective teaching and learning at a distance during COVID-19. This calls for investments in time, finances, and infrastructure to help re-skill the VIS for digitized learning environments.

Moreover, the findings suggest that while the use of mobile phones for educational purposes was a novelty during the adverse period, it also posed challenges as many of the students did not own or have access to even simple phones. The consequence is that only teachers and students who could access digital devices displayed a good level of TK in the sense that they were able to adopt the tools under precarious conditions to continue learning.

The commitment of both teachers and VIS summarizes their resilience strategies during the difficult challenges they faced. The teachers did not only display high levels of both TK and CK, but they also went the extra mile to acquire the needed content to share with their students through phone calls and WhatsApp conference meetings. This epitomizes TPCK, which lies at the heart of the TPACK framework for teachers not only to be acquainted with the knowledge to teach but also to learn how to incorporate appropriate technologies into their teaching. Doing so in adverse circumstances meant teachers needed to be tactful so their students would feel included in their first attempts to learn online. Nonetheless, the digital divide made it impossible for the teachers to serve all their students equally as some could either not access mobile technologies at all or did so at the wrong time.

Finally, the teachers expended their own finances on data due to their school's unstable Internet connectivity while some engaged in intergenerational learning to acquire digital literacy skills needed to be effective online teachers. In effect, one needs to appreciate an assertion by Stringer et al. (2023) that twenty-first-century classrooms will continue to change so teachers need to be more conversant in the use of digital technologies to be able to enhance their chances of performing their roles optimally in line with SDG 4c of the UN agenda 2030. The students, on the other hand, basically relied on family and social networks to access mobile phones so they could join WhatsApp class sessions or obtain information from their teachers. In this case, we can only speculate what happened to the VIS who did not have the economic and cultural capital to access digital devices to facilitate their learning which would be a topic for future studies.

7.9.1 *Implications*

The findings of this study have several significant implications in terms of new knowledge for the field of SEND in Ghana generally and particularly at the study setting. Policy-wise, pre-service training of prospective teachers should incorporate aspects of e-learning and detailed descriptions of convivial technologies that could benefit and enhance the learning of special needs students. The government of Ghana and other stakeholders should provide IT infrastructure to schools while basic digital devices are provided to both teachers and SWVIs. Moreover, policies on inclusion and accommodation should be enforced and online professional training should be mandatory, timely, and dependent on a systematic needs assessment of teachers and schools.

In terms of practice, teachers and school authorities should invest more efforts to ensure that teachers are abreast of developments in digital technology and are using appropriate pedagogical standards both in the physical and online teaching spaces. In the absence of a school learning management system, ICT teachers and other tech-savvy teachers could serve as ambassadors to train, mentor and encourage their counterparts to incorporate simple social media tools to sustain teaching and learning in times of emergency. Overall, this calls for management, teachers and students to be exposed to the elements of the TPACK framework as a tool for evaluating their pedagogical approaches.

7.10 Data Availability Statement

Data for this study is available upon reasonable request from the lead researcher.

References

Adarkwah, M. A. (2020). "I'm not against online teaching, but what about us?": ICT in Ghana post Covid-19. *Education and Information Technologies*, 1–21. https://doi.org/10.1007/s10639-020-10331-z

Adarkwah, M. A. (2021). An outbreak of online learning in the COVID-19 outbreak in Sub-Saharan Africa: Prospects and challenges. *Global Journal of Computer Science and Technology, 21*(2), 1–11.

Adarkwah, M. A., Amponsah, S., Mekonen, Y. K., & Agyemang, E. P. (2021). Exploring mobile technologies as mitigating tools for online learning crisis. In *NOMSA21 open up and connect: Education in a digital era conference* (p. 166).

Agangiba, M., & Agangiba, W. A. (2019). Evaluation of accessibility for the visually impaired-the case of higher education institutions' websites in Ghana. *Ghana Journal of Technology, 3*(2), 58–64.

Agyei, D. D., & Voogt, J. M. (2015). Pre-service teachers' TPACK competencies for spreadsheet integration: Insights from a mathematics-specific instructional technology course. *Technology, Pedagogy and Education, 24*(5), 605–625. https://doi.org/10.1080/1475939X.2015.1096822

Akcil, U. (2018). The use of mobile learning for visually impaired learners school in tolerance education contents. *Quality & Quantity, 52*(2), 969–982. https://doi.org/10.1007/s11135-017-0552-1

Amponsah, S. (2023). The 'shadow pandemic' in online learning: Perspectives of visually impaired students from Ghana and Egypt. *Disability & Society*. https://doi.org/10.1080/09687599.2023.2279934

Amponsah, S., & Bekele, T. A. (2022). Exploring strategies for including visually impaired students in online learning. *Education and Information Technologies*. 1–23.https://doi.org/10.1007/s10639-022-11145-x

Amponsah, S. (2021). Echoing the voices of SWVIs under COVID-19 inspired online learning. *Education and Information Technologies, 26*, 6607–6627. https://doi.org/10.1007/s10639-021-10479-2

Ampratwum, J., Offei, Y. N., & Ntoaduro, A. (2016). Barriers to the use of computer assistive technology among students with visual impairment in Ghana: The case of Akropong school for the blind. *Journal of Education and Practice, 7*(29), 58–61.

Armah, P. (2016). *Teacher professional learning in Ghana: Promoting standards, enhancing professionalism* (Policy Brief). VIAM Africa Centre for Education and Social Policy. https://www.academia.edu/20446885/Teacher_Professional_Learning_in_Ghana_Promoting_standards_enhancing_professionalism?auto=download

Bates, T. (2020). *Crashing into online learning: A report from five continents – and some conclusions.* https://www.tonybates.ca/2020/04/26/crashing-into-online-learning-a-report-from-five-continents-and-some-conclusions/.

Blas, N. D., Paolini, P., Sawaya, S., & Mishra, P. (2014). *Distributed TPACK: Going beyond knowledge in the head*. 2464–2472. https://www.learntechlib.org/primary/p/131154/

Brantley-Dias, L., & Ertmer, P. A. (2013). Goldilocks and TPACK. *Journal of Research on Technology in Education, 46*(2), 103–128. https://doi.org/10.1080/15391523.2013.10782615

Buckner, E., & Kim, P. (2012). Mobile innovations, executive functions, and educational developments in conflict zones: A case study from Palestine. *Educational Technology Research and Development, 60*(1), 175–192.

Choi, B., & Young, M. F. (2021). TPACK-L: Teachers' pedagogical design thinking for the wise integration of technology. *Technology, Pedagogy and Education, 30*(2), 217–234. https://doi.org/10.1080/1475939X.2021.1906312

Churchill, N. (2020). Development of students' digital literacy skills through digital storytelling with mobile devices. *Educational Media International, 57*(3), 271–284.

Corbin, J., & Strauss, A. (2014). *Basics of qualitative research: Techniques and procedures for developing grounded theory*. Sage publications.

Crompton, H. (2013). A historical overview of mobile learning: Toward learner-centered education. In Z. L. Berge & L. Y. Muilenburg (Eds.), *Handbook of mobile learning* (pp. 3–14). Routledge.

Darcy, S., Taylor, T., & Green, J. (2016). 'But I can do the job': Examining disability employment practice through human rights complaint cases. *Disability & Society, 31*(9), 242–1274. https://doi.org/10.1080/09687599.2016.1256807

Durak, H. Y. (2021). Modeling of relations between K-12 teachers' TPACK levels and their technology integration self-efficacy, technology literacy levels, attitudes toward technology and usage objectives of social networks. *Interactive Learning Environments, 29*(7), 1136–1162. https://doi.org/10.1080/10494820.2019.1619591

France, D., Lee, R., Maclachlan, J., & McPhee, S. R. (2021). Should you be using mobile technologies in teaching? Applying a pedagogical framework. *Journal of Geography in Higher Education, 45*(2), 221–237.

Harris, J., Mishra, P., & Koehler, M. (2009). Teachers' technological pedagogical content knowledge and learning activity types. *Journal of Research on Technology in Education, 41*(4), 393–416. https://doi.org/10.1080/15391523.2009.10782536

Hennink, M., & Kaiser, B. N. (2021). Sample size for saturation in qualitative research: A systematic review of empirical tests. *Social Science & Medicine, 292*. https://doi.org/10.1016/j.socscimed.2021.114523

Hersh, M. (2014). Evaluation framework for ICT-based learning technologies for disabled people. *Computers & Education, 78*, 30–47. https://doi.org/10.1016/j.compedu.2014.05.001

Hsu, C.-Y., Liang, J.-C., Chuang, T.-Y., Chai, C. S., & Tsai, C.-C. (2021). Probing in-service elementary school teachers' perceptions of TPACK for games, attitudes towards games, and actual teaching usage: A study of their structural models and teaching experiences. *Educational Studies, 47*(6), 734–750. https://doi.org/10.1080/03055698.2020.1729099

Jang, S.-J., & Tsai, M.-F. (2013). Exploring the TPACK of Taiwanese secondary school science teachers using a new contextualized TPACK model. *Australasian Journal of Educational Technology, 29*(4), Article 4. https://doi.org/10.14742/ajet.282

Kamaghe, J. S., Luhanga, E. T., & Michael, K. (2020). The challenges of adopting M-learning assistive technologies for visually impaired learners in higher learning institutions in Tanzania. *International Journal of Emerging Technologies in Learning*. https://doi.org/10.3991/ijet.v15i01.11453

Kellems, R. O., Charlton, C. T., Black, B., Bussey, H., Ferguson, R., Gonçalves, B. F., Jensen, M., & Vallejo, S. (2022). Social engagement of elementary-aged children with Autism live animation avatar versus human interaction. *Journal of Special Education Technology, 38*(3) https://doi.org/10.1177/01626434221094792.

Kim, P. H. (2009). Action research approach on mobile learning design for the underserved. *Educational Technology Research and Development, 57*(3), 415–435.

Khandkar, S. (2009). *Open coding*. University of Calgary. https://pages.cpsc.ucalgary.ca/~saul/wiki/uploads/CPSC681/open-coding.pdf

Koehler, M. J., Shin, T. S., & Mishra, P. (2012). *How do we measure TPACK? Let me count the ways* [Chapter]. Educational Technology, Teacher Knowledge, and Classroom Impact: A Research Handbook on Frameworks and Approaches; IGI Global. https://doi.org/10.4018/978-1-60960-750-0.ch002

Koehler, M., & Mishra, P. (2009). What is technological pedagogical content knowledge (TPACK)? *Contemporary Issues in Technology and Teacher Education, 9*(1), 60–70.

Koehler, M. J., Mishra, P., Bouck, E. C., DeSchryver, M., Kereluik, K., Shin, T. S., & Wolf, L. G. (2011). Deep-play: Developing TPACK for 21st century teachers. *International Journal of Learning Technology, 6*(2), 146–163. https://doi.org/10.1504/IJLT.2011.042646

Krippendorff, K. (2018). *Content analysis: An introduction to its methodology* (4th ed.). Sage.

Kwarteng, M. A., Mashige, K. P., Naidoo, K. S., Boadi-Kusi, S. B., & Govender-Poonsamy, P. (2021). The prevalence and causes of low vision and blindness amongst learners at the Akropong School for the Blind in Ghana. *African Vision and Eye Health, 80*(1), 7.

Lachner, A., Fabian, A., Franke, U., Preiß, J., Jacob, L., Führer, C., Küchler, U., Paravicini, W., Randler, C., & Thomas, P. (2021). Fostering pre-service teachers' technological pedagogical content knowledge (TPACK): A quasi-experimental field study. *Computers & Education, 174*, Article 104304. https://doi.org/10.1016/j.compedu.2021.104304

Laurillard, D. (2007). Pedagogical forms for mobile learning: Framing research questions. In N. Pachler (Ed.), *Mobile learning: Towards a research agenda* (pp. 153–175). W1.E Centre.

Mailizar, M., Hidayat, M., & Al-Manthari, A. (2021). Examining the impact of mathematics teachers' TPACK on their acceptance of online professional development. *Journal of Digital Learning in Teacher Education, 37*(3), 196–212. https://doi.org/10.1080/21532974.2021.1934613

Maria Galdon, P., Ignacio Madrid, R., De La Rubia-Cuestas, E. J., Diaz-Estrella, A., & Gonzalez, L. (2013). Enhancing mobile phones for people with visual impairments through haptic icons: The effect of learning processes. *Assistive Technology, 25*(2), 80–87.

Merchant, G. (2012). Mobile practices in everyday life: Popular digital technologies and schooling revisited. *British Journal of Educational Technology, 43*(5), 770–782.

Mishra, P., & Koehler, M. (2008). Introducing technological pedagogical content knowledge. *Teachers College Record, 9.*

Mishra, P., & Koehler, M. J. (2006). Technological pedagogical content knowledge: A framework for teacher knowledge. *Teachers College Record, 108*(6), 1017–1054. https://doi.org/10.1111/j.1467-9620.2006.00684.x

Mishra, P., & Warr, M. (2021). Contextualizing TPACK within systems and cultures of practice. *Computers in Human Behavior*, *117*(106673). https://doi.org/10.1016/j.chb.2020.106673

Mohammed, W. F. (2020). What COVID-19 reveals about educational inequality in Ghana. Retrieved from https://www.aljazeera.com/indepth/features/covid-19-reveals-educational-inequality-ghana-200407100729985.html

Muzata, K. K. (2020). The utilisation of computers to improve the quality of learning for students with visual impairment at the University of Zambia. *Zambia Journal of Library & Information Science (ZAJLIS), ISSN: 2708-2695, 4*(2), 34–44.

Omondi, G. (2020, February 11). The state of mobile in Ghana's tech ecosystem. Retrieved from https://www.gsma.com/mobilefordevelopment/blog/the-state-of-mobile-in-ghanas-tech-ecosystem/

Pamuk, S. (2012). Understanding preservice teachers' technology use through TPACK framework. *Journal of Computer Assisted Learning, 28*(5), 425–439. https://doi.org/10.1111/j.1365-2729.2011.00447.x

Parker, E. C., & Draves, T. J. (2018). Tensions and perplexities within teacher education and P–12 schools for music teachers with visual impairments. *Arts Education Policy Review, 119*(1), 42–52. https://doi.org/10.1080/10632913.2016.1201028

Parkin, J., & Smithies, N. (2012). Accounting for the needs of blind and visually impaired people in public realm design. *Journal of Urban Design, 17*(1), 135–149.

Patton, M. (1990). *Qualitative evaluation and research methods* (pp. 169–186). Sage.

Razzaque, A. (2020). M-learning improves knowledge sharing over e-Learning platforms to build higher education students' social capital. *SAGE Open*, 1–9. https://doi.org/10.1177/2158244020926575

Reddy, E., Reddy, P., Sharma, B., Reddy, K., & Khan, M. G. M. (2022). Readiness and perception of Pacific students use of mobile phones for higher education. *Technology, Knowledge and Learning*. https://doi.org/10.1007/s10758-022-09595-w

Reeves, P. M., & Sperling, R. A. (2015). A comparison of technologically mediated and face-to-face help-seeking sources. *British Journal of Educational Psychology, 85*(4), 570–584.

Savage, G. (2018). *Continuing professional development: Past, present and future*. Findcourses.co.uk. https://www.findcourses.co.uk/inspiration/hr-learning-development-articles/continuing-professional-development-cpd-certification-service-9329

Senadza, B., Ayerakwa, M. A., Mill, A. A., Oppong, C. A. & Asare, G. (June 2019). *Inclusive education: Learners with disabilities and special education needs in Ghana* (Research Report). Research Trust Limited.

Sheng, H., Siau, K., & Nah, F. F. H. (2010). Understanding the values of mobile technology in education: A value-focused thinking approach. *ACM SIGMIS Database: The DATABASE for Advances in Information Systems, 41*(2), 25–44.

Tai, H.-C., Pan, M.-Y., & Lee, B.-O. (2015). Applying technological pedagogical and content knowledge (TPACK) model to develop an online English writing course for nursing students. *Nurse Education Today, 35*(6), 782–788. https://doi.org/10.1016/j.nedt.2015.02.016

Thompson, A. D., & Mishra, P. (2007). Editors' Remarks. *Journal of Computing in Teacher Education, 24*(2), 38–64. https://doi.org/10.1080/10402454.2007.10784583

Torff, B., & Sessions, D. (2009). Teachers' attitudes about professional development in high-SES and low-SES communities. *Learning Inquiry, 3*(2), 67–77.

Tuttle, M., & Carter, E. W. (2022). Systematic review of studies addressing computer-assisted instruction for students with visual impairment. *Journal of Special Education Technology, 38*(3) https://doi.org/10.1177/01626434221088026.

UNESCO. (2020). *Adverse consequences of school closures*. UNESCO.

United Nations (2016). Final list of proposed Sustainable Development Goal indicators. Report of the Inter-Agency and Expert Group on Sustainable Development Goal Indicators (E/CN.3/2016/2/Rev.1). https://sustainabledevelopment.un.org/content/documents/11803Official-List-of-Proposed-SDG-Indicators.pdf

Vornholt, K., Villotti, P., Muschalla, B., Bauer, J., Adrienne, C., Zijlstra, F., Uitdewilligen, S., Marc, C. (2018). Disability and employment – overview and highlights. *European Journal of Work and Organizational Psychology, 27*(1), 40–55.https://doi.org/10.1080/1359432X.2017.1387536

Wang, C.-J. (2019). Facilitating the emotional intelligence development of students: Use of technological pedagogical content knowledge (TPACK). *Journal of Hospitality, Leisure, Sport & Tourism Education.* https://doi.org/10.1016/J.JHLSTE.2019.100198

Yeh, Y.-F., Chan, K. K. H., & Hsu, Y.-S. (2021). Toward a framework that connects individual TPACK and collective TPACK: A systematic review of TPACK studies investigating teacher collaborative discourse in the learning by design process. *Computers & Education, 171*, Article 104238. https://doi.org/10.1016/j.compedu.2021.104238

Yin, R. K. (2012). *Applications of case study research* (3rd ed.). Sage.

Chapter 8
Teacher Educators' Perceptions, Readiness, and Use of Generative AI in Enhancing Learning in Universities

Jimmy E. Kihwele, Michael W. Nicodemus, and Solomon T. Jember

Abstract Universities worldwide are encouraged to embrace Artificial Intelligence (AI) in their core functions despite its potential threats. There are debates globally on how to integrate AI decently in universities after the situation proves its inevitability to accommodate AI in learning activities in the technological revolution era. This study explored teacher educators' perceptions, readiness, and the use of generative AI (GenAI). It focused on teacher educators' perceptions of GenAI and their use and control of students' unethical use. A study employed a case study design with 21 teacher educators from Dire Dawa and Mzumbe Universities who participated in interviews. The findings indicate that teacher educators perceive GenAI as a critical and inevitable technological application that requires proper mechanisms to curb indecent use and pose a threat to developing twenty-first-century competencies. Although most teacher educators admit to using GenAI, few use it for teaching purposes, and some do not due to a lack of proper control mechanisms, as they acknowledge the difficulty in identifying students' work written by GenAI. Therefore, universities should capacitate teacher educators and students by devising appropriate guidelines to safeguard the integration of GenAI that diminish the possible threats to enhancing the training of competent, innovative, and employable graduates.

Keywords Teacher educators · Perceptions · Readiness · Generative AI · Tanzania · Ethiopia

---

J. E. Kihwele (✉)
Department of Education and Teaching, Faculty of Social Sciences, Mzumbe University, Morogoro, Tanzania
e-mail: jimmy.kihwele@mu.ac.tz

M. W. Nicodemus · S. T. Jember
Department of Education, College of Social Sciences and Humanities, Dire Dawa University, Dire Dawa, Ethiopia
e-mail: michael.nicodemus@mu.ac.tz

S. T. Jember
e-mail: solomontadele7@gmail.com

M. A. Adarkwah et al. (eds.), *Artificial Intelligence and Human Agency in Education: Volume One*, Future Education and Learning Spaces,
https://doi.org/10.1007/978-981-96-7937-9_8

8.1 Introduction

Despite the perceived threats of Artificial Intelligence (AI) in promoting academic dishonesty, it remains an inevitable technological application in teaching and learning in higher learning institutions (Mohebi, 2024). A simple definition of AI is "a technology that enables machines to imitate various complex human skills" (Sheikh et al. 2023). AI proliferation has ignited a heated debate in academic institutions about whether to integrate them into teaching or ban them. AI has divided teacher educators; others have accepted AI, and some reject it, which has led to its prohibition (Ghafar, 2023). This necessitates an investigation of perceptions, readiness, and use of AI among teacher educators in developing countries where studies indicate low adoption rates (Ezumah, 2020).

Technology companies have advanced their innovations to create AI capable of creating new content such as PPT for presentation, text, audio, pictures, and videos that educators and students can use in teaching and learning (Kalota, 2024). This study refers to these as Generative AI (AI). GenAI emerged in the 1950s but gained momentum in the 2020s when technology companies launched more AI applications with different purposes and uses (Mamo et al., 2024). The propagation of GenAI has brought colossal benefits in enhancing improved teaching and learning in universities. AI assists learners with immediate feedback, promotes personalised learning, enhances language learning through translation, and provides actual scenarios and examples for knowledge construction (Nguyen, 2024; Ghafar, 2023).

Conversely, scholars perceive the spread of AI as a threat to quality education. The threats include unreliability of information, lack of proper citations, plagiarism and academic dishonesty, and lack of technical skills (Kohnke et al., 2023; Meniado, 2023). Again, AI impairs creativity and critical thinking in learning, jeopardising the quality of employable graduates trained (Das & JV, 2024). Another challenge of AI is its failure to interpret social and cultural contexts, which might affect knowledge construction and application in real-life situations (Kohnke, 2023). In light of this context, some academic institutions prohibit using it because of its potential threats to educational activities (Ghafar, 2023). Despite the challenges, possible threats, and prohibition of AI in education for academic activities, AI has proved to be an inevitable technological tool due to its quick spread and penetration. University instructors and students must embrace it as a new normal to enhance teaching and learning but with a calculated mechanism of controlling potential threats that impede quality and equality in learning (Rathore & Dangi, 2021).

8.2 Statement of the Problem

Despite the proliferation and inevitability of AI, specifically GenAI, in the education context, various universities and teacher educators have mixed perceptions that influence their practices (Das & JV, 2024; Meniado, 2023; Amani et al., 2023; Ghafar,

2023). Mixed perceptions have left some institutions enacting laws prohibiting GenAI and teacher educators discouraging students from using AI. However, scholars believe that AI in education should be accommodated as a "new normal", implying that it should be accepted and integrated into teaching and learning (Rathore & Dangi, 2021). Given the situation, it is imperative to study teacher educators' perceptions, readiness, and use of GenAI to enhance university learning. Specifically, the study focused on the following questions.

What are teacher educators' perceptions of using GenAI to facilitate learning?

How do teacher educators use GenAI to facilitate learning?

What mechanisms do teacher educators use to control students' unethical use of GenAI?

8.3 Literature Review

Artificial Intelligence is revolutionising education through personalised learning platforms, automated grading, and facial recognition for student behaviour analysis (Akgun & Greenhow, 2022). GenAI is an advanced form of Artificial Intelligence that autonomously creates content in response to natural language requests via conversational interfaces, unlike traditional methods that curate content from existing sources (Rashid et al., 2024). It generates outputs based on its inputs and deep data understanding acquired through training, enabling it to identify patterns and structures in data (Cao et al., 2023). This AI encompasses various techniques and models designed to create unique, human-like content across multiple media formats, including text, images, audio, video, music, and software codes (Cao et al., 2023; Yusuf et al., 2024). Often employing unsupervised learning methods, these models independently interpret vast amounts of data, resulting in coherent and contextually relevant outputs. Text GenAI uses a type of artificial neural network (ANN) known as a general-purpose transformer, commonly referred to as a Large Language Model (LLM) due to its extensive language capabilities (Rashid et al., 2024). A specific type of LLM used in text generation, such as ChatGPT, is called a generative pre-trained transformer (GPT). ChatGPT, based on GPT-4 developed by OpenAI, shows significant improvements over earlier versions due to enhanced AI architectures and manipulated training methods (Humble & Mozelius, 2019; Murphy, 2019). These advancements make GPT-4 more capable and accurate in text generation, reflecting OpenAI's commitment to advancing AI technology.

Chatbots that mimic natural language conversations for text or voice interaction are increasingly used in education (Yetisensoy & Karaduman, 2024). These AI chatbots enhance the educational experience by adapting to the needs of both teachers and learners, providing personalised tutoring, homework support, concept learning, test preparation, and fostering discussion and collaboration (Bii et al., 2018; Yetisensoy & Karaduman, 2024). Teachers play a crucial role in introducing AI concepts (Ayanwale et al., 2022), while chatbots gain popularity as language learning assistants due to their conversational abilities (Huang et al., 2022). Effective AI integration in education requires collaboration among teachers, researchers, and policymakers (Owolabi et al., 2022). Despite demonstrating significant improvements in learning outcomes (Deng & Yu, 2023), chatbot technology faces challenges, including ethical issues, user attitudes, user training, technological limitations, and the need for proper supervision and maintenance (Okonkwo & Ade-Ibijola, 2021; Pérez et al., 2020; Deng & Yu, 2023). This study's major focus is on GenAI tools, especially chatbots, which are commonly used for learning practices in conducting assignment questions, note preparation, and self-learning.

8.3.1 Teacher Educators' Perceptions of the Use of GenAI

Artificial Intelligence could significantly impact higher education by providing AI assistants, intelligent tutoring systems, and tools for managing student teaching (Crompton & Burke, 2023). This implies that AI could deliver personalised support, guide students through coursework and assessments, and help educators oversee student progress (Rashid et al., 2024; Chan, 2023; Mello et al., 2023). According to Igbokwe (2023) and Karan and Angadi (2024), AI in education offers benefits beyond personalised learning and automated tasks, such as streamlining administrative duties like scheduling, grading, refining teaching strategies, addressing curriculum weaknesses, and managing resources, thereby freeing up educators' time. GenAI can also create intelligent content creation tools, enabling the development of new and adaptable educational materials. AI tools have the potential to positively influence teaching, enhance academic outcomes, and support educators in improving student performance. For example, in Mathematics, teachers view GenAI as a valuable educational tool that can enhance teaching and student performance (Basilo, 2023; Wardat et al., 2024). Educators believe GenAI systems and applications can boost student motivation and engagement by introducing elements of challenge and competition (Mello et al., 2023). Integrating GenAI into higher education could transform teaching and learning approaches, offering personalised learning experiences and 24/7 assistance. Educators recognise the value of AI-based scaffolding in improving students' writing abilities and problem-solving skills, highlighting the importance of individualised support (Doo et al., 2020). GenAI can effectively scaffold writing tasks, providing personalised feedback that enhances students' logical thinking and problem-solving abilities. Embracing GenAI in these ways can improve educational processes, making institutions more efficient, and students can be better prepared for the demands of the modern world.

The acceptance or rejection of AI tools in education largely depends on educators' attitudes. Instructors with favourable views of AI are more likely to integrate it into their teaching, positively influencing students' perceptions and engagement (Ghimire & Edwards, 2024; Bii et al., 2018). Neutral or untrained educators on AI tend to develop a positive attitude after training (Moura & Carvalho, 2024). Opinions on AI's role vary; some see it as a valuable, tailored resource, while others express concerns (Uygun, 2024). Positive perceptions correlate with more significant AI usage, suggesting a shift towards embracing AI in education (Kaplan-Rakowski et al., 2023). However, some studies find no significant demographic differences in attitudes towards AI (Wardat et al., 2024), and educators believe AI can enhance pedagogical practices regardless of background factors (Akanzire et al., 2023). Nonetheless, literature on the impact of GenAI tools remains mixed.

Some sociocultural factors, including digital competence, influence teacher educators' perceptions of the use of GenAI since many educators feel underprepared to integrate GenAI into their curricula, often due to varying levels of digital literacy and confidence across different demographics (Moorehouse & Kohnke, 2024: DfE, 2024). Also, cultural attitudes such as gender, age, and socio-economic background play a critical role in educators' acceptance and usage of GenAI tools, with younger and male educators typically more inclined to adopt these technologies (Lee et al., 2024; Cabero-Almenara et al., 2024; Fahmiyah et al., 2023). However, institutional support, specifically environments that provide robust IT infrastructure and strong leadership backing, is more likely to foster innovation and encourage the integration of GenAI (DfE, 2024; Sharples, 2023). Therefore, contextualising these sociocultural drivers is essential for understanding how those factors shape teacher educators' perceptions, readiness, and GenAI use in enhancing university learning.

8.3.2 *Possible Perils of GenAI in Education*

Scholars have raised concerns about AI in education, focusing on privacy, data accuracy, and its effects on human interaction and personalised relationships (Basilo, 2023). Debates on the pros and cons of GenAI in classrooms persist, with educators citing significant privacy and ethical issues (Salazar et al., 2024; Uygun, 2024). For example, the disadvantages of using ChatGPT include the need for bibliographical sources, incorrect information, and excessive dependence (Moura & Carvalho, 2024). GenAI can disrupt traditional teaching methods and cause overreliance on AI, diminishing educators' roles (Akanzire et al., 2023). Additional challenges include the effort required to use AI tools and the pressure it places on teachers (Alam et al., 2024). AI-assisted testing may only partially assess critical thinking and problem-solving abilities, raising concerns about creativity and honesty (Ghimire & Edwards, 2024). Despite benefits like generating human-like text, accuracy, bias, and reliability issues necessitate caution (Van den Berg, 2024). Overdependence on AI could hinder students' skill development (Cardona et al., 2023). While AI can enhance learning, reduce workload, and assist students, issues of content reliability, overreliance, and academic dishonesty must be addressed (Krause et al., 2024). A balanced approach is needed to leverage AI's benefits while preserving essential conventional teaching methods.

8.3.3 *Teacher Educators' Digital Literacy Skills in Using GenAI*

Technological advancement dictates teacher educators' adaptability in integrating it into teaching and learning. In most cases, educators are behind in technological development, which hinders their practical use. Salazar et al. (2024) underscored that educators can use GenAI platforms in their classroom practices but must follow specific guidelines. These include open dialogue between instructors and students, proper training on using AI as a learning tool, and inclusive practices involving diverse students in the AI conversation. Yusuf et al. (2024) reported that educators demonstrated a high level of understanding and familiarity with GenAI tools acquired through short training and self-learning. In Korea, Lee et al. (2024) depicted that most educators lack formal knowledge of AI and underscored the beneficial impacts of teacher training programs on AI education, enhancing teachers' self-efficacy in teaching AI. However, Ghimire and Edwards (2024) acknowledged that few educators possessed a technical comprehension of GenAI. In contrast, other educators possessed rudimentary knowledge, and most were acutely aware of their lack of knowledge of technical tools. The literature on whether educators acquire AI skills during their formal training at colleges and in-service training is scant.

Educators' popularised GenAI tools include ChatGPT, Gemini (previously called Google Bard), and Microsoft's Bing Chat, and they also use Grammarly's AI-powered syntax and spelling-checking function, enabling academics to review their work rapidly and correct typing errors (Alam et al., 2024). Students primarily utilise ChatGPT for tasks like assignment writing and exam preparation, viewing it as an effective aid in achieving academic goals (Krause et al., 2024). Students' awareness and use of GenAI catapults teacher educators need to adopt and use these technological tools. Teachers use ChatGPT for fast responses, easy searches, summarised information, and originality in the text (Moura & Carvalho, 2024). Educators utilise GenAI for lesson planning, assessment, and personalised learning experiences (Van den Berg, 2024). Yusuf et al. (2024) demonstrated that educators use GenAI mainly for information retrieval and text paraphrase. Sedigheh et al. (2023) revealed that GenAI adoption in higher education can support Sustainable Development Goals and enhance students' skills, engagement, and employability. For successful AI integration in education, fostering teachers' enthusiasm and providing tailored training programs are essential. Polak et al. (2022) highlight that teachers' motivation in AI education is more important than having extensive prior technological knowledge. Wardat et al. (2024) proposed providing necessary technology tools, updating curricula to include AI applications, encouraging teachers to adopt AI-based strategies, and offering training programs to enhance teachers' skills in using AI systems. Lee et al. (2024) and Uygun (2024) recommend developing AI literacy for educators, enabling them to utilise AI tools effectively and ethically. Literature portrayed the need for more practical, hands-on training to bridge the gap between theory and real-world application of AI in education. By offering comprehensive professional development opportunities that familiarise educators with AI tools and their potential benefits, institutions can empower teachers to leverage technology effectively in their teaching.

8.3.4 *Mechanisms Available to Control Students' Dishonest Use of GenAI*

Addressing ethical concerns and providing clear guidelines on using GenAI in educational settings are crucial steps towards its effective adoption. Chan (2023) portrayed that some universities classify GenAI tool use for assignments and tests as academic misconduct, revising plagiarism policies and AI-use guidelines. Cassidy (2023) pointed out the impracticality of banning AI tools as students can bypass restrictions with technology, leading to a return to traditional pen-and-paper exams. Most US and UK universities recognise the value of AI tools, advising their use under academic integrity standards and cautioning against biases, inaccuracies, and privacy breaches (UNESCO, 2023). They allow AI for learning support but forbid copying from AI outputs. In Africa, the clarity of AI guidelines in universities is uncertain. Despite the benefits of AI in education, Institutions and teacher educators must manage challenges such as data protection and student reliance on AI (Kasneci et al., 2023; Salazar et al., 2024). In Japan, Academic institutions restrict AI use to prevent copyright violations, data breaches, and plagiarism, but awareness of AI's pros and cons is encouraged (Lee et al., 2024). UNESCO (2023) recommends regulatory measures, ethical norms, and validation of GenAI systems. The Department of Education at the University of London (DfE, 2024) emphasises a comprehensive long-term strategy for AI in education, addressing academic misconduct, data protection, and effective AI use. Integrating AI requires adjustments in learning objectives, curriculum, and examination approaches while balancing traditional teaching methods to avoid negative impacts on student engagement.

8.4 Methodology

8.4.1 *Study Design*

The study employed a case study design. The design investigates the existing phenomenon or a situation in its real context to have evidence that helps to understand it clearly (Yin, 2018). The design is ideal for this study as it helps investigate teacher educators' familiarity with and use of GenAI in enhancing their teaching, where AI has increased to every corner and penetrated the education context.

8.4.2 Study Area

Studies have indicated a low rate of technology adoption for teaching and learning in African Universities (Amponsah & Bekele, 2023; Jakoet-Salie et al., 2023). Researchers selected Dire Dawa University in Ethiopia and Mzumbe University in Tanzania as the study areas in the departments that offer education programs. These universities have invested in digitalising teaching and learning, yet they face similar challenges, such as reluctance to change among staff, poor infrastructures, and inadequate training (Ergado et al., 2022; Ghasia et al., 2020). The number of undergraduate and postgraduate students using GenAI is increasing, posing a potential threat of academic dishonesty (Crompton & Burke, 2023). These universities are ideal for studg how lecturers perceive the spread of AI, their readiness to use it, and how they use it, despite the reluctance culture and inadequate technology capacity-building training available.

8.4.3 Respondents

The study had 21 teacher educators ten from the Department of Education and Teaching at Mzumbe University and eleven from the Department of Pedagogy and Morality at Dire Dawa University) who consented to participate. The selection criteria of these respondents were all teacher educators teaching in the third-year classes in the second semester of the 2023/2024 academic year. Third-year students have experience in using technology; hence, this quality motivates teacher educators to integrate technology compared to inexperienced first-year students (Byungura et al., 2018; Schmitz & Eisenmann, 2023). Respondents had diversified demographic characteristics, ranging from 25 to 53 years, from the rank of Tutorial Assistant to Senior Lecturers, and had a working experience between two (2) to 31 years. Respondents' demographic characteristics ensured the data triangulation due to the availability of relevant information across age and ranks (Table 8.1).

8.4.4 Data Collection Methods

The study used in-depth interviews to obtain adequate information on teacher educators' perceptions, readiness, and use of GenAI in teaching and learning. The study had seven key interview questions: How do you perceive the existence of GenAI in teaching (and why)? Which GenAI do you use most? How do you learn to use GenAI? In which activities did you use GenAI? What motivated you to learn how to use GenAI? Which mechanism do you use to identify students' work done using GenAI? And which mechanism do you use to control students' dishonesty from

Table 8.1 Demographic characteristics of respondents

S/N	Pseudonym	Age	Gender	Rank	Work experience	Specialisation	Status of AI use
Tanzania							
	Emmanuel	28	M	TA	4	Languages (English and Kiswahili)	Y
	Daudi	53	M	L	31	Education (curriculum)	N
	Maria	50	F	L	20	English and Kiswahili Languages	Y
	Kishazi	42	F	AL	16	English Language	Y
	Malufu	46	M	L	18	Kiswahili Language	N
	Molari	34	M	AL	8	English Language	Y
	Kasokoro	43	F	AL	2	Kiswahili Language	Y
	Lulu	47	F	SL	16	Education management	Y
	Isaya	37	M	L	13	English and Kiswahili Languages	Y
	Phina	25	F	TA	2	Education	Y
Ethiopia							
	Almaz	31	F	L	6	English language and literature	Y
	Kebede	46	M	AL	15	Amharic Language and Literature	N
	Lemlem	27	F	L	7	History and Heritage Management	Y
	Mohammed	32	M	L	9	Chemistry	Y
	Makbael	28	M	L	5	English language and literature	N
	Mustefa	32	M	L	7	Physics	Y
	Serki	28	F	L	6	Biology Education	Y
	Teklu	31	M	L	8	Economics	Y

(continued)

Table 8.1 (continued)

S/N	Pseudonym	Age	Gender	Rank	Work experience	Specialisation	Status of AI use
	Hagos	30	M	L	7	Educational Leadership	Y
	Demeke	48	M	L	17	English language education (TEFL)	N
	Meseret	26	M	L	4	Sport Science	N

GenAI use? Researchers administered interview questions in a face-to-face conversation followed by probing questions to obtain deep information based on respondents' experience and understanding. Collecting information from respondents with diverse demographic characteristics and from different contexts, as well as presenting it with the support of direct quotations, ensures the trustworthiness, transferability, and confirmability of the findings.

8.4.5 Data Analysis

The analysis involved two coding cycles, as Saldana (2013) proposes. The first cycle involved vivo coding, where researchers accustomed themselves to participant perspectives and experiences and gathered information on the phenomenon under study. The second cycle involved eclectic coding in refining and organising the initial codes before presenting them supported with quotations as evidence. In presenting quotations, researchers use pseudonyms to maintain the confidentiality of respondents' identities.

8.5 Findings

The study examined teacher educators' perceptions, readiness, and use of GenAI to enhance university learning. The findings generally indicate that teacher educators in both universities perceive GenAI as a helpful learning tool that needs users' prudence. Teacher educators admitted to using GenAI to verify and complement the content they teach students, and the growing rate of students using such emerging technology is the motivation behind it. Although GenAI use is gaining momentum, educators have yet to find a comprehensive control mechanism to mitigate potential threats of GenAI misuse. Hereunder are the detailed findings with the evidence from teacher educators who participated in the study. In both universities, 15 out of 21 staff use

GenAI in various academic activities, whereas five experienced senior staff and one junior staff with no working experience do not use GenAI.

8.5.1 Teacher Educators' Perception of GenAI Use

The first research question was, what are the teacher educators' perceptions of using GenAI in facilitating learning? The study found a mixed perception of using GenAI in academic activities during the in-depth interview. Teacher educators perceive GenAI as a critically helpful learning tool, which some consider a threat to meaningful learning in constructing twenty-first-century skills, such as critical thinking.

8.5.1.1 GenAI as a Critically Helpful Learning Tool

Teacher educators from both universities agree that GenAI helps teachers and students search for materials and clarify the concepts they learn in the classroom. GenAI saves time that teacher educators and students could use to search for clarifications of concepts from literature. During the interview, Mafulu from Tanzania revealed, "If they use AI with complete professionalism, they [GenAI] simplify tasks for students to search for relevant and self-directed learning information. Tutors can benefit from resources for preparing lessons and conducting research activities". Mustefa from Ethiopia supports that GenAI has simplified the teaching and learning process, making it enjoyable for learners as he said, "We are living in the modern world. As we use technology, AI-powered chatbots simplify teachers' and students' efforts to seek new knowledge".

Molari, an English language instructor from Mzumbe University, also views AI as an essential tool that simplifies language learning, especially for students who learn English as their second and third language. She revealed this during the conversation: "This tool simplifies a lot of work from generating texts, compositions, paraphrasing, grammar checking, and plagiarism checking. I believe that AI has opened a new platform for performing multiple tasks quickly, though it needs professionalism". Lemlem, a teacher educator from Dire Dawa University, cemented this finding by adding that AI allows users to chat with humans like virtual conversation partners by receiving commands and giving prompt responses that mimic real people. She said, "It is a computer program that can chat with humans like a virtual conversation partner. It understands what type or say and responds in a way that mimics a real person".

Teacher educators in STEM subjects believe GenAI could transform pedagogical approaches by bringing real learning into classroom contexts. For example, Serki from Dire Dawa University, who teaches Biology, revealed that "[AI] provides immediate feedback, supports students on answering questions, offering explanations, and providing additional resources to assist study". Through GenAI, students can learn how to plan and conduct experiments with virtual support. Since GenAI offers room for personalised learning, students can practice as often as possible if they have internet access. Teacher educators perceive this as critical to enhancing STEM teaching and learning.

8.5.1.2 AI as a Threat to Teaching Twenty-First-Century Skills

The major AI threat reported by both universities is a control mechanism that will enable its decent use in academic activities. Teacher educators have expressed their worry that AI can negatively impact education apart from technical challenges of access and operational and informational use. In the interview, respondents used phrases like "gives unreliable information", "promotes plagiarism", "disables critical thinking", "affects the assessment of learning", "damaging learning process", "affects the creativity", and "makes learners too reliant on these tools". Hagos from Dire Dawa University believes that GenAI will soon penetrate all aspects that will make it challenging to prohibit its use, hence educating people on proper use. When asked how do you see the future of GenAI in education? He responded that;

While AI-powered chatbots offer exciting benefits for students, issues like data privacy, student consent, and the potential for bias within the algorithms remain critical considerations that teacher educators must address to ensure responsible and ethical implementation in the classroom (Hagos).

Fearing the potential risks, some teacher educators decide not to use GenAI in their teaching and prohibit students from using it in academic activities. Although some are in a transition period from being reluctant to start using as they believe the time has come to venture out and explore what remains, some are still resistant. Kebede, from Dire Dawa University, admitted that:

While AI has the potential to be a helpful tool in education, I'm currently choosing not to integrate it into my teaching. This could be for several reasons, such as a preference for more traditional methods, concerns about student reliance on technology, or a lack of familiarity or support for using AI effectively in the classroom. If I cannot use it well, it will lead to negative impacts rather than positive ones (Kebede).

The response above implies that teacher educators who lack the technical skills to operate GenAI and integrate it into teaching activities are less likely to accept and use it. Teacher educators admit it is shocking if students realise they are less competent in using AI. Possibly, students will maximise GenAI use, believing teachers cannot detect any dishonest acts committed.

8.5.2 Teacher Educators Use GenAI to Facilitate Learning

The second research question was, how can teacher educators use GenAI in facilitating learning? The findings reveal several aspects of teacher educators' use of GenAI. These aspects include commonly used GenAI, how teacher educators learn to use GenAI, in which activities, and what motivates them to learn and keep using GenAI.

8.5.2.1 Common GenAI Teacher Educators Use

We asked teacher educators to mention the common GenAI they frequently use in their teaching activities. The findings show that the majority use ChatGPT (6), Copilot (3), Gemini [previously called Google Bard AI] (3), Ask AI (1), Hybrid Chatbots (1), and Quill Bot (1). The nature of activities that a respective teacher educator wanted to perform influenced the choice of which GenAI to use. Despite their awareness and personal use of these GenAI, some teachers admitted they do not use these in teaching activities but rather for self-learning to enhance their skills in various aspects, such as to improve their language skills and to search materials for their research activities. Kebede, who is a proficient Amharic speaker from Dire Dawa University, confirmed the findings, sag,

AI isn't currently a part of my teaching toolbox, but it's an interesting area with the potential to personalise learning or handle administrative tasks effectively. I only use it to correct grammatical errors in my academic writing and search materials for references, not for teaching purposes (Kebede).

8.5.2.2 Motivations Behind Teacher Educators' Learning and Use of GenAI

We asked teacher educators what motivates them to use GenAI and how they learn. The responses reveal that the fear of being technologically behind their students ignited their need to learn to be on par with students. Emmanuel, a tutorial assistant with four years of experience from Mzumbe University, confirmed the finding as he admitted that:

Since students are using AI, I have to use it too and show them what they need the teacher for clarification, so I have to improve my writing and teaching to meet their needs and interests. You know we cannot escape technological advancement. We must learn what is going on and how it works. It's the pressure, as all my students know, so it is like they indirectly force me to learn it (Emmanuel).

The above response indicates that teacher educators are aware that the sophistication of technology in education is inevitable; hence, they have to cope with the changing world and the needs of students.

Further, teacher educators admitted that the role of GenAI in simplifying academic writing, literature search, obtaining clarification of concepts, and simplifying the composition of some creative literary works for language teachers amplifies their interest in learning and use. These GenAI utilities motivate teachers to learn and use them to advance their practices, shorten the time used in traditional reading, and to organise practical approaches for their students. Mohammed from Dire Dawa University responded in support of the finding, saying,

Using AI chatbots like ChatGPT transforms the classroom by acting as virtual assistants for teachers, freeing us to focus on higher-quality instructions. This improves educators' efficiency and empowers them to personalise the learning experience for students, ultimately leading to better educational outcomes (Mohammed).

Teacher educators mentioned various ways they learned how to use GenAI. Many of them struggle to learn how to use the GenAI from the internet with assistance from their experienced colleagues. Despite the self-learning efforts, most teacher educators at Dire Dawa University perceive they have low-level skills in GenAI use compared to those at Mzumbe University. Then, they practice developing more skills to integrate GenAI into their teaching and effectively guide students. When asked how they learned to use GenAI, they mentioned online platforms such as telegram channels, Coursera, online tutorials from Google and YouTube, and reading articles. For instance, Kasokoro, a Kiswahili language instructor, said, "I just hear from staff mates and learn from some online advertisement. Also, in one conference I attended, we were taught about AI use for language teaching, especially Kiswahili". We obtained a similar response from Almaz of Dire Dawa University, who teaches the English language who said,

My world is a vibrant classroom overflowing with knowledge waiting for us to discover. As a curious learner, I soak up information from every interaction, constantly refining my understanding and expanding my perspective. So, it is a self-effort to learn how to use AI (Almaz).

8.5.2.3 Teaching Activities that Integrate GenAI

Teacher educators revealed which academic activities they use GenAI, including teaching activities and personal issues. In teaching activities, teacher educators search for relevant teaching cases for their lessons, obtaining clear clarifications of concepts and quick answers to some questions. Again, language teachers reported using GenAI to teach grammar issues in Kiswahili for foreign courses, such as clarifying synonyms, identifying their contextual use, comparing sentence structures in different languages, and correcting grammatical errors. Teacher educators in STEM also revealed how GenAI has simplified teaching, primarily to assist students in learning how to plan and conduct various experiments. Teklu from Dire Dawa University reported, "I commonly use AI for Education to educate my students, share learning resources, and educate myself. Students learn how to conduct experiment procedures, clarify questions I couldn't understand clearly, and complement some main points related to the subject matter".

8.5.3 Teacher Educators' Mechanism of Controlling GenAI Use

The third study question was, what mechanisms do teacher educators use to control students' unethical use of GenAI? The findings revealed two main issues: the mechanism teacher educators use to recognise students' work written with GenAI and how they control academic dishonesty.

8.5.3.1 Mechanisms to Identify Students' AI-Written Work

When asked how they identify AI-written work from students, teacher educators reported various techniques they use. These techniques include their experience with GenAI use, adopting technology available to detect (AI detector), how they know their students and GenAI prohibition. Those teacher educators who frequently use GenAI admitted they could realise the GenAI-written work by reading the responses and conversing with students to confirm whether they used them. Features like clarity, lack of citations, and high-quality language might indicate GenAI use in writing. However, this is sometimes ineffective when you have many students. Also, a few respondents indicated they use Turnitin software to detect plagiarism and the per cent written by GenAI. However, some revealed that the subscriptions for plagiarism and GenAI detector platforms are separate, and some institutions could not afford them, making them less effective mechanisms. Maria, one of the respondents, indicated that:

It is very difficult, but when you read, you can see the work and reflect on how you know your students and their fluency and suspect their work. Then, you interrogate them to know if they used AI. Previously, Turnitin had the role of checking AI. We cannot access it now as the university has not subscribed to it (Maria).

Experienced teacher educators revealed that they could tell by looking at some features. Once they realise GenAI has been used in writing the assignment, some penalise students, and some return them for correction and resubmission. At Dire Dawa University, Almaz said, "I am so sympathetic to my learners' current situation with the kneeler. This allows me to read their work carefully. Suppose I encounter an assignment that appears to exceed their current grasp. In that case, I return it for adjustment and correction". However, in both universities, any AI use by students in academic activities is restricted due to fear of its potential threats to the quality of learning. Hagos from Dire Dawa University revealed, "While I can't directly detect AI use, our organisation has a clear and strict policy against it for student work. This policy exists even though there aren't any automated ways to check for it". Although policies prohibit GenAI use, its sophistication and penetration in all corners make those restrictions shadowy.

8.5.3.2 How Teacher Educators Control Academic Dishonesty Among Students

When asked how they control honest GenAI uses among students, teacher educators shared their practical experiences. In both universities, the primary control mechanism reported is providing capacity building on using GenAI to enhance learning and not relying on it as a leading source of knowledge. Teacher educators report that they have proved that GenAI is unreliable in providing trusted information. Hence, learners who use it should verify the information critically and customise it to their needs and interests. At Mzumbe University, Emmanuel shared his experience: "Teacher educators should enhance students' digital literacy specifically on how to use AI platforms". Similarly, at Dire Dawa University, teacher educators have changed teaching approaches to promote group work and open communication between students and instructors to foster a culture of honesty and integrity in academic settings. Teklu revealed that:

To combat potential student dishonesty from AI use, I employ various strategies such as open-ended dialogue prompting explanations without referring to their work, incorporating offline assignments with personal presentations, and cross-referencing students' academic backgrounds with their work to ensure alignment (Teklu).

Apart from enhancing digital literacy skills to promote the decent use of GenAI, teacher educators have now transformed their assessment practices to push students to demonstrate their learning without relying on written assignments. Isaya, a language instructor from Mzumbe University, clarified how transforming assessment practices can help curb AI threats in learning. He said, "To change how we set learning and assessment activities to have critical thinking components. Students write their work and present or demonstrate. Not to have a content-based assessment of relying on written papers".

Some teacher educators have ceased using GenAI due to lacking such control mechanisms. One teacher educator, Lemlem, admitted to having stopped using GenAI in teaching and will resume using it once he finds a better way to control proper use. During the interview, he said, "I have no mechanism to identify, but I plan to get familiar with AI first before I start using it for the desired purpose".

8.6 Discussion and Implications

This study explored teacher educators' perceptions, readiness, and the use of GenAI. Specifically, it explored teacher educators' perceptions of GenAI and their use and control of students' unethical use. A study employed a case study design with 21 teacher educators from Dire Dawa University and Mzumbe University who participated in interviews. In the following section, we present the findings that highlight responses from teacher educators. Despite some teacher educators perceiving it as useful and inevitable, others fear the potential threat of negatively impacting learning.

8.6.1 GenAI Are Useful, but Competence Enhancement Is Vital

Teacher educators from both universities believe GenAI helps find relevant learning materials and solidify their understanding of classroom concepts. The findings resonate with Bii et al. (2018), Walter (2024), and Yetisensoy and Karaduman (2024) studies that indicate GenAI is pivotal in enhancing teachers' and students' access to diverse materials, enhancing their interaction and collaboration that are geared towards knowledge construction through accommodating various learning styles and cognitive states. The result indicates that GenAI provides a space for individualising learning, allowing teachers to assist students in practising as frequently as they want as long as they have internet access. Teacher educators see this as crucial for improving STEM education. This result is similar to Triplett (2023), who asserts that AI plays a vital role in STEM education by enabling personalised learning, refined analytics, and automated instructions. GenAI has the potential to revolutionise STEM education by tailoring learning to individual needs, providing educators with in-depth data analysis, and automating repetitive tasks, ultimately leading to a more effective and successful learning experience for STEM students (Triplett, 2023). Also, Owolabi et al. (2022) similarly reported the importance of collaboration among teachers, researchers, and policymakers for successfully integrating GenAI in educational institutions. This finding implies a need to enhance teacher educators' digital informational literacy to validate information obtained through GenAI for effectively guiding students' learning.

Findings indicate technical and operational skills challenges, implying that teacher educators need capacity building to enhance their skills in using GenAI and a proper mechanism to identify GenAI-written work that needs a GenAI detector and capacity-building support. As a result, universities enact policies prohibiting GenAI use, but they are fruitless, paving the way for detailed studies on proper GenAI integration in teaching and learning. The demographic characteristics indicate that young teacher educators use GenAI more than older colleagues. The observation is similar to Fahmiyah et al. (2023), who found that younger educators are confident and flexible in learning and utilising technology in their teaching activities. Hence, they do not fear any potential that could affect their intention to use technology compared to those aged 36 and above. The findings inform the need to invest more in the new generation of young academicians in integrating modern technology into teaching.

8.6.2 The Need for a Mechanism for GenAI Ethical Use

However, teacher educators are skeptical about using GenAI in their teaching and allowing students to use it for fear of potential risks that might discourage critical learning and the construction of twenty-first-century skills. These teachers believe that GenAI is negatively impacting learning. This research indicated that some teacher educators are hesitant to incorporate GenAI into their teaching and restrict students from using it in academic tasks due to concerns about potential risks. As a result, some teachers have prohibited students' GenAI use in academic activities, reflecting what Ghafar (2023) found in some institutions.

Although teachers fear the risk of GenAI distorting meaningful learning and competency development, its integration into education is inevitable, only requiring proper control mechanisms for their decent use in academics. Working with schools and other educational organisations, teacher educators should develop effective ways to prevent students from misusing GenAI. Academic institutions worry that GenAI might hurt how well students learn and decide to ban it (Ghafar, 2023) or limit how students can use it for schoolwork. Instead, they focus on pedagogical change that allows GenAI to be a helpful tool that does not replace thinking but instead places information at our fingertips. Similarly, Walter (2024) calls for a transformative shift in educational instructional approaches. The findings again indicate that teacher educators are watchful concerning the unreliability of information generated by GenAI. GenAI users must learn to double-check what it tells them and ensure it fits their interests and goals. The study aligns with Bii et al. (2018), who states that instructors with a positive attitude towards a specific technology, such as GenAI, are more likely to integrate it into their instruction practices. The study capitalises on the need for teacher educators to integrate GenAI to harness their potential to simplify and maximise learning.

8.6.3 GenAI as a New Normal for Teacher Educators

Some teacher educators are gradually overcoming their reluctance and recognising the need to embrace new technologies for exploration. Others remain resistant to change. This result is similar to Hashem et al. (2024), whose study emphasises the balanced use of GenAI and its potential for educational reform. Integration AI can optimise teacher planning, enhance instructional support, and refine resource allocation. Findings have indicated that the existence of policies to restrict GenAI use is futile. Teacher educators fear banning GenAI does not work as hundreds of AIs are sophisticated and complex to control. Ghamrawi et al. (2024) and Igbokwe et al. (2023) state that some teacher educators have stopped using AI in their programs because they feel they cannot control it well enough. The lack of GenAI control has led some teacher educators to ditch it altogether. A teacher educator who stopped using GenAI in lessons admits they are open to using it again if they can find a method to ensure effective GenAI use. The findings suggest that universities should develop frameworks to guide the integration of GenAI in academic activities.

The pace of GenAI augmentation has seen it penetrating far corners, making it inevitable to integrate and control it in education. Findings indicate that apart from fear of potential risk, teacher educators lack technical skills in using GenAI. Teacher educators lack confidence in using GenAI due to limited digital literacy, making them hesitant to integrate it into teaching. This finding is similar to Celik et al. (2022), Crompton and Burke (2023), Igbokwe (2023), and Karan and Angadi (2024), and they alerted that teacher educators' programs may be failing behind if teacher educators themselves are not comfortable using GenAI in the classroom, they are less likely to introduce it to future teachers. This situation could create a gap between educators and students. Students, who are likely more comfortable with technology, might leverage GenAI tools in dishonest ways, assuming their teachers cannot detect it, making capacity building for teachers inevitable.

8.7 Conclusion and Recommendations for Future Work

The study examined teacher educators' perceptions, readiness, and use of GenAI to enhance university learning. Findings have revealed that, despite teacher educators perceiving GenAI as a critical tool for teaching and using it, some still fear its negative impact on learning because they lack proper control mechanisms and confidence because of poor technical and operational skills. Although most teacher educators are motivated to learn how to use GenAI because they find their students are far ahead as they fear being behind, some are incapable of integrating them into teaching. The findings imply that to integrate AI fully into teaching and learning, universities should capacitate teacher educators with relevant AI literacy and have proper control mechanisms, such as guidelines and policies, to curb technological perils. The capacity building shall also enhance pedagogical transformation in classroom teaching and assessment for competency development among learners. The study has already revealed that few teacher educators have transformed assessment practices so that they do not rely on written assignments but on demonstrating mastery of knowledge as a control mechanism. The study had a small sample size of 21 teacher educators from two universities with different contexts, making the findings ungeneralisable as they elicited AI use experience of these few respondents. Therefore, the study warrants replication with a larger sample and a different methodological approach for generalisable findings. The study has two recommendations. First, universities should devise frameworks and policies that allow GenAI use while strengthening competency-based approaches in teaching and assessment. Second, universities should provide capacity-building training to teacher educators to elevate their AI literacy skills for their personal AI use and facilitate students' learning. Therefore, universities should uplift policies prohibiting GenAI use and capacitate teachers' and students' ability to use GenAI to improve the quality of learning decently.

Competing Interests Authors declare that they have no conflict of interest.

References

Akanzire, N. B., Nyaaba, M., & Nabang, M. (2023). Perceptions and preparedness: Exploring teacher educators' views on integrating generative AI in colleges of education, Ghana. *SSRN Electronic Journal*. https://doi.org/10.2139/ssrn.4628153

Akgun, S., & Greenhow, C. (2022). Artificial Intelligence in education: Addressing ethical challenges in K-12 settings. *AI and Ethics, 2*(3), 431–440. https://link.springer.com/article/10.1007/s43681-021-00096-7

Alam, S., Hameed, A., Madej, M., & Kobylarek, A. (2024). Perception and practice of using Artificial Intelligence in education: An opinion based study. *XLinguae, 17*(1), 216–233. https://doi.org/10.18355/XL.2024.17.01.15

Amani, S., White, L., Balart, T., Arora, L., Shryock, K., Brumbelow, K., & Watson, K. (2023). *Generative AI perceptions: A survey to measure the perceptions of faculty, staff, and students on generative AI tools in academia*. Cornell University. https://doi.org/10.48550/arxiv.2304.14415

Amponsah, S., & Bekele, T. A. (2023). Technology integration in higher education in Africa: Philosophical, theoretical and policy-practice perspectives. *British Journal of Educational Technology, Editorial,* 437–440. https://doi.org/10.1111/bjet.13368

Ayanwale, M. A., Sanusi, I. T., Adelana, O. P., Aruleba, K. D., & Oyelere, S. S. (2022). Teachers' readiness and intention to teach artificial Intelligence in schools. *Computers and Education: Artificial Intelligence, 3*(100099), 1–11. https://doi.org/10.1016/j.caeai.2022.100099

Basilo, M. B. (2023). *Teachers' perspectives on the integration of ChatGPT in classroom teaching and learning*. Technical Report. https://orcid.org/0009-0002-2785-9109

Bii, P. K., Too, J. K., & Mukwa, C. W. (2018). Teacher attitude towards use of chatbots in routine teaching. *Universal Journal of Educational Research, 6*(7), 1586–1597. https://doi.org/10.13189/ujer.2018.060719

Byungura, J. C., Hansson, H., Muparasi, M., & Ruhinda, B. (2018). Familiarity with technology among first-year students in Rwandan Tertiary education. *The Electronic Journal of e-Learning, 16*(1), 30–45.

Cabero-Almenara, J., Palacios-Rodríguez, A., Loaiza-Aguirre, M. I., & Rivas-Manzano, M. d. R. (2024). Acceptance of educational artificial intelligence by teachers and its relationship with some variables and pedagogical beliefs. *Education Sciences, 14*(7), 740https://doi.org/10.3390/educsci14070740

Cao, Y., Li, S., Liu, Y., Yan, Z., Dai, Y., Yu, P. S., & Sun, L. (2023). A comprehensive survey of AI-generated content (AIGC): A history of generative AI from GAN to ChatGPT. https://doi.org/10.48550/arXiv.2303.04226

Cardona, M. A., Rodríguez, R. J., & Ishmael, K. (2023). Artificial intelligence and the future of teaching and learning: Insights and recommendations. Policy Commons. Retrieved 22 April 2024 from https://policycommons.net/artifacts/3854312/ai-report/4660267/

Cassidy, C. (2023). Australian universities to return to 'pen and paper' exams after students caught using AI to write essays. The Guardian. Retrieved on 21 March 2024 from https://www.theguardian.com/australia-news/2023/jan/10/universities-to-return-to-pen-and-paper-exams-after-students-caught-using-ai-to-write-essays

Celik, I., Dindar, M., Muukkonen, H., & Järvelä, S. (2022). The promises and challenges of artificial Intelligence for teachers: A systematic review of research. *TechTrends, 66*(4), 616–630. https://doi.org/10.1007/s11528-022-00715-y

Chan, C. K. Y. (2023). A comprehensive AI policy education framework for university teaching and learning. *International Journal of Educational Technology in Higher Education, 20*(38).

Crompton, H., Burke, D. (2023). Artificial Intelligence in higher education: the state of the field. *International Journal of Educational Technology in Higher Education, 20*(22). https://doi.org/10.1186/s41239-023-00392-8

Das, S.R. & J.V., M. (2024). Perceptions of higher education students towards ChatGPT usage. *International Journal of Technology in Education (IJTE), 7*(1), 86–106. https://doi.org/10.46328/ijte.583

Deng, X., & Yu, Z. (2023). A meta-analysis and systematic review of the effect of chatbot technology use in sustainable education. *Sustainability, 15*(4), 2940. https://doi.org/10.3390/su15042940

DfE. (2024). Generative AI in education: Educator and expert views. www.gov.uk/government/publications

Doo, M. Y., Bonk, C., & Heo, H. (2020). A meta-analysis of scaffolding effects in online learning in higher education. *The International Review of Research in Open and Distributed Learning, 21*(3), 60–80. https://doi.org/10.19173/irrodl.v21i3.4638

Ergado, A. A., Desta, A., & Mehta, H. (2022). Contributing factors for the integration of Information and Communication Technology into Ethiopian Higher Education Institutions teaching-learning practices. *International Journal of Education and Development Using Information and Communication Technology (IJEDICT), 18*(1), 275–292.

Ezumah, B. A. (2020). Challenges of educational technology adoption in Africa. In M. Thomas & M. Warschauer (Eds), *Critical perspectives of educational technology in Africa. Digital education and learning*. Palgrave Macmillan. https://doi.org/10.1007/978-3-030-53728-9_4

Fahmiyah, I., Utami, I. Q., Ningrum, R. A., Fakhruzzaman, M. N., Pratama, A. I. & Triangga, Y. M. (2023). Examining the effect of teacher's age difference on learning technology adoption using technology acceptance model. *Proceedings of the International Conference on Advanced Technology and Multidiscipline (ICATAM) 2021: "Advanced Technology and Multidisciplinary Prospective Towards Bright Future"* Faculty of Advanced Technology and Multidiscipline, 13–14 October 2021, Surabaya, Indonesia. https://doi.org/10.1063/5.0123943

Ghafar, Z. N. (2023). ChatGPT: A new tool to improve teaching and evaluation of second and foreign Languages a review of ChatGPT: The future of education. *International Journal of Applied Research and Sustainable Sciences (IJARSS), 1*(2), 73–86. https://doi.org/10.59890/ijarss.v1i2.392

Ghamrawi, N., Shal, T., & Ghamrawi, N. A. (2024). Exploring the impact of AI on teacher leadership: Regressing or expanding? *Education and Information Technologies, 29*, 8415–8433. https://doi.org/10.1007/s10639-023-12174-w

Ghasia, M., Machumu, H., Zhu, C., & DePryck, K. (2020). Reflection on e-learning system of the Mzumbe University in Tanzania: Successes, challenges and way. *International Journal of Education and Development Using Information and Communication Technology (IJEDICT), 18*(1), 275–292.

Ghimire, A. & Edwards, J. (2023). Generative AI adoption in classroom in context of Technology Acceptance Model (TAM) and the Innovation Diffusion Theory (IDT). *Computer Science, Computers and Society*. https://doi.org/10.48550/arXiv.2406.15360

Hashem, R., Ali, N., El Zein, F., Fidalgo, P., & Abu Khurma, O. (2024). AI to the rescue: Exploring the potential of ChatGPT as a teacher ally for workload relief and burnout prevention. *Research and Practice in Technology Enhanced Learning, 19*, 023. https://doi.org/10.58459/rptel.2024.19023

Huang, W., Hew, K. F., & Fryer, L. K. (2022). Chatbots for language learning—Are they really useful? A systematic review of chatbot-supported language learning. *Journal of Computer Assisted Learning, 38*(1), 237–257. https://doi.org/10.1111/jcal.12610

Humble, N., & Mozelius, P. (2019). Artificial Intelligence in Education - a Promise, a Threat or a Hype? *Proceedings of the European Conference on the Impact of Artificial Intelligence and Robotics*, EM-Normandie Business School Oxford, UK, 31 October-1 November 2019, 149–156. https://doi.org/10.34190/ECIAIR.19.005

Igbokwe, I. C. (2023). Application of artificial Intelligence (AI) in educational management. *International Journal of Scientific and Research Publications, 13*(3), 300–307. https://doi.org/10.29322/IJSRP.13.03.2023.p13536

Jakoet Salie, A., & Ramalobe, K. (2023). The digitalisation of learning and teaching practices in higher education institutions during the Covid-19 pandemic. *Teaching Public Administration, 41*(1), 59–71. https://doi.org/10.1177/01447394221092275

Kalota, F. (2024). A primer on generative artificial Intelligence. *Education Sciences, 14*(2), 172. https://doi.org/10.3390/educsci14020172

Kaplan-Rakowski, R., Grotewold, K., Hartwick, P., & Papin, K. (2023). Generative AI and teachers' perspectives on its implementation in education. *Journal of Interactive Learning Research, 34*(2), 313–338.

Karan, B., & Angadi, G. R. (2024). Potential risks of artificial intelligence integration into school education: A systematic review. *Bulletin of Science, Technology & Society, 43*(3–4), 67–85. https://doi.org/10.1177/02704676231224705

Kasneci, E., Sessler, K., Küchemann, S., Bannert, M., Dementieva, D., Fischer, F., Gasser, U., Groh, G., Günnemann, S., Hüllermeier, E., Krusche, S., Kutyniok, G., Michaeli, T., Nerdel, C., Pfeffer, J., Poquet, O., Sailer, M., Schmidt, A., Seidel, T., … Kasneci, G. (2023). ChatGPT for good? On opportunities and challenges of large language models for education. *Learning and Individual Differences, 103*, 102274. https://doi.org/10.1016/j.lindif.2023.102274

Kohnke, L. (2023). A pedagogical Chatbot: A supplemental language learning tool. *RELC Journal, 54*(3), 828–838. https://doi.org/10.1177/00336882211067054

Kohnke, L., Moorhouse, B. L., & Zou, D. (2023). ChatGPT for language teaching and learning. *RELC Journal, 54*(2), 537–550. https://doi.org/10.1177/00336882231162868

Krause, S., Panchal, B. H., & Ubhe, N. (2024). The evolution of learning: Assessing the transformative impact of generative AI on higher education. arXiv: 2404.10551v1 [cs.AI]. https://doi.org/10.48550/arXiv.2404.10551

Lee, Y., Davis, R.O., & Ryu, J. (2024). Korean in-service teachers' perceptions of implementing Artificial Intelligence (AI) education for teaching in schools and their AI teacher training programs. *International Journal of Information and Education Technology, 14*(2), 214–219. https://doi.org/10.18178/ijiet.2024.14.2.2042

Mamo, Y., Crompton, H., & Burke, D. (2024). Higher education faculty perceptions of ChatGPT and the influencing factors: A sentiment analysis of X. *TechTrends, 68*, 520–534. https://doi.org/10.1007/s11528-024-00954-1

Mello, R F., Freitas, E L S X., Pereira, F D., Cabral, L., Tedesco, P., & Ramalho, G. (2023). *Education in the age of generative AI: Context and recent developments.* Cornell University. https://doi.org/10.48550/arxiv.2309.12332

Meniado, J. C. (2023). The impact of ChatGPT on English Language teaching, learning, and assessment: A rapid review of literature. *Arab World English Journal, 14*(4), 3–18. https://doi.org/10.24093/awej/vol14no4.1

Mohebi, L. (2024). Empowering learners with ChatGPT: Insights from a systematic literature exploration. *Discover Education, 3*, 36. https://doi.org/10.1007/s44217-024-00120-y

Moorhouse, B., & Kohnke, L. (2024). The effects of generative AI on initial language teacher education: The Perceptions of Teacher Educators. *System, 122*, Article 103290. https://doi.org/10.1016/j.system.2024.103290

Moura, A., & Carvalho, A. A. A. (2024). Teachers' perceptions of the use of artificial Intelligence in the classroom. In *Proceedings of the International Conference on Lifelong Education and Leadership for All (ICLEL 2023), Atlantis Highlights in Social Sciences,* Education and Humanities 17. https://doi.org/10.2991/978-94-6463-380-1_13

Murphy, R. R. (2019). *Introduction to AI robotics.* MIT press

Nguyen, T. C. (2024). University teachers' perceptions of using ChatGPT in Language teaching and assessment. *Proceedings of the AsiaCALL International Conference, 4,* 116–128. https://doi.org/10.54855/paic.2349

Okonkwo, C. W., & Ade-Ibijola, A. (2021). Chatbots applications in education: A systematic review. *Computers and Education: Artificial Intelligence, 2*, Article 100033. https://doi.org/10.1016/j.caeai.2021.100033

Owolabi, K. A., Abayomi, A. O., Aderibigbe, N. A., Kemdi, O. M., Oluwaseun, O. A., & Okorie, C. N. (2022). Awareness and readiness of Nigerian Polytechnic students towards adopting artificial Intelligence in libraries. *SRELS Journal of Information Management, 59*(1), 15–24. https://doi.org/10.17821/srels/2022/v59i1/168682

Pérez, J. Q., Daradoumis, T., & Puig, J. M. M. (2020). Rediscovering the use of chatbots in education: A systematic literature review. *Computer Applications in Engineering Education, 28*(6), 1549–1565. https://doi.org/10.1002/cae.22326

Polak, S., Schiavo, G., & Zancanaro, M. (2022). Teachers' perspective on artificial intelligence education: An initial investigation. *In CHI Conference on Human Factors in Computing Systems Extended Abstracts (CHI '22 Extended Abstracts),* April 29-May 5, 2022, New Orleans, LA, USA. https://doi.org/10.1145/3491101.3519866

Rashid, S. F., Duong-Trung, N., & Pinkwart, N. (2024). Generative AI in education: Technical foundations, applications, and challenges. In S. Kadry, *Artificial Intelligence and Education - Shaping the Future of Learning*. IntechOpen. https://doi.org/10.5772/intechopen.1005402

Rathore, N. P., Dangi, M. (2021). Embedding artificial Intelligence into education: The new normal. In: Hamdan, A., Hassanien, A.E., Khamis, R., Alareeni, B., Razzaque, A., & Awwad, B. (Eds), *Applications of Artificial Intelligence in Business, Education and Healthcare. Studies in Computational Intelligence* (Vol. 954). Springer. https://doi.org/10.1007/978-3-030-72080-3_15

Salazar, L. R., Peeples, S. F., & Brooks, M. E. (2024). Generative AI ethical considerations and discriminatory biases on diverse students within the classroom. In S. Elmoudden & J. Wrench (Eds.), *The role of generative AI in the communication classroom* (pp. 191–213). IGI Global. https://doi.org/10.4018/979-8-3693-0831-8.ch010

Saldana, J. (2013). *The coding manual for qualitative researchers* (2nd ed.). SAGE Publications Ltd.

Schmitz, B., & Eisenmann, S. (2023). Same same but different: Learning with technology – are first-year college students prepared for this? *Journal of University Teaching & Learning Practice, 20*(4). https://doi.org/10.53761/1.20.4.10

Sharples, M. (2023). Towards social generative AI for education: Theory, practices and ethics. *Learning: Research and Practice, 9*(2), 159–167. https://doi.org/10.1080/23735082.2023.2261131

Sheikh, H., Prins, C., & Schrijvers, E. (2023). Artificial Intelligence: Definition and Background. In *Mission AI: The new system technology*. Springer. https://doi.org/10.1007/978-3-031-21448-6

Sedigheh, S., Shakib Kotamjani, S., Shirinova, S., & Fahimirad, M. M. (2023). Lecturers' perceptions of using artificial Intelligence in tertiary education in Uzbekistan. *In The International Conference on Future Networks and Distributed Systems (ICFNDS '23),* December 21–22, 2023, Dubai, United Arab Emirates (p. 9). ACM. https://doi.org/10.1145/3644713.3644797

Triplett, W. J. (2023). Artificial Intelligence in STEM education. *Cybersecurity and Innovative Technology Journal, 1*(1), 23–29.https://doi.org/10.53889/citj.v1i1.296

UNESCO. (2023). *Guidance for generative AI in education and research.* United Nations Educational, Scientific and Cultural Organization. ISBN: 978-92-3-100612-8. https://doi.org/10.54675/EWZM9535

Uygun, D. (2024). Teachers' perspectives on artificial Intelligence in education. *Advances in Mobile Learning Educational Research, 4*(1), 931–939. https://doi.org/10.25082/AMLER.2024.01.005

Van den Berg, G. (2024). Generative AI and educators: Partnering in using open digital content for transforming education. *Open Praxis, 16*(2), 130–141. https://doi.org/10.55982/openpraxis.16.2.640

Walter, Y. (2024). Embracing the future of Artificial Intelligence in the classroom: The relevance of AI literacy, prompt engineering, and critical thinking in modern education. *International Journal of Educational Technology in Higher Education, 21*(5). https://doi.org/10.1186/s41239-024-00448-3

Wardat, Y., Tashtoush, M., Alali, R., & Saleh, S. (2024). Artificial Intelligence in education: Mathematics teachers' perspectives, practices and challenges. *Iraqi Journal for Computer Science and Mathematics, 5*(1), 60–77. https://doi.org/10.52866/ijcsm.2024.05.01.004

Yetişensoy, O., & Karaduman, H. (2024). The effect of AI-powered chatbots in social studies education. *Education and Information Technologies*, 1–35. https://doi.org/10.1007/s10639-024-12485-6

Yin, R. K. (2018). *Case study research and applications: Design and methods* (6th Ed.). SAGE Publications.

Yusuf, A., Pervin, N., & Román-González, M. (2024). Generative AI and the future of higher education: A threat to academic integrity or reformation? Evidence from multicultural perspectives. *International Journal of Educational Technology in Higher Education, 21*(21). https://doi.org/10.1186/s41239-024-00453-6

Chapter 9
Revolutionizing Pedagogy: The Transformative Influence of Artificial Intelligence on Educators' Practices

Mersad Dervić, Senad Bećirović, and Edda Polz

Abstract Artificial intelligence (AI), a rapidly advancing technological phenomenon, has the potential to fundamentally change educational processes, especially following the launch of ChatGPT in late 2022. Its capacity to outperform previous technical breakthroughs presents both opportunities and challenges. However, without meaningful, ethical, and well-regulated applications, AI could pose significant risks, as there are no globally defined regulations, guidelines, or strategies for its use in education. Thus, this study explores the challenges and impediments to the effective integration of AI in education, highlighting both benefits and ethical considerations. Additionally, it offers strategies for harnessing AI's potential to revolutionize teaching and learning, emphasizing personalized learning, administrative automation, professional development, and inclusivity. The findings provide practical insights for improving educational approaches, developing curricula, and equipping educators—both pre-service and in-service—with the skills and knowledge necessary to effectively incorporate AI in the classroom. Furthermore, this study aims to raise students' awareness of the importance of ethical, purposeful, and efficient AI use across educational and non-educational domains.

Keywords Artificial intelligence · AI in education · Educational transformation · Challenges · Benefits · Ethical AI integration · Strategies

---

M. Dervić (✉)
Liberal Arts Department, American University of the Middle East, Egaila, Kuwait
e-mail: mersad.dervic@aum.edu.kw

S. Bećirović · E. Polz
University College of Teacher Education Lower Austria, Baden, Austria
e-mail: senad.becirovic@ph-noe.ac.at

E. Polz
e-mail: edda.polz@ph-noe.ac.at

M. A. Adarkwah et al. (eds.), *Artificial Intelligence and Human Agency in Education: Volume One*, Future Education and Learning Spaces,
https://doi.org/10.1007/978-981-96-7937-9_9

9.1 Introduction

The rapid advancement of technology has profoundly impacted various aspects of human life, playing a pivotal role in the digitalization of socioeconomic sectors, including education (Bećirović, 2023a). Digital technologies are reforming both industry and the public sector by enhancing system efficiency and improving quality of life through streamlined processes. Due to technological breakthroughs, the educational sector is undergoing significant transformations, with Artificial Intelligence (AI) driving some of the most dramatic innovations.

AI-powered technologies have the potential to revolutionize education by inventing new tools, resources, and methodologies. This potential is expected to have a far-reaching impact on teaching, learning, and institutional management than any other technological advancements ever before. However, despite its promise, AI integration in education faces significant challenges, especially in the absence of standardized regulations, strategies, and ethical guidelines. Without careful management, these technologies may lead to unintended consequences that could disrupt educational practices.

This study seeks to address the critical gap in understanding how AI-powered technologies can be meaningfully and ethically integrated into educational systems. More specifically, the article aims to explore the challenges posed by AI in education, while also investigating its potential benefits and applications. The primary objective is to propose actionable strategies for leveraging AI to enhance teaching and learning practices while safeguarding against possible risks. The study is guided by the following research questions:

1. What are the challenges to the successful integration of AI-powered technology in educational settings and how can they be addressed?
2. What are the most potential benefits of AI in the educational systems and how can these benefits assist educators?
3. What are the practical applications of AI-powered technology and what are the future implications and directions for transforming educational practices?

Given the novelty of AI in education and the unyielding need for research in this field, this study focuses on providing a critical analysis of both challenges and opportunities AI presents in education. By narrowing the scope of AI's impact on teaching methodologies and student learning processes, the study aims to contribute significantly to the growing body of literature. Further, the study may inform and assist in improving and developing educational policies, designing curricula, supporting both pre-service and in-service training programs, and equipping educators with the necessary knowledge and skills to integrate AI-powered technologies effectively. Additionally, this study seeks to promote a deeper understanding of the ethical implications of AI in education. The distinction between broader educational systems, teaching practices, and student learning processes will be carefully examined to ensure clarity on how AI affects each component. Moreover, the findings may raise awareness among students and instructors about the responsible, ethical, and meaningful use of AI in an educational context.

9.2 Prior Related Work

The literature review examines the key themes in the research to provide a comprehensive summary of existing studies on the transformative influence of AI on educators' practices in the teaching process. It begins by establishing the background and context of the topic, followed by an exploration of theoretical approaches employed in previous studies. Further, the review analyzes diverse methodological approaches to facilitate a comprehensive understanding of AI in an educational context.

Since high-tech innovations keep altering current systems (Bećirović, 2023b), AI-powered technologies, as the mega-trends in both industry and education, have the potential to enhance system efficiency and improve the quality of educational experiences. Understanding the transformative influence of AI on educators' practices is essential due to its profound implications across socioeconomic sectors and institutions. Particularly notable is the emergence of Generative AI technologies such as OpenAI tools like ChatGPT at the end of 2022, which has catalyzed discussions around AI integration in education. Due to the inadequate current conceptualization of AI chatbots in education, Chang et al. (2023) proposed a new conceptualization by combining Zimmerman's Self-Regulated Learning (SRL) framework and Judgment of Learning (JOL). The aim was to provide educators with guidelines for implementing AI in education through AI-assisted pedagogy and instructional design. Particularly, the alignment of three educational principles—prompting, self-assessment/feedback, and personalization—enabled students to acquire and understand SRL strategies profoundly (Chang et al., 2023).

However, while these tools offer opportunities for personalized learning and innovative educational approaches, they also pose ethical concerns, especially regarding transparency and the development of critical thinking skills (Ahmed et al., 2024; Elbanna & Armstrong, 2024; Huang et al., 2024). More specifically, their limitations are reflected in a lack of factual consistency, profound understanding, and safety mechanisms (Elbanna & Armstrong, 2024).

Previous research (Bulathwela et al., 2024; Onesi-Ozigagun et al., 2024; Saxena et al., 2023; Slimi & Villarejo Carballido, 2023; Vinay & Surendra, 2024) highlights the need for a critical examination of the challenges and promises associated with AI-driven systems within educational settings. Key issues include the risk of exacerbating the digital divide, ethical considerations in AI use, and the necessity for adequate training for educators in AI technologies.

AI-enhanced platforms can assist educators by creating individualized learning experiences tailored to students' unique abilities, needs, interests, styles, pace, and preferences (Ambele et al., 2022; Bulathwela et al., 2024; Demartini et al., 2024; Hashem et al., 2024; Onesi-Ozigagun et al., 2024; Pawar, 2023; Stamper et al., 2024). These systems have the potential to ensure equitable access to quality education, promoting inclusivity for diverse learners (Onesi-Ozigagun et al., 2024; Yu, 2024). This means that everyone, regardless of their background or learning abilities, should have access to countless educational opportunities (Bećirović et al., 2019), particularly in terms of quality and accessibility to personalized learning styles (Mašić et al., 2020). Nonetheless, the ongoing digital divide in education, especially in developing countries, underscores the need for institutions to refine their policies. Enhancing digital literacy and ensuring access to modern technology is vital for achieving equity and inclusivity in education at all levels (Onesi-Ozigagun et al., 2024; Yu, 2024).

Moreover, AI-empowered technology can also help educators to advance their professional development and lifelong learning. Research (Hashem et al., 2024; Onesi-Ozigagun et al., 2024; Vinay & Surendra, 2024) indicates that AI platforms can provide adaptive learning experiences and offer personalized professional development courses tailored to educators' specific needs and interests.

Despite the potential benefits, the integration of AI in education poses significant risks if not approached meaningfully, ethically, and professionally (Bećirović & Dervić, 2022; Bećirović et al., 2022). Therefore, successful AI integration requires the adoption of appropriate educational policies, standardized regulations, and improvement in curricula to equip educators with the necessary knowledge and competencies for effective AI use in the teaching and learning process.

9.3 Method

To explore and identify the transformative influence of AI-powered technology on educators' practices, our literature was conducted as a narrative review. This approach allows for systematic and holistic identification of primary studies on the topic, drawing conclusions based on the researchers' own experiences and existing theories (Demiris et al., 2019) without following a pre-determined protocol.

A comprehensive search strategy was employed across multiple electronic databases (e.g., Scopus, PubMed, Web of Science, ResearchGate, Google Scholar) using relevant keywords such as AI in education, ethical AI in education, AI and pedagogy, AI teaching tools, AI impact on teaching, and personalized and adaptive AI learning. The literature was selected based on recency (2022–2024), relevance to the topic, and publication in peer-reviewed journals. After applying the inclusion and exclusion criteria, a total of 45 publications were included in the final review. The studies represented a diverse geographical distribution, including research from Balkan countries, Canada, Singapore, China, India, the United Kingdom, and the United States which highlights the need for more geographically diverse research on AI in education.

Although the quality of the included studies was not assessed due to the nature of narrative review articles (Demiris et al., 2019), this aspect is acknowledged as a limitation that may impact the findings. However, this approach allowed for a broader thematic synthesis of the current state of AI in education as reflected in recent literature. Furthermore, the researchers performed data extraction by selecting and extracting relevant information (e.g., study aims, methodologies, key results, conclusions, and implications) from each study and by resolving inconsistencies through a consensus decision-making process. A thematic analysis approach was used to synthesize and analyze the findings from selected articles, enabling researchers to profoundly identify and organize common themes related to AI technology in education (Naeem et al., 2023).

This review was guided by our research objectives and the socio-technical system theory, a conceptual framework that is designed to describe and explain the theoretical and practical challenges of integrating technology into educational systems (Ropohl, 1999). This framework, previously employed in studies (Onesi-Ozigagun et al., 2024; Saxena et al., 2023; Vinay & Surendra, 2024) elucidates the reciprocal interrelationship between humans and AI technology integration and its implications for organizational change (Ropohl, 1999). We analyzed studies employing diverse methodological approaches, including theoretical, systematic, and empirical studies (quantitative, qualitative, or mixed-method research), enabling comprehensive data collection and insights into various aspects of AI in education. In terms of ethical considerations, copyright law and the use of published data from the selected studies were observed throughout the review process. As shown in Fig. 9.1, the flowchart illustrates the study selection process for the narrative review, outlining the number of studies identified, screened, excluded, and ultimately included in the analysis.

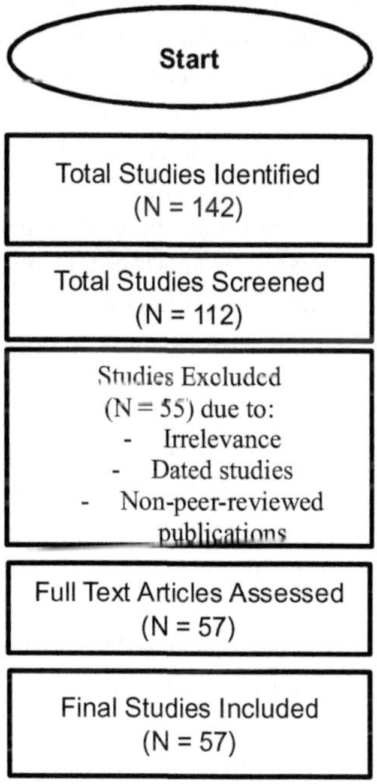

Fig. 9.1 Study selection process

9.4 Findings

9.4.1 Challenges to Successful Integration of AI-Powered Technology in Educational Settings

The most concerning challenges faced by teachers in today's educational landscape mainly revolve around ethical considerations, security, and data privacy issues associated with AI (Saxena et al., 2023; Wu et al., 2024). Since AI can create almost original and natural-sounding text, there is a risk that individuals may misuse it by opting to utilize AI-generated content without proper authorization. This practice undermines issues of copyright, correctness, accuracy, ownership, and authenticity (Saxena et al., 2023; Wu et al., 2024). Thus, it is important to raise awareness that AI operates through algorithms that produce text based on vast and generative input, indicating that all generated information needs to be uncompromisingly verified before its use.

The security risks inherent in AI can be manifested in various forms, including the spread of misinformation, overreliance on AI-generated content, and training data poisoning (Wu et al., 2024). Additionally, by having access to individual's personalized files, the leakage of such records poses high privacy risks through unauthorized access as well as malicious and jailbreaking attacks (Saxena et al., 2023). For instance, these concerns are particularly evident in healthcare AI applications, especially in low-income and middle-income countries. To address such risks, initiatives like RAD-AID have been introduced to tackle disparities in healthcare through an integrated, three-pronged strategy (Mollura et al., 2020). While AI is capable of sharing data with third-party entities without users' consent, privacy leakage also occurs due to the exploitation of personal and public data. This includes leveraging users' input to provide more accurate and unbiased responses or scraping data from various sources such as websites, posts, books, and comments, leading to new privacy attacks on LLMs (Large language models) (Wu et al., 2024). Thus, robust privacy, data protection, and anonymity regulations are crucial to safeguard educators, students, and others against these illicit breaches.

As noted by Slimi and Villarejo Carballido (2023), bias and fairness issues within AI algorithms pose significant challenges for educators. Since AI operates on data-driven from students' personal information, academic performance, and behavior, it may perpetuate and deepen the presence of bias and discrimination even more, which can lead to unfair predictions about certain groups of students and their academic abilities and outcomes (Onesi-Ozigagun et al., 2024; Wu et al., 2024). Wu et al. (2024), pointed out that "the discrimination exhibited by human beings is transmitted to their students, i.e., AI models, which have the ability to further propagate such prejudice" (p. 9). If not addressed appropriately and beforehand, bias in AI models could amplify unfair treatment and exacerbate educational inequalities based on race, gender, or socioeconomic status, ultimately impacting educators, students as well as the entire society in the long run (Bulathwela et al., 2024; Onesi-Ozigagun et al.,

2024; Slimi & Villarejo Carballido, 2023; Stolpe & Hallström, 2024; Wellner & Rothman, 2020; Wu et al., 2024).

Moreover, other significant challenges related to the use of AI-empowered tools in education include job security and a decline in the interpersonal connection between teachers and students (Bulathwela et al., 2024; Slimi & Villarejo Carballido, 2023). Since AI tools can handle many educators' everyday tasks, there is a growing fear within an educational society that the expansion of AI may threaten the long-term sustainability of their role in the classroom. In other words, responsibilities and jobs that are traditionally performed by educators (e.g., course/lesson planning, content creation, grading, providing personalized learning and feedback) might be replaced with automated AI platforms like ChatGPT and CourseAI, which could threaten their current roles within education and reduce demand for their expertise and services (Saxena et al., 2023). For instance, in an attempt to address the teacher shortage, a private school in the UK (David Game College) implemented the first 'Teacherless' classroom using AI technology and VR headsets. This approach has helped students improve faster than with traditional teaching methods and has also saved money on tuition fees.

Another pressing issue stems from AI's current and future aptitudes to provide students with personalized learning experiences in almost every aspect of their academic development (Ambele et al., 2022; Bulathwela et al., 2024; Demartini et al., 2024; Hashem et al., 2024; Onesi-Ozigagun et al., 2024). Inadequate utilization of this potential can lead to negative repercussions for educators in terms of deteriorating their interpersonal cohesion and relations with students, clouding their excelling teaching proficiency, and damaging their educational autonomy and independence. While AI can offer unique experiences and opportunities that advanced technologies lack, such as stimulus, guidance, motivation, encouragement, and a profound understanding of know-how practices, its capabilities may inadvertently underestimate the central role teachers play in education, adversely affecting students' emotional and social development in the long run (Bulathwela et al., 2024; Slimi & Villarejo Carballido, 2023).

In the pursuit of modernizing pedagogy, educators must engage in ongoing professional development focused on advanced AI technologies. Thus, to successfully integrate AI-empowered technologies into teaching practices, it is paramount for all educational bodies to familiarize and equip educators with the necessary tools and knowledge to keep pace with advancements in AI.

Research has highlighted the most common challenges educators face regarding AI integration (Ambele et al., 2022; Bulathwela et al., 2024; Kong & Yang, 2024; Onesi-Ozigagun et al., 2024; Wu et al., 2024), including:

- Keeping pace with rapid AI and technological change (e.g., AI innovative tools and applications),
- Insufficient training opportunities (lack of time, funding, and tailored training courses from educational institutions),
- Understanding and accessing the latest technological trends (challenges digital literacy and technical expertise),

- Overreliance on AI (diminished teacher autonomy and independence in planning, grading, and content delivery),
- Providing systemic and continuous professional development (insufficient emphasis on practical, continuous, and collaborative learning),
- Dealing with institutional barriers (outdated curriculum frameworks or bureaucracies), and
- Facing resistance from administration or colleagues and even fellow educators (lack of support for new AI practices or overlying on traditional teaching methods).

While these challenges are substantial in diverse educational environments, in developing countries, they are frequently convoluted by broader concerns related to infrastructure and security. For example, in countries such as China, India, and Indonesia, major constraints in implementing AI technology include infrastructure issues, lack of Internet access, limited AI expertise, privacy concerns, and the challenge of balancing the development and use of AI in technology-based education (Mustopa et al., 2024).

Given that educators are primarily responsible for guiding and assisting students through their educational journey, AI has the potential to enhance the integration of innovations into classrooms, thereby enriching students' learning experiences. Consequently, a provision of continuous training and professional development with AI and technology trends, capabilities, tools, and interpretations is crucial for sustainable teaching and learning (Bećirović & Mattoš, 2024; Onesi-Ozigagun et al., 2024). In essence, a multi-faceted approach that values educators while effectively integrating AI into education is necessary for promoting a sustainable and equitable educational future. By updating ethical standards, addressing privacy concerns, tackling bias and fairness issues, improving teacher-student relationships, and investing in educators' continuous professional development related to AI, educational institutions can foster effective integration of AI technologies into teaching practices, ultimately mitigating negative impacts while advancing educational outcomes for future generations.

9.4.2 How Can AI-Powered Technology Transform Educators' Practices?

Recent studies (Ambele et al., 2022; Bulathwela et al., 2024; Onesi-Ozigagun et al., 2024; Stolpe & Hallström, 2024) suggest that AI has the potential to revolutionize educational systems worldwide. Its capabilities have been found particularly efficient in assisting educators in pursuing their professional development, while simultaneously enhancing their personal lives. Therefore, addressing the potential promises of AI in pedagogy is crucial not only to educational institutions but also to educators and learners who are eager to improve their academic experiences and personal growth.

The most significant promises of AI include personalized learning experiences for both teachers and students, support with administrative tasks, improved communication and collaboration in the workplace, professional development opportunities, and, ultimately, an enhanced work-life balance. Atlas (2023) notes that "individualized learning focuses on the use of personalized learning, adaptive testing, and intelligent tutoring/advising to enhance the educational experience for all students, including those with disabilities" (p. 79). Furthermore, according to previous studies (Ambele et al., 2022; Atlas, 2023; Bulathwela et al., 2024; Demartini et al., 2024; Hashem et al., 2024; Onesi-Ozigagun et al., 2024; Pawar, 2023; Stamper et al., 2024), AI-powered technology can:

- Personalized practice exercises to help students improve.
- Provide advanced materials to maintain engagement and challenge students appropriately.
- Ensure instant, targeted feedback on quizzes and assignments.
- Enhance academic engagement, retention, motivation, and achievement.
- Facilitate the tracking of students' performance through data-driven insights.

Using data and algorithms, AI's analytical process such as XGBoost (Cosar, 2024) is capable of analyzing educational outcomes to reveal trends and areas needing improvement, subsequently suggesting remedies for students' further academic development (Atlas, 2023; Demartini et al., 2024; Onesi-Ozigagun et al., 2024; Stolpe & Hallström, 2024). Besides, other AI applications like Intelligent Tutoring Systems (ITS), recommendation systems, adaptive assessments, and AI-generated content can significantly help in apt interventions and enhanced development of weak students (Vashishth et al., 2024). Based on these learning analytics that leverages teachers'/students' training, the role of AI transcends traditional boundaries and enables the creation of adaptive learning environments, thereby offering tailored teaching experiences aligned with the needs of both teachers and students (Embarak, 2022; Saxena et al., 2023).

AI-empowered technology is particularly efficient in assisting educators in managing administrative tasks more efficiently, allowing them to dedicate more time to teaching and mentoring rather than dealing with mundane administrative work (Ambele et al., 2022; Bulathwela et al., 2024; Demartini et al., 2024; Onesi-Ozigagun et al., 2024; Vinay & Surendra, 2024). For instance, tasks like lesson planning, assignments grading, real-time feedback, streamlined scheduling, and attendance tracking, can now be completed by AI-enhanced platforms like Teaching Assistant (TA) and MentorAI within minutes (Bagai & Mane, 2023; Sajja et al., 2023). This efficacy enables educators to focus more on:

- Fostering interpersonal relationships with students (e.g., mediating between struggling and excelling students and ensuring a supportive learning environment),
- Providing interactive, engaging, and hands-on learning experiences (e.g., incorporating multimedia elements, simulations, and gamified activities),

- Identifying comprehensive trends and patterns in the teaching process compared to traditional teaching methods (e.g., adoption of a learner-centered approach with innovative tools and techniques to enhance instruction), and
- Enhancing students' critical thinking skills (e.g., problem-solving, creativity, and collaboration).

Another critical aspect of educators' professional development is the ability of AI platforms like the Human-AI Collaboration Platform (HACP), GitHub Copilot, Bing Chat, Bard, ChatGPT to facilitate and establish better communication and collaboration among colleagues (Ashktorab et al., 2024; Hashem et al., 2024; Onesi-Ozigagun et al., 2024; Zheng et al., 2023). This collective approach enhances productivity and promotes effective decision-making, especially in refining and sharing teaching resources, strategies, and practices, improving assessment and feedback mechanisms, and generating innovative ideas in pedagogy (Kong & Yang, 2024; Soofastaei, 2024). AI-driven professional development can also create communities of practice, connecting educators globally and breaking down geographical barriers. This fosters an environment where educators can share their learning experiences and identify areas for improvement (Onesi-Ozigagun et al., 2024; Vinay & Surendra, 2024).

Finally, AI-empowered technology serves as a virtual assistant (e.g., AI Chatbots, adaptive learning platforms, and frameworks like RASA) in developing classroom management strategies, identifying relevant resources, providing feedback on teaching practices, and refining pedagogical approaches (Shekhar et al., 2020; Vinay & Surendra, 2024). By utilizing personalized AI training pathways, educators can track their progress and explore diverse ways to enhance both their professional and personal lives (Onesi-Ozigagun et al., 2024).

Importantly, beyond extensively helping educators professionally, AI-empowered technology can also enhance their personal lives. AI-enhanced systems, such as AI TechWell and PFL framework (Keeley, 2023) create lifelong learning opportunities that make educators' journeys more fulfilling and motivating, while effectively reducing workload and improving work-life balance (Bulathwela et al., 2024; Demartini et al., 2024; Hashem et al., 2024; Onesi-Ozigagun et al., 2024). In other words, incorporating AI pathways into educators' professional lives automatically grants more time for family and personal goals, reduces stress and burnout, and enables a greater focus on student relationships. Overall, the underlying benefits of the transformative nature of AI-empowered applications in the context of education, reside in providing more opportunities for educators' personal and professional lives and creating more dynamic and supportive learning environments for all.

9.4.3 Putting AI-Powered Technologies into Educational Practices

In recent times, AI has increasingly integrated into the education system, with AI-driven solutions witnessing explosive growth. These include student-empowering applications, gamified training, customized teaching systems, and analytical tools (Holmes et al., 2019), which are continually evolving. These technologies can be broadly categorized into those designed to support learning and those intended to analyze and understand the learning process (Holmes et al., 2019). Holmes and Tuomi (2022) further classify these three categories: student-oriented, teacher-oriented, and institution-oriented AI applications.

9.4.3.1 Student-Oriented Applications

Student-oriented applications, such as intelligent tutoring systems like CBM (constraint-based model), CTAT tutor, Andes Physics Tutor, and SQL Tutor have proven to be remarkably effective and particularly efficient on highly structured procedural and open-ended tasks, leading to better learning outcomes (Stamper et al., 2024). In addition, another significant power of AI applications is the development of language learning tools (Natural Language Processing), gamified learning experiences, virtual assistants, and chatbots for students. For example, Han et al., (2023) introduced RECIPE (Revising an Essay with ChatGPT on an Interactive Platform for EFL learners), which enhances English writing skills for EFL learners. Popular AI-powered language learning apps include Duolingo, Memrise, Babbel, Rosetta Stone, HelloTalk, and FluentU, which provide gamified lessons, live tutoring, and real-life dialogues (Kasimova, 2024; Ulfa, 2023).

These apps can monitor students' development, pinpoint their weak points, offer individualized learning advice, simulate real conversations, evaluate speech, and provide tailored recommendations for further development (Kasimova, 2024; Molenaar, 2022; Ulfa, 2023). However, the main shortcomings of these AI-powered language learning and gamified apps reside in their inability to provide a fully immersive cultural experience, personalized feedback, and universally free services (Kasimova, 2024). Thus, while AI-empowered technology serves as a valuable educational tool alongside traditional teaching, it should not be seen as a substitute for educators (Memarian & Doleck, 2023; Yu, 2024).

9.4.3.2 Teacher-Oriented Applications

In supporting teachers, AI-powered systems significantly facilitate educators in pursuing professional development opportunities, enabling them to meet their professional goals at hand. Popular AI tools that can provide educators with plentiful resources and materials to enhance their teaching skills include Google for Education Training Center, Coursera, Udemy, Khan Academy, and IBM Watson Teacher Advisor, which offer free high-quality educational resources.

Furthermore, Sajja et al. (2023) developed an AI-augmented assistance framework based on GPT-3, designed to generate an intelligent teaching assistant (TA) for educators. This virtual TA can help educators reduce logistical workloads, allowing more focus on educational aspects, and identifying learning barriers to enhance engagement and retention (Sajja et al., 2023).

Similarly, Bagai and Mane (2023) introduced MentorAI, an AI-powered mentorship platform, designed to provide tailored mentorship experiences to professionals, fostering skill development and supporting work-life balance. Like the virtual TA (Sajja et al., 2023), MentorAI offers real-time guidance and resources tailored to, users' specific needs and goals (Bagai & Mane, 2023). However, both applications raise concerns regarding data security, protection, and algorithm bias, necessitating proactive measures to ensure user safety (Bagai & Mane, 2023; Sajja et al., 2023).

9.4.3.3 Institution-Oriented Applications

Institution-oriented AI applications focus primarily on ethical aspects and administrative functions (Holmes & Tuomi, 2022). To promote fairness and reduce educational inequality, Li et al. (2022) developed a fair-logistic regression (Fair-LR) algorithm, demonstrating improved predictive accuracy and fairness compared to fairness-unaware AI models. Their findings suggest a methodological shift in the educational community to achieve accurate and fair AI contributions.

Additionally, Saxena et al. (2023) introduced the Ethical Observatory model for AI in Education, which uses a multidisciplinary approach to create comprehensive ethical guidelines and policy frameworks for AI integration. By addressing privacy, bias, transparency, and accountability, this model fosters informed dialogue among educators and policymakers, ensuring educational equity, inclusivity, and outcomes. However, its key drawbacks include limited universal applicability and the need for empirical research to test its effectiveness across various educational contexts, similar to frameworks developed by other researchers (Islam et al., 2022; Shulner-Tal et al., 2023).

9.5 Discussion and Implication

This study highlights several key themes and insights regarding the potential of AI-powered technologies to revolutionize educational practices. More specifically, this paper focuses on AI's potential challenges and benefits and provides strategies for using AI-powered technologies ethically and effectively. Thus, the emphasis is on several potential applications of AI that enable tailored learning, automated administrative work, professional growth, and chances for equity and inclusivity for all.

To fully understand AI's potential and its transformative influence on educators' teaching practices, previous literature has identified several key challenges. Notably, AI integration in teaching and learning poses challenges that are significantly related to data security threats, while other studies emphasized the importance of addressing educators' concerns about their aptitude to integrate AI-powered technology into their practices. Furthermore, important challenges identified in the research include ethical considerations of AI, bias and fairness issues, job security, the relationship between teachers and students, and educators' ability and readiness to cope with its rapid expansion, suggesting a need for further investigation of its impending risks in an educational context.

However, the transformative potential of AI is commonly recognized through providing personalized learning experiences for both educators and students. AI in Education (AIEd) is particularly efficient in tailoring educational content to diverse user profiles, ensuring that their individual needs and interests are adequately met (Ambele et al., 2022; Bulathwela et al., 2024; Demartini et al., 2024; Hashem et al., 2024; Onesi-Ozigagun et al., 2024; Pratama et al., 2023). Based on the use of a constructivist framework (knowledge based on prior experiences and interactions), AI-enhanced systems and algorithms can offer adaptive learning platforms, ITS (intelligent tutoring systems), tailored content delivery, real-time feedback, data-driven insights, personalized practice exercises and resources, and active and interactive engagement in the learning process (Pawar, 2023; Stamper et al., 2024). For instance, ITS models generate feedback using three methods: (1) the expert-created learner model (manual input of models of learners' behaviors or constraints), (2) the data-driven learner model (compiling data from learners' interactions and automatically building a model of learner behavior), and (3) the use of large language models (leveraging LLMs and generating more adaptive feedback with less human labor) (Stamper et al., 2024).

Moreover, AI educational platforms in the United States, such as Dreambox, Blackboard, Arizona State University's OpenAI, and the University of Michigan's Generative AI initiative (GenAI), exemplify how AI can assist both educators and students in adaptive learning environments at all levels. These platforms help in selecting course materials according to individual needs, suggesting pathways based on performance, and providing timely feedback, thereby enhancing both the teaching process and learning outcomes. For instance, the AI platform Dreambox has been created for elementary school students to improve their math and reading skills, personalizing instruction and enabling educators to balance students' differences and needs effectively.

On the other side of the globe, AI educational platforms such as Squirrel AI in China, MyLearn—offered by Torrens University in Australia—and Teacherless from David Game College in the UK represent how educational institutions are swiftly transforming traditional educational settings. These platforms provide more effective, flexible, and student-centered learning environments. For example, Squirrel AI focuses on enhancing students' learning experiences through adaptive technologies. Unlike traditional classroom environments, it demonstrates how AI can transform education by delivering personalized content tailored to students' individual needs and abilities. Furthermore, students who have used the platform have shown significant improvements in their AI literacy and overall learning outcomes, particularly in mathematics (Wang et al., 2023).

Likewise, Pawar (2023) found that students who are engaged with AI-driven personalized learning tools reported higher levels of engagement, motivation, and satisfaction with their educational experiences, demonstrating significant improvements in their academic achievements. For example, in the study conducted by Pratama et al. (2023), the interviews and observations revealed that the majority (97%) of students consider AI as an important aspect of their daily learning process, while 81% view it as an alternative to independent or self-regulated learning. Despite 80% of students disagreeing with the idea that they would replace their educators with AI-powered systems, they still use AI as their virtual smart assistant or tutor whenever possible (Pratama et al., 2023). This indicates that students appreciate educators' dedication and ability to inspire and motivate, cherishing interpersonal connections for emotional and social growth, which ensures educators' long-lasting contributions and legacy in education (Atlas, 2023; Bećirović & Polz, 2021).

While AI-powered technology holds promise, educators must view it as a tool that enhances their roles in personalizing learning, accessing knowledge, offering guidance, strengthening relationships, and promoting creativity (Kasimova, 2024; Pratama et al., 2023). Hence, educators are required to consider the moral side of education (Polz & Bećirović, 2022) and shift their responsibility to the ITS (e.g., DIAG system, LLM-based feedback generation, etc.), which is already used in some educational contexts worldwide (Molenaar, 2022; Stamper et al., 2024). Nevertheless, it is important to note that some of the previously mentioned models lack a solid theoretical foundation and empirical research on their impact on learning (Stamper et al., 2024). Additionally, ethical considerations must be critically examined when developing previously mentioned AI-powered adaptive platforms.

Helping teachers with administrative tasks (e.g., registration, scheduling, record-keeping, and automated assignment grading) is another vital benefit of integrating transformative AI-powered systems and analytics in education. For example, the study conducted by Bryant et al. (2020) surveyed more than 2000 teachers across Canada, Singapore, the United Kingdom, and the United States about the duration of 37 core activities they perform daily (e.g., lesson planning, teaching, grading, and maintaining student records). Their findings revealed that teachers spent equal amounts of time (51%) in direct instruction and engagement with students and on preparation, evaluation, and administrative duties. They concluded that areas with the most potential for automation are preparation, administration, evaluation, and feedback, suggesting that innovative technology could help teachers reallocate 20 to 40% of their time toward activities that support student learning. Thus, to offer practical insights into how AI can enhance personalized feedback and assessment in higher education settings, Vashishth et al. (2024) explored the potential of AI-driven learning analytics (e.g., gather, process, and interpret educational data) in higher education. They found that leveraging AI algorithms and data analytics can provide personalized feedback and adaptive and formative assessments targeting specific strengths and areas for improvement, enabling personalized and accurate evaluation of knowledge and skills. More specifically, they explain that this multi-dimensional approach has promising potential to reduce educators' workload by harnessing data from various sources, including student interactions with digital learning platforms, academic performance records, and behavioral indicators. For future reference, they believe that AI-driven learning analytics can enhance student engagement, support individualized learning, and enhance educational experiences and outcomes. However, successful integration requires addressing ethical considerations, implementation challenges, and faculty training in future research (Vashisth et al., 2024).

An additional important aspect of an AI-powered system is its potential to foster and promote educational inclusivity, equity, and fairness, ensuring alignment with core educational and societal standards as well as safeguarding students and educators to meet their expectations. For instance, Yu (2024) indicates that AI is capable of accommodating the different needs of diverse student demographics, facilitating a more tailored, immersive, and inclusive educational atmosphere. He believes that ChatGPT's contribution to the revolutionizing pedagogy through innovative instruments, platforms, and materials stimulates a contemporary educational environment by "advocating for a more inclusive and enriched educational framework that adopts novel educational philosophies and didactic methodologies" and thus "propelling the amalgamation of technology into instructional practices with heightened proficiency" (Yu, 2024, p. 4). For instance, in an effort to keep pace with AI technologies and bridge the digital divide in countries like India, the government initiated the Atal Innovation Mission (AIM), which established Atal Tinkering Laboratories (ATLs). These laboratories are designed to cultivate cognitive and technical skills among young minds. While ATLs effectively nurture curiosity and creativity, they also instill essential computer literacy skills, including adaptive learning and physical computing. This initiative ensures that students in underserved societies gain access to innovative technologies, promoting inclusivity and fairness in the digital age.

The findings from this review have both theoretical and practical implications. Theoretically, there is a need for innovative and intradisciplinary research frameworks due to the integration of AI into all spheres of human life, especially education. Practically, institutions and policymakers must ensure and consider inclusivity and equity in AI systems by developing regulations that protect users' rights and promote public trust at all times. Since AI's potential can significantly influence the socioeconomic aspect of human lives (e.g., employment, educational attainment, technological literacy, and inequality), comprehensive schemes and solutions are necessary to address and mitigate the negative effects of AI while promoting its inclusive progress.

Even though the previous literature broadly indicated the positive and negative sides of integrating AI in education, further research is needed, primarily due to the rapid growth of AI technologies, hindering the development and implementation of already established ethical guidelines and frameworks (Saxena et al., 2023). Other limitations include a lack of empirical studies testing the effectiveness of AI frameworks in diverse educational settings and examining the long-term influence of AI on teachers' and learners' interrelationships, a delay in the applicability and adoption of the universal guidelines for AI use in diverse educational systems across different regions, and a lack of exchange of best practices concerning AI ethical standards, challenges, and promises in a technologically transformative educational context (Bulathwela et al., 2024; Onesi-Ozigagun et al., 2024; Saxena et al., 2023; Vinay & Surendra, 2024). Thus, to provide a more holistic understanding of AI's impact on educators' practices, future research should address the previously mentioned limitations by seeking more empirical research on AI's effects on educators and learners individually and their interrelationships and by developing up-to-date ethical guidelines promoting equity and inclusivity across diverse educational settings and regions (Yu, 2024). Thereby, such studies would provide insights and understanding of AI's dimensions and its implications for revolutionary pedagogy.

9.6 Conclusion and Recommendations for Future Work

AI in Education (AIEd) revolutionizes the process of teaching and learning, as well as the structure of education. With deep learning algorithms and data-driven insights, its expectations to completely transform how current educational systems function theoretically and practically are higher than those of any previous technological advancements.

This article aimed to explore AI-powered technology challenges, and promises and provide strategies for AI's effective integration and use in transforming educational practices. The study identified several key aspects of lAI that may greatly impact educational systems, including personalized learning experiences, professional development opportunities, automated administrative tasks, and inclusivity and equity. However, successful implementation is hindered by challenges such as data privacy regulations, ethical considerations, teachers' attitudes and skills, and algorithm bias tendencies.

The ground-breaking potential of AI in education offers revolutionary opportunities that could transform current pedagogy for the better. Firstly, the integration of AI-powered technology into teaching can provide personalized and tailored learning experiences for all learners regardless of their abilities, knowledge, and experience. This would not only allow learners to experience more dynamic and student-driven learning environments, but it would also enable them to navigate learning according to their preferences and needs. By the same token, allowing AI-powered technology to deal with administrative tasks would not only help educators spend more time interacting with their students, but it would also reduce their daily workload and, consequently, improve their professional as well as personal lives.

As for professional development, AI-powered technology offers endless opportunities for educators' lifelong learning improvement, ensuring their sustainable growth in the transformative wave of technological trends, especially AI-powered systems. Additionally, the most transformative promise of AI resides in its capability to promote inclusivity, equity, and fairness by fostering equal and improved digital and AI literacy opportunities and access to modern technologies for all in future educational environments. However, to fully benefit from AI-powered technology integration and to ensure fair access to AI technologies, the previously mentioned challenges (e.g., ethical, security, data, and algorithm concerns) need to be adequately addressed.

Since AI-powered technology keeps developing rapidly, these concerns should first be faced by continually developing up-to-date ethical guidelines and frameworks. This should be followed by conducting more empirical studies that offer insights into the effectiveness and the long-term influence of such frameworks on students' learning outcomes. AI's sustainability in an educational context is only attainable by constantly ensuring equal, fair, and inclusive educational opportunities for everyone. In the end, AI's future in the educational context heavily depends on how efficient we are at addressing its impending challenges and threats, as its revolutionary and transformative potential in educational practices, whether positive or negative, is inevitable.

In an attempt to provide a comprehensive overview of the previous literature on the topic, the review's progress did not develop without limitations. Since the study deployed a narrative review to address the existing literature on the transformative influence of AI on educators' practices in education, it may have failed to disclose the validity of the included literature and/or include all relevant and related studies regarding the topic in a broader context. Also, the consistency of synthesized findings could have been compromised due to the variety of the existing studies reviewed (e.g., qualitative, quantitative, systematic reviews, etc.), and down to the evolving nature of AI, meaning some recent findings might have been overlooked.

To address these limitations, the following suggestions for future research need to be taken into consideration. Initially, ethical considerations of AI should be carefully observed and developed, particularly in an educational context, by frequently implementing and improving existing or new ethical guidelines and frameworks. Additionally, future research should focus on conducting more empirical, interdisciplinary, and longitudinal studies to address the multi-faceted challenges that AI poses and provide more insights into how AI influences educational practices across educational sectors. Lastly, including geographical diversity in research could help to identify gaps in the existing literature and ensure that AI's potential is explored in a global context. More diverse types of studies (e.g., experimental, observational, cross-sectional, and case studies) would provide us with additional insights into how we can leverage AI's full potential for better education and society in the end.

References

Ahmed, Z., Shanto, S. S., Rime, M. H. K., Morol, M. K., Fahad, N., Hossen, M. J., & Abdullah-Al-Jubair, M. (2024). The generative AI landscape in education: Mapping the terrain of opportunities, challenges and student perception. *IEEE Access*. https://doi.org/10.1109/ACCESS.2024.3461874

Ambele, R. M., Kaijage, S. F., Dida, M. A., Trojer, L., & Kyando, N. M. (2022). A review of the development trend of personalized learning technologies and its applications. *International Journal of Advances in Scientific Research and Engineering, 8*(11), 75–91.

Ashktorab, Z., Bansal, G., Buçinca, Z., Holstein, K., Hullman, J., Smith-Renner, A. M., Wu, T., & Zhang, W. (2024). Trust and reliance in evolving human-AI workflows (TREW). *Conference on Human Factors in Computing Systems—Proceedings*. https://doi.org/10.1145/3613905.3636319

Atlas, S. (2023). *ChatGPT for higher education and professional development: A ChatGPT for higher education and professional development: A guide to conversational AI guide to conversational AI*. Notion Press. https://digitalcommons.uri.edu/cba_facpubs/548

Bagai, R., & Mane, V. (2023). Designing an AI-powered mentorship platform for professional development: Opportunities and challenges. *International Journal of Computer Trends and Technology, 71*(4), 108–114. https://doi.org/10.14445/22312803/IJCTT-V71I4P114

Bećirović, S. (2023a). Digital pedagogy: The use of digital technologies in contemporary education. *Springer Nature*. https://doi.org/10.1007/978-981-99-0444-0

Bećirović, S. (2023b). Examining learning management system success: A multiperspective framework. *Education and Information Technologies,* 1–25. https://doi.org/10.1007/s10639-023-12308-0

Bećirović, S., Ahmetović, E., & Skopljak, A. (2022). An examination of students online learning satisfaction, interaction, self-efficacy and self-regulated learning. *European Journal of Contemporary Education, 11*(1), 16–35. https://doi.org/10.13187/ejced.2022.1.16

Bećirović, S., Brdarević Čeljo, A., & Zavrl, I. (2019). Research into intercultural effectiveness in a multicultural educational milieu in Bosnia and Herzegovina. *Economic Research-Ekonomska Istraživanja, 32*(1), 1336–1351. https://doi.org/10.1080/1331677X.2019.1629329

Bećirović, S., & Dervić, M. (2022). Students' perspectives of digital transformation of higher education in Bosnia and Herzegovina. *The Electronic Journal of Information Systems in Developing Countries, 89*(2), 1–22. https://doi.org/10.1002/isd2.12243

Bećirović, S., & Mattoš, B. (2024). Artificial intelligence in the transformation of higher education: Threats, promises and implementation strategies. In L. Miltiadis D., A. C. Serban, E. Alkhalidi, M. Sawsan, & T. Aldosemani (Eds.), *Digital Transformation in Higher Education, Part A: Best Practices and Challenges* (pp. 23–43). Emerald Publishing.

Bećirović, S., & Polz, E. (2021). *Fostering giftedness: Challenges and opportunities.* Nova Science Publishers.

Bryant, J., Heitz, C., Sanghvi, S., & Wagle, D. (2020). *How artificial intelligence will impact K–12 teachers.* McKinsey & Company. https://www.mckinsey.com/industries/education/our-insights/how-artificial-intelligence-will-impact-k-12-teachers/

Bulathwela, S., Pérez-Ortiz, M., Holloway, C., Cukurova, M., & Shawe-Taylor, J. (2024). Artificial intelligence alone will not democratise education: On educational inequality, techno-solutionism and inclusive tools. *Sustainability, 16*(2), 781. https://doi.org/10.3390/su16020781

Chang, D. H., Lin, M. P.-C., Hajian, S., & Wang, Q. Q. (2023). Educational design principles of using AI Chatbot that supports self-regulated learning in education: Goal setting, feedback, and personalization. *Sustainability (Switzerland), 15*(17). https://doi.org/10.3390/su151712921

Cosar, M. (2024). Utilizing the eXtreme gradient boosting algorithm for artificial intelligence-supported learning analytics application. *The Eurasia Proceedings of Science Technology Engineering and Mathematics, 28*, 277–285. https://doi.org/10.55549/epstem.1521844

Demartini, C. G., Sciascia, L., Bosso, A., & Manuri, F. (2024). Artificial intelligence bringing improvements to adaptive learning in education: A case study. *Sustainability, 16*(3), 1347. https://doi.org/10.3390/su16031347

Demiris, G., Oliver, D. P., & Washington, K. T. (2019). Defining and analyzing the problem. In *Behavioral intervention research in hospice and palliative care* (pp. 27–39). Elsevier. https://doi.org/10.1016/B978-0-12-814449-7.00003-X

Elbanna, S., & Armstrong, L. (2024). Exploring the integration of ChatGPT in education: Adapting for the future. *Management and Sustainability, 3*(1), 16–29. https://doi.org/10.1108/MSAR-03-2023-0016

Embarak, O. H. (2022). Internet of behaviour (IoB)-based AI models for personalized smart education systems. *Procedia Computer Science, 203*, 103–110. https://doi.org/10.1016/j.procs.2022.07.015

Han, J., Yoo, H., Kim, Y., Myung, J., Kim, M., Lim, H., Kim, J., Lee, T. Y., Hong, H., Ahn, S. Y., & Oh, A. (2023). RECIPE: How to integrate ChatGPT into EFLwriting education (pp. 1–8). https://doi.org/10.1145/3573051.3596200

Hashem, R., Ali, N., El Zein, F., Fidalgo, P., & Abu Khurma, O. (2024). AI to the rescue: Exploring the potential of ChatGPT as a teacher ally for workload relief and burnout prevention. *Research and Practice in Technology Enhanced Learning, 19*, 023. https://doi.org/10.58459/rptel.2024.19023

Holmes, W., Bialik, M., & Fadel, C. (2019). *Artificial intelligence in education. Promise and implications for teaching and learning*. Center for Curriculum Redesign.

Holmes, W., & Tuomi, I. (2022). State of the art and practice in AI in education. *European Journal of Education, 57*(4), 542–570. https://doi.org/10.1111/ejed.12533

Huang, C.-W., Coleman, M., Gachago, D., & Van Belle, J.-P. (2024). Using ChatGPT to encourage critical AI literacy skills and for assessment in higher education. *Communications in Computer and Information Science, 1862*, 105–118. https://doi.org/10.1007/978-3-031-48536-7_8

Islam, S. R., Russell, I., Eberle, W., & Dicheva, D. (2022). Incorporating the concepts of fairness and bias into an undergraduate computer science course to promote fair automated decision systems. In *Proceedings of the 53rd ACM technical symposium on computer science education V. 2* (pp. 1075–1075). https://doi.org/10.1145/3478432.3499043

Kasimova, M. A. (2024). The implementation of artificial intelligence in teaching foreign languages. *Mental Enlightenment Scientific—Methodological Journal,* 71–79. https://doi.org/10.37547/mesmj-V5-I1-11

Keeley, K. (2023). AI-assisted teacher wellness: Theory and practice. In *Generative AI in teaching and learning* (pp. 201–216). https://doi.org/10.4018/979-8-3693-0074-9.ch008

Kong, S.-C., & Yang, Y. (2024). A human-centered learning and teaching framework using generative Artificial Intelligence for self-regulated learning development through domain knowledge learning in K–12 settings. *IEEE Transactions on Learning Technologies, 17*, 1588–1599. https://doi.org/10.1109/TLT.2024.3392830

Li, C., Xing, W., & Leite, W. (2022). Using fair AI to predict students' math learning outcomes in an online platform. *Interactive Learning Environments, 32*(3), 1117–1136. https://doi.org/10.1080/10494820.2022.2115076

Mašić, A., Polz, E., & Bećirović, S. (2020). The Relationship between learning styles, GPA, school level and gender. *European Researcher, 11*(1), 51–60. https://doi.org/10.13187/er.2020.1.51

Memarian, B., & Doleck, T. (2023). ChatGPT in education: Methods, potentials, and limitations. *Computers in Human Behavior: Artificial Humans, 1*(2), Article 100022. https://doi.org/10.1016/j.chbah.2023.100022

Molenaar, I. (2022). Towards hybrid human-AI learning technologies. *European Journal of Education, 57*(4), 632–645. https://doi.org/10.1111/ejed.12527

Mollura, D. J., Culp, M. P., Pollack, E., Battino, G., Scheel, J. R., Mango, V. L., Elahi, A., Schweitzer, A., & Dako, F. (2020). Artificial intelligence in low- and middle-income countries: Innovating global health radiology. *Radiology, 297*(3), 513–520. Scopus. https://doi.org/10.1148/radiol.2020201434

Mustopa, M., Nasikhin, N., Chamami, R., Nihayah, H., Habibullah, M. R., & Manshur, A. (2024). Challenges in artificial intelligence development in higher education in China, India, and Indonesia: International students' perspectives. *International Journal of Learning, Teaching and Educational Research, 23*(2), 354–373. https://doi.org/10.26803/ijlter.23.2.17

Naeem, M., Ozuem, W., Howell, K., & Ranfagni, S. (2023). A step-by-step process of thematic analysis to develop a conceptual model in qualitative research. *International Journal of Qualitative Methods, 22*, 16094069231205788. https://doi.org/10.1177/16094069231205789

Onesi-Ozigagun, O., Ololade, Y. J., Eyo-Udo, N. L., & Ogundipe, D. O. (2024). Revolutionizing education through AI: A comprehensive review of enhancing learning experiences. *International Journal of Applied Research in Social Sciences, 6*(4), Article 4. https://doi.org/10.51594/ijarss.v6i4.1011

Pawar, P. B. (2023). AI-enhanced education: Personalized learning and educational technology. In *Fusion of knowledge* (1st ed., pp. 1–8). Red'shine Publication Pvt. Ltd.

Polz, E., & Bećirović, S. (2022). *Competency-based teaching and learning.* MAP Multidisciplinary Academic Publishing.

Pratama, M. P., Sampelolo, R., & Lura, H. (2023). Revolutionizing education: Harnessing the power of artificial intelligence for personalized learning. *Klasikal: Journal of Education, Language Teaching and Science,* 5(2), 350–357. https://doi.org/10.52208/klasikal.v5i2.877

Ropohl, G. (1999). Philosophy of socio-technical systems. *Philosophy of Socio-Technical System, 4*(3), 59–71.

Sajja, R., Sermet, Y., Cwiertny, D., & Demir, I. (2023). Platform-independent and curriculum-oriented intelligent assistant for higher education. *International Journal of Educational Technology in Higher Education, 20*(1), 42. https://doi.org/10.1186/s41239-023-00412-7

Saxena, A. K., García, V., Amin, M. R., M. R., Salazar, J. M. R., & Day, S. (2023). Structure, objectives, and operational framework for ethical integration of artificial intelligence in educational. *Sage Science Review of Educational Technology, 6*(1), 88–100.

Shekhar, G., D'Souza, R., & Fernandes, K. (2020). AI-driven contextual virtual teaching assistant using RASA. In *Proceedings of the 21st annual conference on information* (p. 346). https://doi.org/10.1145/3368308.3415442

Shulner-Tal, A., Kuflik, T., & Kliger, D. (2023). Enhancing fairness perception—Towards human-centred AI and personalized explanations understanding the factors influencing laypeople's fairness perceptions of algorithmic decisions. *International Journal of Human-Computer Interaction, 39*(7), 1455–1482. https://doi.org/10.1080/10447318.2022.2095705

Slimi, Z., & Villarejo Carballido, B. (2023). Navigating the ethical challenges of artificial intelligence in higher education: An analysis of seven global AI ethics policies. *TEM Journal,* 590–602. https://doi.org/10.18421/TEM122-02

Soofastaei, A. (2024). *Advanced virtual assistants—A window to the virtual future.* IntechOpen.

Stamper, J., Xiao, R., & Hou, X. (2024). *Enhancing LLM-based feedback: Insights from intelligent tutoring systems and the learning sciences (Version 2).* arXiv. https://doi.org/10.48550/ARXIV.2405.04645

Stolpe, K., & Hallström, J. (2024). Artificial intelligence literacy for technology education. *Computers and Education Open, 6,* Article 100159. https://doi.org/10.1016/j.caeo.2024.100159

Ulfa, K. (2023). The transformative power of artificial intelligence (AI) to elevate English language learning. *Majalah Ilmiah METHODA, 13*(3), 307–313. https://doi.org/10.46880/methoda.Vol13No3.pp307-313

Vashishth, T. K., Sharma, V., Sharma, K. K., Kumar, B., Panwar, R., & Chaudhary, S. (2024). AI-driven learning analytics for personalized feedback and assessment in higher education: In T. V. T. Nguyen & N. T. M. Vo (Eds.), *Advances in media, entertainment, and the arts* (pp. 206–230). IGI Global. https://doi.org/10.4018/979-8-3693-0639-0.ch009

Vinay, S., & Surendra, R. (2024). Impact of artificial intelligence on teacher education. *Shodh Sari-An International Multidisciplinary Journal, 03*(01), 243–266. https://doi.org/10.59231/SARI7669

Wang, S., Christensen, C., Cui, W., Tong, R., Yarnall, L., Shear, L., & Feng, M. (2023). When adaptive learning is effective learning: Comparison of an adaptive learning system to teacher-led instruction. *Interactive Learning Environments, 31*(2), 793–803. https://doi.org/10.1080/10494820.2020.1808794

Wellner, G., & Rothman, T. (2020). Feminist AI: Can we expect our AI systems to become feminist? *Philosophy & Technology, 33*(2), 191–205. https://doi.org/10.1007/s13347-019-00352-z

Wu, X., Duan, R., & Ni, J. (2024). Unveiling security, privacy, and ethical concerns of ChatGPT. *Journal of Information and Intelligence, 2*(2), 102–115. https://doi.org/10.1016/j.jiixd.2023.10.007

Yu, H. (2024). The application and challenges of ChatGPT in educational transformation: New demands for teachers' roles. *Heliyon, 10*(2), Article e24289. https://doi.org/10.1016/j.heliyon.2024.e24289

Zheng, Q., Gou, J., Camarinha-Matos, L. M., Zhang, J. Z., & Zhang, X. (2023). Digital capability requirements and improvement strategies: Organizational socialization of AI teammates. *Information Processing and Management, 60*(6). https://doi.org/10.1016/j.ipm.2023.103504

Part III
Psychological Context

Chapter 10
Ethics and Privacy in AI Education: Prospects and Challenges in Higher Education

Yvonne Appiah Dadson, Zacharia Mohammed, Barak Hussein, Yaa Essah Armah, and Alex Kumi-Yeboah

Abstract Artificial intelligence (AI) in education is a field of study that integrates the applications of machine learning, technological tools, algorithm productions, and natural language processing. Recently, there has been a surge of AI technologies such as ChatGPT and personalized learning platforms to help students' learning, assessment systems to support faculty and students, and other systems to generate deeper understanding of students' behavior. Despite the benefits of AI technologies in education to support students' learning experiences, and best practices for faculty, there are concerns about the ethical and privacy challenges associated with the application of these AI technologies in higher education settings. Further, not much is known about the ethical and privacy in AI education and challenges students and faculty experience with the use and application of AI technologies, implications on students and faculty, and its challenges in higher education institutions. This chapter provides a comprehensive exploration of the key ethical and privacy issues

Y. A. Dadson (✉) · B. Hussein
College of Emergency Preparedness, Homeland Security, and Cybersecurity, University at Albany- SUNY, New York, United States
e-mail: ydadson@albany.edu

B. Hussein
e-mail: bhussein@albany.edu

Z. Mohammed
School of Education, Department of Educational Psychology, University at Albany- SUNY, New York, United States
e-mail: zmohammed@albany.edu

Y. E. Armah
School of Education, Department of Educational Policy & Leadership, University at Albany-SUNY, New York, United States
e-mail: yarmah@albany.edu

A. Kumi-Yeboah
School of Education, Department of Educational Theory & Practice, University at Albany-SUNY, New York, United States
e-mail: akumi-yeboah@albany.edu

M. A. Adarkwah et al. (eds.), *Artificial Intelligence and Human Agency in Education: Volume One*, Future Education and Learning Spaces,
https://doi.org/10.1007/978-981-96-7937-9_10

raised by the use of AI in higher education, including algorithmic bias and fairness, transparency and explainability, accountability and human oversight, data privacy and security, and student autonomy and consent. We analyze how these challenges can impact student learning, academic performance, well-being, and the comprehensive educational experience, with particular attention to the differential effects on vulnerable and underrepresented student populations. The chapter also examines the crucial role of institutional policies, governance frameworks, and participatory design practices in mitigating risks and fostering trust. Finally, we offer actionable recommendations for addressing these challenges through a combination of technical, educational, and policy interventions, and highlight priority areas for future research and collaboration. The chapter also examines the crucial role of institutional policies, governance frameworks, and participatory design practices in mitigating risks and fostering trust. Finally, we offer actionable recommendations for addressing these challenges through a combination of technical, educational, and policy interventions, and highlight priority areas for future research and collaboration. By proactively engaging with the ethical and privacy implications of AI, higher education institutions can harness the benefits of these powerful technologies while upholding fundamental values of fairness, transparency, accountability, and respect for student rights and agency. Recommendations for future studies and a conclusion are discussed.

Keywords Artificial intelligence · ChatGPT · Ethics · Chatbots · Personalized learning

10.1 Introduction

The rapid advancement and widespread adoption of artificial intelligence (AI) technologies in higher education are transforming the landscape of teaching, learning, and institutional decision-making (Bates et al., 2020; Goksel & Bozkurt, 2019; Popenici & Kerr, 2017; Zawacki-Richter et al., 2019; Katsamakas et al., 2024; Kumar et al., 2024). AI-powered tools and systems, such as adaptive learning platforms, intelligent tutoring systems, predictive analytics, and automated assessment, are increasingly being integrated into various aspects of educational practice and administration (Lin et al., 2023; Slimi, 2023; Kabudi et al., 2021; Alkhatlan & Kalita, 2018; Baker & Hawn, 2021; Hinojo-Lucena et al., 2019; Kulik & Fletcher, 2016; Luckin & Holmes, 2016; Reilly et al., 2016; Shute & Rahimi, 2021; Tuomi, 2018; Wilson & Czik, 2016). Proponents argue that AI has the potential to revolutionize higher education by enabling personalized and adaptive learning experiences, improving student outcomes, enhancing institutional efficiency, and supporting data-driven decision-making (Alkhatlan & Kalita, 2018; El-Sabagh, 2021; Gligorea et al., 2023; Holmes et al., 2019; Kye et al., 2021; Luckin et al., 2022; Xie et al., 2019).

However, the rapid growth of AI in higher education also raises significant ethical and privacy concerns that must be carefully addressed to ensure responsible and equitable implementation (Nyugen et al., 2023; Aiken & Epstein, 2000; Berendt et al., 2019; Jones & McCoy, 2019; Kitto et al., 2017; Prinsloo & Slade, 2017; Rubel & Jones, 2016; Slade & Prinsloo, 2013; Tsai et al., 2020; West et al., 2020; Harishbhai Tilala et al., 2024; Akgun & Greenhow, 2022; Al-Zahrani & Alasmari, 2024). As institutions increasingly rely on AI systems to collect, analyze, and make decisions based on vast amounts of student data, concerns arise around algorithmic bias and fairness, transparency and explainability, accountability and human oversight, data privacy and security, and student autonomy and consent (Barmaki & Hughes, 2015; Brasca et al., 2022; Drachsler & Greller, 2016; Dwivedi et al., 2021; Kizilcec et al., 2017; Pardo & Siemens, 2014; Prinsloo & Slade, 2017; Bart et al., 2020; Selwyn, 2019; Tsai et al., 2020; Zhai et al., 2024; Holmes et al., 2022; Al-Zahrani, 2024). These ethical and privacy issues have profound implications for student learning, academic success, well-being, and educational equity, particularly for vulnerable and underrepresented populations who may be disproportionately affected by AI-driven inequities and harms (Kizilcec & Lee, 2020; Ocumpaugh et al., 2014; Ogan et al., 2015, Akgun & Greenhow, 2022; Abulibdeh et. al, 2024; Nguyen et al., 2023; Al-Zahrani & Alasmari, 2024).

The COVID-19 pandemic has further accelerated the adoption of AI and digital technologies in higher education, as institutions have rapidly transitioned to remote and hybrid learning models (Imran et al., 2023; Turnbull et al., 2021; Bashir et al., 2021; Chen et al., 2020; Daniel, 2020; Aleem et al., 2023). This sudden shift has heightened the urgency of addressing the ethical and privacy challenges of AI, as the reliance on data-driven systems and online learning platforms has increased, while the capacity for human oversight and student support has been strained (Aleem et al., 2023; Hilliger et al., 2020; Dhawan, 2020; Khogali & Mekid, 2023; Williamson & Eynon, 2020). In this context, it is crucial for institutions to proactively develop policies, practices, and safeguards that prioritize student privacy, agency, and well-being in the design and deployment of AI technologies (Adams et al., 2023; Berendt et al., 2019; Jones, 2019; Mennella et al., 2024; Pardo et al., 2019; Prinsloo & Slade, 2017; West & Huijser, 2019).

This paper provides a comprehensive examination of the use of AI in higher education, exploring its potential benefits, techniques, and challenges. The paper begins by reviewing the current landscape of AI applications in higher education and their implications for teaching and learning. Furthermore, it delves into the key ethical and privacy issues raised by these technologies, analyzing their impact on students and educational practices. Moreover, the paper considers the role of institutional policies, governance frameworks, and participatory design approaches in mitigating risks and promoting responsible AI deployment. Subsequently, it offers recommendations for addressing these challenges through a multi-stakeholder approach that combines technical solutions, educational interventions, policy development, and ongoing research and assessment.

By critically engaging with the ethical and privacy implications of AI, higher education institutions can proactively navigate the challenges and opportunities presented by these technologies, ensuring that their implementation aligns with fundamental values of fairness, transparency, accountability, and respect for student rights and agency (Al-Zahrani & Alasmari, 2024; Aoun, 2017; Dabis & Csáki, 2024; Hartman et al., 2020; Luckin & Cukurova, 2019; Prinsloo & Slade, 2017; Slimi and Villarejo Carballido, 2023). This paper aims to contribute to the growing dialogue around responsible AI in education and provide actionable insights for educators, administrators, policymakers, and researchers working to harness the transformative potential of AI while safeguarding the integrity and inclusivity of the educational enterprise.

10.2 Issues of Ethics and AI in Higher Education

The increasing adoption of AI in higher education raises significant ethical concerns that must be carefully addressed to ensure responsible and equitable implementation. As institutions integrate AI systems into various aspects of educational practice and decision-making, they face complex challenges related to data privacy, algorithmic bias, transparency, accountability, and the changing roles of educators and students (Aiken & Epstein, 2000; Akgun & Greenhow, 2022; Al-Zahrani & Alasmari, 2024; Berendt et al., 2019; Bélanger & Crossler, 2011; Corrin et al., 2019; Prinsloo & Slade, 2017; Rubel & Jones, 2016; Slimi and Villarejo Carballido, 2023; West et al., 2020).

10.2.1 Data Privacy and Security

One of the primary issues is the privacy and security of student data, as AI systems rely on the collection, storage, and analysis of vast amounts of personal information (Bélanger & Crossler, 2011; Grosso et al., 2024; Huang, 2023; Liu et al., 2023; Rubel & Jones, 2016). AI systems rely on the collection, storage, and analysis of vast amounts of personal information, including demographic details, academic records, learning behaviors, and even biometric data (Chui & Sarakatsannis, 2015; Ifenthaler & Schumacher, 2016; Kaur et. al., 2023; Khalid et al., 2023; Liu et al., 2023; Menard & Bott, 2024; Pardo & Siemens, 2014; Slade & Prinsloo, 2013; Wang et al., 2022). The aggregation and use of such sensitive data raise concerns about informed consent, transparency, compliance with privacy regulations, and the potential for breaches, misuse, or unauthorized access (Chatti et al., 2014; Drachsler & Greller, 2016; Hoel & Chen, 2016; Rubel & Jones, 2016; Williamson and Prybutok, 2024).

To address these challenges, institutions must develop robust data governance policies and practices prioritizing student privacy (Jones & Salo, 2018; Prinsloo & Slade, 2017; Tsai et al., 2020). This includes implementing strict security measures, providing clear information about data collection and usage, obtaining informed consent, and ensuring compliance with relevant regulations such as the Family Educational Rights and Privacy Act (FERPA) in the United States and the General Data Protection Regulation (GDPR) in the European Union (Gagliardi & Turk, 2017;

Hoel & Chen, 2018; Kay et al., 2012; Regan & Jesse, 2019; Privacy Technical Assistance Center, U.S. Department of Education, 2015; Zhai et al., 2024;).

There are concerns about how student data is being collected, used, and shared, as well as the potential for data breaches, misuse, or unauthorized access (Chui & Sarakatsannis, 2015; Gagliardi & Turk, 2017; Regan & Jesse, 2019). Institutions must develop robust data governance policies and practices that prioritize student privacy, obtain informed consent, and provide transparency about data usage (Jones & Salo, 2018; Tsai et al., 2020). Another critical ethical issue is algorithmic bias and fairness in AI systems used in education (Kizilcec & Lee, 2020; O'Neil, 2017). AI algorithms can perpetuate or amplify existing societal biases and discriminatory practices, leading to unequal treatment and opportunities for certain groups of students based on their race, gender, socioeconomic status, or other characteristics (Alahmed et al., 2023; Belenguer, 2022; Chen, 2023; Ferrara, 2023; Yaghmaei & Poel, 2021). Bias can be introduced through the training data, model design, or the interpretation and application of AI-generated insights (Mehrabi et al., 2022; Suresh & Guttag, 2021). To mitigate these risks, institutions must ensure that AI systems are developed and deployed in a fair, inclusive, and equitable manner, with regular audits and monitoring for potential biases (Baker & Hawn, 2022; The White House, 2023; Wachter et al., 2020; Yelne et al., 2023).

Transparency and accountability in AI-based decision-making are also crucial ethical considerations (Shin & Park, 2019). As AI systems become more complex and autonomous, it can be challenging to understand how they arrive at specific recommendations or predictions (Felzmann et al., 2019; Mittelstadt et al., 2016). This lack of transparency can undermine trust in AI systems and make it difficult to hold them accountable for their impacts on students (Prinsloo & Slade, 2017; Tsai et al., 2020). Institutions must strive to develop explainable and interpretable AI models, provide clear information about their functioning and limitations, and establish mechanisms for redress and human oversight (Arrieta et al., 2020; Chamola et al., 2023; Panigutti et al., 2023).

The use of AI in education also raises questions about the changing roles and responsibilities of educators (Guilherme, 2019; Herodotou et al., 2019). As AI systems take on tasks such as grading, feedback provision, and student support, there are concerns about the potential displacement of human teachers and the erosion of the student–teacher relationship (Popenici & Kerr, 2017; Zawacki-Richter et al., 2019). It is essential to recognize that AI should be designed to augment and support human educators, rather than replace them entirely (Baker, 2016; Lai & Bower, 2019). Institutions must invest in professional development and training programs to help educators effectively integrate AI into their teaching practices and develop the skills needed to work alongside these technologies (Luckin & Cukurova, 2019; Pedro et al., 2019).

Moreover, the adoption of AI in education can have unintended consequences and raise broader societal and ethical questions (Aoun, 2017; Selwyn, 2019). For example, the use of predictive analytics to identify at-risk students may lead to stigmatization, self-fulfilling prophecies, or the allocation of resources away from those deemed less likely to succeed (Kizilcec et al., 2017; Wang, 2019). The increasing reliance on AI systems in education may also exacerbate existing inequalities in access to technology and digital skills, creating new forms of exclusion and marginalization (Holmes et al., 2022; Tang, 2024). Institutions must consider these broader ethical implications and work to develop inclusive, equitable, and socially responsible approaches to AI implementation (Castañeda & Selwyn, 2018; Prinsloo, 2017).

To address these ethical challenges, higher education institutions must develop comprehensive ethical frameworks and guidelines for the use of AI in education (Bates et al., 2020; Prinsloo, 2017). These frameworks should be grounded in principles such as privacy, fairness, transparency, accountability, and human-centeredness, and should involve all relevant stakeholders, including students, educators, administrators, and technology providers (Gašević et al., 2015; Holmes et al., 2022; Mikroyannidis et al., 2015). Institutions should also establish ethics review boards or committees to oversee the development, deployment, and monitoring of AI systems in education (Tsai et al., 2020; Willis et al., 2016).

Furthermore, there is a need for ongoing research and public dialogue about the ethical implications of AI in higher education (Aoun, 2017; Selwyn, 2019). Researchers should investigate the long-term impacts and unintended consequences of AI adoption, as well as develop new methodologies and frameworks for ethical AI design and evaluation (Holmes et al., 2022). Institutions should also engage in open and transparent communication with students, educators, and the broader public about the use of AI in education, fostering awareness, trust, and collaborative problem-solving (Bates et al., 2020; Gašević et al., 2015).

10.3 Addressing Ethics and Privacy in the Era of AI-Based Education in Higher Education

The rapid advancement of artificial intelligence (AI) is revolutionizing various aspects of society, and higher education is no exception. AI-powered tools, such as personalized learning platforms, intelligent tutoring systems, chatbots, and automated grading software, are being increasingly adopted by colleges and universities to enhance student learning experiences, improve educational outcomes, increase administrative efficiency, and reduce costs (Becker et al., 2018; Popenici & Kerr, 2017; Zawacki-Richter et al., 2019). However, the proliferation of AI in higher education also raises significant ethical and privacy concerns that must be carefully addressed to ensure the responsible and equitable use of these technologies (Corrin, 2021; Corrin et al., 2019; Tsamados et al., 2022).

One of the primary ethical challenges surrounding AI in higher education is the risk of algorithmic bias and discrimination. Many AI systems are trained on historical datasets that may reflect societal biases and inequities related to factors such as race, gender, socioeconomic status, and disability (Conitzer et al., 2017; Kizilcec & Lee, 2020; Ntoutsi et al., 2020). If these biases are not identified and mitigated, AI tools could inadvertently perpetuate or even amplify discrimination against certain groups of students (Naudé, 2020). For instance, an AI-based admissions system that relies on historical data might unfairly disadvantage applicants from underrepresented communities, while an AI-powered predictive analytics tool could discourage underprivileged students by reinforcing achievement gaps and creating self-fulfilling prophecies (Kizilcec & Lee, 2020; Schwartz et al., 2022; Xue et al., 2023). To address these risks, it is imperative that the datasets and algorithms underpinning AI-based educational tools are carefully audited for bias and that there is transparency and accountability in how they are developed and applied (Ahmad et al., 2020; Holstein et al., 2019). Higher education institutions should establish clear ethical guidelines and oversight mechanisms to ensure that AI systems are designed and used in a fair, inclusive, and non-discriminatory manner (Prinsloo & Slade, 2017; Radanliev et al., 2024).

Another critical ethical consideration is the protection of student privacy and data security. AI-based learning systems often collect and analyze vast amounts of sensitive data about students' academic performance, learning behaviors, engagement patterns, personal backgrounds, and even emotional states (Gašević et al., 2015; Ifenthaler & Schumacher, 2019; Pardo & Siemens, 2014). This data can be used to provide personalized feedback, adapt learning content, and identify students who may be at risk of falling behind. However, there are also significant risks associated with the collection, storage, and use of student data (Drachsler & Greller, 2016; Rubel & Jones, 2016). Not properly secured, this data could be vulnerable to hacking, unauthorized access, or misuse for commercial purposes.

There are also concerns about the potential for student data to be exploited to manipulate students' behaviors, decisions, or even their personal beliefs and values (Regan & Jesse, 2019; Roberts et al., 2016). To mitigate these risks, higher education institutions must implement robust data governance frameworks that prioritize student privacy and data protection (Tsai et al., 2020). This includes establishing clear policies and procedures for data collection, storage, and use, as well as ensuring compliance with relevant privacy regulations such as the Family Educational Rights and Privacy Act (FERPA) in the United States and the General Data Protection Regulation (GDPR) in the European Union (Hoel & Chen, 2018; Khalil et al., 2018). Students should also be provided with clear information about what data is being collected, how it will be used, and given meaningful control over their personal information (Slade & Prinsloo, 2013).

In addition to privacy concerns, the use of AI in higher education also raises questions about student agency, autonomy, and the development of critical thinking skills. As AI-powered tools become more sophisticated and ubiquitous, there is a risk that students may become overly reliant on these technologies for guidance, feedback, and decision-making (Baker, 2016). This could potentially undermine students' ability to engage in independent problem-solving, critical analysis, and self-directed learning (Guilherme, 2019; Peters, 2017). To counter this, educators must strive to use AI in ways that empower students and foster the development of essential twenty-first-century skills such as creativity, collaboration, and adaptability (Luckin & Holmes, 2016). Rather than replacing human instruction and interaction, AI should be leveraged as a complementary tool that enhances the learning experience and supports students in their academic and personal growth (Holmes et al., 2019, 2022). Educators should also prioritize the teaching of digital literacy and critical thinking skills to help students navigate the complexities of AI and make informed decisions about its use (Pangrazio & Sefton-Green, 2021).

Another significant challenge in the era of AI-based education is the widening digital divide and inequities in access to advanced educational technologies. Students from disadvantaged backgrounds, including those from low-income families, rural communities, and underfunded schools, may lack the necessary devices, internet connectivity, or digital literacy skills to fully benefit from AI-powered learning tools (Castañeda & Selwyn, 2018; Resta & Laferrière, 2015; Van Dijk, 2017). If these disparities are not addressed, the uneven adoption of AI in higher education could exacerbate existing achievement gaps and further marginalize underserved populations (Goldin & Katz, 2018). To promote digital equity, colleges and universities should work to ensure that all students have access to the technological infrastructure, resources, and support needed to effectively engage with AI-based learning systems (Smyrnova-Trybulska, 2022). This may involve providing subsidized devices, expanding broadband access, offering digital literacy training, and designing AI tools with accessibility and cultural inclusivity in mind (Aagaard & Lund, 2020; Resta et al., 2018).

Finally, the ethical implementation of AI in higher education requires ongoing collaboration and dialogue among a wide range of stakeholders, including educators, administrators, technology developers, ethicists, policymakers, and students themselves. Higher education institutions should establish interdisciplinary ethics committees or advisory boards to guide the development and deployment of AI systems, ensuring that they align with institutional values, academic integrity, and the public good (Berendt et al., 2020; Prinsloo & Slade, 2017). These groups should also engage in regular monitoring and evaluation of AI tools to assess their impact on student learning, well-being, and equity (Dawson et al., 2017). Additionally, there is a need for greater public awareness and engagement around the ethical implications of AI in education (Whittlestone et al., 2019). Higher education leaders should foster open and inclusive conversations about the benefits, challenges, and potential risks of these technologies, seeking input from diverse perspectives and working to build trust and accountability (Floridi & Cowls, 2019).

10.4 Prospects/Significance of AI Education in Higher Education

As AI continues to advance and permeate different aspects of society, it is crucial for higher education institutions to adapt their curricula and equip students with the knowledge and skills necessary to thrive in an AI-driven world (Kamalov et al., 2023; Pinski & Benlian, 2024). This section explores the prospects and significance of AI education in higher education, highlighting the potential benefits, challenges, and strategies for effective implementation.

10.4.1 Preparing Students for the AI-Driven Workforce

One of the primary reasons for integrating AI education into higher education curricula is to prepare students for the rapidly evolving job market. As AI technologies continue to transform industries and create new job roles, it is essential for graduates to possess a strong foundation in AI concepts, tools, and applications (Aoun, 2017; Frey & Osborne, 2017; Gagne, 2023; Southworth et al., 2023). By incorporating AI education into various disciplines, such as computer science, engineering, business, and social sciences, higher education institutions can equip students with the interdisciplinary skills needed to leverage AI in their future careers (Grosz et al., 2018; Ng et al., 2023; Parviz, 2024; Walter, 2024).

Moreover, AI education can foster the development of critical twenty-first-century skills, such as computational thinking, problem-solving, data literacy, and creativity (Celik, 2023; Luckin et al., 2022; Walter, 2024; Weng et al., 2024; Zawacki-Richter et al., 2019). These skills are not only valuable in AI-related fields but also transferable to various other domains, enhancing students' adaptability and resilience in the face of technological disruption (Khogali & Mekid, 2023; Păvăloaia & Necula, 2023; Schintler & McNeely, 2022; Shiohira, 2021). AI-assisted technologies, such as personalized learning platforms and adaptive pacing, can further enhance the learning experience and cater to individual learning needs (Bhutoria, 2022; Kabudi et al., 2021).

10.4.2 Enhancing Research and Innovation

The integration of AI education in higher education also has significant implications for research and innovation. By exposing students to cutting-edge AI technologies and methodologies, universities can cultivate a new generation of researchers and innovators who can push the boundaries of AI and contribute to its advancement (Abulibdeh et al., 2024; Aiken & Epstein, 2000; Al-Zahrani, 2024; Cardona et al., 2023; Ng et al., 2023; Wang et al., 2024; Xu et al., 2021). AI education can inspire students to pursue research careers in AI and related fields, driving scientific discovery and technological breakthroughs (Cardona et al., 2023; Xu & Ouyang, 2022; Yin, 2024).

Furthermore, AI education can foster interdisciplinary collaboration and knowledge exchange among students, faculty, and industry partners (Abulibdeh et al., 2024; Cardona et al., 2023.; Passey et al., 2004; Wang et al., 2024). By bringing together experts from diverse backgrounds, such as computer science, psychology, neuroscience, and ethics, higher education institutions can promote the development of innovative AI solutions that address complex societal challenges (Bouhouita-Guermech et al., 2023; Grace et al., 2018; Kamalov et al., 2023; Luan et al., 2020). The use of AI tools, such as IBM's Watson supercomputer, in partnership with universities for digitizing administrative tasks exemplifies the potential for collaboration and innovation (IBM, 2024; Pise, 2024).

AI-assisted technologies also significantly impact faculty efforts through the automation of administrative tasks, such as grading and scheduling, allowing educators to focus on classroom pedagogy and mentoring students (Ghamrawi et al., 2024; Luckin & Cukurova, 2019). The use of AI-driven assessment tools offers more accurate and timely feedback, facilitating effective interactions between students and faculty and ultimately enhancing the quality of education (Kamalov et al., 2023; Swiecki et al., 2022; Wang et al., 2024).

10.4.3 Ethical and Responsible AI Development

As AI technologies become more pervasive and influential, it is crucial to ensure that they are developed and deployed in an ethical and responsible manner. Higher education institutions have a critical role to play in promoting ethical AI education and fostering a culture of responsible innovation (Al-Zahrani, 2024; Greene et al., 2019; Nguyen et al., 2023; Wachter et al., 2017). By integrating ethics and social responsibility into AI curricula, universities can equip students with the moral framework and critical thinking skills necessary to navigate the complex ethical dilemmas posed by AI (Akgun & Greenhow, 2022; Bostrom & Yudkowsky, 2018; Grosz et al., 2018; Usher & Barak, 2024).

AI education in higher education should address topics such as algorithmic bias, data privacy, transparency, accountability, and the social implications of AI (Akgun & Greenhow, 2022; Al-Zahrani & Alasmari, 2024; Fjeld et al., 2020; Memarian & Doleck, 2023). The potential abuse of data privacy, misinformation, consent, and perceived biases in AI algorithms must be regulated by policies and compliance (Belenguer, 2022; Díaz-Rodríguez et al., 2023; The White House, 2023). To prevent potential misuse and ensure data collection privacy and student rights are protected, higher education institutions must implement robust privacy protection systems. Additionally, AI algorithms must be transparent to avoid biases that can disproportionately affect certain student groups and undermine the fairness of educational opportunities (Balaban, 2024; Park & Vance, 2021).

By engaging students in discussions and projects related to these issues, universities can foster a sense of social responsibility and empower students to become ethical leaders in the development and deployment of AI technologies (Abulibdeh et al., 2024; Akgun & Greenhow, 2022; Berendt et al., 2020; Loui et al., 2024; Park & Vance, 2021).

10.4.4 Challenges and Strategies for Implementation

Integrating AI education into higher education curricula comes with its own set of challenges. One of the primary challenges is the lack of qualified faculty with expertise in AI (Grunhut et al., 2022; Holmes et al., 2019; Lee et al., 2024; Popenici & Kerr, 2017; Southworth et al., 2023). Higher education institutions need to invest in faculty development programs and recruit AI experts to ensure that students receive high-quality education and mentorship (Aoun, 2017; Robert & McCormack, 2024; Southworth et al., 2023).

Another challenge is the need for infrastructure and resources to support AI education, such as computing facilities, software tools, and datasets (Ali et al., 2024; Cardona et al., 2023; Ridsdale et al., 2015; Xu et al., 2021). Universities must prioritize investments in AI infrastructure and collaborate with industry partners to provide students with access to cutting-edge technologies and real-world datasets (George & Wooden, 2023; Southworth et al., 2023).

To overcome these challenges and effectively implement AI education, higher education institutions can adopt several strategies. One approach is to develop interdisciplinary AI programs that bring together faculty from different departments and foster cross-disciplinary collaboration (Abulibdeh et al., 2024; Bates et al., 2020; Cardona et al., 2023; Grosz et al., 2018; Ng et al., 2023). Universities can also leverage online learning platforms and open educational resources to expand access to AI education and support self-paced learning (Cardona et al., 2023; Chen et al., 2020; Gligorea et al., 2023).

Furthermore, higher education institutions should actively engage with industry partners, government agencies, and research organizations to establish AI education ecosystems (Al-Zahrani & Alasmari, 2024; Cardona et al., 2023; Chan, 2023; Pantanowitz et al., 2022). These partnerships can provide students with internship and research opportunities, facilitate knowledge transfer, and ensure that AI curricula align with industry needs and emerging trends (Kamalov et al., 2023; Lin et al., 2024; Pantanowitz et al., 2022).

10.5 Addressing Ethics and Privacy in the Era of AI-Based Education in Higher Education

As with several other technology-based resources, the use of AI in higher education comes with some ethical concerns that should not be ignored. O'Dea and O'Dea (2023) discussed the likelihood that text generated using AI cannot be detected, coined as the 'hallucination effect.' This difficulty in detection increases the likelihood that further work by students will involve the misuse of AI to complete assignments. This takes away the element of intellectual integrity and academic rigor meant to be associated with academic work, as students use less and less of their critical thinking skills (Cotton et al., 2023).

Findings from Essien et al.'s (2024) study revealed that the use of AI text generators also delineates the individual from process of reading and understanding information presented. In effect, students' assignments may be completed devoid of any actual intellectual effort as expected of learners and work produced may not necessarily reflect their academic achievement or levels of understanding, as traditionally viewed. Contrary to common knowledge, digital illiteracy still exists among educators and students, and this tends to influence their understanding of AI tools and how to use them ethically (Lincoln & Kearney, 2019). Additionally, students with low skills in the use of AI tools may end up with lower grades than those savvy with them, implying a subtle form of injustice and unfairness when the same work is graded among students.

10.6 Discussion and Conclusion

10.6.1 AI in Education: Definition and Origins.

The inception of AI can be traced back to 1956 when John McCarthy organized a two-month seminar at Dartmouth College in the United States. McCarthy initially introduced the phrase artificial intelligence in the workshop proposal (Russell & Norvig, 2010). He believes that it is possible to explain every part of learning or any other intelligence attribute with such precision that a computer can be created to imitate it. Hence, the task at hand would involve discovering methods to enable computers to utilize language, develop abstractions and notions, solve problems that are currently exclusive to humans, and enhance their capabilities. Baker et al. (2019) provide a comprehensive definition of AI as computer systems that carry out cognitive functions typically attributed to human minds, specifically in the areas of learning and problem-solving. According to Vinuesa et al. (2020), AI encompasses a diverse array of technologies and approaches, including machine learning, natural language processing, data mining, neural networks, and many algorithms. It is not limited to a particular technology.

The field of AI has its roots in computer science and engineering, but it is strongly shaped by various other fields. AI experts lack consensus over a potential standardized definition and comprehension of AI, as well as intelligence in a broader sense. Within the realm of higher education, it is a fact that numerous instructors lack a comprehensive understanding of its extent and, more importantly, its composition (Vinuesa et al., 2020).

10.7 Possible Areas of Application

Ifenthaler and Yau (2019) suggest that there is a growing consensus on the benefits of using AI in educational settings. These benefits include a) enhancing students' learning experiences and effectiveness, as well as their motivation to learn, thereby reducing drop-out rates and increasing completion rates, and b) offering personalized and flexible learning paths based on specific goals set by either the teacher or the student to support the learning process. The potential advantages of utilizing artificial intelligence in the field of education are substantial. AI in education offers personalized learning, which is a major benefit. This approach allows students to learn at their speed and in a manner that aligns with their learning preferences, resulting in improved student results (Shrivastava et al., 2023). Intelligent tutoring systems, chatbots, and automated grading and evaluation have the potential to enhance efficiency, reduce teachers' workload, and deliver more precise and uniform feedback (Shrivastava et al., 2023).

Baker et al. (2019) categorizes the applications of AI in higher education based on the individuals who benefit from it: (a) the student, (b) the teacher, and (c) the AI system itself.

Student-oriented AI tools refer to computer applications specifically designed for students to enhance their learning experience. These tools can include adaptive or personalized learning management systems. Teacher-centric systems provide support to teachers and alleviate their workload by automating functions such as administration, evaluation, feedback, and plagiarism detection. AI systems also furnish data on students' learning progress, enabling teachers to offer proactive support and guidance as necessary. System-oriented applications are software tools designed to furnish administrators and managers at the institutional level with information that aids in their decision-making processes. This information is derived from data on student behavior, courses, and programs (Baker et al., 2019).

Nevertheless, other obstacles are linked to the utilization of AI in education. Challenges such as privacy and security problems, lack of confidence, expense, and potential prejudice must be resolved (Jarrah, Wardat, & Gningue, 2022). It is important to consider ethical factors such as accessibility, openness, and justice when implementing AI-based education systems (AlArabi, Tairab, Wardat, Belbase, & Alabidi, 2022) (Tariq et al., 2022). Outside of Australia, the UK, and the United States, AI utilization remains uncommon (Ifenthaler & Yau, 2019).

10.8 Challenges of AI in Education

To fully harness the power of AI in higher education, institutions need to be aware of and proactively address several challenges. One key concern is the ethical and legal implications of handling vast amounts of student data. As AI systems often require access to personal information to offer personalized learning experiences, there is a heightened risk of this data being exposed to unauthorized individuals, either through cyberattacks or internal negligence. Such breaches could lead to privacy violations and potentially harm students' academic and personal lives. Therefore, educational institutions must implement stringent security measures to protect this data. This includes using encryption, secure data storage practices, and regular audits to prevent breaches and ensure compliance with data protection regulations like GDPR.

Another challenge involves student trust in AI-based systems. While AI can enhance grading, feedback, and support, some students may be skeptical of the results generated by these systems. They might question the fairness, accuracy, or impartiality of AI-based assessments compared to those conducted by human instructors. This skepticism could lead to resistance to adopting AI-driven tools, especially in critical areas like grading, where students expect human judgment and empathy. As such, institutions need to focus on building trust by increasing transparency—explaining how AI algorithms work, ensuring students understand the criteria for assessments, and offering avenues for human oversight when necessary. Therefore, fostering a sense of comfort with technology is crucial to smooth integration. Some students may be unfamiliar with AI systems and require training or reassurance to interact effectively with them. Providing clear guidance and ensuring the technology is user-friendly will help ease concerns and promote acceptance. As AI becomes more integrated into education, institutions must prioritize not only technical safeguards but also the psychological and emotional factors that influence student engagement with these tools (Harry, 2023).

Finally, realizing AI's potential in higher education demands a comprehensive approach that balances innovation with ethical responsibility. This involves safeguarding privacy, building trust, ensuring fairness, and helping students feel at ease with the new technology to foster a supportive learning environment.

10.8.1 Data Collection, Student Privacy, and Safety

An important issue regarding AI-powered educational systems is the extensive collection of student data they gather. This dataset includes a wide range of information, including academic achievements, learning preferences, behavioral tendencies, and social contacts. The gathering of such delicate information gives rise to apprehensions over the absence of openness and informed permission (Office of the Victorian Information Commissioner, 2018), adherence to data privacy legislation (The Ark HQ., 2023), and data security and the possibility of exploitation (Politico, 2023).

10.8.2 Lack of Transparency and Informed Consent

Students and parents may lack a comprehensive understanding of the nature of the data being gathered, its utilization, and the parties it is shared. The gathering and examination of such data give rise to significant privacy concerns. Improper handling of data may result in security breaches, identity theft, or unlawful profiling. Additionally, the delicate nature of educational data requires strict privacy protections to protect students' rights and mitigate the risk of potential discrimination (Office of the Victorian Information Commissioner, 2018). The absence of openness impedes the ability to give informed consent and undermines confidence in educational institutions. AI systems should possess transparency, providing explicit elucidations of their decision-making processes and rationales. Developing trust with pupils and ensuring their comprehension of the technology can be facilitated by this approach (Harry, 2023).

10.8.3 Compliance with Data Privacy Regulations

Educational institutions face the challenge of complying with various data privacy rules, including the Family Educational Rights and Privacy Act (FERPA) and the General Data Protection Regulation (GDPR) (The Ark HQ., 2023). Unintentional failure to comply might result in legal and financial consequences.

10.8.4 Data Security and Potential for Misuse

The vast volume of student data accumulated by AI systems presents an attractive opportunity for cybercriminals seeking financial gain. Data breaches have the potential to expose confidential information, which can result in identity theft, social engineering attacks, and harm to one's reputation (Politico, 2023). One must also consider the ethical issues that emerge when dealing with the extensive gathering, creation, examination, and distribution of data concerning individuals about AI's potential. Nevertheless, it is important to acknowledge that the pursuit of comprehending the moral implications of emerging technology is not a recent objective (Pedró, 2020). When developing AI-based education systems, it is crucial to prioritize accessibility to ensure that all students, including those with disabilities, can effectively utilize the technology (Harry, 2023). In the last thirty years, scholars and professionals have endeavored to establish a framework for information ethics, which may be summed in a single query: What constitutes an ethical utilization of technology? Data science's advent has redirected the conversation from ethics around information to ethics surrounding data. According to experts, the origin of ethical dilemmas lies not in the hardware itself, but rather in how the hardware interacts with the software and data, which gives rise to new challenges (Mittelstadt et al., 2016).

10.9 Cost, Potential Bias, and Fairness

Harry (2023) identifies expense, potential prejudice, and fairness as additional problems associated with the implementation of AI in education. Implementing and maintaining AI systems can be a financial burden for educational institutions, particularly when they are already dealing with budget limitations. It is imperative for institutions to thoroughly evaluate the advantages and disadvantages of incorporating AI technologies in their courses. Artificial intelligence systems have the potential to exhibit bias, especially when they are trained on biased data. This can lead to the unjust treatment of specific students and perpetuate preexisting disparities. Institutions must guarantee that their AI systems are impartial and do not perpetuate preexisting disparities. AI-powered educational systems must adhere to principles of fairness, guaranteeing equitable treatment for all pupils, regardless of their ethnicity, gender, or other relevant variables (Harry, 2023).

Notwithstanding these difficulties, the capacity of artificial intelligence (AI) in the field of education is vast (M Al-Bahrani et al., 2018). Artificial intelligence can enhance data analysis, empowering educators to make facts-based decisions. Additionally, it can enhance student involvement by offering interactive and captivating educational encounters (Yang et al., 2022) (Wardat et al., 2022). AI can enhance the accessibility and inclusivity of education, allowing individuals from diverse backgrounds to obtain high-quality education easily.

10.10 Implications of Integrating AI in Higher Education

AI integration in higher education underscores the dual-edge nature of this technology and the potential wide-ranging impacts of AI innovation in higher education. The benefits are crucial, offering relatively transformative possibilities for personalized learning, efficient administrative duties, and harnessing educational outcomes. However, ethical and privacy challenges presented by adopting AI require careful consideration and proactive management. Shaw, M. (2003). Revealed that the proliferation of AI technologies has led to an unprecedented level of connectivity, offering new opportunities and challenges. While the benefits of inter-connected systems are evident, the potential risks to user privacy and security demand a thorough investigation. Also, variability in access to AI technologies widens the gap between those that have access to its use, and those who do not, what Hohlfeld et al., (2008) theorized as the digital divide. Addressing these challenges in higher educational institutions, through effective policies and regulations, can unlock the full potential benefits of AI and pave the way for an inclusive educational future.

10.11 Development of Enhanced-AI Educational Policy:

Fundamentally, one major implication of these studies is to investigate how robust policy frameworks can safeguard AI's ethical use in education. Educational institutions are foremost responsible for making rules and regulations to govern the ethical use of AI in education. Institutions are mandated to develop comprehensive guidelines that address particularly, data privacy, consent, and transparency. Such policy frameworks must address Student data and the responsible use of AI with clear protocols for obtaining informed consent. Furthermore, these policies should incorporate frequent auditing of AI tools so that inherent bias associated with such tools can be mitigated to ensure fair and equitable treatment and inclusivity among all students and faculty.

It is important that students and faculty consider the advantages and limitations of incorporating AI in university administrative procedures. For the smooth implementation of AI-supported teaching and learning procedures, effective faculty training is essential in the adoption and use of AI technology. Higher education professionals should be encouraged to equip themselves with the knowledge and skills for the efficient utilization of AI tools in teaching and learning. The institutionalization of professional development programs is encouraged to help faculty understand the intricacies and ethical dimensions of the use of AI in higher education. Professional development is relevant due to the potential ethical concerns associated with integrating AI tools in teaching and learning. Continuous support and resources are useful in assisting educators to navigate the challenges and complexities of AI implementation within their institutions.

10.12 Implications for Student Engagement and Awareness

The importance of student engagement and creating awareness of the ethical ramifications of AI technologies cannot be overemphasized. This is because as end users, students are also directly affected by policy and the technological climate within higher education. Hence the need to carry students along significant changes that can impact on their learning. As with faculty, students also need to be educated on the benefits and risks of AI, as well as their rights concerning data privacy and other reporting procedures. In promoting transparency in AI operations, higher education institutions need to make the effort to involve students in AI ethics and privacy-related discussions at all levels. These interactions with students not only ensure confidence but also enable students to make informed decisions about their interactions with AI tools and advocate for their rights.

10.13 Directions for Future Research

Further research in AI in education should focus on investigating the long-term impact of AI use on student outcomes, the effectiveness of different AI tools across various disciplines, and the development of ethical AI assessment frameworks. To promote equity and an inclusive learning environment in higher education institutions, attention must be given to research that investigates the impact of AI on marginalized groups. Research that looks into access and influence of AI technologies on student outcomes in different parts of the world is an under researched area in the AI discourse.

Higher education institutions must ensure continuous assessment, evaluation, and monitoring of AI tools in use within their institutions. To achieve this, it is recommended that a mechanism for regularly reviewing the performance and impact of AI systems should be established. This involves collecting feedback from both students and faculty, monitoring outcomes, and making data-driven decisions to refine AI applications. Such a culture of continuous improvement ensures that AI tools remain effective and relevant, adapting to the evolving educational and technological landscape. Finally, the implications and impact of AI integration in higher education are extensive. The development of robust policies, faculty training, continuous assessment and evaluation, engagement of students, and directions for future research are crucial to optimize the benefits of AI while addressing its challenges.

10.14 Conclusion

In conclusion, while AI has the potential to transform and enhance higher education in numerous ways, it also presents complex ethical and privacy challenges that must be proactively addressed (Shneiderman, 2020). To harness the benefits of AI while mitigating its risks, higher education institutions must prioritize issues of fairness, transparency, accountability, privacy protection, student agency, and digital equity (Dignum, 2018). This requires a comprehensive approach that involves establishing clear ethical guidelines, implementing robust data governance frameworks, promoting digital literacy and critical thinking skills, ensuring equitable access to technology, and fostering ongoing collaboration and dialogue among stakeholders (Mittelstadt, 2019; Taddeo & Floridi, 2018). By taking these steps, the higher education sector can responsibly leverage AI to support student success, enhance educational quality, and ultimately advance the mission of teaching, learning, and public service in an increasingly digital world (Holmes et al., 2019). Further, there are numerous advantages to integrating AI in education; there are also various obstacles and apprehensions that must be tackled. It is imperative for institutions to thoroughly evaluate the expenses and advantages of incorporating AI systems in their classes, while also ensuring they are adopting necessary safeguards to safeguard students' privacy and mitigate bias. By carefully considering the advantages and difficulties of

AI in education, we may establish a learning environment that is tailored, streamlined, and highly productive for every student.

References

Aagaard, T., & Lund, A. (2020). *Digital agency in higher education: Transforming teaching and learning*. Routledge.

Abulibdeh, A., Zaidan, E., & Abulibdeh, R. (2024). Navigating the confluence of artificial intelligence and education for sustainable development in the era of industry 4.0: Challenges, opportunities, and ethical dimensions. *Journal of Cleaner Production, 437*, 140527. https://doi.org/10.1016/j.jclepro.2023.140527

Academic Integrity and Artificial Intelligence in Higher Education (HE) Contexts: A Rapid Scoping Review | Canadian Perspectives on Academic Integrity (ucalgary.ca)

Adejo, O. W., & Connolly, T. (2018). Predicting student academic performance using multi-model heterogeneous ensemble approach. *Journal of Applied Research in Higher Education, 10*(1), 61–75. https://doi.org/10.1108/JARHE-09-2017-0113

Ahmad, M. A., Teredesai, A., & Eckert, C. (2020). Fairness, accountability, transparency in AI at scale: Lessons from national programs. *Proceedings of the 2020 Conference on Fairness, Accountability, and Transparency*, 690–690. https://doi.org/10.1145/3351095.3375690

Aiken, R., & Epstein, R. (2000). Ethical guidelines for AI in education: Starting a conversation. *International Journal of Artificial Intelligence in Education, 11*, 163–176.

Akgun, S., & Greenhow, C. (2022). Artificial intelligence in education: Addressing ethical challenges in K-12 settings. *Ai and Ethics, 2*(3), 431–440. https://doi.org/10.1007/s43681-021-00096-7

Alahmed, Y., Abadla, R., Ameen, N., & Shteiwi, A. (2023). Bridging the gap between ethical AI implementations. *International Journal of Membrane Science and Technology, 10*(3), 3034–3046. https://doi.org/10.15379/ijmst.v10i3.2953

AlArabi, K., Tairab, H., Wardat, Y., Belbase, S., & Alabidi, S. (2022). Enhancing the learning of Newton's second law of motion using computer simulations. *Journal of Baltic Science Education, 21*(6).

Al-Bahrani, M., Gombos, Z. J., & Cree, A. (2018). The mechanical properties of functionalized MWCNT infused epoxy resin: A theoretical and experimental study. *International Journal of Mechanical and Mechatronics Engineering, 18*, 76–86.

Ali, O., Murray, P. A., Momin, M., Dwivedi, Y. K., & Malik, T. (2024). The effects of artificial intelligence applications in educational settings: Challenges and strategies. *Technological Forecasting and Social Change, 199*, Article 123076. https://doi.org/10.1016/j.techfore.2023.123076

Alkhatlan, A., & Kalita, J. (2018). *Intelligent tutoring systems: A comprehensive historical survey with recent developments*. http://arxiv.org/abs/1812.09628

Al-Zahrani, A. M. (2024). Unveiling the shadows: Beyond the hype of AI in education. *Heliyon, 10*(9), Article e30696. https://doi.org/10.1016/j.heliyon.2024.e30696

Al-Zahrani, A. M., & Alasmari, T. M. (2024). Exploring the impact of artificial intelligence on higher education: The dynamics of ethical, social, and educational implications. *Humanities and Social Sciences Communications, 11*(1), 1–12. https://doi.org/10.1057/s41599-024-03432-4

Aoun, J. E. (2017). *Robot-proof: Higher education in the age of artificial intelligence*. The MIT Press. https://doi.org/10.7551/mitpress/11456.001.0001

Arrieta, A. B., Díaz-Rodríguez, N., Del Ser, J., Bennetot, A., Tabik, S., Barbado, A., Garcia, S., Gil-Lopez, S., Molina, D., Benjamins, R., Chatila, R., & Herrera, F. (2020). Explainable Artificial Intelligence (XAI): Concepts, taxonomies, opportunities and challenges toward responsible AI. *Information Fusion, 58*, 82–115. https://doi.org/10.1016/j.inffus.2019.12.012

Baker, T., Smith, L., & Anissa, N. (2019). Educ-AI-tion rebooted? Exploring the future of artificial intelligence in schools and colleges. https://www.nesta.org.uk/report/education-rebooted/

Baker, R. S. (2016). Stupid tutoring systems, intelligent humans. *International Journal of Artificial Intelligence in Education, 26*(2), 600–614. https://doi.org/10.1007/s40593-016-0105-0

Baker, R. S., & Hawn, A. (2022). Algorithmic bias in education. *International Journal of Artificial Intelligence in Education, 32*(4), 1052–1092. https://doi.org/10.1007/s40593-021-00285-9

Balaban, D. (2024, March 29). *Privacy and security issues of using AI for academic purposes.* Forbes. https://www.forbes.com/sites/davidbalaban/2024/03/29/privacy-and-security-issues-of-using-ai-for-academic-purposes/

Barmaki, R., & Hughes, C. E. (2015). Providing real-time feedback for student teachers in a virtual rehearsal environment. *Proceedings of the 2015 ACM on International Conference on Multimodal Interaction*, 531–537. https://doi.org/10.1145/2818346.2830604

Bates, T., Cobo, C., Mariño, O., & Wheeler, S. (2020). Can artificial intelligence transform higher education? *International Journal of Educational Technology in Higher Education, 17*(1), 42, s41239-020-00218–x. https://doi.org/10.1186/s41239-020-00218-x

Becker, S. A., Brown, M., Dahlstrom, E., Davis, A., DePaul, K., Diaz, V., & Pomerantz, J. (2018). NMC horizon report: 2018 higher education edition. In *Educause.* Educause.

Berendt, B., Littlejohn, A., & Blakemore, M. (2020). AI in education: Learner choice and fundamental rights. *Learning, Media and Technology, 45*(3), 312–324. https://doi.org/10.1080/17439884.2020.1786399

Bélanger & Crossler. (2011). Privacy in the digital age: A review of information privacy research in information systems. *MIS Quarterly, 35*(4), 1017. https://doi.org/10.2307/41409971

Belenguer, L. (2022). AI bias: Exploring discriminatory algorithmic decision-making models and the application of possible machine-centric solutions adapted from the pharmaceutical industry. *AI and Ethics, 2*(4), 771–787. https://doi.org/10.1007/s43681-022-00138-8

Bhutoria, A. (2022). Personalized education and artificial intelligence in the United States, China, and India: A systematic review using a Human-In-The-Loop model. *Computers and Education: Artificial Intelligence, 3*, Article 100068. https://doi.org/10.1016/j.caeai.2022.100068

Bostrom, N., & Yudkowsky, E. (2018). *The ethics of artificial intelligence* (pp. 57–69). https://doi.org/10.1201/9781351251389-4

Bouhouita-Guermech, S., Gogognon, P., & Bélisle-Pipon, J.-C. (2023). Specific challenges posed by artificial intelligence in research ethics. *Frontiers in Artificial Intelligence, 6*, 1149082. https://doi.org/10.3389/frai.2023.1149082

Brasca, C., Kaithwal, N., Krishnan, C., Lam, M., Law, J., & Marya, V. (2022). *Machine learning in higher education | McKinsey.* https://www.mckinsey.com/industries/education/our-insights/using-machine-learning-to-improve-student-success-in-higher-education

Cardona, M. A., Rodríguez, R. J., & Ishmael, K. (n.d.). *Artificial intelligence and the future of teaching and learning.*

Castañeda, L., & Selwyn, N. (2018). More than tools? Making sense of the ongoing digitizations of higher education. *International Journal of Educational Technology in Higher Education, 15*(1), 22. https://doi.org/10.1186/s41239-018-0109-y

Celik, I. (2023). Exploring the determinants of Artificial Intelligence (AI) literacy: Digital divide, computational thinking, cognitive absorption. *Telematics and Informatics, 83*, Article 102026. https://doi.org/10.1016/j.tele.2023.102026

Chamola, V., Hassija, V., Sulthana, A. R., Ghosh, D., Dhingra, D., & Sikdar, B. (2023). A review of trustworthy and explainable artificial intelligence (XAI). *IEEE Access, 11*, 78994–79015. https://doi.org/10.1109/ACCESS.2023.3294569

Chan, C. K. Y. (2023). A comprehensive AI policy education framework for university teaching and learning. *International Journal of Educational Technology in Higher Education, 20*(1), 38. https://doi.org/10.1186/s41239-023-00408-3

Chen, Z. (2023). Ethics and discrimination in artificial intelligence-enabled recruitment practices. *Humanities and Social Sciences Communications, 10*(1), 1–12. https://doi.org/10.1057/s41599-023-02079-x

Chen, X., Xie, H., & Hwang, G.-J. (2020). A multi-perspective study on artificial intelligence in education: Grants, conferences, journals, software tools, institutions, and researchers. *Computers and Education: Artificial Intelligence, 1*, Article 100005. https://doi.org/10.1016/j.caeai.2020.100005

Chu, S.-T., Hwang, G.-J., & Tu, Y.-F. (2022). Artificial intelligence-based robots in education: A systematic review of selected SSCI publications. *Computers and Education: Artificial Intelligence, 3*, Article 100091. https://doi.org/10.1016/j.caeai.2022.100091

Chui, M., & Sarakatsannis, J. (2015). *Protecting student data in a digital world | McKinsey*. https://www.mckinsey.com/industries/education/our-insights/protecting-student-data-in-a-digital-world/

Conitzer, V., Sinnott-Armstrong, W., Schaich Borg, J., Deng, Y., & Kramer, M. (2017). Moral decision making frameworks for artificial intelligence. *Proceedings of the AAAI Conference on Artificial Intelligence, 31*(1). https://doi.org/10.1609/aaai.v31i1.11140

Corrin, L. (2021). Shifting to digital: A policy perspective on 'Student perceptions of privacy principles for learning analytics' (Ifenthaler & Schumacher 2016). *Educational Technology Research and Development, 69*(1), 353–356. https://doi.org/10.1007/s11423-020-09922-x

Corrin, L., Kennedy, G., French, S., Buckingham Shum, S., Kitto, K., Pardo, A., West, D., Mirriahi, N., & Colvin, C. (2019). *The ethics of learning analytics in australian higher education. Discussion Paper Prepared By.*

Cotton, D. R. E., Cotton, P. A., & Shipway, J. R.. (2023). Chatting and cheating: Ensuring academic integrity in the era of ChatGPT. *Innovations in Education and Teaching International*, 1–12. https://doi.org/10.1080/14703297.2023.2190148.

Díaz-Rodríguez, N., Del Ser, J., Coeckelbergh, M., López de Prado, M., Herrera-Viedma, E., & Herrera, F. (2023). Connecting the dots in trustworthy Artificial Intelligence: From AI principles, ethics, and key requirements to responsible AI systems and regulation. *Information Fusion, 99*, Article 101896. https://doi.org/10.1016/j.inffus.2023.101896

Dawson, S., Jovanovic, J., Gašević, D., & Pardo, A. (2017). From prediction to impact: Evaluation of a learning analytics retention program. *Proceedings of the Seventh International Learning Analytics & Knowledge Conference*, 474–478. https://doi.org/10.1145/3027385.3027405

Dignum, V. (2018). Ethics in artificial intelligence: Introduction to the special issue. *Ethics and Information Technology, 20*(1), 1–3. https://doi.org/10.1007/s10676-018-9450-z

Drachsler, H., & Greller, W. (2016). Privacy and analytics: It's a DELICATE issue a checklist for trusted learning analytics. *Proceedings of the Sixth International Conference on Learning Analytics & Knowledge - LAK '16*, 89–98. https://doi.org/10.1145/2883851.2883893

Dwivedi, Y. K., Hughes, L., Ismagilova, E., Aarts, G., Coombs, C., Crick, T., Duan, Y., Dwivedi, R., Edwards, J., Eirug, A., Galanos, V., Ilavarasan, P. V., Janssen, M., Jones, P., Kar, A. K., Kizgin, H., Kronemann, B., Lal, B., Lucini, B., … Williams, M. D. (2021). Artificial Intelligence (AI): Multidisciplinary perspectives on emerging challenges, opportunities, and agenda for research, practice and policy. *International Journal of Information Management, 57*, 101994. https://doi.org/10.1016/j.ijinfomgt.2019.08.002

El-Sabagh, H. A. (2021). Adaptive e-learning environment based on learning styles and its impact on development students' engagement. *International Journal of Educational Technology in Higher Education, 18*(1), 53. https://doi.org/10.1186/s41239-021-00289-4

Felzmann, H., Villaronga, E. F., Lutz, C., & Tamò-Larrieux, A. (2019). Transparency you can trust: Transparency requirements for artificial intelligence between legal norms and contextual concerns. *Big Data & Society, 6*(1), 205395171986054. https://doi.org/10.1177/2053951719860542

Ferrara, E. (2023). *Fairness and bias in artificial intelligence: a brief survey of sources, impacts, and mitigation strategies*. https://arxiv.org/pdf/2304.07683

Fjeld, J., Achten, N., Hilligoss, H., Nagy, A., & Srikumar, M. (2020). Principled artificial intelligence: mapping consensus in ethical and rights-based approaches to principles for AI. *SSRN Electronic Journal*. https://doi.org/10.2139/ssrn.3518482

Floridi, L., & Cowls, J. (2019). A unified framework of five principles for AI in society. *Harvard Data Science Review, 1*(1). https://doi.org/10.1162/99608f92.8cd550d1

Frey, C. B., & Osborne, M. A. (2017). The future of employment: How susceptible are jobs to computerisation? *Technological Forecasting and Social Change, 114*, 254–280. https://doi.org/10.1016/j.techfore.2016.08.019

Gagliardi, J. S., & Turk, J. M. (2017). *The-data-enabled-executive.pdf*. https://www.acenet.edu/Documents/The-Data-Enabled-Executive.pdf

Gagne, J. C. D. (2023). The state of artificial intelligence in nursing education: Past, present, and future directions. *International Journal of Environmental Research and Public Health, 20*(6). https://doi.org/10.3390/ijerph20064884

Gašević, D., Dawson, S., & Siemens, G. (2015). Let's not forget: Learning analytics are about learning. *TechTrends, 59*(1), 64–71. https://doi.org/10.1007/s11528-014-0822-x

George, B., & Wooden, O. (2023). Managing the strategic transformation of higher education through artificial intelligence. *Administrative Sciences, 13*(9), 196. https://doi.org/10.3390/admsci13090196

Ghamrawi, N., Shal, T., & Ghamrawi, N. A. R. (2024). Exploring the impact of AI on teacher leadership: Regressing or expanding? *Education and Information Technologies, 29*(7), 8415–8433. https://doi.org/10.1007/s10639-023-12174-w

Gierl, M. J., Latifi, S., Lai, H., Boulais, A.-P., & De Champlain, A. (2014). Automated essay scoring and the future of educational assessment in medical education. *Medical Education, 48*(10), 950–962. https://doi.org/10.1111/medu.12517

Gligorea, I., Cioca, M., Oancea, R., Gorski, A.-T., Gorski, H., & Tudorache, P. (2023). Adaptive learning using artificial intelligence in e-learning: A literature review. *Education Sciences, 13*(12), 1216. https://doi.org/10.3390/educsci13121216

Gningue, S. M., Peach, R., Jarrah, A. M., & Wardat, Y. (2022). The relationship between teacher leadership and school climate: Findings from a teacher-leadership project. *Education in Science, 12*, 749.

Goldin, C., & Katz, L. F. (2018). The race between education and technology. In D. B. Grusky & J. Hill (Eds.), *Inequality in the 21st century* (1st ed., pp. 49–54). Routledge. https://doi.org/10.4324/9780429499821-10

Grace, K., Salvatier, J., Dafoe, A., Zhang, B., & Evans, O. (2018). Viewpoint: When will AI exceed human performance? Evidence from AI experts. *Journal of Artificial Intelligence Research, 62*, 729–754. https://doi.org/10.1613/jair.1.11222

Greene, D., Hoffmann, A., & Stark, L. (2019). *Better, nicer, clearer, fairer: A critical assessment of the movement for ethical artificial intelligence and machine learning*. https://doi.org/10.24251/HICSS.2019.258

Grosso, D. P., Bowling, M. R., Chun, S. S., & Delaney, B. M. (2024). *Protecting student data privacy in light of artificial Intelligen*. Retrieved May 20, 2024, from https://natlawreview.com/article/development-ai-and-protecting-student-data-privacy

Grosz, B. J., Grant, D. G., Vredenburgh, K., Behrends, J., Hu, L., Simmons, A., & Waldo, J. (2018). *Embedded EthiCS: Integrating ethics broadly across computer science education*. http://arxiv.org/abs/1808.05686

Grunhut, J., Marques, O., & Wyatt, A. T. M. (2022). Needs, challenges, and applications of artificial intelligence in medical education curriculum. *JMIR Medical Education, 8*(2), Article e35587. https://doi.org/10.2196/35587

Guilherme, A. (2019). AI and education: The importance of teacher and student relations. *AI & SOCIETY, 34*(1), 47–54. https://doi.org/10.1007/s00146-017-0693-8

Harry, A. (2023). Role of AI in education. *Interdiciplinary Journal and Hummanity (INJURITY), 2*(3), 260–268.

Herodotou, C., Hlosta, M., Boroowa, A., Rienties, B., Zdrahal, Z., & Mangafa, C. (2019). Empowering online teachers through predictive learning analytics. *British Journal of Educational Technology, 50*(6), 3064–3079. https://doi.org/10.1111/bjet.12853

Hinojo-Lucena, F.-J., Aznar-Díaz, I., Cáceres-Reche, M.-P., & Romero-Rodríguez, J.-M. (2019). Artificial intelligence in higher education: A bibliometric study on its impact in the scientific literature. *Education Sciences, 9*(1), 51. https://doi.org/10.3390/educsci9010051

Holmes, W., Persson, J., Chounta, I.-A., Wasson, B., & Dimitrova, V. (2022). *Artificial intelligence and education: A critical view through the lens of human rights, democracy and the rule of law.* Council of Europe.

Holmes, W., Bialik, M., & Fadel, C. (2019). *Artificial intelligence in education.*

Hoel, T., & Chen, W. (2018). Privacy and data protection in learning analytics should be motivated by an educational maxim—towards a proposal. *Research and Practice in Technology Enhanced Learning, 13*(1), 20. https://doi.org/10.1186/s41039-018-0086-8

Holstein, K., Wortman Vaughan, J., Daumé, H., Dudik, M., & Wallach, H. (2019). Improving fairness in machine learning systems: What do industry practitioners need? *Proceedings of the 2019 CHI Conference on Human Factors in Computing Systems*, 1–16. https://doi.org/10.1145/3290605.3300830

IBM. (2024, April 2). *IBM watsonx.ai.* https://www.ibm.com/products/watsonx-ai

Ifenthaler, D., & Schumacher, C. (2019). Releasing personal information within learning analytics systems. In D. Sampson, J. M. Spector, D. Ifenthaler, P. Isaías, & S. Sergis (Eds.), *Learning technologies for transforming large-scale teaching, learning, and assessment* (pp. 3–18). Springer International Publishing. https://doi.org/10.1007/978-3-030-15130-0_1

Jones, K., & Salo, D. (2018). Learning analytics and the academic library: Professional ethics commitments at a crossroads. *College & Research Libraries, 79*(3), 304–323. https://doi.org/10.5860/crl.79.3.304

Kabudi, T., Pappas, I., & Olsen, D. H. (2021). AI-enabled adaptive learning systems: A systematic mapping of the literature. *Computers and Education: Artificial Intelligence, 2*, Article 100017. https://doi.org/10.1016/j.caeai.2021.100017

Kamalov, F., Santandreu Calonge, D., & Gurrib, I. (2023). New era of artificial intelligence in education: Towards a sustainable multifaceted revolution. *Sustainability, 15*(16), 12451. https://doi.org/10.3390/su151612451

Khalil, M., Wong, J., De Koning, B., Ebner, M., & Paas, F. (2018). Gamification in MOOCs: A review of the state of the art. *IEEE Global Engineering Education Conference (EDUCON), 2018*, 1629–1638. https://doi.org/10.1109/EDUCON.2018.8363430

Khalifa, M., & Albadawy, M. (2024). Using artificial intelligence in academic writing and research: An essential productivity tool. *Computer Methods and Programs in Biomedicine Update, 5*, Article 100145. https://doi.org/10.1016/j.cmpbup.2024.100145

Khogali, H. O., & Mekid, S. (2023). The blended future of automation and AI: Examining some long-term societal and ethical impact features. *Technology in Society, 73*, Article 102232. https://doi.org/10.1016/j.techsoc.2023.102232

Kizilcec, R. F., & Lee, H. (2020). *Algorithmic fairness in education* (version 3). https://doi.org/10.48550/ARXIV.2007.05443

Kizilcec, R. F., Saltarelli, A. J., Reich, J., & Cohen, G. L. (2017). Closing global achievement gaps in MOOCs. *Science, 355*(6322), 251–252. https://doi.org/10.1126/science.aag2063

Kulik, J. A., & Fletcher, J. D. (2016). Effectiveness of intelligent tutoring systems: A meta-analytic review. *Review of Educational Research, 86*(1), 42–78. https://doi.org/10.3102/0034654315581420

Kye, B., Han, N., Kim, E., Park, Y., & Jo, S. (2021). Educational applications of metaverse: Possibilities and limitations. *Journal of Educational Evaluation for Health Professions, 18*, 32. https://doi.org/10.3352/jeehp.2021.18.32

Lai, J. W. M., & Bower, M. (2019). How is the use of technology in education evaluated? A systematic review. *Computers & Education, 133*, 27–42. https://doi.org/10.1016/j.compedu.2019.01.010

Lee, D., Arnold, M., Srivastava, A., Plastow, K., Strelan, P., Ploeckl, F., Lekkas, D., & Palmer, E. (2024). The impact of generative AI on higher education learning and teaching: A study of educators' perspectives. *Computers and Education: Artificial Intelligence, 6*, Article 100221. https://doi.org/10.1016/j.caeai.2024.100221

Lin, X., Chan, R., Sharma, S., & Bista, K. (2024). *The impact of Artificial Intelligence (AI) on global higher education: opportunities and challenges of using ChatGPT and generative AI* (pp. 1–17). https://doi.org/10.32674/rh27qv16

Lincoln, D., & Kearney, M.-L. (2019). Promoting critical thinking in higher education. *Studies in Higher Education., 44*(5), 799–800. https://doi.org/10.1080/03075079.2019.1586322

Liu, M., Ren, Y., Nyagoga, L. M., Stonier, F., Wu, Z., & Yu, L. (2023). Future of education in the era of generative artificial intelligence: Consensus among Chinese scholars on applications of ChatGPT in schools. *Future in Educational Research, 1*(1), 72–101. https://doi.org/10.1002/fer3.10

Loui, M. C., Bosch, N., Chan, A. S., Davis, J. L., Gutiérrez, R., He, J., Karahalios, K., Koyejo, S., Mendenhall, R., Sanfilippo, M. R., Tong, H., Varshney, L. R., & Wang, Y. (2024). Artificial intelligence, social responsibility, and the roles of the university. *Communications of the ACM, 67*(8), 22–25. https://doi.org/10.1145/3640541

Luan, H., Geczy, P., Lai, H., Gobert, J., Yang, S. J. H., Ogata, H., Baltes, J., Guerra, R., Li, P., & Tsai, C.-C. (2020). Challenges and future directions of big data and artificial intelligence in education. *Frontiers in Psychology, 11*. https://doi.org/10.3389/fpsyg.2020.580820

Luckin, R., & Cukurova, M. (2019). Designing educational technologies in the age of AI: A learning sciences-driven approach. *British Journal of Educational Technology, 50*(6), 2824–2838. https://doi.org/10.1111/bjet.12861

Luckin, R., Cukurova, M., Kent, C., & du Boulay, B. (2022). Empowering educators to be AI-ready. *Computers and Education: Artificial Intelligence, 3*, Article 100076. https://doi.org/10.1016/j.caeai.2022.100076

Luckin, R., & Holmes, W. (2016). *Intelligence unleashed: An argument for AI in education.*

Memarian, B., & Doleck, T. (2023). Fairness, Accountability, Transparency, and Ethics (FATE) in Artificial Intelligence (AI) and higher education: A systematic review. *Computers and Education: Artificial Intelligence, 5*, Article 100152. https://doi.org/10.1016/j.caeai.2023.100152

Mehrabi, N., Morstatter, F., Saxena, N., Lerman, K., & Galstyan, A. (2022). A survey on bias and fairness in machine learning. *ACM Computing Surveys, 54*(6), 1–35. https://doi.org/10.1145/3457607

Mikroyannidis, A., Gomez Goiri, A., Domingue, J., Tranoris, C., Pareit, D., Vanhie-Van Gerwen, J., & Marquez-Barja, J. (2015). *Deploying learning analytics for awareness and reflection in online scientific experimentation*. 105–111.

Mittelstadt, B. (2019). Principles alone cannot guarantee ethical AI. *Nature Machine Intelligence, 1*(11), 501–507. https://doi.org/10.1038/s42256-019-0114-4

Mittelstadt, B. D., Allo, P., Taddeo, M., Wachter, S., & Floridi, L. (2016). The ethics of algorithms: Mapping the debate. *Big Data & Society, 3*(2), 205395171667967. https://doi.org/10.1177/2053951716679679

Moroianu, N., Iacob, S.-E., & Constantin, A. (2023). *Artificial intelligence in education: A systematic review* (pp. 906–921). https://doi.org/10.2478/9788367405546-084

Mousavinasab, E., Zarifsanaiey, N., R. Niakan Kalhori, S., Rakhshan, M., Keikha, L., & Ghazi Saeedi, M. (2021). Intelligent tutoring systems: A systematic review of characteristics, applications, and evaluation methods. *Interactive Learning Environments, 29*(1), 142–163. https://doi.org/10.1080/10494820.2018.1558257

Naudé, W. (2020). Artificial intelligence vs COVID-19: Limitations, constraints and pitfalls. *AI & Society, 35*(3), 761–765. https://doi.org/10.1007/s00146-020-00978-0

Ng, D. T. K., Leung, J. K. L., Su, J., Ng, R. C. W., & Chu, S. K. W. (2023). Teachers' AI digital competencies and twenty-first century skills in the post-pandemic world. *Educational Technology Research and Development, 71*(1), 137–161. https://doi.org/10.1007/s11423-023-10203-6

Nguyen, A., Ngo, H. N., Hong, Y., Dang, B., & Nguyen, B.-P.T. (2023). Ethical principles for artificial intelligence in education. *Education and Information Technologies, 28*(4), 4221–4241. https://doi.org/10.1007/s10639-022-11316-w

Ntoutsi, E., Fafalios, P., Gadiraju, U., Iosifidis, V., Nejdl, W., Vidal, M., Ruggieri, S., Turini, F., Papadopoulos, S., Krasanakis, E., Kompatsiaris, I., Kinder-Kurlanda, K., Wagner, C., Karimi, F., Fernandez, M., Alani, H., Berendt, B., Kruegel, T., Heinze, C., … Staab, S. (2020). Bias in data-driven artificial intelligence systems—An introductory survey. *WIREs Data Mining and Knowledge Discovery, 10*(3), e1356. https://doi.org/10.1002/widm.1356

Nye, B. D., Graesser, A. C., & Hu, X. (2014). AutoTutor and family: A review of 17 years of natural language tutoring. *International Journal of Artificial Intelligence in Education, 24*(4), 427–469. https://doi.org/10.1007/s40593-014-0029-5

Office of the Victorian Information Commissioner. (2018). Artificial intelligence and privacy – issues and challenges. https://ovic.vic.gov.au/wp-content/uploads/2021/04/Artificial-Intelligence-and-Privacy-Issues-And-Challenges.docx

O'Neil, C. (2017). *Weapons of math destruction: How big data increases inequality and threatens democracy* (First paperback edition). B/D/W/Y Broadway Books.

Pantanowitz, L., Bui, M. M., Chauhan, C., ElGabry, E., Hassell, L., Li, Z., Parwani, A. V., Salama, M. E., Sebastian, M. M., Tulman, D., Vepa, S., & Becich, M. J. (2022). Rules of engagement: Promoting academic-industry partnership in the era of digital pathology and artificial intelligence. *Academic Pathology, 9*(1), Article 100026. https://doi.org/10.1016/j.acpath.2022.100026

Panigutti, C., Hamon, R., Hupont, I., Fernandez Llorca, D., Fano Yela, D., Junklewitz, H., Scalzo, S., Mazzini, G., Sanchez, I., Soler Garrido, J., & Gomez, E. (2023). The role of explainable AI in the context of the AI Act. *2023 ACM Conference on Fairness, Accountability, and Transparency*, 1139–1150. https://doi.org/10.1145/3593013.3594069

Pangrazio, L., & Sefton-Green, J. (2021). Digital rights, digital citizenship and digital literacy: What's the difference? *Journal of New Approaches in Educational Research, 10*(1), 15. https://doi.org/10.7821/naer.2021.1.616

Pardo, A., & Siemens, G. (2014). Ethical and privacy principles for learning analytics. *British Journal of Educational Technology, 45*(3), 438–450. https://doi.org/10.1111/bjet.12152

Park, J., & Vance, A. (2021, February 11). *Data privacy in higher education: Yes, students care*. EDUCAUSE Review. https://er.educause.edu/articles/2021/2/data-privacy-in-higher-education-yes-students-care

Parviz, M. (2024). AI in education: Comparative perspectives from STEM and Non-STEM instructors. *Computers and Education Open, 6*, Article 100190. https://doi.org/10.1016/j.caeo.2024.100190

Passey, D., Rogers, C., Machell, J., & McHugh, G. (2004). *The Motivational effects of ICT on pupils.*

Păvăloaia, V.-D., & Necula, S.-C. (2023). Artificial intelligence as a disruptive technology—A systematic literature review. *Electronics, 12*(5), Article 5. https://doi.org/10.3390/electronics12051102

Peters, M. A. (2017). Technological unemployment: Educating for the fourth industrial revolution. *Educational Philosophy and Theory, 49*(1), 1–6. https://doi.org/10.1080/00131857.2016.1177412

Pedró, F. (2020). Applications of artificial intelligence to higher education: Possibilities, evidence, and challenges. *IUL Research, 1*(1), 61–76.

Pedro, F., Subosa, M., Rivas, A., & Valverde, P. (2019). *Artificial intelligence in education challenges and opportunities for sustainable development.pdf*. http://repositorio.minedu.gob.pe/bitstream/handle/20.500.12799/6533/Artificial%20intelligence%20in%20education%20challenges%20and%20opportunities%20for%20sustainable%20development.pdf

Pinski, M., & Benlian, A. (2024). AI literacy for users – A comprehensive review and future research directions of learning methods, components, and effects. *Computers in Human Behavior: Artificial Humans, 2*(1), Article 100062. https://doi.org/10.1016/j.chbah.2024.100062

Pise, D. A. (2024, February 26). IBM: Watson to Watsonx journey. *Medium.* https://anilpise7.medium.com/ibm-watson-to-watsonx-journey-4d0df10bb351

Politico. (2023, December 29). Artificial intelligence stirs privacy challenges for schools. https://www.politico.com/news/2024/02/04/how-ai-is-quietly-changing-everyday-life-00138341penspark

Popenici, S. A. D., & Kerr, S. (2017). Exploring the impact of artificial intelligence on teaching and learning in higher education. *Research and Practice in Technology Enhanced Learning, 12*(1), 22. https://doi.org/10.1186/s41039-017-0062-8

Prinsloo, P. (2017). Fleeing from Frankenstein's monster and meeting Kafka on the way: Algorithmic decision-making in higher education. *E-Learning and Digital Media, 14*(3), 138–163. https://doi.org/10.1177/2042753017731355

Prinsloo, P., & Slade, S. (2017). *Ethics and learning analytics: Charting the (Un)Charted.* https://www.researchgate.net/publication/317092406_Ethics_and_Learning_Analytics_Charting_the_UnCharted

Radanliev, P., Santos, O., Brandon-Jones, A., & Joinson, A. (2024). Ethics and responsible AI deployment. *Frontiers in Artificial Intelligence, 7*, 1377011. https://doi.org/10.3389/frai.2024.1377011

Radianti, J., Majchrzak, T. A., Fromm, J., & Wohlgenannt, I. (2020). A systematic review of immersive virtual reality applications for higher education: Design elements, lessons learned, and research agenda. *Computers & Education, 147*, Article 103778. https://doi.org/10.1016/j.compedu.2019.103778

Ramesh, D., & Sanampudi, S. K. (2022). An automated essay scoring systems: A systematic literature review. *Artificial Intelligence Review, 55*(3), 2495–2527. https://doi.org/10.1007/s10462-021-10068-2

Regan, P. M., & Jesse, J. (2019). Ethical challenges of edtech, big data and personalized learning: Twenty-first century student sorting and tracking. *Ethics and Information Technology, 21*(3), 167–179. https://doi.org/10.1007/s10676-018-9492-2

Reilly, E. D., Wiliams, K. M., Stafford, R. E., Corliss, S. B., Walkow, J. C., & Kidwell, D. K. (2016). Global times call for global measures: Investigating automated essay scoring in linguistically-diverse MOOCs. *Online Learning, 20*(2). https://doi.org/10.24059/olj.v20i2.638

Ridsdale, C., Rothwell, J., Smit, M., Bliemel, M., Irvine, D., Kelley, D., Matwin, S., Wuetherick, B., & Ali-Hassan, H. (2015). *Strategies and best practices for data literacy education knowledge synthesis report.* https://doi.org/10.13140/RG.2.1.1922.5044

Rienties, B., Køhler Simonsen, H., & Herodotou, C. (2020). Defining the boundaries between artificial intelligence in education, computer-supported collaborative learning, educational data mining, and learning analytics: A need for coherence. *Frontiers in Education, 5*, 128. https://doi.org/10.3389/feduc.2020.00128

Robert, J., & McCormack, M. (2024, May 23). *2024 EDUCAUSE action plan: AI policies and guidelines.* EDUCAUSE. https://www.educause.edu/research/2024/2024-educause-action-plan-ai-policies-and-guidelines

Rubel, A., & Jones, K. M. L. (2016). Student privacy in learning analytics: An information ethics perspective. *The Information Society, 32*(2), 143–159.

Russell, S., & Norvig, P. (2010). The nature of environments. *Artificial intelligence: A modern approach* (3rd ed.). Pearson Education.

Sarker, I. H. (2022). AI-based modeling: techniques, applications and research issues towards automation, intelligent and smart systems. *Sn Computer Science, 3*(2). https://doi.org/10.1007/s42979-022-01043-x

Schintler, L. A., & McNeely, C. L. (2022). Artificial intelligence, institutions, and resilience: Prospects and provocations for cities. *Journal of Urban Management, 11*(2), 256–268. https://doi.org/10.1016/j.jum.2022.05.004

Shaw, M. (2003). Writing good software engineering research papers. In *25th International Conference on Software Engineering*, (pp. 726–736). Portland.

Selwyn, N. (2019). *Should robots replace teachers?* Polity Press.

Shermis, M. D., & Burstein, J. (Eds.). (2013). *Handbook of automated essay evaluation* (0 ed.). Routledge. https://doi.org/10.4324/9780203122761

Shin, D., & Park, Y. J. (2019). Role of fairness, accountability, and transparency in algorithmic affordance. *Computers in Human Behavior, 98*, 277–284. https://doi.org/10.1016/j.chb.2019.04.019

Shiohira, K. (2021). https://files.eric.ed.gov/fulltext/ED612439.pdf

Shrivastava, A., Suji P. S. J., Yeruva, A. R., Mani, P., Nagpal, P., & Chaturvedi, A. (2023). IoT-based RFID attendance monitoring system of students using Arduino ESP8266 & Adafruit. io on defined area. *Cybernetics and Systems*, 1–12.

Shute, V. J., & Rahimi, S. (2021). Stealth assessment of creativity in a physics video game. *Computers in Human Behavior*, *116*, 106647. https://doi.org/10.1016/j.chb.2020.106647

Slade, S., & Prinsloo, P. (2013). Learning analytics: Ethical issues and dilemmas. *American Behavioral Scientist, 57*(10), 1510–1529. https://doi.org/10.1177/0002764213479366

Slimi, Z. (2023). The impact of artificial intelligence on higher education: An empirical study. *European Journal of Educational Sciences, 10*(1). https://doi.org/10.19044/ejes.v10no1a17

Southworth, J., Migliaccio, K., Glover, J., Glover, J., Reed, D., McCarty, C., Brendemuhl, J., & Thomas, A. (2023). Developing a model for AI across the curriculum: Transforming the higher education landscape via innovation in AI literacy. *Computers and Education: Artificial Intelligence, 4*, Article 100127. https://doi.org/10.1016/j.caeai.2023.100127

Suresh, H., & Guttag, J. (2021). A framework for understanding sources of harm throughout the machine learning life cycle. *Equity and Access in Algorithms, Mechanisms, and Optimization*, 1–9. https://doi.org/10.1145/3465416.3483305

Swiecki, Z., Khosravi, H., Chen, G., Martinez-Maldonado, R., Lodge, J. M., Milligan, S., Selwyn, N., & Gašević, D. (2022). Assessment in the age of artificial intelligence. *Computers and Education: Artificial Intelligence, 3*, Article 100075. https://doi.org/10.1016/j.caeai.2022.100075

Tang, K. H. D. (2024). Implications of artificial intelligence for teaching and learning. *Acta Pedagogia Asiana, 3*(2), 65–79. https://doi.org/10.53623/apga.v3i2.404

Tariq, S., Samad, A., Hamza, M., Ahmer, A., Muazzam, A., Ahmad, S., & Amhabj, A. M. A. (2022). Salmonella in poultry; An overview. *International Journal of Multidisciplinary Sciences and Arts, 1*(1), 80–84.

The Ark HQ. (2023, September 27). Privacy concerns in the age of AI-driven education: A guide for school leaders. https://thearkhq.com/contact-the-ark-hq/

The White House. (2023, October 30). *Executive order on the safe, secure, and trustworthy development and use of artificial intelligence*. The White House. https://www.whitehouse.gov/briefing-room/presidential-actions/2023/10/30/executive-order-on-the-safe-secure-and-trustworthy-development-and-use-of-artificial-intelligence/

Tsai, Y.-S., Whitelock-Wainwright, A., & Gašević, D. (2020). The privacy paradox and its implications for learning analytics. *Proceedings of the Tenth International Conference on Learning Analytics & Knowledge*, 230–239. https://doi.org/10.1145/3375462.3375536

Tuomi, I. (2018). *The impact of artificial intelligence on learning, teaching, and education.* Publications Office. https://data.europa.eu/doi/https://doi.org/10.2760/12297

Usher, M., & Barak, M. (2024). Unpacking the role of AI ethics online education for science and engineering students. *International Journal of STEM Education, 11*(1), 35. https://doi.org/10.1186/s40594-024-00493-4

Vinuesa, R., Azizpour, H., Leite, I., Balaam, M., Dignum, V., Domisch, S., & Nerini, F. F. (2020). The role of artificial intelligence in achieving the sustainable development goals. *Nature Communications, 11*(1), 1–10.

Wachter, S., Mittelstadt, B., & Russell, C. (2020). Why fairness cannot be automated: Bridging the gap between EU non-discrimination law and AI. *SSRN Electronic Journal*. https://doi.org/10.2139/ssrn.3547922

Walter, Y. (2024). Embracing the future of Artificial Intelligence in the classroom: The relevance of AI literacy, prompt engineering, and critical thinking in modern education. *International*

Journal of Educational Technology in Higher Education, 21(1), 15. https://doi.org/10.1186/s41239-024-00448-3

Wang, P. (2019). On defining artificial intelligence. *Journal of Artificial General Intelligence, 10*(2), 1–37. https://doi.org/10.2478/jagi-2019-0002

Wardat, Y., Belbase, S., & Tairab, H. (2022). Mathematics teachers' perceptions of trends in international mathematics and science study (TIMSS)-related practices in Abu Dhabi Emirate schools. *Sustainability, 14*(9), 5436.

Weng, X., Ye, H., Dai, Y., & Ng, O. (2024). Integrating artificial intelligence and computational thinking in educational contexts: A systematic review of instructional design and student learning outcomes. *Journal of Educational Computing Research, 62*(6), 1640–1670. https://doi.org/10.1177/07356331241248686

Willis, J. E., Slade, S., & Prinsloo, P. (2016). Ethical oversight of student data in learning analytics: A typology derived from a cross-continental, cross-institutional perspective. *Educational Technology Research and Development, 64*(5), 881–901.

Wilson, J., & Czik, A. (2016). Automated essay evaluation software in English Language Arts classrooms: Effects on teacher feedback, student motivation, and writing quality. *Computers & Education, 100*, 94–109. https://doi.org/10.1016/j.compedu.2016.05.004

Xie, H., Chu, H.-C., Hwang, G.-J., & Wang, C.-C. (2019). Trends and development in technology-enhanced adaptive/personalized learning: A systematic review of journal publications from 2007 to 2017. *Computers & Education, 140*, Article 103599. https://doi.org/10.1016/j.compedu.2019.103599

Xu, W., & Ouyang, F. (2022). The application of AI technologies in STEM education: A systematic review from 2011 to 2021. *International Journal of STEM Education, 9*(1), 59. https://doi.org/10.1186/s40594-022-00377-5

Xu, Y., Liu, X., Cao, X., Huang, C., Liu, E., Qian, S., Liu, X., Wu, Y., Dong, F., Qiu, C.-W., Qiu, J., Hua, K., Su, W., Wu, J., Xu, H., Han, Y., Fu, C., Yin, Z., Liu, M., … Zhang, J. (2021). Artificial intelligence: A powerful paradigm for scientific research. *The Innovation, 2*(4), 100179. https://doi.org/10.1016/j.xinn.2021.100179

Yang, X., Hesami, M. D., Nazemipool, E., Bahadoran, A., Al-Bahrani, M., & Azizi, B. (2022). Fabrication of $CuCo_2S_4$ yolk-shell spheres embedded with S-scheme V_2O_5-deposited on wrinkled g-C_3N_4 for effective promotion of levofloxacin photodegradation. *Separation and Purification Technology, 301*, Article 122005.

Yaghmaei, E., & van de Poel, I. (Eds.). (2021). *Assessment of responsible innovation: Methods and practices.* Routledge.

Yelne, S., Chaudhary, M., Dod, K., Sayyad, A., & Sharma, R. (2023). Harnessing the power of AI: A comprehensive review of its impact and challenges in nursing science and healthcare. *Cureus, 15*(11), Article e49252. https://doi.org/10.7759/cureus.49252

Yin, W. J. (2024, January 24). *Will our educational system keep pace with AI? A Student's perspective on AI and learning.* EDUCAUSE Review. https://er.educause.edu/articles/2024/1/will-our-educational-system-keep-pace-with-ai-a-students-perspective-on-ai-and-learning

Youvan, D. C. (2024). *The role of AI in revolutionizing academic publishing and knowledge dissemination.* https://doi.org/10.13140/RG.2.2.35215.76962

Zawacki-Richter, O., Marín, V. I., Bond, M., & Gouverneur, F. (2019). Systematic review of research on artificial intelligence applications in higher education—where are the educators? *International Journal of Educational Technology in Higher Education, 16*(1), 39. https://doi.org/10.1186/s41239-019-0171-0

Zhu, X., Li, C., & Bao, M. (2024). Research on the application and future trend of artificial intelligence in education and teaching. *SHS Web of Conferences, 187*, 04017. https://doi.org/10.1051/shsconf/202418704017

Chapter 11
Navigating the Digital Shift: An Analysis of the Psychological Impact of AI Adoption on Lecturers' Job Security in Zimbabwe

Clemenciana Mukenge

Abstract The rise of Artificial Intelligence (AI) has sparked intense debate about its potential impact on various professions, including education. In Africa, where education is critical for economic development and social mobility, concerns about AI's effect on teacher job security are particularly high. This qualitative study explores the benefits and challenges of AI adoption, and its impact on lecturers' job security in Zimbabwe. A qualitative approach was employed, utilizing a purposive sampling technique to select 30 lecturers from various disciplines in a Zimbabwean university. Semi-structured interviews were conducted to collect data, which were then analyzed using a mixed methods approach, combining thematic analysis and descriptive statistics. The findings indicate that lecturers are resilient and adaptable to the revolving technological landscape, and can balance the benefits and challenges of AI adoption. Significant implementation challenges include limited training and support, and students' overreliance on AI. The study concludes that, despite adoption challenges, AI implementation has a positive impact on lecturers' job security, enabling a focus on high-touch, high-value tasks that require human skills. Recommended is that universities should prioritize the provision of comprehensive AI training and support to lecturers, and take steps to mitigate the potential risks of student dependency on AI.

Keywords Artificial intelligence · Higher education · Technology adoption · University lecturers · Job security · Zimbabwe

C. Mukenge (✉)
Department of Creative Media and Communication, University of Zimbabwe, Harare, Zimbabwe
e-mail: cmukenge@arts.uz.ac.zw

M. A. Adarkwah et al. (eds.), *Artificial Intelligence and Human Agency in Education: Volume One*, Future Education and Learning Spaces,
https://doi.org/10.1007/978-981-96-7937-9_11

11.1 Introduction

The rise of Artificial Intelligence (AI) has sparked intense debate about its potential impact on various professions, including education (Das, Malaviya & Singh, 2023). In Africa, where education is critical for economic development and social mobility, concerns about AI's effect on teacher job security are particularly high. One of the primary concerns is that the automation of certain teaching tasks through AI could potentially lead to the displacement of human educators as "this recalibrates the role of instructors as well as optimizes the teaching–learning environment for a better learning experience" (Bhutoria, 2022: 100,068). Bhutoria insists that, as AI continues to evolve and become more proficient at tasks traditionally performed by teachers, there is a worry that educators may face job loss or reduced job opportunities in the future. Given the teacher shortages in Africa, AI could exacerbate the problem by reducing the demand for human instructors (UNESCO, 2019). For instance, the African Development Bank estimates that Africa needs to recruit over 10 million new teachers by 2030 to meet the demand for education (AfDB, 2019). Thus, while AI presents opportunities for educators to focus on high-value tasks, expand access to education, and improve student outcomes, it also poses challenges to teacher job security in Africa (Kaswan et al. (2024). This solicits questions about how educators can adapt to these changes and what the future role of teachers will be in an AI-driven educational landscape.

Despite job security concerns, AI's integration into educational practices has brought about numerous benefits including personalized learning experiences, improved efficiency in grading, circumvention of anticipated learning difficulties, and enhanced educational outcomes (Dimla et al., 2024; Ghamrawi et al., 2024; Walter, 2024; Das et al., 2023; Bhutoria, 2022). This personalized learning approach is believed to improve learners' participation, performance, and overall satisfaction (Das et al., 2023). It can expand access to education in the African continent, particularly in rural or underserved areas where qualified teachers may be scarce (UNESCO, 2019). Online and blended learning platforms, powered by AI, can provide high-quality educational content and instruction to students who may not have access to them otherwise (Kinyanjui, 2018). Moreover, AI can also augment teacher capabilities, freeing them to focus on high-touch, high-value tasks that require empathy, creativity, and human interaction (Burgess & Sievert, 2017). According to Kaswan et al. (2024), AI-powered tools can help teachers with tasks such as student assessment, feedback, and personalized learning plans. In situations where teacher workload and class sizes are often high, AI can help alleviate some of these pressures (Hashem et al., 2024).

11.2 Research Gap

Despite the growing interest in AI's impact on employment in the education sector, there remains a notable gap in the existing literature concerning this phenomenon, especially in Africa. As Gwagwa et al. (2020: 2) observe, "there is a dearth of data on all aspects of artificial intelligence (AI) in Africa, and much of the available information is thus anecdotal." Precisely, in Zimbabwe, where the adoption of AI in universities is gradual (Maphosa, 2023), research into how this digital shift is influencing educators' perceptions of work satisfaction is scarce. To address this gap, this study aims to delve into the complex interplay between AI integration in universities and its impact on lecturers' job security, shedding light on the challenges and opportunities that arise from this digital shift. Through exploring this under-researched topic, this study seeks to provide valuable insights that can inform policy decisions and strategies to support educators in navigating the evolving educational landscape amidst technological variabilities in Zimbabwe. The study addresses the following pertinent questions:

How has the adoption of AI in Zimbabwean universities affected the lecturers' roles and responsibilities?

What concerns do lecturers have regarding job security owing to AI integration?

What navigation strategies are employed to manage the digital shift?

11.3 Methodology

This study was conducted at a Zimbabwean university, which has been actively integrating AI into its educational landscape, providing a unique context to examine lecturers' job security views in the wake of AI-assisted learning. A thorough understanding of the methodology used, including the research design, participant selection, data collection, and analysis procedures, is essential to appreciate the study's findings.

11.3.1 Research Design and Participants

This qualitative study adopted an exploratory design to execute its objectives. It targeted lecturers with diverse experiences from various academic disciplines in a conveniently selected university, including STEM and humanities, ensuring diverse perspectives. A purposive sample of 30 lecturers, evenly split between 15 males and 15 females, was chosen to participate. This sample size was deemed sufficient to achieve data saturation, allowing for an in-depth exploration of the participants' perceptions. Table 11.1 below highlights the participants' demographic traits.

Table 11.1 Participants' demographic information

Variable	Category	Frequency
Age (Years)	25–35 35–45 45–55	6 17 7
Gender	Male Female	15 15
Experience (Years)	0–5 5–10 10–15 15–20	10 13 5 2
Highest qualification	Doctorate Masters	25 5
Discipline	Education and Law Science and Engineering Veterinary and Health Sciences Humanities and Behavioral Sciences Commerce and Business Studies	6 6 6 6 6

11.3.2 Data Collection Instrument

A semi-structured interview guide served as the primary data collection instrument for this study. The guide consisted of ten open-ended questions that were designed to explore the experiences and perspectives of university lecturers regarding the adoption of AI technologies in their teaching practices and impact on job security. The interview questions corresponded to the three research questions and were organized around three themes (the impact of AI integration on job roles and responsibilities; concerns about job security; and coping mechanisms and support systems) which were further sub-divided into ten sub-themes, producing ten questions. Probing questions were also used to gather in-depth information from participants and to provide context to their responses.

11.3.3 Data Collection Procedures

The semi-structured interviews were conducted from 15 May to 14 June 2024 at the selected university, ensuring flexible scheduling and participant comfort. Participants granted permission for audio recording to ensure accurate data capture. The interview protocol consisted of a brief introduction, a 25–30-min semi-structured discussion guided by open-ended questions, and a conclusion. Probing questions encouraged participants to elaborate on their responses. Post-interview, transcripts were prepared, stored securely, and shared with participants for validation. This rigorous procedure yielded high-quality, reliable data, providing valuable insights into lecturers' job security concerns amidst AI adoption.

11.3.4 Data Trustworthiness

To ensure data trustworthiness, the study employed several strategies including audio recordings of interviews to ascertain accuracy in data capture and verbatim transcriptions of the interviews to maintain data integrity. In addition, member checking involving sharing transcripts with participants for validation, enhanced validity, and thick descriptions of the research context and methodology facilitated transferability. These measures ensured that the data accurately reflected participants' experiences and perceptions.

11.3.5 Data Analysis Strategy

This study employed deductive thematic analysis to identify patterns and themes in the interview data, guided by the research questions. The analysis began with data familiarization, where transcripts were repeatedly reviewed to gain a comprehensive understanding. Codes were then manually developed based on the three research questions and applied to relevant segments of the transcripts. The coded data was subsequently categorized into three broad themes, which were further sub-divided into several corresponding sub-themes as demonstrated in the table below. The sub-thematic data was presented and subjected to critical analysis, drawing on findings from existing literature and theoretical perspectives, to provide deeper insights and meaning (Table 11.2).

To complement the thematic analysis, descriptive statistical analysis was used to arrive at frequencies of participants' responses. This involved calculating the number and percentage of participants who reported specific experiences, attitudes, or perceptions related to AI adoption. The use of descriptive statistics strengthened the data analysis by providing a quantitative perspective on the data, and enabling the identification of patterns and trends that may not have been apparent through thematic analysis alone.

11.3.6 Ethical Considerations and Clearance

This study was conducted in strict adherence to the principles outlined in the Declaration of Helsinki of 1964. Approval to carry out research in the selected university was obtained from the institutional Research and Innovation Board on 10 May 2024 (Approval number: UZRIB 0038/24). In addition, informed consent was obtained

Table 11.2 Research questions and corresponding themes and sub-themes

Research question	Broad theme	Sub-themes
How has the adoption of AI in Zimbabwean universities affected the lecturers' roles and responsibilities?	Impact of AI on Lecturers' Roles and Responsibilities	-Evolving Lecturers' Roles and Responsibilities -Teaching Practices and Experiences -Student Dependence on AI-Enabled Learning Tools -Transformations in Teaching and Learning Methodologies
What concerns do lecturers have regarding job security owing to AI integration?	Job Security Concerns	-Adaptation to AI Implementation -Effects of AI on Job Security and Career Prospects -Personal Experiences of Job Insecurity
What navigation strategies are employed to manage the digital shift?	Coping Mechanisms and Support Systems	-Strategies for Managing AI-Driven Change -Training and Support for AI Integration -Balancing AI Integration with Job Security

from all participants prior to the interviews, ensuring confidentiality, anonymity, and the right to withdraw from the study without consequences. Participants were assured that their responses would remain confidential and anonymous and that the data would be stored securely.

11.4 Findings and Discussions

This section presents and discusses qualitative data that was collected from semi-structured interviews with selected Zimbabwean lecturers, designed to elicit insightful perspectives on job satisfaction during the ongoing AI implementation in education. The data is categorized into three overarching themes: Impact of AI on Lecturers' Roles and Responsibilities; Job Security Concerns; and Coping Mechanisms and Support Systems. The findings are organized and presented under relevant thematic subheadings, providing a clear and concise overview of the participants' experiences and perceptions as delineated in their responses to the interview questions. To maintain participant anonymity and confidentiality, each participant is assigned a unique alphanumeric code (M1-M15 for male participants and F1-F15 for female participants).

11.4.1 Impact of AI on Lecturers' Roles and Responsibilities

This is a critical theme that corresponds to the study's first research question: "How has the adoption of AI in Zimbabwean universities influenced the lecturers' job experiences?". It further explores four key sub-themes, illuminating the complex interplay between AI adoption and lecturers' professional experiences in Zimbabwe as outlined in the following paragraphs.

11.4.1.1 Evolving Lecturers' Roles and Responsibilities

Question 1: How would you describe your current roles and responsibilities as a lecturer at the university and how have these been impacted by the integration of AI?

The participants emphasized the multifaceted nature of lecturers' responsibilities, which can be categorized into four primary areas: teaching, curriculum development, assessment and feedback, and student support. These responsibilities encompass a range of tasks, including delivering lectures, designing course materials, conducting assessments, and providing guidance on academic and personal issues. According to the majority of participants (23 out of 30), the integration of AI into the education system has positively impacted these roles and responsibilities. For instance, AI has automated administrative tasks such as grading and data analysis, enabled teaching with AI-powered tools such as virtual simulations and adaptive learning systems, informed curriculum development with AI-driven content recommendations, and supported student feedback with AI-generated insights and suggestions. Participant F10 noted, "*Since AI has taken over grading and data analysis, I've been able to focus more on teaching and providing feedback to students.*" Similarly, Participant M5 stated, "*AI-powered tools have enhanced my teaching, allowing me to create more interactive and engaging learning experiences for my students.*" These responses illustrate how AI integration has influenced lecturers' responsibilities, freeing up time for more critical tasks and enabling innovative teaching approaches.

Although the majority of respondents report significant changes, a minority (7 out of 30) indicate that AI integration has had minimal or no impact on their job responsibilities. These respondents argue that they remain in control of their roles and have historically utilized AI tools, thereby experiencing no substantial changes. For instance, Participant F5 from the Engineering discipline noted, "*I've been using AI tools for years, so the integration of AI hasn't really changed my job responsibilities.*" Similarly, Participant M3 from Medical Sciences stated, "*I'm still in charge of my teaching and research, and AI has just become another tool to support my work.*" Participant F2 from Earth Sciences also shared, "*I don't see AI as a replacement for my role, but rather as a means to enhance my teaching and student engagement.*" These responses reflect the perspective that AI integration has not significantly altered lecturers' responsibilities, particularly in the STEM discipline, instead it has been incorporated as a complementary tool to support work.

11.4.1.2 Teaching Practices and Experiences

Question 2: Can you share your thoughts on the increasing integration of AI technologies in the educational sector, particularly concerning your teaching practices?

Most of the participants (21 out of 30) expressed a positive outlook on the integration of AI technologies in education, viewing it as a promising tool to enhance teaching practices and experiences, improve student engagement, and facilitate personalized learning experiences. This perspective highlights the potential benefits of AI for improving learning outcomes, increasing efficiency, enhancing student support, enabling data-driven decision-making, promoting accessibility, and fostering innovation and collaboration in the academic landscape. The following are some of the significant responses capturing this sentiment:

M12: *AI-powered tools can help me adapt learning to student needs, identify knowledge gaps, and develop more effective lectures.*

M3: *I can now use data analytics to track student progress, identify areas where students need extra support, and adjust my teaching strategies accordingly.*

While there was a generally positive attitude toward the integration of AI technologies in education, there were also repressed negative views against the technological shift from 9 out of 30 respondents. For example; Participant F5 noted: "*I believe the integration of AI technologies in higher education comes with significant risks and drawbacks.*" Similarly, Participant F15 expressed that, "*The integration of AI technologies at university raises concerns about privacy and data security.* These views highlight signs of subtle resistance to incorporating new technology into educational settings and to better understand and address the challenges and opportunities associated with the espousal of AI.

11.4.1.3 Students' Dependence on AI-Enabled Learning Tools

Question 3: What are your perceptions of students' reliance on AI tools and technologies for their academic work?

Responses to this question were varied. While students' reliance on AI tools was revealed to aid efficient information access and enhance productivity, strong concerns were also raised by the majority of the participants (18 out of 30) about the risk of overdependency, lack of understanding, and the possible erosion of critical thinking skills. Some of the outstanding responses indicating the perceived two-fold effect of dependence on AI in education include the following:

F11: *Students' reliance on AI tools and technologies for their academic work is a growing trend. While it can help streamline tasks and boost productivity, there is a concern that excessive dependence on AI may hinder critical thinking and creativity among students.*

F3: *While AI tools certainly provide access to information, students mustn't become overly reliant on them.*

Upon further probing, the participants suggested that, to gain AI's benefits and mitigate its risks, it is essential to teach AI literacy, encourage critical thinking and thorough monitoring, and provide feedback to ensure understanding and original thought. Overall, the participants indicated readiness to guide students in navigating the complexities of AI-aided learning, fostering efficiency and intellectual growth.

11.4.1.4 Transformations in Teaching and Learning Methodologies

Question 4: How do you believe the use of AI impacts traditional teaching and learning methodologies?

A total of 25 out of 30 participants acknowledged that AI complements and enhances traditional teaching methods by providing data-driven insights, automating administrative tasks, and delivering personalized learning experiences. However, some of these participants also noted that this integration might require a shift in the role of lecturers toward facilitation and mentorship. The following are some of the most prominent views:

M4: *AI integration can supplement traditional teaching, but it needs us to focus more on facilitation, mentorship, and providing context, rather than just delivering content.*

M10: *AI can take over routine tasks, freeing us up to focus on what matters most - student engagement, guidance, and development. Our role evolves into more of coaching rather than just a lecturer.*

These findings indicate that the lecturers believe that AI's impact on traditional teaching methods and their role in the classroom is multifaceted; both complementary and requiring a role shift. To adapt to this shift, participants further suggest professional development (Participants F6, F8, & M15), redefining roles and responsibilities (Participants M1 & M9), emphasizing human skills that AI cannot replicate such as empathy (Participants F7, M11, & M12), creativity, and critical thinking (Participants M3, M8, F13, & M4).

11.4.1.5 Summary of Findings

The data presented in this section, corresponding to four interview questions reveals a multifaceted impact of AI implementation on lecturers' roles and responsibilities. While AI has enhanced teaching practices and complemented traditional teaching methods, participants raised concerns about the potential risk of overreliance on AI by students, which they argued may erode critical thinking skills. Figure 11.1 below provides a statistical overview of the participants' perspectives on this issue.

11.4.1.6 Discussions

The indication that the majority of Zimbabwean lecturers are still able to effectively carry out their multifaceted teaching roles and responsibilities in a technologically

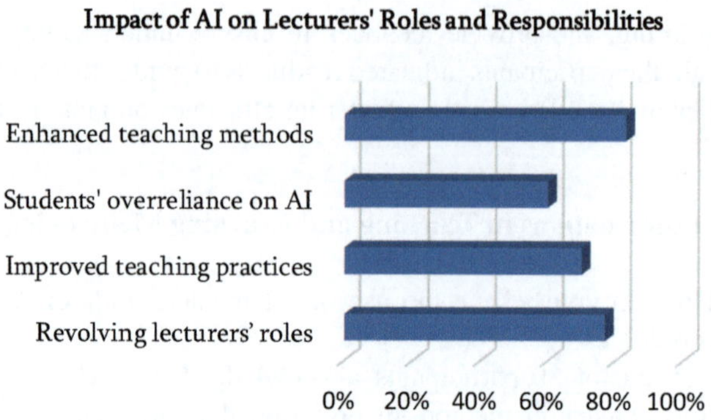

Fig. 11.1 Impact of AI on lecturers' roles and responsibilities

advancing environment, despite the rise of AI in academia, sheds light on the opportunity presented by the adoption of AI in higher education. It demonstrates the lecturers' resilience and adaptability in the face of evolving technology. It also suggests that Zimbabwean lecturers have developed the necessary skills to navigate and utilize technology in their teaching and research activities. Further, the lecturers' ability to handle their tasks in a technologically advancing landscape reflects positively on the quality of education provided to students. It indicates that these lecturers can integrate technological tools into their work to enhance the learning experience and keep pace with the changing academic scenery. Given the perception that the teacher's AI digital competencies signify competitiveness (Ng et al., 2023), this outcome could also suggest that Zimbabwean lecturers are competitive and hence relevant in the global academic arena, where advancements in AI and technology are shaping the future of education. Further, as suggested by Kamalov et al. (2023), the outcome of the study highlights the context-specific factors in Zimbabwe such as policies and practices that enable lecturers to navigate the evolving technological space effectively.

The potential of AI technologies to revolutionize teaching practices and enhance student learning experiences is a significant outcome of this study. Lecturers' indication that AI tools can improve teaching experiences, increase student engagement, and provide personalized learning experiences tailored to individual student needs is crucial evidence suggesting that educators recognize the potential benefits of incorporating AI technologies into their teaching practices. Evidently, those in the Science disciplines who were already using AI proclaimed continued practice. This positive outlook can contribute to the widespread adoption of AI tools in educational settings in Zimbabwe, ultimately enhancing the quality of education and improving student learning outcomes. Furthermore, this development can also positively impact lecturers' job security, as their roles evolve to focus on high-touch, high-value tasks that complement AI-powered tools. As lecturers adapt to these changes, they can leverage AI to enhance their teaching practices, ultimately strengthening their professional identities and job security. This perspective is supported by global contemporary research findings, which highlight the role of AI in personalized learning (Grájeda et al., 2023; Pesovski et al., 2024; Ezeoguine & Eteng-Uket, 2024; Dimla et al., 2024; Ghamrawi et al., 2024; Walter, 2024; Marzuki et al., 2023). For instance, Dimla et al., (2024: 8495) emphasize that "Educators see both opportunities and challenges, but agree AI can personalize learning through student data," and Walter (2024: 1) posits that "the introduction of AI into education marks a significant departure from conventional teaching methods, offering personalized learning and support for diverse educational requirements, including students with special needs." Further, Pesovski et al., (2024: 3034) concur that "the introduction of accessible generative artificial intelligence opens promising opportunities for the implementation of personalized learning methods in any educational environment."

The integration of AI technologies in education has necessitated lecturers to adapt their teaching methodologies to effectively leverage these tools. While AI can streamline administrative tasks, provide data-driven insights, and offer personalized learning experiences (Ghamrawi et al., 2024), it may also lead to a shift in the role of lecturers toward facilitation and mentorship, as highlighted by the participants. Such a shift would imply a fundamental change in the traditional approach to university education and pedagogy. It suggests that AI technologies could take over certain tasks currently performed by lecturers, such as content delivery and assessment, enabling lecturers to focus more on other tasks such as guiding students, providing personalized support, and fostering critical thinking skills. This shift could have wide-reaching implications for the higher education sector, including changes in the way educational institutions are structured, how courses are designed and delivered, and how lecturers are trained (Grájeda et al., 2023). Pesovski et al. (2024) add that a shift in the lecturers' teaching methodologies consequent to AI implementation may also impact student engagement, learning outcomes, and the overall quality of education. In consistency with Chan (2023) and Itse, Yahaya and Uzoigwe (2024), these findings suggest that while AI may change the nature of lecturers' work, it is unlikely to replace them entirely. Instead, AI can augment lecturers' capabilities, enabling them to focus on other tasks requiring human skills.

Concerns were raised regarding students' overreliance on AI tools, which could potentially hinder the development of critical thinking skills and independent learning. This outcome underscores not only the value of human educators but also the importance of developing critical thinking skills in students, which will help them navigate an increasingly complex and data-driven world. Furthermore, it accentuates the importance of harmonizing the use of AI tools with the cultivation of critical thinking skills and independent learning. Excessive dependence on AI tools could lead to a decline in students' ability to think critically, problem-solve, and engage deeply with course material. Grájeda et al. (2023) agree that overreliance on AI tools creates a passive learning environment where students simply seek quick answers rather than engage in active discovery, analysis, and reflection. Ezeoguine and Eteng-Uket (2024) also observe that students' overdependence on AI hinders their ability to adapt to new challenges and develop a deeper understanding of complex concepts.

This dual nature of AI's impact on education suggests a need for a balanced approach, where AI is used as a complement to traditional teaching methods, rather than a replacement.

11.4.2 Job Security Concerns

This section addresses the study's second research question: "What concerns do lecturers have regarding job security owing to AI integration?" It examines the anxieties and uncertainties lecturers face amidst AI integration in Zimbabwean universities. It explores three pivotal sub-themes emerging from the interview data as demonstrated in the proceeding text.

11.4.2.1 Adaptation to AI Implementation

Question 5: Have you experienced any changes in your day-to-day work environment as a result of AI implementation?

The majority of the participants (19 out of 30) revealed that they have experienced significant changes in their day-to-day work environment due to AI implementation. The cited changes were experienced in content delivery, assessment and feedback, and teaching and learning methodologies. In terms of content delivery, the participants noted that they are slowly transitioning from traditional lectures to more interactive and personalized approaches, incorporating AI-generated multimedia content, such as videos and simulations and using AI-powered tools to supplement teaching (Participants M12, M9, F4, & M8). Adjustments in assessment and feedback include utilizing AI-driven assessment tools to evaluate student progress and understanding, receiving AI-generated insights to inform feedback and improve student outcomes, and implementing peer review and self-assessment strategies facilitated by AI platforms (Participants M2, F1, M10, & F9). Teaching and learning methodologies were indicated to shift from a solely instructor-centric approach to a more student-centered and collaborative model, incorporating AI-facilitated group work and discussions to enhance student engagement (Participants F8, M8, M6, & M11), and using AI to support project-based learning and problem-solving activities (Participants M14, M5, & M7). Examples of these perceptions include the following:

M14: *Absolutely, AI implementation has transformed my teaching approach. I now use AI-powered interactive simulations to deliver content, making lectures more engaging and interactive. Assessments are also more efficient, with AI grading tools providing instant feedback.*

F8: *I have adapted by incorporating AI-powered platforms for student engagement and administrative tasks and enhancing the feedback process through intelligent tutoring systems.*

To adapt to these changes, the participants indicated that they need to develop new skills and strategies such as learning to effectively integrate AI-powered tools into their teaching practices (Participant M10), develop methods to ensure AI-generated content aligns with learning objectives (Participant F7), and stay updated on the latest AI advancements and best practices in education (Participants F13, M12, F4, M8, & M5).

However, a notable proportion of participants (11 out of 30) indicated challenges, citing that they have not fully integrated AI into their work due to various constraints. Specifically, participants from disciplines such as humanities and commerce mentioned that the nature of their subjects makes it challenging to fully incorporate AI. Additionally, network challenges, limited access to digital resources, and the digital divide were identified as significant barriers to AI adoption. The digital divide, in particular, was seen as a major obstacle, as it restricts access to AI-powered tools, training, and support, thereby hindering the participants' ability to fully adapt to AI. Examples of responses from these participants include: "*I teach in the humanities department, and application of AI to my subject area is limited.*" (Participant F6); "*Our university's network infrastructure is not reliable, making it difficult for me to consistently use AI-powered tools in my teaching.*" (Participant M9).

11.4.2.2 Effects of AI on Job Security and Career Prospects

Question 6: How do you think the utilization of AI affects your job security and career prospects as a lecturer in Zimbabwe?

While concerns about potential job automation due to AI were minimal (9 out of 30), the majority of the participants (21 out of 30) expressed confidence in the enduring need for human educators to offer guidance, support, and mentorship. The following are some of the striking responses corresponding to this sentiment:

M6: *I believe that the role of a lecturer involves a significant level of interaction, creativity, and critical thinking that may not be easily replaced by AI.*

M15: *While the advancements in AI are changing the education landscape in Zimbabwe, I believe that the unique human qualities and experiences that lecturers bring to the table cannot be fully substituted with technology.*

These responses suggest a belief in the irreplaceable human touch in the educational sphere. The participants strongly believed that AI cannot adequately replace human capital. The general contention is that, in addition to the intellectual support offered to the students, lecturers must acquire new skills to leverage the evolving AI tools, without having to lose their jobs or change careers. Contrary, participants who expressed concerns that AI integration poses a threat to their job security, cited risks such as potential replacement of lecturers by AI-powered systems (Participant M3), loss of autonomy in teaching and assessment (Participants M1, F5, & F2), and increased reliance on technology that may diminish the need for human instructors (Participant F12). Additionally, the potential for AI to assume tasks traditionally performed by lecturers such as grading and content creation was a concern. One participant stated that "*I'm concerned that if AI takes over tasks like grading and content creation, universities might see lecturers as less essential, and that could lead to job losses*" (Participant M7).

11.4.2.3 Personal Experiences of Job Insecurity

Question 7: Have you had any specific experiences or instances where you felt your job security was compromised due to the increasing reliance on AI in education?

Direct job security concerns attributed to AI implementation were limited among the participants. Only 4 out of 30 participants reported experiences of significant job insecurity due to AI implementation. The majority of the participants (26 out of 30) mainly perceived AI as a tool to augment teaching, rather than replace human instructors. However, a sense of vigilance toward the evolving landscape and the necessity for continuous upskilling and adaptability were emphasized. For example;

M9: *I have not experienced any direct instances where my job security was compromised due to AI implementation. However, the rapid pace of technological change has highlighted the importance of continuous professional development and staying abreast of emerging AI trends in education.*

F8: *Although I do not feel like my job security is compromised at the moment, there is a growing concern about the potential long-term impacts of AI on the need for human educators in the education system.*

11.4.2.4 Summary of Findings

The data presented in this section on job security concerns reveals that while most lecturers have successfully adapted to AI implementation in education and have had no experiences of direct job insecurities, the minority have expressed concerns about the potential impact of AI on their job security and have faced challenges in adapting to AI implementation. Moreover, the data highlights the importance of professional development and upskilling in technologies to ensure that lecturers remain relevant in an AI-driven education system. Figure 11.2 below presents a statistical overview of the participants' views on these aspects.

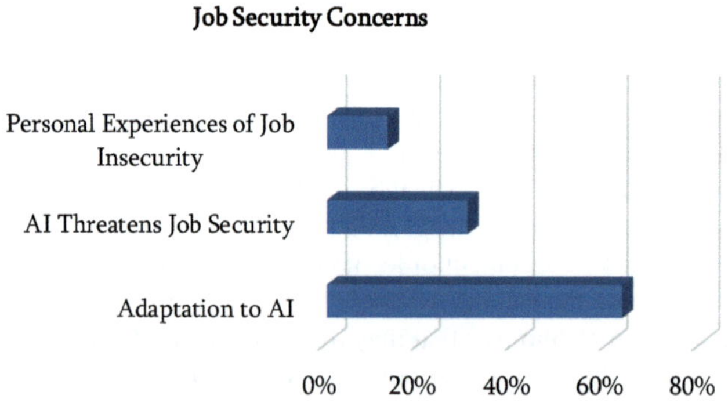

Fig. 11.2 Lecturers' job security concerns

11.4.2.5 Discussions

While the majority of lecturers acknowledge successful adaptation to AI implementation, job security concerns among lecturers regarding the automation of certain tasks traditionally performed by educators have been revealed to be very minimal. The general sentiment is that human educators will always be indispensable for providing guidance, support, and mentorship to students, thus emphasizing the enduring value of human interaction in education. The nominal job security threat among lecturers in Zimbabwe suggests that these are not overly worried about AI taking over their roles completely, which could indicate a level of confidence in the value of human resource in the educational process. It also implies that lecturers see opportunities for collaboration with AI rather than outright replacement. Nonetheless, Ng et al. (2023) warn that, while minimal job security concerns may be a positive sign, it is crucial to monitor how the landscape of education evolves with AI integration and ensure that educators are equipped with the necessary skills to work alongside these technologies effectively. Most of the AI tools are novel to the educators, who may lack the technical skills to use them for instruction or develop students' AI digital skills. "As such, there is a growing need for teachers to equip themselves with adequate digital competencies so as to use and teach AI in their teaching environments" (Ng et al., 2023: 137).

Significant is the emphasis on the importance of continuous professional development and upskilling programs for lecturers to effectively integrate AI tools into their teaching practices. This outcome is consistent with research findings from recent studies underscoring the importance of enhancing the teachers' AI competencies through training to improve job security. For instance, Kitcharoen et al. (2024) study revealed that Artificial Intelligence Internet of Things (AIoT) training workshops were crucial in significantly improving the teacher's AI knowledge, helping them to effectively execute their teaching duties using these digital tools. Nyaaba and Zhai (2024) highlight the significance of institutional support for teachers' training and development in AI tools, to strengthen their skills in innovative teaching practices. Das et al. (2023) note the importance of upskilling programs for educators as signifying a positive recognition of the need for ongoing learning and growth in response to technological advancements. Further, the perception that institutions should invest in lecturer training shows that the lecturers in Zimbabwe understand the value of staying updated and acquiring new skills to enhance their teaching methods with AI tools. This interpretation implies a proactive approach among lecturers toward embracing innovation and technology to improve the quality of education they provide and safeguard their job security in the digital era. Concurringly, Kamalov et al., (2023: 12,451) sustain that in the wake of AI technologies, "the only way forward is to embrace the new technology, while implementing guardrails to prevent its abuse."

11.4.3 Coping Mechanisms and Support Systems

This section focuses on the strategies Zimbabwean lecturers employ to navigate the challenges of AI integration, and addresses the third research question, "What navigation strategies are employed to manage the digital shift?". Three key sub-themes guide this exploration as demonstrated below.

11.4.3.1 Strategies for Managing AI-Driven Change

Question 8: How do you manage the potential stress, anxiety, or uncertainties caused by the digital shift toward AI in your role as a lecturer?

The majority of the participants (17 out of 30) reported successful management of AI-related stresses and anxieties. However, these also highlighted the significance of staying informed about technological advancements (Participants F11 & M15), engaging in upskilling through training programs (Participant F5), and embracing the opportunities that AI presents to enhance teaching practices and student learning outcomes (Participants M14, F2, & F7). Outstanding responses capturing these views include the following:

F5: *Managing the potential stress and uncertainties associated with the digital shift toward AI requires a proactive approach to skill development, collaboration with tech experts, and open communication with colleagues to address concerns and explore new opportunities for professional growth.*

F11*: Managing the digital shift toward AI involves staying informed about technological advancements, improving skills through training programs, and embracing the opportunities that AI offers to enhance teaching practices and student learning outcomes.*

The cited views about how to manage anxiety caused by the shift toward AI highlight the proactive approach needed to navigate the digital transition effectively. They also climax the fact that lecturers in Zimbabwe are gradually embracing the digital shift.

11.4.3.2 Training and Support for AI Integration

Question 9: Do you receive any training or support to adapt to the changes brought about by the implementation of AI technologies in teaching?

The majority of the participants (27 out of 30) noted that the training programs for lecturers were still scarce, with the minority (3 out of 30) indicating ongoing engagement in self-improvised training. The participants emphasized the importance of providing training and support for lecturers to effectively integrate AI technologies into their teaching practices. Continuous professional development emerged as a crucial component in keeping educators abreast of educational innovations. Examples of the responses that sufficiently capture this sentiment include the following:

M12: *Currently, there are limited training programs or support mechanisms in place to help lecturers adapt to the changes brought about by AI technologies in teaching. As educators, we must advocate for targeted training initiatives and resources to build digital literacy and AI competencies.*

M7: *Training and support for adapting to AI technologies are essential to ensure lecturers can effectively integrate these tools into their teaching practices. Continuous professional development is crucial to staying abreast of changes and innovations in education.*

Comprehensive training and support for lecturers by educational institutions was perceived by most participants as empowering to confidently adapt to AI-driven changes.

11.4.3.3 Balancing AI Integration with Job Security

Question 10: To what extent do you think there is a balance between AI integration and job security for lecturers in Zimbabwe, and what strategies or measures could be implemented to ensure its sustainability?

Most of the participants (26 out of 30) believed that, thus far, there is a good balance between AI implementation and job safety as lecturers are able to adapt without experiencing significant job displacements. Views about how to strike a balance between AI integration and lecturers' job security included investing in upskilling programs (Participant F5), outlining clear career pathways for educators in the digital era (Participant M8), fostering collaboration between AI systems and human instructors (Participant F2), and prioritizing academic quality amidst technological disruptions (Participant M1). These strategies were indicated to enable harmonizing technological progress with the preservation of job stability in the educational sector. The following are some of the key responses in relation to this notion:

F13: *To ensure a balance between AI integration and job security for lecturers in Zimbabwe, it is essential to foster a culture of innovation, collaboration, and lifelong learning within the academic community.*

F5: *To balance AI integration and job security for lecturers, institutions can invest in training programs, provide clear career pathways for educators in the digital era, forge a collaboration between AI systems and human instructors, and prioritize maintaining academic quality in the face of technological disruptions.*

11.4.3.4 Summary of Findings

The data presented in this section reveals that while most participants have successfully managed AI-related stress and anxiety, some face challenges in adapting to AI implementation. The findings also suggest that training programs for AI are limited in universities, highlighting a need for increased support and resources. Furthermore, the data indicates that although most of the participants seem to effectively balance between AI implementation and job security, these emphasize the importance

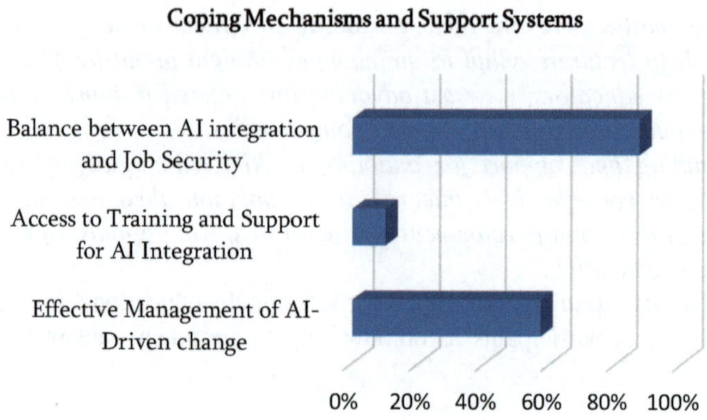

Fig. 11.3 Coping mechanisms and support systems for AI integration

of addressing concerns around job safety. Figure 11.3 below presents a statistical overview of the participants' perspectives on this issue.

11.4.3.5 Discussions

The finding that most participants have successfully managed AI-related stress and anxiety is a positive indication that lecturers are resilient and adaptable in the face of technological change. This ability to cope with AI-related stress and anxiety is crucial for lecturers' job security as it enables them to maintain their well-being and continue to perform their duties effectively (Itse et al., 2024). Moreover, this finding suggests that lecturers are proactive in seeking out support and resources to manage AI-related stress and anxiety, which is essential for their job security and overall well-being. This proactive approach is a testament to the lecturers' commitment to their profession and willingness to adapt to changing circumstances. As Shakib et al. (2023) posit, by seeking out support and resources, lecturers can better navigate the challenges associated with AI implementation and maintain their job security.

Furthermore, the limited availability of training programs for AI in Zimbabwean universities is a significant concern that needs to be addressed. The lack of training programs can exacerbate lecturers' anxiety and stress related to AI, ultimately affecting their job security (Hopcan et al., 2024). To mitigate this risk, universities must invest in providing lecturers with comprehensive training and support to develop the necessary skills to effectively integrate AI into their teaching practices. This investment will not only enhance lecturers' job security but also improve the overall quality of education (Pesovski et al., 2024). Moreover, providing lecturers with AI training programs can also foster a culture of innovation and continuous learning within universities. By investing in lecturers' professional development, universities can ensure that their staff remain adaptable and responsive to the changing needs of students and the education sector as a whole.

Moreover, the outcome that participants expressed a good balance between AI implementation and job safety is reassuring. This suggests that lecturers can adapt to the changing technological landscape without experiencing significant job displacements. However, this finding also highlights the importance of addressing concerns around job safety. As AI continues to advance, universities must prioritize transparency and communication with lecturers regarding the impact of AI on their roles and responsibilities (Chan, 2023). By doing so, universities can alleviate lecturers' concerns about job security, foster a culture of trust and collaboration, and promote a smooth transition to an AI-driven education system. This proactive approach can help universities retain top talent and maintain a stable workforce, which according to Mohiuddin et al. (2022), is essential for providing high-quality education. Additionally, by prioritizing transparency and communication, universities can demonstrate their commitment to supporting lecturers' career development and well being (Hopcan et al., 2024).

11.5 Conclusions and Recommendations

This study has provided valuable insights into the experiences of university lecturers in Zimbabwe regarding the adoption and implementation of AI technologies in their teaching practices. Despite the rise of AI in academia, the majority of lecturers are still able to effectively carry out their teaching roles and responsibilities, and job security concerns are minimal. However, the study has also highlighted the need for universities to provide adequate training and support to lecturers to effectively manage AI integration into the education system, as well as to address the challenge of students' overreliance on AI.

Based on these findings, it is recommended that universities should prioritize the provision of comprehensive training and support programs for lecturers to develop the necessary skills to effectively integrate AI into their teaching practices. To address the challenge of students' overreliance on AI, universities should incorporate critical thinking and media literacy skills into the curriculum, and encourage lecturers to design learning activities that promote human-AI collaboration. Finally, universities should prioritize transparency and communication with lecturers regarding the impact of AI on their roles and responsibilities, and work to address concerns about job security. These steps would enhance the teaching and learning experiences and also promote the lecturers' job security.

11.6 Limitations

This study has several limitations that should be acknowledged. Firstly, the sample size of 30 lecturers, although demographically diverse, may not represent the entire university population, limiting the generalizability of the findings. Nonetheless, no new themes or insights emerged from the data, indicating that the sample was adequate for exploring the research questions. Secondly, reliance on interviews as the primary data collection tool may have introduced biases, such as social desirability bias, where participants provide responses that they think are expected of them. To address this restraint, the study employed mixed analysis methods, combining qualitative and quantitative approaches to triangulate the data and increase the validity of the findings. The study's findings should be interpreted in light of these limitations, and future research should build upon this study using larger and more diverse samples.

References

AfDB (African Development Bank). (2019). African Development Bank Group Annual Report 2019. https://www.afdb.org/en/documents/annual-report-2019-0

Bhutoria, A. (2022). Personalized education and Artificial Intelligence in the United States, China, and India: A systematic review using a Human-In-The-Loop model. *Computers and Education: Artificial Intelligence, 3*(2022), 100068. https://doi.org/10.1016/j.caeai.2022.100068

Burgess, A., & Sievert, M. (2017). AI in education: A review of the literature. *Journal of Educational Data Mining, 9*(1), 1–24.

Chan, C. K. Y. (2023). A comprehensive AI policy education framework for university teaching and learning. *International journal of Educational Technology in Higher Education, 20*(1), 38. https://doi.org.https://doi.org/10.1186/s41239-023-00408-3

Das, A., Malaviya, S., & Singh, M. (2023). The impact of AI-driven personalization on learners' performance. *International Journal of Computer Sciences and Engineering, 11*, 15–22. https://doi.org/10.26438/ijcse/v11i8.1522

Dimla, C. Y., Sumaway, M. D., Torres, J. M. T., & Cruz, C. A. B. D. (2024). The role of Artificial Intelligence in personalized learning: Enhancing student engagement and academic performance. *International Journal of Research Publications and Reviews, 5*(5), 8495–8505.

Ezeoguine, E. & Eteng-Uket, S. (2024). Artificial intelligence tools and higher education student's engagement. *Edukasiana: Jurnal Inovasi Pendidikan, 3*, 300–312. https://doi.org/10.56916/ejip.v3i3.733.

Ghamrawi, N., Shal, T., & Ghamrawi, N. A. (2024). Exploring the impact of AI on teacher leadership: Regressing or expanding? *Education and Information Technologies, 29*, 8415–8433. https://doi.org/10.1007/s10639-023-12174-w

Grájeda, A., Burgos, J., Córdova, P., & Sanjinés, A. (2023). Assessing student-perceived impact of using artificial intelligence tools: Construction of a synthetic index of application in higher education. *Cogent Education, 11*(1), 1–24. https://doi.org/10.1080/2331186X.2023.2287917

Gwagwa, A., Kraemer-Mbula, E., Rizk, N., Rutenberg, I. & De Beer, J. (2020). Artificial intelligence (AI) deployments in Africa: Benefits, challenges, and policy dimensions. *The African Journal of Information and Communication* (AJIC), *26*, 1–28. https://doi.org/10.23962/10539/30361

Hashem, R., Ali, N., El Zein, F., Fidalgo, P., & Khurma, O. A. (2024). AI to the rescue: Exploring the potential of ChatGPT as a teacher ally for workload relief and burnout prevention. *Research & Practice in Technology Enhanced Learning, 19*, 1–26. https://doi.org/10.58459/rptel.2024.19023

Hopcan, S., Türkmen, G., & Polat, E. (2024). Exploring the artificial intelligence anxiety and machine learning attitudes of teacher candidates. *Education and Information Technologies, 29*(6), 7281–7301. https://doi.org/10.1007/s10639-023-12086-9

Itse, Y. I., Yahaya, I., & Uzoigwe, T. L. (2024). Empirical assessment of artificial intelligence anxiety, associated factors among university employees in Nasarawa, Nigeria. *Psychology Nexus, 1*(1), 37–47. https://nex.reapress.com/journal/article/view/18

Kamalov, F., Santandreu, C. D., & Gurrib, I. (2023). New era of artificial intelligence in education: Towards a sustainable multifaceted revolution. *Sustainability, 15*(16), 12451. https://doi.org/10.3390/su151612451

Kaswan, K. S., Dhatterwal, J. S., & Ojha, R. P. (2024). AI in personalized learning. In A. Garg, B. V. Babu, & V. E. Balas (Eds.), *Advances in Technological Innovations in Higher Education* (1st ed., pp. 103–117). CRC Press.

Kinyanjui, P. E. (2018). The impact of artificial intelligence on education in Africa. *Journal of Educational Technology Development and Exchange, 10*(1), 1–12.

Kitcharoen, P., Howimanporn, S., & Chookaew, S. (2024). Enhancing teachers' AI competencies through artificial intelligence of things professional development training. *International Journal of Interactive Mobile Technologies (IJIM), 18*(2), 4–15. https://doi.org/10.3991/ijim.v18i02.46613

Maphosa, V. (2023). The impact of digital transformation on institutional growth. A case of Zimbabwean Universities. Paper Presented at the African Conference on Information Systems and Technology. Available at: https://digitalcommons.kennesaw.edu/acist/2023/presentations/17

Marzuki, W. U., Rusdin, D., & Darwin, & Indrawati, I. (2023). The impact of AI writing tools on the content and organization of students' writing: EFL teachers' perspective. *Cogent Education, 10*(2), 1–17. https://doi.org/10.1080/2331186X.2023.2236469

Mohiuddin, M., Hosseini, E., Faradonbeh, S. B., & Sabokro, M. (2022). Achieving human resource management sustainability in universities. *International Journal of Environmental Research and Public Health, 19*(2), 928. https://doi.org/10.3390/ijerph19020928

Ng, D. T. K., Leung, J. K. L., Su, J., Ng, R. C. W., & Chu, S. K. W. (2023). Teachers' AI digital competencies and twenty-first-century skills in the post-pandemic world. *Educational Technology Research and Development: ETR & D, 71*(1), 137–161. https://doi.org/10.1007/s11423-023-10203-6

Nyaaba, M. & Zhai, X. (2024). Generative AI professional development needs for teacher educators. *Journal of AI*, 8(1), 1–13. https://doi.org/10.61969/jai.1385915

Pesovski, I., Santos, R., Henriques, R., & Trajkovik, V. (2024). Generative AI for customizable learning experiences. *Sustainability, 16*(7), 3034. https://doi.org/10.3390/su16073034

Shakib Kotamjani, S., Shirinova, S., & Fahimirad, M. (2023). Lecturers' perceptions of using Artificial Intelligence in Tertiary Education in Uzbekistan. In *Proceedings of the 7th International Conference on Future Networks and Distributed Systems* (pp. 570–578). https://doi.org/10.1145/3644713.3644797

UNESCO (United Nations Educational, Scientific and Cultural Organization). (2019). Global Education Monitoring Report 2019: Migration, displacement and education: Building bridges, not walls. https://www.right-to-education.org/resource/global-education-monitoring-report-2019-migration-displacement-and-education-building

Walter, Y. (2024). Embracing the future of artificial intelligence in the classroom: The relevance of AI literacy, prompt engineering, and critical thinking in modern education. *International Journal of Educational Technology in Higher Education, 21*(15), 1–29. https://doi.org/10.1186/s41239-024-00448-3

Chapter 12
Artificial Intelligence (AI) and Human Mind: Struggles and Strengths in the Education Sector

Syeda Tafseer Zahra, Erum Bibi, and Zainab Younus

Abstract Artificial Intelligence (AI) has become a revolutionary force impacting society and human existence in recent years. While AI and human interactions frequently promote emotional attachment, trust, and social closeness, the changing nature of work after the advent of AI tools has caused workers to experience stress, anxiety, and unemployment. The fear is as a result of their concerns about automation and AI integration-related job displacement and skill obsolescence. Job transitions and upskilling may also increase psychological stress. To address ethical and psychological difficulties scholars and developers, as well as policymakers must understand how AI influences the human mind. To build a future that promotes human well-being, we must recognize and lessen the detrimental psychological consequences of AI technology while maximizing its positive aspects. This study aims to present a broad overview of the influence of Artificial intelligence (AI) on the human mind particularly concerning cognition, memory, learning, and mental health. Semi-structured interviews were used to generate data from teachers, IT professionals and students regarding the impact of AI on the human mind. The study also offers further recommendations to guide readers towards a more dynamic use of AI.

Keywords Artificial intelligence · Cognition · Memory · Mental health · Learning · Social life · Teachers

S. T. Zahra (✉) · E. Bibi · Z. Younus
National University of Modern Languages, Rawalpindi, Pakistan
e-mail: tafseer.zahra@numl.edu.pk

E. Bibi
e-mail: erum.bibi@numl.edu.pk

Z. Younus
e-mail: zainab.younus@numl.edu.pk

M. A. Adarkwah et al. (eds.), *Artificial Intelligence and Human Agency in Education: Volume One*, Future Education and Learning Spaces,
https://doi.org/10.1007/978-981-96-7937-9_12

12.1 Introduction

In the contemporary world, the pervasive growth of Artificial Intelligence (AI) in every field of human life has profoundly influenced an individual's mental health, and it is hard to negate its impact. Even within the field of psychology, AI-based services are becoming increasingly commonplace. AI-based services are defined as those practices that utilize computer systems to perform various tasks that would usually require uniquely human interpretive skills; for instance decision-making, visual perception, and the processing of language (Singh & College, 2023). It would not be an exaggeration to say that AI has the potential to allow machines to imitate those skills that were previously thought to require human input. It is not surprising that the European Commission (EC) now defines AI as Systems that display intelligent behaviour by analyzing their environment and taking actions—with some degree of autonomy—to achieve specific goals (Sheikh et al., 2023).

Cyberpsychology, also known as the psychology of technology, is a field of study that emphasizes the impact of technology on mental health and human behaviour with a paradigmatic focus on the psychological effects of virtual environments, online communication systems, digital devices, and internet-related behaviours. In this growing technological world, Digital Learning is now not only shaping our cognition, but is also influencing our implicit and explicit memories. In short, while AI is a technological marvel, on the other hand, it can also alter our higher functionality as humans with time (Khadse et al., 2023a, 2023b).

The field of mental illness is one sector in which the application of AI is progressing rapidly. AI-driven technologies can detect mental health issues early on, and can potentially allow scientists to provide healthcare to individuals in a feasible way. For instance, when an individual needs psychological support and therapy, virtual assistants and chatbots can be available for instant responses. This creates a sense of intimacy and emotional connection between the user and the technology which eliminates the feelings of social isolation and loneliness (Khadse et al., 2023a, 2023b). By gathering data through algorithms, new interventions and therapies utilizing AI are now available to deal with anxiety, stress, and post-traumatic stress disorder (PTSD) (Dwivedi et al., 2021).

Contemporary researchers are today also extremely concerned with the utilization of AI in the workplace especially in educational settings, which poses a variety of possible drawbacks and risks to one's mental health. One of the dominating parameters of these concerns is the workers' experience of stress, anxiety, and fear of unemployment because they are concerned about automation and AI integration-related job displacement and skill obsolescence (Khadse et al., 2023a, 2023b).

Consequently, an employee's job performance is now being determined by to what degree he/she possesses the ability to synthesize and summarize information by utilizing automated processes for routine work. This is also true with the professionals working in the educational sector. AI is now prepared to take their place at any time. The dilemma is made worse by the amazing advancements in AI technologies, which cause some occupations to become obsolete and require machine labour while simultaneously creating new ones (Dumitru & Halpern, 2023).

The majority of a student's day is spent in educational institutions, which directly supervise their training. AI is quickly becoming a prerequisite for the learning process. We can now see how the learning process is becoming more efficient and accessible, learning is becoming customized, which leads to increased motivation and involvement of the youth (Săseanu et al., 2024).

Although the invention of AI is the latest achievement, its quick spread in all domains of education has nevertheless surprised the experts. AI is used in the identification and remediation of knowledge and skill gaps, the organization and accessibility of information, the facilitation of education for individuals with special needs and access to distant socialization are all marks of AI success (Felea et al., 2021). Further, the use of interactive learning techniques and real-time feedback, the rapid updating of information content, learning through simulations of real-life scenarios, and closing the gap between students' socioeconomic circumstances, geographic location, age, and gender are also the latest milestones of AI (Moonpreneur, 2023).

On the one hand, while a significant number of employees are grateful for the productivity improvements, there is a considerable subgroup of individuals who are apprehensive that technology will completely take their positions in future. Professionals and scholars are speculating that within the technology sector, the abundance of automated tasks within several departments—especially the Human Resource domain will increasingly lead to job reductions. Academic scholars are of the view that monitoring employees with algorithms to minimize human biases can have possible risks as well. It would not be wrong to say that every single advancement in the domain of artificial intelligence (AI) is unsurprisingly impacted by many psychological characteristics inherent to human beings that can be intricate and often contradictory responses.

As human psychology and learning vary from individual to individual even despite underlying interconnectedness; everyone's capacity for short-term technological adoption and its long-term implications will require further observation and research before any concrete conclusions can be reached. It can be inferred that in terms of adopting new technology, a person's psychological tendencies and cognitive predispositions often make them vulnerable—resulting in a potentially unfavourable and adverse future. While it cannot be denied that AI has opened new avenues for learning and excelling at the workplace in the last two years; it has nonetheless also been the main source of stress, depression, anxiety, and uncertainty among certain employees making them apprehensive about job loss and replacement (Shankar, 2023). Therefore, this book chapter attempts to shed light on the use of AI in an individual's work life and underlines areas where positive interaction and advancements are possible.

12.1.1 Statement of the Problem

This study attempts to emerge from the limited exploration of how artificial intelligence (AI) impacts specific cognitive functions such as memory, learning, socialization, and mental health, especially in real-world environments like workplaces and educational settings. While there has been substantial research on the technical aspects and potential benefits of AI, less attention has been given to its psychological implications, particularly concerning long-term effects on cognitive abilities and emotional well-being. The existing studies largely focus on generalized mental health outcomes, such as anxiety or stress due to job displacement, but there is a notable lack of in-depth examination of how AI-driven technologies influence cognitive processes like memory retention and critical thinking, especially in contexts where individuals are highly dependent on these technologies. Moreover, the nuances of human-AI interaction, including the role of emotional attachment and trust formed with AI systems. The field also lacks comprehensive data that examines both the positive and negative consequences of AI, particularly from the perspectives of teachers, IT professionals, and students.

This study aims to fill this gap by investigating the detailed psychological and cognitive effects of AI, employing a qualitative approach to gather nuanced insights, and offering practical recommendations for integrating AI in ways that support mental well-being.

The research, undertaken with the collaboration of psychologists, engineers, and teachers contributing their input can help more effectively counter the negative effects of AI on mental health to guarantee a responsible and successful implementation of the findings. It can potentially provide policymakers with reliable data to make educated decisions based on scientific facts and the opinions of experts. Thus, this study hopes to showcase not only how to maintain a balance between human interaction with AI and the responsibility of human psychologists to deliver comprehensive and ethically sound health care.

12.1.2 Objectives of the Study

The existing literature comprehensively supports the concerns of educationists to deeply explore the role of AI in the education sector especially in the mental health domain. Students' cognition, learning, memory, and socialization are the few factors that are directly influenced by AI that are explored in this chapter in detail.

So the following primary objectives were devised to meet the above purpose.

1. To explore artificial intelligence's (AI) contributions to human mental health.
2. To discover AI technology's detrimental psychological consequences on human cognitive process; (secondary objectives)

    - Memory formation and retrieval?

- Learning acquisition and retention?
- Executive functions (attention, decision-making, problem-solving)?

3. To find out the contribution of AI to the social domain of students, teachers, and IT professionals.

12.2 Review of Past Studies

AI technology has significant impacts on technological advancement. Its usage has in recent studies been linked to mental health-related issues within the academic setup. For instance, healthcare policymakers are concerned with the consequences of AI's wider ethical development and application; as well as the obligation for interdisciplinary collaboration in tackling the complicated and complex mental challenges that emerge from it (Bharthi et al., 2023). A study by Shanker et al. (2023) suggests that there exists a direct and significant association between excessive usage of AI in terms of digital technology and social media, and the harms associated with one's overall mental health. As far as the benefits of AI are concerned, it has been proven helpful in detecting and treating such illnesses in most users of diagnostic tools that are powered by AI technology.

Not only this, AI is also shaping our educational systems worldwide. The majority of teachers do not consider AI tools to be a reliable pedagogical source for learning, believing that it limits intellectual and critical thinking ability. However, students are not only uncritically utilizing AI technology but also passing over what they consider to be unnecessary cognitive work onto the machine. The reality is that students are not aware that the information provided by most AI tools may not be reliable or true—consider the problems researchers have faced with Chat GPT—but the fact remains that students tend to believe that AI-generated information is reliable and it is often available in a format that can make it sound highly convincing. This blind trust in AI-generated material which lacks quality and critical evaluation is undermining the integrity of academic work. On the other hand, if students learn how to use AI tools sensibly and responsibly by understanding the limitations and utilizing AI tools in their full capacity, AI can foster one's critical thinking, learning, and skills without minimizing one's efforts (Walter, 2024). Thus, it can be said that AI is directly or indirectly influencing our neuroplasticity (the brain's dynamic capability to rewire and adapt) as the updated versions of AI are becoming a mirror reflecting how our brains might work (Perwej & Parwej, 2012).

If we look into the history of how humans access knowledge and memory, a human being is solely responsible for digging into his memories through cognitive processes. In contrast, the modern humans' external hard drive for memories is the internet. The way we have started putting the production of our memories into the hands of deep learning and automated systems is impacting our short-term and long-term memory by depriving us of the natural procedure of remembering events (Farinella, 2024). The impact of AI is thus not only limited to a person's overall mental and cognitive health, rather it also influences one's cognitions in terms of decision-making, job satisfaction, and the perception of AI as a threat to their job.

Cognition in the context of work extends beyond the limitations of living organisms if defined in broader terms (Seni & Seni, 2010). Some organizations have a basic structure and objective revolving around the cognitive development of their employees. Another influential study (Dienlin & Johannes, 2020) highlighted the impression of artificial intelligence (AI) on the overall well-being of individuals especially related to students. The findings suggested a complicated association between the usage of digital technology and well-being. The frequent consumption of digital screens has also been found to be an unfavourable influence on a person's global well-being (Rayhan, 2023).

AI and automation have potential benefits and limitations across various job categories and businesses. They have the potential to supplant several industrial tasks like; manual labour, healthcare and legal services, data analysis, roles and manufacturing, customer service, and occupations. The rule-based processes categorized by reliance, repetition, and routine nature can be codified by algorithms. However, human cognitions and attributes comparatively offer a diverse advantage (Urwin, 2024). The study suggests that despite the dynamic potential of artificial intelligence (AI), human skills comprising flexibility, creativity, emotional intelligence, and sophisticated problem-solving cannot be replaced by robots or automated processes. Therefore, the need is to utilize automation and artificial intelligence tools to augment human capabilities rather than substitute them. The partnership between humans and artificial intelligence has been shown to enhance productivity and efficiency. The potential inclusion of AI systems in future jobs necessitates the need for individuals to be adequately prepared through education and training (Ojiyi et al., 2023). For instance, the examination conducted by McKinsey Quarterly (2018) focused on the intricate interplay among automation, artificial intelligence, and the workforce. The study concluded that while technology can supplant certain tasks, it is unable to replicate the unique skills and characteristics possessed by humans in the workplace. To maintain a competitive edge in a dynamic labour market, it is anticipated that the future of work will necessitate collaboration between humans and artificial intelligence, the transformation of job roles, and the enhancement of human skills.

This chapter is structured in four sections, the first detailed introduction was presented with summaries of relevant past research. The next section includes a detailed presentation of the methodology of the research performed—emphasizing the aspects related to research design, sample details, instrument complete description and analysis. The results and discussions section is presented in detail followed by the conclusion, which shows the interdependency and impact of using AI in the education sector with relevance to the mental health and social life of its users.

12.3 Methodology

The review of past literature shows the diverse findings related to the impact of artificial intelligence on the human mind in an educational domain. As technology continues to permeate educational environments, there is a pressing need to understand whether these tools enhance student understanding and academic performance or present unforeseen challenges.

This exploratory research is designed to understand how artificial intelligence relates to the human mind and explore its struggles and strengths concerning cognition, memory, mental health, and social life of students, teachers, and IT professionals working in Pakistan. The selection of variables and questions makes this study unique and innovative. Demographics like—gender, profession, and education are used to highlight the profile of the respondents. Further in-depth content analysis uncovered the asked questions. The research questions that were explored in the analysis were:

1. How artificial intelligence (AI) is related to human mental health, especially concerning the educational field of Pakistan;
2. What are the negative impacts of AI on learners' cognitive processes like memory and learning?
3. How does AI affect the Social lives of students, teachers and IT workers?

Based on the above research it can be easily figured out how AI-related perceptions can lead to psychological and mental health-related issues in educational institutes. As such, the study illustrates the following conceptual model: this proposed model will be tested through qualitative research. Semi-structured questions helped to understand the dynamics underlying socio-cognitive learners' perspectives (Fig. 12.1).

Under qualitative research design, a semi-structured interview method was used to collect data from students, teachers, and IT professionals using an online platform. Artificial intelligence is a relatively new concept and a small number of research is available worldwide. In Pakistan, both quantitative as well as quantitative studies related to AI were also very limited. This study has been planned under the paradigm of qualitative research because this approach allows the researcher to uncover the intrinsic and contextual connotations attached to situations or a person that are not

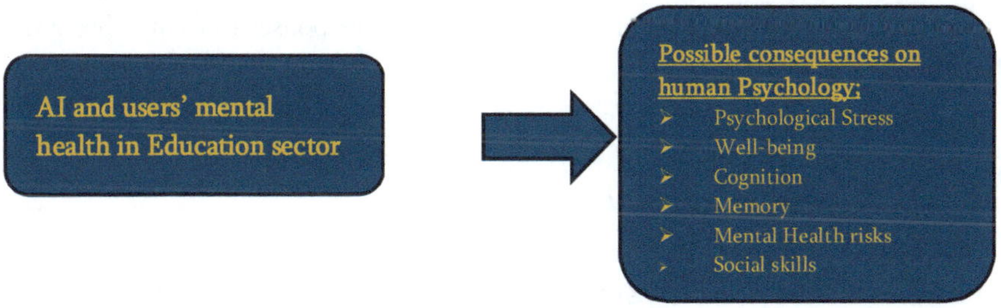

Fig. 12.1 Perceptual Model to the role of AI in mental health domain of education sector

readily possible through a quantitative approach that focuses solely on the coded response method. Qualitative research methods help to frame research questions using the "how" and "why" approach, consequently enabling a deeper understanding of any experiences, or phenomena, in multiple contexts (Cleland, 2017). Therefore, a semi-structured interview method under qualitative research design has been used.

12.3.1 *Instruments for Data Collection*

To conduct the exploratory study regarding the role of AI on mental health, semi-structured interview guideline was designed for the students, teachers, and IT professionals with the help of expert opinion and a comprehensive literature review. The beauty of the semi-structured design is that it allows the researcher to fix the response category wherever required as well as further explore the answer at any point through open-ended questions. The online method of tool dissemination was selected due to easy access to the participants and because of the lack of resources to physically reach out to the participants.

Four questions were finalized and framed in the English language. A thorough literature review was done to finalize these questions in our Indigenous setup. All the participants were university graduates with a good command of English language.

The form starts with a brief introduction of the purpose of the research, ensuring participants the confidentiality and anonymity of the data. Demographic questions about age, profession, and education were asked (See Annex A) which led to open and closed-ended questions. The first question was "Is Artificial Intelligence (AI) good for mental health? It was framed to check whether the topic itself was significant to the participants or not. The second question, "How is AI harmful to our mental health?" was designed for those who think that AI is not good for mental health. This gave an in-depth insight into the participants' thoughts on this perception. The third question, "Does AI lead to psychological problems" was framed to check any connection between AI and mental health issues which is the main objective of this study.

Further insight was taken by asking Question 4 "How does AI affect students' cognition, memory and Learning?". Also in Question 5 "How does AI affect the social life of learners?" was asked. Detailed responses to these questions highlighted the significance of these domains and provided detailed responses (in-depth discussion is available in the discussion.

12.3.2 *Sample of the Study*

Utilizing convenience sampling as a method, a sample of 115 participants comprising: teachers (40), IT professionals (35), and students (40) were approached through an online survey. As the research was planned to check the possible role of AI in the

Table 12.1 Showing sample distribution ($N = 115$)

Students ($N = 40$)		Teachers ($N = 40$)		IT professionals ($N = 35$)	
Male	Female	Male	Female	Male	Female
14	26	16	24	22	13

mental health of its users in academic settings therefore the most relevant persons were approached along with experts of AI who design such tools for the target sample. All the students and teachers who were contacted were from different Pakistani universities based in Rawalpindi, Islamabad, and Lahore. It was requested to share the email IDs of the respondents (professionals, teachers, and students). Semi-structured questionnaires were disseminated through emails. Only 115 respondents filled out the forms and sent them back.

The IT professionals were from Rawalpindi and Islamabad and are working as full-time employees in private and public sector institutions (Table 12.1).

12.3.3 Method of Data Collection

The present research is about the impact of AI on our mental health, particularly as related to cognition, memory, and learning within higher education environments. Semi-structured interview guidelines have been developed for this purpose. In addition, online interviews were held with every participant after obtaining their informed consent. The privacy and anonymity of the participants have also been ensured.

In each interview, the participants of the study were asked to submit their responses in written form. The format also contained a survey of their demographic information. As a protocol of the interview method, first informed consent was taken from each participant which led to demographic information. After the demographic information, four core questions were asked of each participant. The whole procedure was designed to be completed in 20–25 min. All the participants have been acknowledged for their participation in the research at the end. Appreciation emails were also sent to the participants. Confidentiality and anonymity were also ensured.

12.3.4 Framework/Method of Data Analysis

The framework used to analyze the data collected is based on the statistical modelling given in the interpretative phenomenological analysis (IPA) approach given by Willig (2001). According to this approach, the analysis is carried out using a systemic procedure to investigate lived experiences. This in turn helps to ground the interpretive analysis by presenting factual evidence (Eatough & Smith, 2006; Willig, 2001). In this study, the researchers are using the text-based answers provided by the participants as well as the transcribed version of the semi-structured interview. This is also why the interpretative phenomenological analysis structure is most suitable for the current study.

The analysis has been carried out in various steps to ensure a thorough and rich interpretation and discussion of the collected data. The validation of the study was ensured through these steps. The stages of analysis in the current study are:

1. Firstly, a close reading of the written responses that were collected through the semi-structured interview.
2. Secondly, based on the close reading, a thematic analysis was carried out to determine the overarching themes collectively identified in the responses. This helped to establish the common grounds and trends within the data pool.
3. Thirdly, the researchers endeavoured to create an organizational structure within the identified thematic trends to create correlations that would link the themes to create a cluster of shared meanings or attempt to note any hierarchical relationships that are demonstrated within the data collected. The discussion section of the study is organized according to these identified shared trends.
4. Fourthly, a visual presentation of the data is given in Table form to help collate the themes with the overall pool of collected data. This holistic presentation as well as a detailed discussion of selected key responses for each thematic strand helps lay the grounding for the findings of the study. The choice of themes included in the Table is dictated by the research questions of the study.

To ensure the validity of the data collection and analysis as it is carried out under the parameters for qualitative research, the study adapts the methods suggested by Creswell (2007). Two out of the eight procedures given by Cresswell have been opted for in this study:

1. In the first stage, a peer review was conducted that cross-checked the thematic labels that have been utilized in the coding of the data by a pool of six peers. The peer reviewers were given sample quotes selected at random from the data pool and asked to place them within the given labels. Any incongruities or inconsistencies in the label categories were resolved based on the feedback received. After incorporating the feedback, revised labels and organizational structure were created, which were put through a peer review for a second time to ensure no further refinement was needed.
2. In the second stage, a detailed interpretive analysis has been carried out based on the selected quotes from the responses that best showcase the observed themes of the study. This will provide the readers with an opportunity to consider the thematic codes and decide the extent to which they can be considered representative of the overall responses of the participants of the study. To ensure the discussion presented is as objective as possible for a diversity of applicable contexts, the collected data has also been categorized into three sections: student perspective, teacher perspective & the perspective of IT professionals.

12.4 Findings and Discussion

The world is switching and adopting quite quickly to the new wave of AI and AI-powered tools and technologies, though this shift was initially criticized for many reasons. The adoption of AI in different tasks as well as professions means that within the field of cyberpsychology, we need to determine its long-term effects on memory, neuroplasticity, learning, and overall mental health of those who are related to the field of education. While AI has the potential to advance social closeness, trust, and emotional attachment, the darker side of the picture is that it may foster anxiety, distress, skill undesirability, job displacement, and greater levels of unemployment.

The following discussion of the participants' responses is carried out to ascertain the links that may exist between the use of AI tools and technologies with their cognitive and psychological impacts on users within the context of Higher Education Institutions.

12.4.1 Question 1: Is Artificial Intelligence (AI) Good for Mental Health?

Globally we can witness that mental health issues are arising and becoming a topic of concern with a steady 13% prevalence over the past 10 years. Statistically, it is also estimated that nearly one in four people worldwide will be affected by a mental or neurological disorder at some point in their lives (World Mental Health Report, 2022). Alongside, it has been proven that the use of AI tools in the education and learning process is related to the mental health domain and has a contradictory impact on users: carrying both advantages and limitations (Săseanu et al., 2024).

Based on this prevalence, detailed answers were elicited from the respondents. All respondents answered the question and scrutiny of the data showed that the majority (61%) reported that AI does not harm mental health; while 39% of respondents viewed AI's role as negative. Most IT Professionals and students believe that AI is good for mental health. Their given responses were studied in detail and the following themes emerged from the collected responses.

12.4.1.1 Theme: Decreases Cognitive Load

Thirty-seven respondents mentioned this theme—reduction in cognitive load after taking assistance from AI. The help of artificial intelligence made complex tasks easy, leading to mental comfort and a strong sense of relaxation (Braga & Logan, 2017). As can be seen in the following responses:

One Software Engineer believed that,

> AI helps in doing multiple tasks leading free humans to focus on higher-level activities.

As one student also reported,

> Life is easy after AI; we have less mental burden now.

12.4.1.2 Theme: Empowers Human Beings

Empowering human beings is the second theme. 69% responses were in line with the idea that AI has empowered humans and made tasks easy for them. The availability of the latest technological tools like Chabot's and virtual assistants provides fast replies, fostering a sense of accomplishment and producing a sense of community by giving quick access to the masses and people from far-flung areas. All these possibilities make humans empowered in their choices (Braga & Logan, 2017). The present data from this study also reflects this as different participants reported:

One teacher said,

> With the invention of AI lot of work can be done independently without any delay.

On the other hand, IT professional added that,

> Now we feel that we can handle a lot of data and can do multiple tasks without any delay.

Further latest research proves that AI increases accessibility to the learning process and its efficiency (Moonpreneur, 2023). It provides ways for learners to customize learning and train themselves as per requirement. All this ultimately leads to the youth's motivation and involvement in the learning process (Săseanu et al., 2024).

12.4.1.3 Theme: Helps in Screening and Treatment of Mental Disorders

The latest era of advanced technology also witnessed the addition of a third member in the patient-doctor dyad which is AI. Screening and diagnosis procedures were not so streamlined before. Twenty-three participants reported their opinions related to this theme that AI is assisting medical professionals in screening and treatment. One Psychologist and teacher stated,

> AI assists medical workers in diagnosis and treatment of different illnesses especially related to mental disorders.

One Engineer reported,

> AI is very helpful in performing professional tasks. Even doctors are taking help in screening and diagnosis.

The above views are also supported by the Research done by Ettman and Galea (2023), who argue that AI prevents more severe mental illness from developing by identifying higher-risk populations which leads to quicker intervention (Tielman et al., 2020). These tools assist mental health professionals in making decisions by analyzing a patient's previous medical records, behavioural patterns, and social media activity (Oladimeji et al., 2023).

12.4.2 Question 2: How is AI Harmful to Our Mental Health?

Despite the numerous benefits of AI in mental health, there are still concerns about building trust in this new technology, especially in the next wave of adoption of digital health (O'Dell, 2022). The second question, focusing on whether the participants believed that AI is not favourable to our mental health, asked them for their detailed viewpoints the responses were thoroughly studied and it was noted that many participants mentioned multiple opinions that fall under different themes. Interestingly, the second question was also answered by those participants who primarily do not agree with the stance that AI is harmful to our mental health so their opinions are also incorporated. Each of the identified themes is discussed below in detail.

12.4.2.1 Theme: Slowing Down Intellectual Thinking/Creativity

Many participants reported that AI significantly influences our thinking abilities as we spend hours and hours taking AI assistance. One student stated that,

> As we are completely relying on using AI it's making us lazier and there's no critical thinking

Similarly, a teacher believed,

> It is slowing down our Intellectual thinking process

IT professional further stated that,

> Our mind is bounded near AI problem-solving techniques and we couldn't solve our daily life issues with our mind that we're only human mind works not AI.

Despite the ease of working through AI, face-to-face interaction and actual experiences were believed integral to promote the quality of imagination, increase the sense of in-depth exploration, and enhance pictorial imaging ability. The frequent interaction via screens and taking help from AI in the form of quick fixes and solutions can diminish these human mental capacities (Braga & Logan, 2017). Therefore, it is important to use the latest technologies cautiously.

12.4.2.2 Theme: Reliance/Inappropriate Use of AI Can Cause Stress

For the learners it is easy to use different AI tools which result in their over dependence on it, which may hinder their ability to be independent, think creatively, solve problems, and apply lateral thinking (Stevenson et al., 2023).

An in-depth analysis of the transcriptions also reveals that 43% of the respondents reported the use of AI as inappropriate, as well as exhibiting the belief that heavy reliance on it can cause stress. A teacher stated,

> AI is harmful to us. Because Students completely rely on AI-based information.

While a student replied,

> We are getting dependent on it and stop doing reading which affects our memory.

Research also supports the above stance as Meyer et al. (2020) found that AI systems routinely collect and analyze enormous amounts of personal data. An individual may feel more anxious and may lose control over their private information by an extensive use of AI-based technologies. Over-reliance on AI in mental health care could also potentially result in a decline in empathy and human connection, which could worsen feelings of loneliness or isolation (Khadse, 2023a, 2023b).

12.4.2.3 Theme: Reduces Neuroplasticity

Science has proven that the brain is remarkably adaptable. It can rearrange itself in reaction to novel experiences, forming new pathways in the brain and changing the ones that already exist. Our brains learn new abilities and adjust to changes in the environment due to a phenomenon called neuroplasticity. One such development that is felt to have such an impact on the brain is interactions with AI. AI is believed to alter our thought processes and information processing capability (Pantev et al., 2001). The data collected in response to this question was interpreted and twelve participant responses came under the theme of "Reduces neuroplasticity". In line with this discussion, a teacher mentioned,

> AI will have negative long-term effects on our learning and neuroplasticity.

In this context, an IT professional viewed,

> AI changes the way we think and imagine leading to a decrease in the brain capacity of neuroplasticity.

12.4.3 Question 3: Does AI Lead to Psychological Problems?

Although the advent of artificial intelligence-based technologies and tools is quite recent, its impact on the human psyche is becoming quickly evident. A study done by Turkle (2011) reported that the heavy use of social media and other kinds of virtual environments is leading to an increased risk of anxiety, fewer real social interactions, lack of social skills and human empathy. This in turn is creating difficulties in handling solitude and other psychological issues. Based on this scenario, the last question was framed as: "Does the Constant use of AI lead to different psychological Problems like cognitive processes, especially memory and learning?" The responses were restricted to a YES or NO option. 90% of respondents opted for Yes, while 10% selected No.

12.4.4 Question 4: AI and Psychological Problems: Effect on Cognitive Processes like Memory and Learning

It is observed in the literature that the duration of the use of AI and its tools is also related to the negative impact on learners' psychological health. Senior students are mostly aware of this impact and consider it damaging to their health (Săseanu et al., 2024).

In this given survey, the second last question is quite direct and completely open-ended. To gain a deeper understanding of the phenomena under study, participants were asked "How can AI lead to different psychological problems like cognition, memory and learning?" All participants opted for the question and responded based on their own personal or professional experiences. After a careful reading and examination of the transcriptions and consultation of expert opinion, the following themes surfaced.

12.4.4.1 Theme: Negative Impact on Critical Thinking Ability

The ability to analyze data, assess claims, and reach well-informed conclusions is based on logic and understanding of supporting evidence—all of which are components of critical thinking. There is fear that as people would depend more and more on AI systems to make decisions, they will lose the ability to fully comprehend the reasons behind these decisions as AI systems take on the roles that are typically linked with critical thinking. This is believed to result in a loss of opportunities for critical analysis and autonomous cognitive processes, as well as a restriction in perspectives for the users of these technologies (Jarrahi, 2018). 44% of the responses within this study also showed that people take its adverse effects very seriously. As one teacher said,

> Making assignments using AI is all about copy-pasting and students aren't using critical thinking to solve problems and making their assignments and other academic work.

On the other hand, a student responded,

> It is easy to do assignments and projects while just giving commands to AI. We no longer need to be bookworms…AI is real magic.

While for the IT experts, the responses emphasized the necessity of setting time limits for using AI,

> Adverse effects of AI on the learning and analysis of data should be minimized by setting time limits

This study proposes that promoting people to actively pursue creative endeavours, investigate others' viewpoints, and develop their analytical abilities can help lessen the possible harm that artificial intelligence (AI) may cause to human cognition and critical thinking.

12.4.4.2 Theme: Limiting Brainstorming and Learning

Humans think they are getting benefits and saving time by using AI in their decision-making process. However, AI limits and replaces the human's role in decision-making. Human mental capabilities like intuitive analysis, critical thinking, and creative problem-solving are being left out of decision-making (Ahmad et al., 2023). 38% of the responses were noted down as falling under this theme. 6 IT professionals, 18 teachers, and 14 students in total responded in detail in this regard.

One teacher reported,

> Instead of learning the basics of a technique or subject, people rely on using AI tools to solve a problem which is limiting the brainstorming.

A student also commented,

> Relying on technology inhibits human self-abilities.

While another said,

> People rely on using AI tools to solve a problem which is limiting brainstorming.

Research has shown that the human brain is designed so that neural pathways get stronger after each stimulation and neuron fire. However, when skills like reading are not taking place at the required pace then neural tracts between the language areas are not developed to their full extent (Hutton et al., 2020). AI is thus serving as a replacement for the human biological processors and is doing so through lowering our cognition capabilities (Jarrahi, 2018).

12.4.4.3 Theme: Making Us Anti-social

One of the primary areas of concern regarding the impact that artificial intelligence will have on mental health and well-being is the fact that it can add to feelings of isolation, anxiety, and hopelessness in individuals (Khadse, 2023a, 2023b). 51 participants believed that AI technology is making us lonely or anti-social. 17 IT professionals, 14 teachers, and 20 students reported that we are forgetting about social and experiential learning due to the long interaction with machines and lack the skills related to human dealing. One IT professional said,

> Everybody left doing hard work, teamwork they simply take help from AI

One student replied,

> Yes, too much use of it can make us feel stressed and lonely, only relying on machines instead of people.

These findings were also supported by the study conducted on 285 students from different universities in Pakistan and China, which found that AI significantly impacts the loss of human decision-making and makes humans lazy. It also impacts security and privacy. The findings show that 68.9% of laziness in humans, 68.6% in personal privacy and security issues, and 27.7% of the loss of decision-making is due to the impact of artificial intelligence in Pakistani and Chinese society (Ahmad et al., 2023).

12.4.4.4 AI-induced Cognitive Fatigue: Impacts on Memory, Focus, and Deep Processing

Interactions with artificial intelligence that are inadequately planned or poorly conceived might lead to frustration, discontent, and possibly even harmful psychological impacts like depression can lead to anxiety and sleep disorders while the reduction in working memory capacity and influence on the level of text comprehension was also noted in research (Khadse, 2023a, 2023b). Forty-five responses were received to within this theme and participants from all categories expressed their opinions. One Student reported,

> We use AI for our queries which reduced our habit of reading which affect our learning and memory

A teacher said,

> Constant use of AI can potentially impact memory, learning, and remembering because relying too much on AI for information can reduce our brain's natural ability to retain and process information

IT professionals believed that,

> Non-stop use of screen decreases the ability of focus and attention span while also make senses heavily loaded

The above opinions were also supported by the study of the language scientist Naomi Baron (2018) who claims that Digital environments encourage a surface-level involvement with text analysis due to the differences in reading patterns. This possibly depends on the fact that most digital media users glance at and multitask from one item to the next—a habit that might reduce attention span.

12.4.5 *Question 5: How Does AI Affect the Social Life of Learners?*

12.4.5.1 Theme: Social Isolation

It is scientifically observed that the constant interaction with screens and the lucrative possibilities of AI tools enable students to get a better understanding of concepts, while at the cost of a higher rate of individualization and isolation (Mou, 2019), this segregation from their fellow beings minimized their skill of social adaptability (Lai et al., 2023).

A total of 85 responses come under this category, in which 25 IT professionals, 31 teachers, and 29 students reported that the frequent and constant usage of AI and its tools is becoming the obvious reason for social isolation and loneliness. Attractive and sensational programs directly capture the attention of users and tame them to their frequent use. As the tools are user-friendly and now worldwide available so makes it more vulnerable to avoid or limit their use.

12.4.5.2 Limited Role of Teachers

One of the fields in which AI has a significant presence in the education market. Sophisticated and intelligent training tools are now changing the whole scenario of classrooms (Moonpreneur, 2023). Students' dependency on modern technology to access AI tools in the learning process is increasing day by day (Ahmad et al., 2023) However experts believe that the role of the teacher continues to be essential (Cope et al., 2020).

79 total responses come under this theme. 21 IT professionals, 30 teachers, and 28 students believe that the growing use of AI and its easy availability limits the role of teachers in classrooms. Further advancement in the field of Robotics also replaces teachers in many subjects worldwide.

One teacher reported,

> jobs of teachers are at risk.

One student added,

> through AI we can have a complete demonstration of the topic and it is also available every time

Another student thought that,

> learning experience is cool through AI tools

Despite the crucial role of artificial intelligence in classroom learning, the importance of teachers cannot be denied. It is a well-established fact that students who receive feedback and guidance from teachers show superior accomplishments and educational goals to those who solely rely on machine learning (Rapanta et al., 2020) (Tables 12.2, 12.3 and Graph 12.1).

12.5 Implications of the Study

The present chapter sheds light on a detailed understanding of the interplay between AI and mental health. The research conducted has shown that using AI carries the possibility of excessive dependence on technology, which may result in eliminating human interaction and the absence of empathy. AI assistance is beyond our expectations and provides remarkable assistance in every field of life. The present study will help us understand the role of AI concerning psychological health and well-being. This high majority of the response showcases the public perception regarding the impact of AI in these areas, which are also the key focus of the study. The public perception, backed up by past studies and the currently collected data shows that this is going to be a long-term concern within the field and that the findings of this study can be applied at home, in academic and professional settings which makes it equally helpful for all individuals.

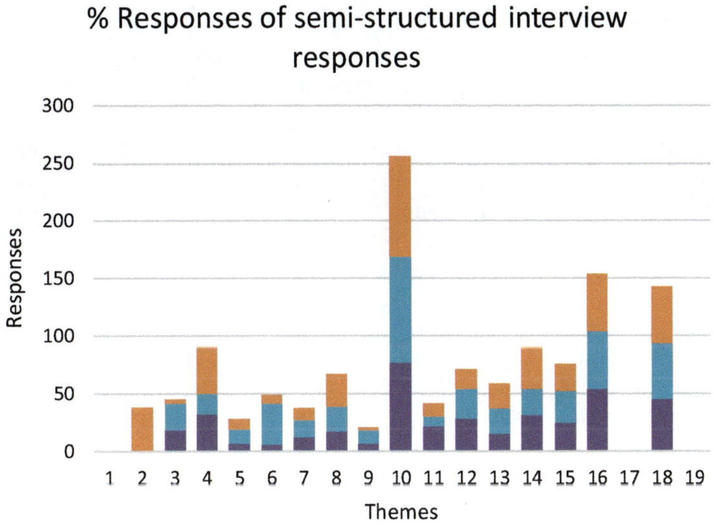

Graph 12.1 Showing the responses of semi-structured interview responses

12.6 Conclusion

The application of artificial intelligence (AI) in a wide variety of fields, including mental health, has become increasingly commonplace in today's quickly developing technology landscape. It is becoming necessary to investigate and gain a better understanding of these dangers to guarantee a responsible and successful implementation and integration of AI into our daily lives. To further study these claims, an exploratory study was designed to understand AI's role in human mental health and cognitive processes. Semi-structured interviews were designed and given to the students, teachers, and IT professionals. Their responses were taken through an online survey method. Analysis of the collected data supported the above notion that AI has a significant role in students' lives and learning processes. Students, teachers, and professionals highlighted their concerns and applauded for the contributions of AI. This work will be proved as a foundation stone for further exploration in Pakistan.

12.6.1 Limitations and Recommendation(S) for Future Work

There are many limitations in this research which are required to be dealt in future studies. First physical interview techniques are better than the online method. Due to the limitation of resources, we opted online method which can introduce subjectivity as well as the issues of communication and language cannot be solved. Secondly, convenience sampling technique was used instead of random sampling which also

Table 12.2 Responses of semi-structured interviews ($N = 115$)

Questions	Themes		IT professionals ($n = 35$)	Teachers ($n = 40$)	Students ($n = 40$)	Total responses ($N = 115$)
1. Is AI good for mental health?	Yes		28	8	32	68
	How?	Decrease cognitive load	15	20	3	38
		Empowering human beings	25	15	35	75
		Helps in screening and treatment of mental disorders	6	10	8	24
	No		5	30	6	41
2. How AI is harmful to our mental health?	Slowing down Intellectual thinking/creativity		8	11	7	26
	Reliance/inappropriate use of AI can cause stress		11	16	18	45
	Reduces neuroplasticity		5	08	2	15
3. Does AI affect cognitive processes, (like memory, and learning)?	Yes		30	33	31	94
	No		9	3	5	17
4. If yes in Q-3, explain how	Negative impact on critical thinking ability		18	19	11	48
	Limiting the brainstorming and learning		10	16	14	40
	Anti-social behaviours/ learnings		20	17	22	59
	Reducing attention span, focus, and memory		16	20	15	51
5. How does AI affect the social lives of learners?	Social isolation		25	31	29	85
	Limit the role of teachers		21	30	28	79

Table 12.3 Percentage responses of semi-structured interviews ($N = 115$)

Questions	Themes		IT professionals ($n = 35$)	Teachers ($n = 40$)	Students ($n = 40$)
	Yes		35%	9%	38
1. Is AI good for mental health?	How?	Decrease cognitive load	18	24	3
		Empowering human beings	32	18	41
		Helps in screening and treatment of mental disorders	7	12	9
	No		6	36	7
2. How AI is harmful to our mental health?	Slowing down Intellectual thinking/creativity		12	15	11
	Reliance/inappropriate use of AI can cause stress		17	22	28
	Reduces neuroplasticity		7	11	3
3. Does AI affect cognitive processes (like memory, and learning?	Yes		77	92	87
	No		22	8	12
4. If yes in Q-3, explain how	Negative impact on critical thinking ability		28	26	17
	Limiting the brainstorming and learning		15	22	22
	Anti-social behaviours/ learnings		31	23	35
	Reducing attention span, focus, and memory		25	27	24
5. How does AI affect the Social lives of learners?	Social isolation		54	50	50
	Limit the role of teachers		45	49	49

increased the chances of systematic error. Lastly, sample categories can be increased which can give a variety of perspectives on the asked questions. Lastly, the use of self-reported measures in our study raises the possibility of bias. Future research should take into account objective assessments of AI exposure and the effects on cognitive and mental health domains.

Based on the conducted research and literature review, it is highly recommended to limit the use of AI to fields which are completely mechanical or technical whereas all those fields that need human interaction like education must retain human elements.

Ethically, it may be more sound to be listened to and treated by individuals rather than by robots or machines. The research in this domain with the collaboration of psychologists, educationists, and legislators giving viewpoints and expertise can help counter the negative effects of AI on mental health, especially in the field of education. It can provide policymakers the ability to make educated decisions based on scientific facts and the opinions of experts. Thus, it is imperative to maintain a balance between human interactions with AI and reinforce the responsibility of human psychologists to deliver comprehensive and ethically sound health care.

Annexure-A

Interview Guideline

Thank you for agreeing to participate in this research interview. The purpose of this study is to explore university graduates' perceptions of the impact of Artificial Intelligence (AI) on mental health, cognition, memory, and social well-being—particularly in the context of higher education and learning environments.

We are particularly interested in understanding how individuals perceive the psychological effects of AI tools such as ChatGPT, AI-based educational platforms, and automated systems used in academic settings.

Informed Consent:

Before we begin, please note the following:

- Your participation in this interview is entirely voluntary.
- You may choose not to answer any question and may withdraw from the interview at any point without any penalty.
- All responses will be treated with strict confidentiality and anonymity. No personally identifiable information will be shared or published.

Section A: Demographic Information

1. Age: __________
2. Gender: __________
3. Current Profession or Occupation: ____________________________
4. Highest Level of Education Completed: ______________________
5. Experience with AI Tools (e.g., ChatGPT, AI learning platforms):
   ☐ Frequently ☐ Occasionally ☐ Rarely ☐ Never

Section B: Interview Questions

1. Opening Question (Engagement):

In your opinion, is Artificial Intelligence (AI) beneficial for mental health? Why or why not?

2. Perceived Risks:
How, if at all, do you think AI can be harmful to our mental health?(Prompt: Think about stress, isolation, overreliance, anxiety, etc.)

3. Core Inquiry—Mental Health Linkage:
Do you believe that AI contributes to psychological problems such as anxiety, depression, or cognitive overload? Please explain.

4. Cognitive Impact:
In your experience or observation, how does the use of AI affect students' cognitive abilities—such as cognition, memory and learning?

5. Social Impact:
How do you think AI affects the social life of learners, especially in university or academic contexts?

References

Ahmad, S. F., Han, H., Alam, M. M., Rehmat, M. K., Irshad, M., Arraño-Muñoz, M., & Ariza-Montes, A. (2023). Impact of artificial intelligence on human loss in decision making, laziness and safety in education. *Humanities & Social Sciences Communications, 10*, 311. https://doi.org/10.1057/s41599-023-01787-8

AI, automation, and the future of work: Ten things to solve for. (2018, June 1). McKinsey & Company. https://www.mckinsey.com/featured-insights/future-of-work/ai-automation-and-the-future-of-work-ten-things-to-solve-for

Baron, N. S. (2018). Do students lose depth in digital reading? *The Conversation*. https://theconversation.com/do-students-lose-depth-in-digital-reading-99355

Bharthi, D., Poonam, Bajaj, K. K., Babu, S. A., & Singh, G. (2023). AIS effect on human behavior and well-being: An empirical analysis. *Tuijin Jishu, 44*(3), 2033–2042. https://doi.org/10.52783/tjjpt.v44.i3.650

Braga, A., & Logan, R. K. (2017). The emperor of strong AI has no clothes: Limits to artificial intelligence. *Information, 8*(4), 156. https://doi.org/10.3390/info8040156

Cleland, J. A. (2017). The qualitative orientation in medical education research. *Korean Journal of Medical Education, 29*(2), 61–71. https://doi.org/10.3946/kjme.2017.53

Cope, B., Kalantzis, M., & Searsmith, D. (2020). Artificial intelligence for education: Knowledge and its assessment in AI-enabled learning ecologies. *Educational Philosophy and Theory, 53*(12), 1229–1245. https://doi.org/10.1080/00131857.2020.1728732

Creswell, J. W. (2007). *Qualitative inquiry and research design: Choosing among five approaches* (2nd ed.). Sage Publications, Inc.

Dienlin, T., & Johannes, N. (2020). The impact of digital technology use on adolescent well-being. *Dialogues in Clinical Neuroscience, 22*(2), 135–142. https://doi.org/10.31887/DCNS.2020.22.2/tdienlin.

Dumitru, D., & Halpern, D. F. (2023). Critical thinking: Creating job-proof skills for the future of work. *Journal of Intelligence, 11*(10), 194. https://doi.org/10.3390/jintelligence11100194

Dwivedi, Y. K., Hughes, L., Ismagilova, E., Aarts, G., Coombs, C., Crick, T., Duan, Y., Dwivedi, R., Edwards, J., Eirug, A., Galanos, V., Ilavarasan, P. V., Janssen, M., Jones, P., Kar, A. K., Kizgin, H., Kronemann, B., Lal, B., Lucini, B., … Williams, M. D. (2021). Artificial intelligence (AI): Multidisciplinary perspectives on emerging challenges, opportunities, and agenda for research, practice and policy. *International Journal of Information Management, 57*, 101994. https://doi.org/10.1016/j.ijinfomgt.2019.08.002

Eatough, V., & Smith, J. (2006). I was like a wild wild person: Understanding feelings of anger using interpretative phenomenological analysis. *British Journal of Psychology, 97*(4), 483–498. https://doi.org/10.1348/000712606X97831

Ettman, C., K., & Galea, S. (2023). The potential influence of AI on population mental health. *JMIR Mental Health*. https://doi.org/10.2196/49936

Farinella, F. (2024). Artificial intelligence and the right to memory. *Research Gate*. https://doi.org/10.21202/2949-2483.2024.2

Felea, M., Bucur, M., Negruțiu, C., Nițu, M., & Stoica, D. A. (2021). Wearable technology adoption among Romanian students: A structural model based on TAM. *Amfiteatru Economic, 23*(57), 376–391. https://doi.org/10.24818/EA/2021/57/376

Hutton, J., Dudley, J., Horowitz-Kraus, T., DeWitt, T., & Holland, S. K. (2020). Associations between screen-based media use and brain white matter integrity in preschool-aged children. *JAMA Pediatrics, 174*(1), e193869. https://doi.org/10.1001/jamapediatrics.2019.3869

Jarrahi, M. H. (2018). Artificial intelligence and the future of work: Human-AI symbiosis in organizational decision making. *Business Horizons, 61*(4), 1–15. https://doi.org/10.1016/j.bushor.2018.03.007

Khadse, K., Malhotra, S., Priyadharshini, S. L., & Singh, A. (2023a). Cyberpsychology and the impact of AI on mental health. *Research Gate*. https://www.researchgate.net/publication/373097637

Khadse, K., Malhotra, S., Priyadharshini, S., Bharthi, D., & Singh, A. (2023b). Cyberpsychology and the impact of AI on mental health. *Journal for ReAttach Therapy and Developmental Diversities, 6*(10), 276–287.

Lai, T., Xie, C., Ruan, M., Wang, Z., Lu, H., & Fu, S. (2023). Influence of artificial intelligence in education on adolescents' social adaptability: The mediatory role of social support. *PLoS ONE, 18*(3). https://doi.org/10.1371/journal.pone.0283170

Meyer, J., Smith, A., Johnson, B., & Davis, C. (2020). Privacy and data security concerns in the era of AI-driven technologies. *Journal of Privacy and Data Protection, 8*(3), 123–140.

Moonpreneur. (2023). *AI's negative and positive impact on education industry*. https://moonpreneur.com/blog/ai-negative-and-positive-impact-oneducation-industry

Mou, X. (2019). *Artificial intelligence, No 32652. World Bank Publications—Reports*. The World Bank Group. https://EconPapers.repec.org/RePEc:wbk:wboper:32652

O'Dell, B., Stevens, K., Tomlinson, A., Singh, I., & Cipriani, A. (2022). Building trust in artificial intelligence and new technologies in mental health. *BMJ Mental Health, 125*(2), 45–46.

Ojiyi, G. K., Ayegbusi, W. E., Oji, I., & Aikabeli, B. O. (2023). Job security in the artificial intelligence and automation era. *Research Gate*. https://doi.org/10.13140/RG.2.2.36551.47528/2

Oladimeji, K. E., Nyatela, A., Gumede, S., Dwarka, D., & Lalla-Edward, S. T. (2023). Impact of artificial intelligence (AI) on psychological and mental health promotion: An opinion piece. *New Voices in Psychology, 13*, 14548. https://doi.org/10.25159/2958-3918/14548

Pantev, C., Engelien, A., Candia, V., & Elbert, T. (2001). Representational cortex in musicians. *Annals of the New York Academy of Sciences, 930*(1), 300–314. https://doi.org/10.1111/j.1749-6632.2001.tb05740.x

Perwej, Y., & Parwej, F. (2012). A neuroplasticity (brain plasticity) approach to use in artificial neural network. *International Journal of Scientific & Engineering Research (IJSER), 3*(6). https://hal.science/hal-03362902/document

Rapanta, C., Botturi, L., Goodyear, P., Guàrdia, L., & Koole, M. (2020). Online university teaching during and after the covid-19 crisis: Refocusing teacher presence and learning activity. *Post Digital Science and Education, 2*(3), 923–945.

Rayhan, A. (2023). The future of work: How AI and automation will transform industries. *ResearchGate*. https://doi.org/10.13140/RG.2.2.36092.51848

Săseanu, A. S., Gogonea, R. M., & Ghiță, S. I. (2024). The social impact of using artificial intelligence in education. *Amfiteatru Economic, 26*(65), 89–105. https://doi.org/10.24818/EA/2024/65/89

Seni, D. A. & Seni, A. G. (2010). Do modern neurosciences herald a new cognition model for companies? *Gestion 2000, 27*(6), 131–144.

Shankar, S. (2023). Artificial intelligence's effects on mental health, human behaviour and well-being—An empirical study. *Tuijin Jishu, 44*(4), 1302–1309. https://doi.org/10.52783/tjjpt.v44.i4.1013

Sheikh, H., Prins, C., & Schrijvers, E. (2023). Artificial intelligence: Definition and background. *Research for Policy,* 15–41.

Singh, S., & College, A. (2023). Role of artificial intelligence in psychological and mental well-being: A quantitative investigation. *Journal for Re Attach Therapy and Developmental Diversities, 6*(9s2), 149–156. https://doi.org/10.13140/RG.2.2.28769.28004

Stevenson, C., Smal, I. M., Grasman, R. P. P. P., Baas, M., & van der Maas, H. (2023). *Putting GPT-3's creativity to the (alternative uses) test.* https://doi.org/10.17605/OSF.IO/VMK3C

Tielman, M. L., Neerincx, M. A., van Meggelen, M., Franken, I. H. A., & Brinkman, W. P. (2020). The effect of empathy in an automated virtual reality based therapist: An interview study. *Computers in Human Behavior, 107*, 106–273. https://doi.org/10.1016/j.chb.2020.106273

Turkle, S. (2011). Alone together: Why we expect more from technology and less from each other. *Choice/choice Reviews, 48*(12), 48–7239. https://doi.org/10.5860/choice.48-7239

Urwin, M. (2024, February 23). AI taking over jobs: What to know about the future of jobs. *Built-In.* https://builtin.com/artificial-intelligence/ai-replacing-jobs-creating-jobs

Walter, Y. (2024). Embracing the future of artificial intelligence in the classroom: The relevance of AI literacy, prompt engineering, and critical thinking in modern education. *International Journal of Educational Technology in Higher Education, 21*(1). https://doi.org/10.1186/s41239-024-00448-3

Willig, C. (2001). *Introducing qualitative research in psychology adventures in theory and method.* Open University Press.

World Mental Health Report. (2022). *Transforming mental health for all.* World Health Organization. https://www.who.int/publications/i/item/9789240049338

GPSR Compliance

The European Union's (EU) General Product Safety Regulation (GPSR) is a set of rules that requires consumer products to be safe and our obligations to ensure this.

If you have any concerns about our products, you can contact us on ProductSafety@springernature.com

In case Publisher is established outside the EU, the EU authorized representative is:

Springer Nature Customer Service Center GmbH
Europaplatz 3
69115 Heidelberg, Germany

Batch number: 10704039

Printed by Printforce, the Netherlands